Teaching with Digital Humanities

TOPICS IN THE DIGITAL HUMANITIES

Humanities computing is redefining basic principles about research and publication. An influx of new, vibrant, and diverse communities of practitioners recognizes that computer applications are subject to continual innovation and reappraisal. This series publishes books that demonstrate the new questions, methods, and results arising in the digital humanities.

Series Editors
Susan Schreibman
Raymond G. Siemens

Teaching with Digital Humanities

Tools and Methods for Nineteenth-Century American Literature

Edited by Jennifer Travis
and Jessica DeSpain

UNIVERSITY OF ILLINOIS PRESS
Urbana, Chicago, and Springfield

Publication of this book was supported by funding
from Southern Illinois University Edwardsville and
St. John's University

Library of Congress Cataloging-in-Publication Data
Names: Travis, Jennifer, 1967– editor. | DeSpain, Jessica, editor.
Title: Teaching with digital humanities : tools and methods for
    nineteenth-century American literature / edited by Jennifer
    Travis and Jessica DeSpain.
Description: Urbana : University of Illinois Press, [2019] | Series:
    Topics in the digital humanities | Includes bibliographical
    references and index.
Identifiers: LCCN 2018041455 | ISBN 9780252042232 (hardcover :
    alk. paper) | ISBN 9780252083983 (pbk. : alk. paper)
Subjects: LCSH: American literature—19th century—Study and
    teaching—Technological innovations. | American literature—
    19th century—Computer-assisted instruction. | Digital
    humanities.
Classification: LCC PS44 .T43 2019 | DDC 810.71—dc23
LC record available at https://lccn.loc.gov/2018041455

ISBN 9780252050978 (e-book)

Contents

Acknowledgments

EDITING AND COMPILING this manuscript was a truly collaborative project; contributors read and responded to each other's work and fine-tuned their essays in conversation with one another. We would like to thank our contributors and their students for sharing their ideas and experiences with us. Thanks also goes to our own students, whose enthusiasm and experimentation with digital humanities tools and methods inspired the collection. We are grateful to Kathryn Krueger and Jill Anderson, who read portions of the manuscript; peer reviewers for their helpful feedback; and University of Illinois Press senior acquisitions editor Dawn Durante for her insightful advice throughout the publication process. Southern Illinois University Edwardsville and St. John's University helped offset the publication cost of the manuscript, without which we would not have been able to develop the comprehensive companion website with sample teaching materials.

INTRODUCTION

Digital Humanities and the Nineteenth-Century American Literature Classroom

Jessica DeSpain and Jennifer Travis

THIS COLLECTION REPRESENTS the changing shape of what it means to engage in academic research and to share, teach, and collaborate with our students in the digital age. The essays offer theoretical perspectives and practical case studies for teaching American literature of the long nineteenth century using the tools and methods of the digital humanities (DH). The collection brings together scholars who are foundational to the development of digital humanities and to the building of nineteenth-century American digital archives alongside scholars who have made digital tools and methods central to their American literature pedagogy. In doing so, the essays bring an important shift in emphasis to DH pedagogy, moving from a focus on digital humanities writ large to how particular DH methods and practices operate at a field-specific level.[1] By emphasizing an approach centered on American literature of the long nineteenth century, the collection invites conversations among scholars of other disciplines and literary specializations about how digital pedagogies can deepen their own objectives for student learning and scholarship. Rather than limiting the collection's use, the disciplinary practices showcased here offer strategies for literature and digital humanities scholars, practitioners, and instructors regardless of specialty or discipline.

This applied approach provides case studies for how digital humanities pedagogy can enrich student experiences of reading, writing, and researching. Contributors discuss concepts such as design thinking and archival theory, demonstrating their relevance to the American literature classroom and to pedagogy and scholarship in the field. DH in the classroom can introduce students to texts beyond those anthologized in *Norton* and expose them to archival documents previously accessible only to credentialed scholars. The accompanying assignments and readings foster classroom discussions about the constructed nature of the canon, the networked development of nineteenth-century activist movements, and the nuanced comparison of nineteenth-century society with our current moment. From the study of ephemera and bioregional archives, to the recovery and analysis of texts by women and minority authors, to new methods for teaching already canonical digital projects such as *The Walt Whitman Archive*, this collection transforms how we approach the field, engage our students, and facilitate our classrooms.

Contributors bring their research into the classroom and bring their students into their research, demonstrating what Emily Renker, in a commentary on the state of American literary studies, has called the academy's "greatest power—political, ethical, [and] global": to bring the undergraduate classroom, still largely "invisible" in the profession, into sharper focus. The essays here demonstrate how DH pedagogy renders our work "meaningful and coherent" as it empowers students to become reciprocal, collaborative partners in our scholarship.[2] Even Augusta Rohrbach's essay on embracing DH in a graduate seminar reenvisions the mission of graduate teaching by introducing students to pedagogical theory and helping them frame their identity as future instructors. This book takes seriously the call for scholars to make our classrooms visible, our pedagogy accountable, and our research meaningful and accessible. Though the digital humanities at first struggled to define its relationship to the undergraduate classroom,[3] pedagogy became more central after a 2011 Modern Language Association panel, "History and Future of Digital Humanities," wherein scholars argued for more critical attention to the importance of teaching. Katherine D. Harris, for example, discussed the limitations of engaging in DH scholarship at her institution, San Jose State University, including funding, institutional support, research time, and access to graduate assistants. Harris was among an initial group of scholars to integrate digital pedagogy as it had long been practiced in the teaching of writing and other fields into the digital humanities.[4] Bringing attention to DH pedagogy opened the field to faculty at a wider sampling of institutions.[5]

As the number of books that address DH pedagogy continues to grow, most seek broad coverage, focusing on wide-reaching digital humanities skills rather than field-specific methods and content. Brett D. Hirsch's *Digital Humanities Pedagogy: Practices, Principles and Politics* (2012) includes a comprehensive selection of essays targeting basic DH practices for undergraduates.[6] Rebecca Frost Davis, Matthew K. Gold, Katherine D. Harris, and Jentery Sayers have recently partnered to develop *Digital Pedagogy in the Humanities: Concepts, Models, and Experiments* (2015), which organizes DH pedagogy artifacts by keywords such as *video, praxis,* and *hybrid* that have broad applicability across disciplines.[7] We are indebted to the work initiated by these collections, as well as to many journals and blogs such as ProfHacker, *JiTP*, *Hybrid Pedagogy*, *Transformations*, *Kairos*, *Radical Teacher*, HASTAC, NINES (Nineteenth-Century Scholarship Online), and (un)conferences such as THATCamp Pedagogy.[8] We build on this groundwork to discuss how DH might engage students with core issues in studies of the long nineteenth century and so that others might imagine new uses for digital pedagogy in their own subject areas. Topics covered in the essays include race and ethnicity, the history of the book and print culture, democracy, citizenship and activism, Indigenous cultures, gender, sexuality, regionalism, class, theories of the archive, periodization, the canon, the spatial turn, and more.

This collection aims to support instructors at a variety of institutions and levels of expertise. It is understandable that instructors may be wary of the time and skill it takes to include DH in their classrooms and to help students build technological dexterity in the context of literary study. They may not have the infrastructure, classroom resources, or support for instructional development. Our students may have limited access to technology or broadband. Moreover, there may be little incentive to experiment pedagogically in institutional cultures that continue to perpetuate academic hierarchies regarding scholarship and teaching, particularly in relation to tenure, promotion, and career advancement. Mindful of these possibilities, essays offer readers step-by-step guidelines, sample assignments, and minute-to-minute timeframes for introducing DH into the curriculum. Some assignments rely on in-class use of technology; however, some, like Edward Whitley's assignments in which students analyze social movements on Twitter, require little more than the ubiquitous smartphone. Many of the authors focus on freely available tools, archives, and digital resources. Duncan Faherty and Ed White reflect on their *Just Teach One* project, which sits at the intersection of print and digital publishing so that students can easily read newly recovered texts online or via printed copies distributed by their instructor. Some assignments are capstone projects for the semester and are scaffolded as such, while others can be incorporated in a day, in a week, or in short units. Catherine Waitinas's essay describes how to introduce students to the study of Walt Whitman's manuscripts in as little as one class period. Tisha M. Brooks's assignment in which students create visual and textual anthologies of African American literature could be adapted to any learning environment. Taken together, the essays model how to engage students in the study of nineteenth-century American literature and culture in ways that reflect the dynamism of the field as well as their own skills and interests.

Notably, several of the essays interrogate the very idea of the classroom, preferring to think about spaces of teaching and learning as labs or studios. DH pedagogy defies conventional notions of classroom space and time and the idea that knowledge flows one way, from lectern to students. Essays throughout the collection consider how to create a culture of play and experimentation, how to assess process rather than product, and how to reward risk and teach students to learn from failure. Amy E. Earhart, for instance, discusses how to blend a studio model where students learn by doing and act as apprentices with an in-depth examination of primary sources. Yet, it is also a fallacy to assume that students enter learning spaces as confident digital makers who require little guidance. Tisha M. Brooks models how mindful pedagogical practices can "bridge multiple literacies—those originating within the academy and those from without." By fostering a "culture of collaboration and openness, rather than hierarchy" we may draw out the best work from our students and recognize the same in ourselves. Embracing a collaborative classroom in which neither student nor teacher is certain of the outcome can be intimidating for everyone. The essay "Reading Macro and Micro Trends in Nineteenth-Century Theater History," written collaboratively by Robert Davis and his students, demonstrates the rich outcomes of such a model while also highlighting how instructors and students must adapt to new discoveries as well as project pitfalls.

The essays are organized by five keywords that we've called *tags*, a term borrowed from the practice of crowdsourcing the organization of online content. Our organization builds on several recent works in American studies and digital cultures that have used keywords as a dynamic way to arrange, critique, and understand linguistic, cultural, and social change.[9] We use verbs for the tags, emphasizing how the active pedagogical practices of the digital humanities can transform teaching and scholarship in the field. In addition to the five organizing tags, readers will encounter many more exemplifying methods of active learning that contributors advocate throughout the collection, including *play*, *collaborate*, *participate*, *curate*, and *fail*, to name a few. Additional tags after the introduction provide readers with multiple methods of accessing the collection. Users of the companion website (www.press.uillinois.edu/books/TeachingWithDH) will be able to participate in this process, adding their own tags to classify the essays. Substantial appendixes of syllabi and assignments that will make it easy for readers to integrate DH into any classroom are also available online.

Make, Read, Recover, Archive, and *Act* are the action-based tags that constitute the book's arrangement. The essays in Make illustrate the pedagogical value of project-based, collaborative, and interactive learning. They also challenge students to actively *make* connections between nineteenth-century technologies, literatures, and cultures as they reflect on and inform the present. The essays in Read describe assignments in which students engage in multiple reading practices, from traditional close reading to collaborative and computational reading, or what Franco Moretti has coined "distant reading."[10] The essays illustrate, for example, how distant reading, in which students mine text to identify literary patterns, as they do in Cynthia L. Hallen's seminar on Emily Dickinson and Eliza R. Snow, or compile and machine-read large data sets, as students do in Robert Davis's class on nineteenth-century American theater, often brings students back to the work of detailed textual analysis. The essays in Recover place the recovery of works by women and minority writers at the center of the American literature classroom, showing how DH approaches substantially aid in the scholarly consideration of marginalized or forgotten American texts. Projects like *Just Teach One* and *Just Teach One: Early African American Print* consider how central DH pedagogy can be to the work of recovery. As students and instructors alike discover neglected authors and texts, they animate scholarly debates surrounding recovery practices and the canon. In Archive contributors inspire students to act as archivists in a community beyond the classroom and to select and organize materials with an ethics of care. The final section, Act, advocates for an activist approach to DH pedagogy, demonstrating the ways in which DH can bring new insight to debates central to the study of the long nineteenth century, particularly concerning difference.

Make

The essays in Make unite theory with practice. In this section readers learn how to create a classroom environment that encourages content-based instruction through tinkering. Tinkerers experiment with materials and ideas to understand their capacities and find solutions to problems. As Jentery Sayers explains, tinkering brings to mind child's play, and yet the term is useful for imagining a pedagogy that focuses on the ways in which the act of creation encourages learning through haptic memory.[11] For authors Ryan Cordell, Benjamin J. Doyle, Elizabeth Hopwood, Ashley Reed, and Augusta Rohrbach, working hands-on with nineteenth- and twentieth-century materials and technologies results in pedagogy that blends content with process. Their students become editors and producers to understand literature and scholarly practices anew.

This section melds cultural and literary analysis with the processes of making as it is theorized and practiced in DH pedagogy. By visiting a printing press and setting type, undergraduate students in Ryan Cordell's American literature class engage with nineteenth-century print culture in ways that complicate their understanding of books as technical and material objects. Ashley Reed draws on local history and archives to immerse her students in the collaborative creation and annotation of an online edition of a nineteenth-century scrapbook. Graduate students in Augusta Rohrbach's course crowdsource wikis and build *Digital Emerson: A Collective Archive* as a means of interrogating hierarchical distinctions between student and instructor. These essays exemplify process-oriented learning at its best: students and instructors alike take risks with new platforms and work in visual, textual, aural, and haptic modes. Students also become project managers, tasked with planning and executing work that is publicly accessible.

The essays in Make also ask how the use of digital tools can encourage students to recognize the sociocultural impact of technology historically and today. Many of the practices in our web-based culture, from information retrieval and circulation to social bookmarking, as Reed describes, mirror nineteenth-century forms of the "culture of reprinting."[12] Moreover, as Cordell reminds us, debates that seem unique to the twenty-first century, including information overload, textual authority, and intellectual property, gained prominence in the nineteenth century. Learning the history of copyright, writes Reed, encourages students to reflect on the importance of attribution practices and inspires discussion of open-access publication and the freedom of information. The comparative approach to technologies described in Make reveals the continuities and commonalities between nineteenth-century texts and our current cultural moment.

Ryan Cordell, Benjamin J. Doyle, and Elizabeth Hopwood's essay seizes a nineteenth-century invention, the kaleidoscope, as a model and metaphor for pedagogical practices and learning spaces that encourage play and experimentation. Chapter 1 describes how making can bridge rhetorical divides between the analog and the digital. Through examples that involve setting letterpress type, the Text Encoding Initiative (TEI) encoding of texts as an interpretive process, and the collaborative creation of Wikipedia pages, the authors describe how experiments with contemporary technologies help students claim scholarly agency over the texts and tools central to their study of the nineteenth century. When one class's Wikipedia entry was cited by the Wikipedia community as lacking "notability," students learned about the dynamics of race, class, and gender at work in the online encyclopedia as they made a successful case for the entry's importance. Hopwood designed a TEI assignment in which students tagged themes, characters, and other textual elements to, as she puts it, "tease apart the layers of the text and arrive at interpretive distinctions." In learning to code poetry Twitterbots, students in Cordell's class discovered the hidden workings of web services like Twitter while analyzing the building blocks of nineteenth-century poems in ways that allowed them to see literary texts anew. In examples like these, kaleidoscopic pedagogy encourages students to discover how such nineteenth-century competencies as close reading and contemporary methods of coding and data analysis have the potential to be mutually constitutive, inspiring a more nuanced understanding of both periods.

Making an annotated digital edition of a nineteenth-century scrapbook offers an opportunity to introduce students to an array of concepts related to the study of nineteenth-century literature in its relation to the twenty-first century, from the culture of reprinting to the history of intellectual property. In chapter 2, Ashley Reed writes about a project inspired by Ellen Gruber Garvey's work in *Writing with Scissors* (2012) on the culture of scrapbooks and the ways in which readers curated and remixed their own collections of literary artifacts.[13] Reed details her work with students to create an annotated online edition of a scrapbook by Prudence Person, a member of a prominent North Carolina family. She also outlines the lessons she learned as the project progressed from its first phase in a classroom of nineteen students to an independent study with only two. When the smaller group integrated more field-specific knowledge, the students and the project thrived: they visited historic sites, presented at undergraduate research forums, and took ownership of the content. This is a running thread throughout the essays: when students become makers, they invest rigorously in their work. Reed frankly addresses the difficulties and benefits of launching a context-rich DH project in a general education classroom, and she imagines its future iteration as the centerpiece of an intensive upper-level course on nineteenth-century print culture.

Augusta Rohrbach writes of making in the context of graduate education where students learn to rethink the role of scholarship, pedagogy, and research. In chapter 3, Rohrbach details her collaborative work with six graduate students to build *Digital Emerson: A Collective Archive*. Rohrbach uses a set of theoretical and critical readings that engage students in reflections about Emerson's conscious rupture of pedagogical barriers and how his philosophy might be realized in digital environments. In so doing, Rohrbach's students learn about the value of pedagogical theory for their own research and teaching and begin considering, even at an early point in their careers, how the two support each other. Using collective knowledge against the privileging of the individual scholar, Rohrbach and her students learn to think outside argument-based rhetoric and explore the importance of visual literacy and design thinking. In this way, her graduate students imagine an audience beyond academia for their work, one that includes a broad community of interested readers.

The essays in Make describe the challenges of working with new platforms and the mishaps related to the advent and emendation of digital tools. Experimenting and taking risks increases the likelihood of encountering setbacks, and these essays emphasize the learning potential in failure and the value of pedagogical flexibility. As Reed describes, she and her students practiced an "increasingly essential skill in our computer-assisted world: the art of dealing with unexpected technological breakdown." Embracing DH pedagogy means learning to anticipate obstacles and seeing them as opportunities for innovation and growth. Rohrbach and her students also learned this lesson well when one of their video technologies for *Digital Emerson: A Collective Archive* became obsolete. Students working with Wikipedia in Ryan Cordell's class learned how quickly work shared publicly might be critiqued and edited, and in some cases might disappear from view. Regardless of experience or comfort with digital technologies, the essays show makers at all levels encountering failure and thriving in the face of challenges.

Read

The essays in Read describe how computational analysis can bring students to close intimacy with and insight about nineteenth-century texts. In "How We Read: Close, Hyper, Machine," N. Katherine Hayles describes the expansion of reading practices in the digital age, from the tradition and practice of close reading to the recognition and incorporation of new computer-aided methods.[14] Jerome McGann has also urged more nuanced approaches to traditional reading practices, arguing as early as 1991 in *The Textual Condition* for the teaching of "radial reading," a method that accounts for a text's multiple versions, discursive fields, and historicity, which has become especially relevant with the advent of digital archives.[15] Of course, these practices are not mutually exclusive. Essays in this section model how new reading methods enhance and deepen students' engagement with literary texts, encouraging them to find new meanings in and methods for assessing old texts.

This is particularly noteworthy given the student populations in these courses: nonhumanities majors in a Melville seminar, theater majors and actors-in-training with limited knowledge of nineteenth-century American literature and culture in a theater history course, and a mix of English and linguistics majors in a course on Emily Dickinson. In Cynthia L. Hallen's Dickinson and Snow seminar, students use computational methods to identify literary patterns and word usage across authors and their works, discovering "new dimensions of the author's craft, culture, and circumference." "Distant reading and close reading shouldn't be thought of as opposite forces—both need each other," write the authors/collaborators of chapter 6, "Reading Macro and Micro Trends in Nineteenth-Century Theater History." They advocate for "hybrid reading practices" that enable students to develop their own "relationships with texts and textual data." Distant reading promotes literary study through the aggregation and analysis of large amounts of data; although, as the essays here show, bringing meaning to large data sets often requires close reading practices.

Because of the scale of reading projects underway in Kelley, Hallen, and Davis's classrooms, these essays offer instructive models for practicing collaboration among students and instructors. In classes like these, students depend upon one another to complete the work, and they bring diverse sets of skills to their projects. Wyn Kelley's essay demonstrates how students can collaborate across digital platforms to crowdsource the reading of *Moby Dick* (1851). Using the social reading tool *Annotation Studio*, students grapple with their classmates' multiple interpretations and divergent readings of the same passage and learn meaningful collaboration often relies on the unique attributes of each member of a collective. Kelley's students also develop the Locast *Moby-Dick* site by adding images, links, and comments for other students (current and future) to see and use. Robert Davis's students and cowriters undertake a variety of collaborative projects, discussing how they divided their work and considered individual expertise in the assignment of roles and responsibilities. Both Davis and Hallen discuss the benefits of equal collaboration with their students. Hallen and one of her students presented their work at the American Literature Association Conference. Davis and his students wrote their contribution to this collection collectively, with each class member adding to the conception and methodology of the class project and the composition of the essay.

Wyn Kelley describes how students in her seminar Mapping Melville use tools developed in MIT's HyperStudio to make new and surprising discoveries of deeply canonical texts. Chapter 4 begins by asking why students should spend an entire semester reading Melville, given that most were not humanities majors. Kelley describes how students' reading of Melville led them to rethink global geographies, deep histories, and broad social concerns. The seminar emphasized a diverse array of reading practices and modeled the classroom space as a design studio where students might "iterate and test," where "process is favored over product, versioning and extensibility are favored over definite editions," and students are "active participants and stakeholders in the creation and preservation of cultural materials."[16] Mapping Melville became a place where students could "engineer—hack and redesign—the reading process for themselves and their peers." As students experimented with digital tools for reading, mapping, editing, and comparing texts, they expanded their power to track verbal patterns, share comments, and develop reports and essays. Kelley thinks of her pedagogical methods as a platform for design thinking in the humanities classroom, and she demonstrates how nineteenth-century American literature is especially hospitable to such an approach.

In chapter 5, Cynthia L. Hallen describes her launch and development of the *Emily Dickinson Lexicon (EDL)* project, a dictionary of all the words in the poet's collected verse. With English and linguistics majors volunteering as apprentice collaborators, Hallen, starting in the 1990s, began the ambitious project of digitizing the Franklin edition of Dickinson's poems and using the newly developed WordCruncher concordance program to amass the lexicon.

Hallen describes her use of the *EDL* along with other digital philological tools in a senior capstone course where students learned principles of philology as well as skills of lexicography, etymology, exegesis, rhetoric, style, translation, discourse analysis, and literary interpretation. As in Kelley's class, digital tools used for close textual study brought students to the materiality of the texts themselves.

Chapter 6, coauthored by students Blair Best, Madeleine G. Cella, Rati Choudhary, Kayla C. Coleman, Ella L. Gill, Clayton Grimm, Malin Jörnvi, Philip Kenner, Patrick Korkuch, Mahayla Laurence, Joanna Pisano, Teagan Rabuano, Lawrence G. Richardson, Haley Sakamoto, and Victoria K. Sprowls and their instructor, Robert Davis, in a theater class at New York University, describes the interdependence of close and distant reading practices in their creation and analysis of a representative corpus of nineteenth-century drama using corpus linguistic and spatial analysis tools. U.S. theater history is complicated by a problematic critical heritage and long-running stigma associating pre-twentieth-century productions with commerce and cheap melodrama. With irregular scholarly and theatrical attention given to nineteenth-century American theater, the archive of plays and productions is frustratingly fragmented with few playbooks and only limited accounts of their staging. The collaborators' work demonstrates how students and scholars might leverage digital tools to recover and reignite readership of a neglected century of drama. Rather than plotting a clear path through the substantial corpus of antebellum playbooks or beginning with hypotheses, they loaded their texts into visualization tools such as Voyant, Antconc, and Tagxedo and viewed their work as an invitation to create and play. Play—improvising without expectations and goals, allowing failure to see what you might discover—is exactly what the authors have done together. Although digital methods could not repair all the gaps in the century's theater archive, the students found the use of digital tools to perform text analysis, mapping, and network visualization sparked new scholarly ideas about nineteenth-century theater.

In these essays, we see the deep commitment to project-oriented learning. Students not only study nineteenth-century writers; they too become authors. Indeed, the role of authorship, central to the content of all three courses on canonical and noncanonical texts, is a framework through which to understand the collaborative process of writing as well as textual discovery and scholarly invention. All three essays describe a vision of peer-to-peer learning that builds upon the insights of student work and articulates its applicability for students and instructors in future semesters. It is important to note that not every assignment or project described in this section includes specialized tools with steep learning curves. Davis's students, for example, used Google Maps and word clouds. For instructors who want to begin experimenting with DH in their classrooms, these tools can teach students how to "prepare, refine, and interpret data" with applicability to many kinds of scholarship.

Recover

Scholars of the long nineteenth century have harnessed digital resources to expand the canon and recover texts that have been neglected and ignored, challenging the defining features and pedagogical practices of the field itself. Of the sixty keywords curated in the first iteration of MLA Commons's *Digital Pedagogy and the Humanities*, recovery is not featured, reinforcing the importance of this field-specific approach toward DH pedagogy. In her book *Traces of the Old, Uses of the New* (2015), Amy E. Earhart presents an intellectual history of digital recovery projects from the 1980s and 1990s that listed and often reproduced in full the texts of little-known nineteenth-century writers.[17] Much of this early recovery work is now lost because of institutional and fiscal constraints, and today few scholars are building upon these early projects. The essays in Recover imagine and implement textual recovery projects in the classroom as a sustainable model for present and future canon expansion work.

Just Teach One (*JTO*), a project spearheaded by Duncan Faherty and Ed White, leads the way in these efforts, demonstrating why digital pedagogy must be at the center of recovery work and how the adoption and circulation in the classroom of noncanonical texts reinforces the mutually constitutive relationship between pedagogy and scholarship. *Just Teach One* recovers neglected early American texts and provides free, downloadable editions of out-of-print materials for classroom use. The project also provides an on-site blog for instructors to share resources and discuss their methods for teaching each recovered text. *JTO* raises important questions about the availability of digital editions, as the project was born after publishers declined to publish print-based editions of noncanonical works. *JTO* and its sister project, *Just Teach One Early African American Print* (*JTO: EAAP*), demonstrate the value of building a pedagogical community around newly circulated texts to ensure their future sustainable use. Inspired by these efforts, Caroline M. Woidat's essay asks students to consider the politics of canon formation and to investigate forms of labor and collaboration in the writing, editing, and dissemination of texts that have been traditionally overlooked.

In chapter 7, Faherty and White describe the history and evolution of their project, from early efforts to publish print-based editions of recovered texts to their discovery that going digital offers the greatest reach to scholars, instructors, and students. In 2012, in conjunction with the online journal *Common-place* and the American Antiquarian Society, *JTO* was born. To date the project has produced free editions of eight early American texts and recruited volunteers to experiment with and blog about their teaching experiences with these new editions. While Faherty and White imagined graduate students would be their most receptive audience, this turned out not to be the case; rather, the most enthusiastic participants were undergraduate students excited by the experimental nature of the project and the opportunity to be part of a larger collective from across institutions simultaneously interacting with the same recovered text. Faherty and White's essay analyzes data about the sixty-five instructors (from almost as many colleges and universities) who took part in *JTO* across its first five semesters and imagines the potential evolution of the project, including the development of a new platform to encourage students from multiple institutions to collaborate as they read each *JTO* text.

Just Teach One: Early African American Print adopts and augments the charge of *JTO*. Recognizing the relatively narrow way in which the field of pre-twentieth-century African American literature has been defined, *JTO: EAAP* develops a more diverse and inclusive approach to pre-twentieth-century American culture and focuses on texts excluded from critical and historical narratives of black literature, a philosophy modeled in Nicole N. Aljoe's experiences teaching the project's pilot text "Theresa" (1827). Chapter 8 describes the team's plans to link its work with other evolving DH projects such as the *Early Caribbean Digital Archive* and the *Colored Conventions Project*, and to build bridges to lesser-known collections, including smaller historically black colleges and universities (HBCUs) and church collections, in order to aid text sharing, identification, preservation, and technological engagement. Recognizing its responsibility to preserve African American cultural heritage, *JTO: EAAP* employs TEI standards to encode texts on the site, a decision process explored in the essay.

Digital recovery initiatives like *JTO* and *JTO: EAAP* are central to Caroline M. Woidat's upper-level undergraduate literature course devoted to the study and practice of recovery of American women writers. In chapter 9, Woidat describes how classroom "archival explorations" can transform the ways that students think about literary texts, American history, and their roles as scholars. Animated by feminist scholarship and pedagogy, Woidat's course aims to recover certain roles that literary editors, critics, and communities perform—the vital work that is often effaced or demeaned as "secondary" and peripheral—along with "primary" texts by women authors. Students in Woidat's class become editors engaged in literary recovery, learning to negotiate and participate in the politics and practices of textual recovery and recognizing that the results of recovery go far beyond just one text taught in a single class. Recovered texts reframe approaches to canonical works and inspire reevaluation of the canon's primacy.

The essays in Recover demonstrate the interconnected relationship of scholarship and pedagogy. Faherty and White describe the ways in which recovery, paraphrasing Theresa Gaul, is a "chicken and egg puzzle: recovered texts which do not inspire a sustained critical conversation seldom manage to achieve regularized course adoption, and texts that are not often taught receive only fitful critical attention." Textual recovery shapes communities of scholars, instructors, and editors who restore marginalized texts to the field of literary studies. Projects like these that crowdsource the recovery of texts and the teaching of recovery not only transform central disciplinary concerns, but they also have the potential to impact humanities pedagogy and scholarship writ large.

Archive

To archive is an action fraught with meaning. An archive is a repository and a practice, a means of storage, and a method of curation. How archives, as sites of knowledge production and retrieval, are designed, collected, organized, stored, appraised, sustained, and retrieved are interpretive acts that shape what counts as knowledge and who has access to it. Archives can fill students with wonder and the excitement of discovery. Digital archives bring students close to hands-on archival experiences often reserved for scholars and introduce them to underlying questions about the selection, curation, and preservation of artifacts.

Open-access digital archives provide unprecedented opportunities for students to engage with manuscripts, multiple editions, and primary documents, challenging them to become more proficient readers of primary source materials. Catherine Waitinas, for example, describes students' profound experiences examining Whitman's manuscripts on *The Walt Whitman Archive* as they "see literature not only or even at all as the product of a burst of inspiration but, instead, as the result of recurring acts of creation and re-creation." Building a digital archive alongside students, as Ken Cooper and Elizabeth Argentieri describe, can engage students in meaningful local research and encourage them to broach a world beyond the classroom and to take ownership of their education, as they become project managers and collaborators with local organizations. These projects can also expand students' understanding of the canon in experiential ways. Archivists and librarians have used the term *ephemera* to describe material objects and documents labeled miscellaneous or of questionable historical significance. Projects like *Open Valley* curate and articulate the value of this material as a means for students to learn about the literary, cultural, and ecological history of their region. Celeste Tường Vy Sharpe and

Timothy B. Powell describe their co-taught course in which students build an Omeka site to showcase significant Indigenous materials. Because Omeka's timeline features do not allow for the tagging of nonchronological temporal elements, students struggled with how to present the materials responsibly and were compelled to reflect on the impact of Eurocentrism in digital design.

In chapter 10, Catherine Waitinas leads readers step-by-step through a digital manuscript project on Walt Whitman's poetry that she created for a variety of courses from general education to graduate seminars. Using handwritten manuscripts digitized in *The Walt Whitman Archive*, Waitinas's students blend old and new technologies, placing penmanship and the "physical marks of human hesitation and intention" in conversation with big data analysis and *The Walt Whitman's Archive*'s tools. Waitinas focuses on the best practices behind digital manuscript study in literature classrooms, demonstrating how teaching with digital manuscripts engages students in "original, textually grounded, technologically savvy work." The project is infinitely scalable; it can be used in relation to many other archives, and Waitinas gives suggestions for one-day to full-unit versions of the assignment. Like many of the essays in the collection, Waitinas likes to defamiliarize content through her DH projects. She recommends assigning students lesser-known Whitman poems to deter them from seeking online commentaries to inform their arguments. In this way, Waitinas recognizes the importance of letting students flail and fail as a method of reorienting themselves as experts who have something to contribute to scholarly conversations.

Just as many of the essays in Recover consider how to use teaching as a method for reshaping scholarly inquiry, Celeste Tường Vy Sharpe and Timothy B. Powell's students learn about the limitations of existing DH platforms for archiving Indigenous cultural materials. In chapter 11, Sharpe and Powell explain how they used the design of digital platforms as teachable problems to engage students in a DH course about the stories of Indigenous peoples and the Eurocentric "control over time." Sharpe and Powell tasked students with creating a digital project that explored a more culturally specific and nuanced model of Iroquois or Haudenosaunee temporality. Students and instructors alike imagined solutions that may enable digital humanities tools to more accurately represent how Indigenous peoples tell their histories. The course design corrects a noted absence in DH pedagogy by encouraging more rigorous cultural critique of the technological platforms used for the accumulation and dissemination of knowledge while reflecting on how to represent Indigenous artifacts and narratives ethically and respectfully. Their work calls for the mindful use and description of artifacts, the formats we use to share them, and the tools we use to understand them.

In chapter 12, Ken Cooper and Elizabeth Argentieri discuss their collaborative project about the Genesee region of western New York, which invites students not just to think and act locally, but, less obviously, to gather in one location otherwise unconnected types of knowledge: literary, economic, ecological, and historical. As a place-specific conception of knowledge, their emphasis on bioregionalism shares many assumptions with kindred methodologies like environmental studies, ecocriticism, and sustainability studies. Engaging students in archival projects that stretch the possibilities of the academic term, *OpenValley* invites them to connect with institutions beyond the college campus by collaboratively analyzing commercial documents, building a digital map of nineteenth-century food infrastructure, and editing as-yet unpublished diaries from a local farming family. Combining in real life (IRL) experiences for students in the form of community-engaged service learning with digital humanities pedagogy, students bring local materials to new and wider audiences. Much like in Sharpe and Powell's classes, Cooper and Argentieri's students also learn that the digital is not a substitute for emplaced and embodied knowledge. Against the potential pitfalls of digital humanities work, they consider how the growing screen time of modern academic scholarship can lead to unmindful harvesting of IRL materials for transformation into virtual "objects." *OpenValley*, by contrast, guides students in the work of sustainability and the recovery of local knowledge.

Essays in this section demonstrate the critical thinking that attends the curatorial work of constructing and interacting with archives. A project the size of *OpenValley*, involving community partners and a variety of digital platforms, can certainly be intimidating even to experienced practitioners. However, the essays' authors provide detailed project management suggestions. They offer advice for structuring service learning commitments to ensure equal partnerships with the community and the engaged, responsible actions of students. Contributors design assignments that provide students with a sense of completion and accomplishment at the end of the course while allowing for the evolution of the archive across semesters.

Act

The essays in this concluding section consider what it means to reframe the field with an activist DH pedagogy, one that encourages reflection on the sociocultural implications of DH practices in the classroom. In Act, contributors reflect on how questions of difference impact the American literature classroom, where race, gender, sexuality, and class intersect with nation, place, and identity. Earhart, Whitley, and Brooks, like so many of the contributors to the collection, describe assignments and classroom environments that put students in charge of selecting historical and contemporary artifacts, introducing curation as an activist practice. In this way, their essays are positioned within a tradition of Americanists dedicated to a particular form of pedagogy, one that shapes the field through teaching.

Prominent scholars such as Alondra Nelson and Lisa Nakamura have problematized the role of difference in digital spaces beginning in the late 1990s; however, the relevance of difference studies within the digital humanities has centered, most prominently, on questions of scholarship, from Tara McPherson's "Why Are the Digital Humanities So White" to Amy E. Earhart's work on the digital humanities canon.[18] The essays in Act theorize how DH can teach students about political agency, especially in relation to the curation of materials that explore difference. Students in Earhart's African American literature survey course research and select newspapers, political documents, and images pertaining to the 1868 Millican race "riot" that occurred fifteen miles from what is now the campus of Texas A & M University, where Earhart teaches. Edward Whitley's students learn how "studying the activism of the past helps to understand the activism of the present" as they examine how Harriet Beecher Stowe carefully curated the version of slavery she presented in her popular novel *Uncle Tom's Cabin* (1852) by examining her archive of influences in *A Key to "Uncle Tom's Cabin"* (1853). Students later study the Twitter feeds of prominent social movements such as Black Lives Matter to consider how organizers document and circulate their messages. Students in Tisha M. Brooks's survey course construct anthologies of African American literature that contain textual and visual primary source materials with the aim of bridging the gap between the past and the present and between print and visual literacies. As Julia Flanders explains in *Digital Pedagogy and the Humanities*, curation "licenses students to intervene in the artifact's fortunes, and it reminds students that their interventions will also have an impact on other participants. Perhaps most importantly, curation activities are situational and pose questions about how objects circulate and signify in different contexts."[19] Learning spaces led by Earhart, Whitley, and Brooks make it clear that choices matter.

In chapter 13, Earhart shows how the connection between DH and American literature is intimately linked to the historical development of activist DIY (do-it-yourself) digital projects built by scholars to provide alternatives to a predominantly white, Eurocentric canon. Earhart's students construct a digital archive that puts Texas's 1868 Millican race "riot" in broader cultural context by using historical newspaper articles about lynchings and editorials about voter rights. As with Cooper and Argentieri's *OpenValley* project, Earhart's students grapple with how sociocultural problems addressed in literature manifest themselves locally. They read nineteenth- and early twentieth-century texts emphasizing "African Americans' responses to white violence" as they curate materials related to the Millican "riot," animating a period in African American literature and history currently being recovered by scholars as a period of resistance. Earhart's essay shows how structural hierarchies, in the biases of historical newspapers and in the technologies we employ today, can limit access to the literary voices that once animated the period.

Edward Whitley, in chapter 14, proposes studying the curatorial work of Harriet Beecher Stowe in *The Key to "Uncle Tom's Cabin"* alongside current examples of digital activism to understand how groups mobilize and share information to effect change. Students in Whitley's class "reverse engineer" the composition of *Uncle Tom's Cabin* by searching through digital archives of abolitionist texts and images to discover how Stowe's inclusion of some materials and exclusion of others shaped her novel. Students then consider how social activists similarly sort, organize, select, and reject the documentary record of social injustice appearing online in real time. Whitley's students discovered the distance between nineteenth-century abolitionism and online activism is much shorter than we might think. In researching the effort to end the global trafficking of minors, one student found an organization called Operation Underground Railroad, which "works to end the sex trafficking of children in large part by retracing the link back to slavery in the United States." The organization asks for donations to "Give a Lincoln, Save a Slave." Whitley's student concluded that the organization "wants to bring Stowe's very archive into the twenty-first century. . . . The message: this is the *same* issue that was supposedly resolved." By encouraging his students to compare historical periods and media forms—and using the archive as a conceptual link between these disparate modes—Whitley fosters an environment where students can reflect on the processes through which texts are created, disseminated, structured, stored, and used to change the world.

The collection concludes with Tisha M. Brooks's use of multiple literacies to help students value their own assets as visual readers and bring them to bear on scholarly practices that may seem, at first, more foreign to them. In chapter 15, Brooks writes about a digital anthology assignment in her 200-level African American literature survey in which students act as "knowledge curators," while mindful of P. Gabrielle Foreman's clarion call about the responsibilities that attend fields that study "the lives and the literary productions" of disempowered groups. Brooks's assignment on the Middle Passage pairs the Schomburg Center's digital archive *In Motion: African American Migration Experience* with Markus Rediker's *The Slave Ship: A Human History* (2007) to help students make connections between literary and visual texts, to "bridge multiple literacies and historical gaps," and to encourage students to think critically about the representations of violence against black bodies. After a visual interpretation exercise in which students analyze visual artifacts, the class turns its attention to Frederick Douglass's Aunt Hester passage and Saidiya Hartman's 2007 book *Lose Your Mother* to consider what Douglass means in this passage by being both a "witness" and a "participant" in slavery. Students then return to the archive focused on how they, as viewers, are implicated in the violence and spectacle of slavery. Their work culminates in group digital anthology projects that help them "move from mere consumers of knowledge to critical thinkers who use the archive to make meaning of its artifacts and the history and literature connected to them." By selecting multimedia artifacts across periods, students become adept at representing the historical continuities between past and present.

Across all three essays in Act, students read nineteenth-century texts forward to understand the power of interpretive acts in our own moment. Earhart critiques canonicity and models textual recovery. She engages her students in the discovery of local knowledge, and she decenters the traditional classroom. Whitley guides his students to reflect on practices of inclusion and exclusion and the resonances between nineteenth- and twenty-first-century activism as he builds assignments around students' digital lives. Brooks concludes with a wide-reaching charge for instructors and scholars in the digital age to "recognize an evolving definition of literacy that is not tied strictly to a traditional and highly specialized canon of literature (i.e., printed books)." All three essays think deeply about race, culture, history, and textuality in ways that reflect and engage the collection's manifold field-based inquiries and digital humanities practices.

As they engage digital humanities practices and pedagogies writ large and small, the essays in the collection model inventive strategies and rethink what is possible in the American literature classroom. The act of building an archive using digital tools, as several of the essays attest, invites students to interrogate the canon and explore textual variants. Introducing students to the transcription of handwritten manuscripts and the coding of printed texts teaches them that careful attention to details can dramatically transform a text's meaning. Annotating texts with a community of readers (both within and beyond the walls of the traditional classroom) teaches students about the multiple uses of literary analysis while strengthening their close-reading skills. Aggregating and analyzing disparate archives with distant-reading methods reframes students' understanding of noncanonical texts and underrepresented genres. Visualizing the imaginative landscape of a text using maps and other digital tools asks students to see and think about literary invention in novel ways. We invite readers to explore the additional tags we've provided, interact with the many supplementary materials on the companion website, and contribute their own insights about how to interact with the many models of field-specific DH pedagogy presented in the collection.

Notes

1. Lauren F. Klein and Matthew K. Gold identify a similar shift in scholarship "from congregating in the big tent to practicing DH at a field-specific level, where DH work confronts disciplinary habits of mind." Lauren F. Klein and Matthew K. Gold, "Digital Humanities: The Expanded Field," in *Debates in the Digital Humanities 2016*, ed. Klein and Gold (Minneapolis: University of Minnesota Press, 2016), http://dhdebates .gc.cuny.edu/debates/2.

2. Emily Renker, "What Is American Literature," *American Literary History* 25, no. 1 (2013): 255.

3. *Hacking the Academy*, a book crowdsourced over one week in 2010 includes only a small section on pedagogy with very little field-specific analysis. *Hacking the Academy*, Roy Rosenzweig Center for History and New Media, George Mason University, May 21–28, 2010, accessed March 26, 2017, http://hackingtheacademy.org. The first *Debates in the Digital Humanities* collection, a foundational text in the digital humanities, sparingly addresses pedagogy. Matthew K. Gold, ed., *Debates in the Digital Humanities* (Minneapolis: University of Minnesota Press, 2012), http://dhdebates.gc.cuny.edu /debates. See especially essays by Gold, Jim Groom, and Stephen Brier for discussions of pedagogy.

4. The terms *digital humanities pedagogy* and *digital pedagogy* are often used interchangeably, though it is most accurate to think of digital pedagogy as an umbrella term covering multiple disciplines that, according to *Hybrid Pedagogy*, is "precisely not about using digital technologies for teaching and, rather, about approaching those tools from a critical pedagogical perspective. . . . It is as much about using digital tools thoughtfully as it is about deciding when not to use digital tools." "What Is Digital Pedagogy," *Hybrid Pedagogy: A Digital Journal of Learning, Teaching, and Technology*, accessed March 26, 2017, http://www.digitalpedagogylab.com/hybridped/digitalpedagogy/.

5. Harris's subsequent essay in *Polymath* provides a longer meditation on the need to engage students at the nexus of digital humanities and literary studies. Katherine D. Harris, "Play, Collaborate, Break, Build Share: 'Screwing Around' in Digital Pedagogy," *Polymath: An Interdisciplinary Arts and Sciences Journal*, 3, no. 3 (2013), https://ojcs .siue.edu/ojs/index.php/polymath/article/view/2853/0.

6. Brett D. Hirsch ed., *Digital Humanities Pedagogy: Practices, Principles and Politics* (Cambridge: Open Book, 2012).

7. Rebecca Frost Davis, Matthew K. Gold, Katherine D. Harris, and Jentery Sayers, eds., *Digital Pedagogy in the Humanities: Concepts, Models, and Experiments*, MLA Commons, Modern Language Association, accessed March 26, 2017, https://digital pedagogy.mla.hcommons.org/keywords/.

8. See, for example, Rebecca Frost Davis, *Liberal Education in a Networked World* (blog), https://rebeccafrostdavis.wordpress.com/; Mark Sample, *SampleReality* (blog), http://www.samplereality.com/; and Brian Croxall, *Brian Croxall* (blog), http://www .briancroxall.net/.

xxviii DESPAIN & TRAVIS

9. In addition to the *Digital Pedagogy in the Humanities* project on MLA Commons arranged by keywords, see Raymond Williams, *Keywords: Vocabulary of Culture and Society*, rev. ed. (New York: Oxford University Press, 1985); Bruce Burgett and Glenn Hendler, eds. *Keywords for American Cultural Studies* (New York: New York University Press, 2007), and the expanded online edition, http://keywords.nyupress.org/american-cultural-studies; Rebecca Frost Davis et al., *Digital Pedagogy in the Humanities*; and Benjamin Peters, ed., *Digital Keywords: A Vocabulary of Digital Information, Society & Culture* (Princeton, N.J.: Princeton University Press, 2016).

10. Franco Moretti, *Distant Reading* (London: Verso, 2013). As the book goes to press, allegations against Moretti regarding sexual assault and harassment raise questions about his academic career and scholarship. While the term *distant reading* has become a useful shorthand among digital humanities scholars, the work of N. Katherine Hayles, also discussed in this introduction and in several of the essays, is equally useful for understanding reading informed by large data sets and algorithms.

11. Jentery Sayers, "Tinker-Centric Pedagogy in Literature and Language Classrooms," in *Collaborative Approaches to the Digital in English Studies*, ed. Laura McGrath (Logan: Utah State University Press / Computers and Composition Digital Press, 2011), 27, http://ccdigitalpress.org/cad/index2.html.

12. Meredith McGill, *American Literature and the Culture of Reprinting, 1834–1853* (Philadelphia: University of Pennsylvania Press, 2007).

13. Ellen Gruber Garvey, *Writing with Scissors: American Scrapbooks from the Civil War to the Harlem Renaissance* (New York: Oxford University Press, 2012).

14. N. Katherine Hayles, "How We Read: Close, Hyper, Machine," *ADE Bulletin* no. 150 (2010): 62–79.

15. Jerome McGann, *The Textual Condition* (Princeton, N.J.: Princeton University Press, 1991), 122–125.

16. Johanna Drucker, "Designing in the Digital Humanities," in *Digital_Humanities*, ed. Anne Burdick, Johanna Drucker, Peter Lunenfeld, Todd Presner, and Jeffrey Schnapp (Cambridge, Mass.: MIT Press, 213), 13.

17. Amy E. Earhart, *Traces of the Old, Uses of the New: The Emergence of Digital Literary Studies*. Ann Arbor, MI: University of Michigan Press, 2015.

18. See Tara McPherson, "Why Are the Digital Humanities So White? or Thinking the Histories of Race and Computation," and Amy E. Earhart, "Can Information Be Unfettered? Race and the New Digital Humanities Canon," in Gold, *Debates in the Digital Humanities*.

19. Julia Flanders, "Curation," in *Digital Pedagogy in the Humanities: Concepts, Models, and Experiments*, MLA Commons, ed. Rebecca Frost Davis, Matthew K. Gold, Katherine D. Harris, and Jentery Sayers, Modern Language Association, accessed March 26, 2017, https://digitalpedagogy.mla.hcommons.org/keywords/.

Additional Tags

THERE ARE A VARIETY of pathways through the essays that supplement and enhance the collection's organization. We include here additional tags that organize the essays by DH pedagogical practices. Despite the richness of the contributions, fifteen essays in any combination could not hope to fully address the ways that DH pedagogy impacts American literary studies. The collection does not claim to be comprehensive, but it is our hope that the essays will inspire efforts to broaden our disciplinary methodologies and instructional tools. Visitors to our companion website can suggest their own tags for the collection's essays.

Begin

Readers new to DH may want to begin with some of the user-friendly tools described in chapter 6, the step-by-step instructions offered in chapter 10, or the social media assignment in chapter 14. See chapters 9 and 10 for instructors who come to DH by "happy accident" as they seek ways to teach the content of their classes more effectively.

Build

Readers interested in the best methods for incorporating students in the work of constructing digital archives should turn to chapters 2, 3, 5, 11, 12, and 13. For readers interested in building projects on particular platforms, see chapter 4 for TextLab; chapters 3, 11, 12, and 13 for Omeka; chapters 2 and 11 for Scalar; and chapter 11 for TimelineJS. Chapter 2 is instructive for those learning how to choose the best platform for a given project.

Code

Chapter 1 is best suited for learning how to integrate code into the humanities classroom, particularly Cordell's Twitterbot assignment.

Collaborate

Most of the essays describe collaborative classroom practices and assignments. For student and instructor collaborations, see chapters 2, 3, 5, 6, 11, and 12. For peer-to-peer collaboration, see chapters 1, 2, 3, 4, 10, 12, 13, and 15.

Crowdsource

Chapters 1, 2, 3, 4, and 6 consider how to use digital tools for public and peer-produced student work only possible through the combined efforts of multiple participants. Chapters 2 and 4 discuss the benefits of crowdsourced annotation.

Edit

For teaching students about editorial methods, see chapters 2, 7, 9, and 15. For approaches to TEI and textual editing, see chapters 1, 4, and 8.

Engage

For ways to build on student success and to encourage research opportunities outside the classroom, see chapters 2, 4, 5, 6, and 9. Chapters 11 and 12 explore service learning and community-engaged pedagogy.

Experiment

A reconfiguration of traditional classroom spaces and the relationship between student and instructor is central to chapters 1, 2, 4, and 13.

Fail

Practicing a pedagogy that encourages risk and finds ways to mitigate and leverage failure is central to chapters 1, 2, 3, 5, 6, 10, and 11.

Interact

Several of the essays discuss how best to interact with digital resources in the classroom. See chapter 5 for the *Emily Dickinson Archive*; chapter 7 for *Just Teach One*; chapter 8 for *Just Teach One: Early African American Print*; chapter 9 for *JTO, JTO: EAAP*, and the teaching resources at the *Society for the Study of American Women Writers*; chapter 10 for *The Walt Whitman Archive*; and chapter 15 for *In Motion: African American Migration Experience* and *DocSouth*.

Map

Readers interested in assignments exploring the use of maps to visualize networks of influence or the geographical expansiveness of a text's content should read chapters 4, 6, and 12.

Network

For discussions of social media and social networks, see chapters 1, 14, and 15. Chapters 1 and 14 discuss Twitter in particular.

Play

For discussions of play and tinkering, see chapters 1, 3, 6, and 10. For easy-to-incorporate DH tools, see chapters 4, 6, 10, 11, and 12. Chapter 6 is instructive for understanding the importance of and time commitment required for establishing clean data before beginning play.

Research

Chapters 9, 10, 11, 13, 14, and 15 discuss using research in primary documents as a means of reinvigorating the undergraduate classroom.

Scaffold

For guidance in scaffolding DH projects, see chapters 2, 9, 10, 13, 14, and 15. For projects that think beyond the semester and continue to build on student work, see chapters 4, 6, 11, and 12.

Write

For assignments that use DH pedagogy to create more audience-based writing assignments, see chapters 1, 3, 11, 12, and 13. For introducing students to genres of writing other than the argumentative essay, see chapters 1, 2, 3, 9, 12, and 13. Chapter 4 discusses how using digital tools throughout the semester can strengthen final, argumentative papers.

PART ONE

Make

1. Kaleidoscopic Pedagogy in the Classroom Laboratory

Ryan Cordell, Benjamin J. Doyle,
and Elizabeth Hopwood

The name Kaleidoscope, which I have given to a new
Optical Instrument, for creating and exhibiting beautiful
forms, is derived from the Greek καλός, beautiful; εἶδος,
a form; and σκοπέω, to see.
—David Brewster, *The Kaleidoscope: Its History, Theory,
and Construction* (1855)

IN RECENT YEARS, the term *laboratory* has become a keyword in discussions of digital learning environments in the humanities.[1] The laboratory is not an entirely new concept to humanities education and pedagogical models, as discussions of writing laboratories in rhetoric and composition indicate.[2] However, the term *laboratory* is increasingly posited and applied as an innovation in instructors' and students' approach to humanistic inquiry. We seek in this essay to delineate a more deliberate application of the term that does more than rhetorically align the humanities with the sciences. In fact, we argue that *laboratory* can connote a deeply historicized and media-focused learning environment for studying the nineteenth century. To frame this conversation, we propose a model of laboratory-based learning we are calling a "kaleidoscopic" pedagogy, which emphasizes not only the site of a laboratory space but the experiences that such a site engenders.

In a science laboratory, students might use a microscope to more closely investigate an object of study. A grain of pollen, for instance, becomes delicately intricate, complicated, unnerving. By contrast, we draw our central metaphor for the laboratory from a nineteenth-century tool: the kaleidoscope. Whereas the microscope, as both tool and metaphor, enables the researcher to see and know what they could not see or know before, the kaleidoscope fractures an otherwise singular entity into an array of seemingly disparate parts that remain in intimate relation. In literature classrooms, students and instructors are familiar with the microscopic framework, which we engage through close reading and related interpretive practices. In this chapter, we propose a complementary kaleidoscopic framework for the laboratory classroom. Adopting a kaleidoscopic perspective, we argue, productively unsettles our and our students' familiar ways of knowing and doing literary studies. A kaleidoscopic pedagogy adds building and experimentation to reading and interpretation, blends digital and analog media as tools and objects of our analyses, and repositions students as necessary and integral collaborators in the knowledge-making processes of the field.

The kaleidoscope offers a deeply humanistic metaphor for imagining classrooms as laboratories. In David Brewster's account of his invention of the kaleidoscope—quoted above as our epigraph—he describes it as "a new Optical Instrument, for creating and exhibiting beautiful forms."[3] It is, in other words, an instrument that blends optics and aesthetics, symmetry and surprise, structure and creation. A kaleidoscopic laboratory challenges students to both "explore unfamiliar technologies" and to "defamiliarize those we think we already know," such as the book.[4] In such labs, students build in two distinct ways: as an experiential learning practice (e.g., understanding early nineteenth-century book production by setting type and operating a letterpress printer) and as a method of knowledge production (e.g., from bibliographic metadata research to mapping the movements of an enslaved person using geospatial software). Such acts of making can bridge rhetorical divides between the digital and the analog, help students understand nineteenth-century technologies, deepen their engagement with books as material and technological objects, and push them to think critically about both the words and the media through which they present their own ideas about the period. Indeed, many debates that seem unique to the twenty-first century—over privacy, intellectual property, information overload, and textual authority—rose to prominence during the nineteenth century. By engaging directly with the technologies that spurred such debates then and now, students come to insights unavailable through reading alone.

We conceive of these activities under the term *laboratory* not to mark off a separate, more "objective" space for humanities work. With Amy E. Earhart, we believe "it is important not to romanticize the [scientific] lab."[5] In some classroom or institutional contexts, the more familiar *studio* or *workshop* might be equally effective spaces for fostering the activities and learning goals we describe here. Indeed, our central metaphor deliberately troubles such distinctions. The kaleidoscope itself was, through the course of the nineteenth century, a scientific instrument, a device for creative provocation, an objet d'art in Victorian parlors, and, just as importantly, a toy. As Jason Farman describes, Sir David Brewster developed the kaleidoscope during experiments on "the relationships between optics, light, and mirrors," and it was soon adopted by scientists who "found it useful as a tool to visualize massive numbers."[6] From the optics laboratory, the kaleidoscope flourished in studios, workshops, and even industry, where it was used to create patterns for cloth and housewares. Indeed, Farman demonstrates how the kaleidoscope became a popular mobile device, critiqued for distracting the public in ways analogous to critiques of mobile computing technology today. Ultimately, however, Farman argues, "it was the way that this new mobile device brought together these elements (the science of optics, industrial utility, and symmetrical beauty through a visual instrument) that captured the attention of the nineteenth century."

Likewise, the kaleidoscopic laboratory encourages students to experiment— often beginning in quite procedural ways—to foster work that refracts into analysis, creativity, building, and play. In the following pages, we first outline discussions in the digital humanities community (and beyond) around ideas of *building*, *making*, or *tinkering* as both research and pedagogical practices. While acknowledging the political and epistemological limitations of these conversations thus far, we advocate a vision of building in the classroom that we see as liberating and generative for students. Echoing Earhart, we advocate the kaleidoscopic laboratory as "a space into which we can imagine our hopes for new practices" in the classroom.[7] In the rest of the article, we delineate the kaleidoscopic outcomes a laboratory-oriented course can meet for students, illustrating each point with examples from our own classes. We offer these points as provocations, not inflexible principles, and hope they can generate discussion within the context of particular courses and curricula.

Building the Kaleidoscope

In a fall 2014 class, we accompanied a group of undergraduates enrolled in an upper-level English course, Technologies of Texts, to the Museum of Printing in North Andover, Massachusetts, a twenty-five-minute bus ride from Northeastern University in Boston. While there, students set lines of movable type, which they then printed on nineteenth-century proof presses under the supervision of museum volunteers. By the end of this brief letterpress laboratory, students had composed and printed a single word or phrase, which they could take with them to hang on a dorm wall or give as a present. To complete the letterpress assignment, students published lab reports on the course blog in which they "use[d their] brief experience working in a print shop to think about very small details of printing and compositing work." We asked them, "What is apparent to you now that wasn't before this trip, and how might those details help you (re)consider class concepts and/or texts?" The assignment encouraged students to focus on specifics, write about observations rather than emotions (e.g., "the type was smaller in size than I had imagined" rather than "I really had fun at this lab"), and to use the environment of the print shop to consider the material aspects of printing.

One student, Lauren Smith, wrote the following in her lab report:

> A lot of what I learned at the Museum of Printing were things that we had already covered to a certain extent during class, but were really cemented in my mind while we were there, and the implications of them became clearer. . . . [For instance,] the only interaction one has with the ink with modern printing is buying a new cartridge, and then once it's already dry, or mostly so, on the printed page. For this lab, I had to roll out the ink on a roller and roll it onto the type. Where most errors with a printer would only come from a broken printer or low ink, here, there are more variables. If I missed a spot while rolling the ink, it wouldn't show on the printed version. Some errors in my pieces of type meant that there were some slight imperfections in the printing. The second print of one came out lighter, which implies that not only does the ink have to be reapplied frequently, but that it's very unlikely that any editions of a book are exactly identical. Also, there's much more room for error–I not only decorated my hands with ink, but also my sweatshirt. (It's okay. Now it looks more vintage.) But it's surprising to me that the books we've seen at the Rare Books Room weren't more smudged with ink and makes me wonder if printers were so adept that they didn't get ink on their own hands, didn't get it on the printing, or if there really is no such thing as an identical edition.[8]

Smith's reflection aptly illustrates the multiple effects of the kaleidoscopic laboratory. Specifically, we want to call attention to how her experience operating a printing press refracts into insights that connect a range of course materials and allows her to inhabit, albeit partially and anachronistically, the physical and mental spaces of a nineteenth-century printer. Smith recalls the readings and videos we watched about letterpress print practices ("things that we had already covered to a certain extent in class"), but these recollections are extended by observations made in the print shop. By comparing letterpress printing to her own experiences with inkjet or laser printing, she connects her lab activities and readings with in-class discussions in which students paralleled their understanding of modern technologies with historical print technologies. From here she moves to a specific, material observation about the messiness of ink in the letterpress process, which is an element of print that our readings and in-class discussions did not illuminate for her. Finally, Smith links her new synthesis to an earlier class trip to the Boston Public Library's Rare Books Room. Her comment that "it's surprising to me that the books we've seen at the Rare Books Room weren't more smudged with ink" surfaces a small but salient material-textual detail that had not been evident to her during the BPL trip, but that became apparent through her work in the print shop. Indeed, Lauren's final point reaches toward a sophisticated bibliographical question, as she extrapolates from her new insight about ink to wonder "if there really is no such thing as an identical edition." This one laboratory activity becomes a locus around which Smith can gather a cluster of ideas about the larger course, its activities, and its subjects. The work of the lab allows her to place previously studied materials in new and meaningful configurations by bringing together both familiar and novel facets of print technology and asking her to make something, both literally and figuratively, of them.

But what does this experience have to do with *digital* pedagogies, and how does it differ from activities or field trips in nineteenth-century literature classes that would not be classified as laboratories? Considered as an isolated class event, the answer to those questions would be "very little"—there is, we suppose, a blog involved—and "nothing." Many instructors incorporate hands-on activities and field trips into their classes. In the kaleidoscopic classroom we advocate here, however, such hands-on assignments constitute a core, sustained, organizing element of the course. The classroom laboratory spans archival research; hands-on experiments with both historical and modern technologies; and media-focused assignments that ask students to craft arguments in textual, aural, visual, and haptic modes. Though literature is most typically a discipline of the book, we insist that nineteenth-century books are themselves sophisticated technologies—"machine[s] of knowledge"—created through and often composed in response to a constellation of other technologies.[9] Within the laboratory environment, the book's own technologies become more visible and available for critique. Indeed, the larger mediascape of the nineteenth century comes into sharper focus for students for whom its innovations are so routine as to seem, without conscious effort, invisible.

Such ideas of *making* or *building* have been central to discourse in the growing field of digital humanities. Stephen Ramsay—whether famously or infamously—argued that a "commonality to everyone who finds their way to dh" involves "moving from reading and critiquing to building and making." For Ramsay, this movement constitutes "a new kind of hermeneutic" central to the field:

> As humanists, we are inclined to read maps (to pick one example) as texts, as instruments of cultural desire, as visualizations of imperial ideology, as records of the emergence of national identity, and so forth. This is all very good. In fact, I would say it's at the root of what it means to engage in humanistic inquiry.... But *making* a map (with a GIS system, say) is an entirely different experience. DH-ers insist—again and again—that this process of creation yields insights that are difficult to acquire otherwise. It's the thing I've been hearing for as I long as

I've been in this. People who *mark up* texts say it, as do those who *build* software, *hack* social networks, *create* visualizations, and pursue the dozens of other forms of haptic engagement that bring DH-ers to the same table.[10]

Ramsay's hermeneutic of building has been vigorously debated, particularly by scholars concerned that it eschews the necessary interventions of critical theory or even reinforces the inequities those theories seek to address.[11] Certainly ideas of *building* or *making* can reinscribe dominant cultural modes and economic discrepancies, particularly when taken up uncritically, as self-evident goods.

Nevertheless, we are convinced, largely through the classroom experiences we describe throughout this essay, by the core of the building argument. Students gain insights that cannot be had otherwise through sustained, haptic engagement with nineteenth-century subjects, archives, and technologies. As Jentery Sayers argues of *tinkering* in English studies classrooms, we mark a profound benefit to "inexpert, tactical, and situational experimentation" in the classroom. Sayers's theorization of tinkering is particularly compelling as an iterative mode in which "a dusty Humanities 1.0 expertise is not rendered retrograde by a shiny Humanities 2.0 toolkit." Instead, "Competencies generally associated with the study of literatures and languages are . . . mobilized in new domains and situations, with different effects."[12] Likewise, we do not here advocate that the typical competencies central to literature classrooms, such as reading, contemplation, or writing, be replaced by data analysis, quantification, or coding. However, we do recognize those latter activities as existing on a continuum of student engagement with the former, with the potential to be mutually constitutive in students' burgeoning understanding of nineteenth-century texts and cultures. The comparative approach to both nineteenth- and twenty-first-century technologies "emphasizes their historical and technological specificity," leading to a more nuanced understanding of both periods.[13]

A kaleidoscopic laboratory framework helps investigations with primary materials resonate with students as something more than antiquarianism. In "The Histories of Computing(s)," Michael S. Mahoney describes his own realization that to effectively teach his students a history of technology, they needed to work directly with machines: "The sources I needed were not texts about these machines, but the machines themselves, to be found not in a library but in a museum. Technology is not a literate enterprise, but a visual, tactile one. . . . We do not read about them, we act with, in and through them."[14] Our laboratories, then, might be described as another kind of course text. In them, the printed book and letterpress become lenses through which students can test ideas that echo and refract from the technological nineteenth century through to our technological present. Indeed, we argue that the laboratory setting can structure such investigations in ways that push students beyond historical tourism—in which the archival book or device registers primarily as an object of awe—and toward comparative interpretation. Moreover, students' experiments with contemporary technologies—from TEI encoding to Python programming—help them claim scholarly agency over both the texts and tools central to their educations.

In his essay "Building and Sharing (When You're Supposed to Be Teaching)," Mark Sample argues that *building* can operate as both an alternative and spur to the *thinking* that typically dominates the humanities classroom. Sample conceptualizes building in terms of work, by which he means "the opposite of thinking." Sample insists "tortured and laborious thinking does not automatically translate into anything of importance" and can manifest primarily as delay, waiting for a brilliant idea to descend from on high. Ultimately, Sample values the interpretive force and public resonance of his students' building: "As my students build—both collaboratively and creatively—they are also reshaping, and that very reshaping is an interpretative process. It is not writing, or at least not only writing. And it is certainly not only thinking. It is work, it has an audience, and it is something my students never expected."[15]

The kaleidoscopic classroom incorporates many aspects of Sample's building ethos, though we would clarify that perhaps the most salutary effect of classroom building is that recontextualizing course materials through building generates new thinking. Building a digital exhibit necessarily raises questions about representation and reading that can only be answered through design and writing together. By asking students to *make* and *do* (and indeed often to "make do"), we seek to instill "a kind of productive unease that results from the encounter and from its product. This unease registers," as Julia Flanders notes of humanities scholars using digital tools, "as a sense of friction between familiar mental habits and the affordances of the tool, but it is ideally a provocative friction, an irritation that prompts further thought and engagement."[16] Whether the tool in question is a papermaking screen or computer screen, we see the laboratory as a space for students to engage consciously with modes of production that make clearer affordances and limitations of media that might otherwise escape notice.

Keywords for a Kaleidoscopic Pedagogy

What, then, are the central values or outcomes we see emerging from laboratory work in classrooms learning about nineteenth-century literature and culture? In this section we offer three key concepts for a kaleidoscopic pedagogy, illustrating each with specific examples from our classroom activities and assignments. We offer these concepts as prompts for reflection and, we hope, as models for others to test and refine. A kaleidoscopic pedagogy seeks to inspire students toward a more intimate appreciation for the material conditions of textual production through *defamiliarization, experimentation,* and *contribution,* which we argue emerge at the intersections between immersion and reorientation. We provide students opportunities for intellectual contribution by bringing them closer to a history of literary material culture and its technologies of production, which helps them reconceptualize their objects of study while also calling on their existing knowledge, experiences, and interests. Indeed, we argue that a kaleidoscopic laboratory invites students to a more active relationship with their objects of study. Within a hybrid analog-digital laboratory setting, the process of experimentation operates both as a method for validating hypotheses and discovering possible variations. It is this intimate overlap between thesis and hypothesis that enables students to locate opportunities for genuine contribution.

Defamiliarization

During the first week of the course "Technologies of Text," Cordell introduced students to a cutting-edge technology that redefined the experience and practice of reading. Students were given the opportunity to handle the device, testing out its features. They were then asked to describe any benefits or advantages this reading platform had over others. Some praised its portability and lightness, and others noted that it caused less eye and neck strain than alternative interfaces. One student appreciated the device's ease for habitual readers, which made it simple to bookmark a spot for later reference. This cutting-edge device Cordell passed around was, of course, a printed book, or codex. But when students were asked to engage with it as an unfamiliar—even innovative—development, they were able to see it not as "just a book," but as a technology that carries with it particular sets of values, assumptions, meaning, and histories. Throughout the rest of this semester, this engagement with a printed book as an object of uncertainty helped students develop a vocabulary for discussing the affordances and limitations of other textual media, including blogs and ebooks.

We see this activity—or, more specifically, the framing of this activity—as an example of *defamiliarization,* which we identify as the core of a kaleidoscopic laboratory pedagogy. In practice, defamiliarization can take several forms in the literature laboratory. An instructor might ask students to read across digital and analog archives; create their own scholarly editions; examine the material form of books and their historical development; and/or look at different editions of texts to demonstrate variations in content, reception, and reading experience. In the laboratory classroom, defamiliarizing a student's relationship to a text can unsettle the typical relationship between students and their objects of study. This practice resonates with the idea of "deformance" posited by Jerome McGann and Lisa Samuels, reading texts "backward"—both literally and figuratively—to critically resituate a reader to a text, or perhaps to Emily Dickinson's poetic injunction to "Tell all the truth but tell it slant."[17] We advocate practices of making as a way of giving students a sideways view at objects with which they are otherwise familiar.

For instance, we might ask students to study and then edit primary documents for the web, rather than only reading in anthologies or edited editions. In an undergraduate seminar at Northeastern University called Race and Slavery (taught by Nicole N. Aljoe, a contributor to this volume), Hopwood worked with a small group of students who chose to mark up texts using the Text Encoding Initiative (TEI) for their final assignment (see Appendix 1.1). TEI is a set of scholarly encoding guidelines for machine-readable texts in the humanities and social sciences.[18] These students were asked to read and analyze a novel not only as the bounded codex with which they were familiar but also as an XML document that tests given assumptions about the form and structure of the text. There are many challenges to working with TEI in the literature classroom, particularly when TEI is not the main learning objective.[19] Even opening an XML file, with its red error messages and angle brackets, can be an uncomfortable—and sometimes stilting—experience for students who have only composed in a WYSIWYG editor.[20] In many cases, this activity is as unfamiliar for the instructor as it is for the student. However, such acts of making can be incredibly valuable and result in an intense form of close reading that is instantiated in the encoding. Asking students to work with markup is to ask them to impose a set of ideas directly onto the text and to think about the text as content *and* as data that represents structure. There is a pedagogical imperative in asking students to engage in close reading in a way that is unfamiliar: the text looks different on screen, its paragraphs and sections demarcated with division tags. For the instructor, the challenge of defamiliarization might occur in the negotiation between teaching new media while maintaining the learning objectives of the literary classroom.

To respond to this learning curve, the students met with Hopwood over the course of several weeks for an introduction to the markup, including using the oXygen text editor.[21] Hopwood first sought to de-emphasize TEI as an XML language. One might easily spend a semester or more training and working with TEI, and the instructor, as Hopwood found, must continually bring the focus back to the goals of the course.[22] They kept literary analysis as the primary focus but also discussed how XML facilitated or, in some cases, shaped that analysis. Much as a student might mark up their copy of a novel with sticky notes and highlighter, students used XML markup to tease apart different layers of the text to arrive at a set of interpretative distinctions. For example, in tagging the names of people in the anonymously authored 1808 novel *The Woman of Colour*, one student, Lizzie Seaburg, contended with how to treat named characters, references to characters, and unnamed or anonymous characters, as well as what these naming systems might suggest about the text. Seaburg marked characters to indicate interpretative categories related to race.[23] Across her markup, Seaburg used the "comment out" feature of XML to encode her own annotations about the text and her process of marking it up.[24]

Seaburg located segments of texts (<seg>) and applied her own analytical category of #race to mark moments of racial difference. She then used these segments to identify moments where the language seemed to indicate a character's inclusion or exclusion from their larger community. She found that racial designations continuously overlapped with moments of exclusivity, particularly regarding Olivia, the biracial "Woman of Colour" at the center of the narrative. But what was more surprising to Seaburg were the moments when characters seemed to push back against these designations. Seaburg's markup led her to a counterreading wherein particular instances of racial separation are followed by examples of inclusive language. The constraints and the customizations of TEI require that a student not only make but also provide a rationale for their editorial decisions. Viewing the text through the lens of XML, and armed with only a minimal set of approaches to markup, the students could engage in an alternative form of exploratory reading of their text. They developed a list of interpretive categories that they then marked within the text and also moved into more focused interpretations of the text's meaning. The students' final product comprised a package consisting of an XML file, the output rendered with simple CSS (Cascading Style Sheets),[25] and a reflective essay, which together resulted in new questions, observations, and arguments. In her reflection piece, Seaburg reported:

> I've found in regular close readings, I tend to focus on the quotes I'm analyzing as a whole, but in order to do this markup I had to look closer at individual words, what they meant, and who was saying them. Throughout the process of encoding this text and doing the markup, I have discovered a lot about how the different characters interact and the way in which the text can interact with and contradict itself. We were able to analyze elements such as "race" and "commodities" and see how these two ideas connect, but also branch off to other ideas. Some categories, which seemed like they would be opposites, such as "inclusive" and "exclusive" language ended up being linked more than I expected. As an English major, I'm used to analyzing text, but there is something about marking up a text that allows me to look at it in a different light than I normally would. While we are working within a certain set of parameters and working to label particular things, I

found that learning what doesn't fit into the established interpretive categories is just as important as finding out what does. I could go over this section of text multiple times and always discover new ways of marking it up and keep adding to my work until I had more tags than text.

Seaburg's reflection illustrates how this type of exercise promotes close reading, though she draws a distinction between "regular close readings" and the reading that she did with TEI, which brought her closer to the text itself, as well as the text's "individual words, what they meant, and who was saying them." Seaburg's encoding experience demonstrates the close connection between defamiliarization and experimentation. Seaburg's findings indicate an element of surprise; she points to how interpretive "categories which seemed like they would be opposite . . . ended up being linked more than I expected." We asked Seaburg and her classmates to undertake this activity not knowing what they might find. It was up to students to make encoding decisions and, from their markup, make meaning from patterns and discrepancies.

Encoding in TEI was for our students, as Kate Singer argues about encoding poetry in the classroom, an act of "rescripting the scene of reading as a collaborative, social, and descriptive one rather than something more hermetic, fixed, and prescriptive."[26] For her students as for ours, "The physical, hands-on nature of a project where students literally rebuilt pieces of a poem and painstakingly marked it by hand resonated with them in ways that 'analogue' reading did not." The act of adding anachronistic angle brackets provides a way, paradoxically, to generate analytical distance from nineteenth-century texts while compelling students to pay close attention to details. Of course, a TEI-centered activity is only one way in which to bring a sense of defamiliarization into the literary classroom. What we hope to illustrate is how approaching a novel, short story, or poem kaleidoscopically can reposition and reinvigorate students' understandings of historical texts. The digital itself defamiliarizes and deforms, as TEI serves as an apparatus or a lens through which to see a text anew.

Experimentation

Defamiliarization opens space in the classroom for students and instructors to experiment together—we might imagine turning the kaleidoscope this way and that, watching how the colors rearrange themselves and then testing new arrangements. A kaleidoscopic pedagogy requires students and instructors to welcome serendipity, to anticipate surprise, differing outcomes, and sometimes even failure in activities and assignments. This can be particularly true when working with digital tools that may be new even to the instructor. For instance, in a fall 2014 assignment in his Technologies of Text class, Cordell worked with students to write "Twitterbot" scripts in the Python programming language that would remix nineteenth-century poems and post them to accounts on the microblogging platform.[27] These Twitterbots were themselves quite simple, taking a stanza from students' chosen poems (only a stanza, given Twitter's 140-character limit in 2014) and replacing some of its key words with new words of the appropriate grammatical kind drawn randomly from Wordnik, an online dictionary. Each time the program ran, a new version of the poem would be produced and posted on the Twitter account students created for the assignment. While the computational work required was relatively simple, the assignment was complex, requiring students to choose a poem; identify its significant structural elements; gain access to the APIs (application programming interfaces) for Wordnik and Twitter; learn basic Python syntax; restructure a model Python poetry-bot program to accommodate their chosen poem; debug the resulting program; and run their new poetry-bot program successfully. The randomized poems created through this process were sometimes nonsensical, often humorous, and occasionally oddly poignant. Either way, the strict and formal process through which students constructed these Twitterbots required them to attend closely to their chosen poem, and the new versions their bots produced offered refracted vantages—whether hilarious or profound—on the originals from which they iterated.

Cordell's Twitterbot assignment did not emerge from a longstanding proficiency on his part. On the contrary, he had learned to build such programs only weeks before and was excited to share this new knowledge with his students. As a result, this laboratory required willingness on the part of both students and instructor to test ideas that sometimes failed and to work together to find answers (in this case, often on programming websites like Stack Overflow). Several students took it upon themselves to write more complex poetry bots than the model, a welcome development that signaled their intellectual ambition and the value they placed in gaining new technical skills. Some students, for instance, wished to incorporate a trending hashtag from Twitter into their poems, so their Twitterbots would insert themselves into live conversations about news, celebrity culture, or other hot topics on the platform. The assignment required collaboration among groups of students and Cordell, with the end goal being not (just) a good grade but a particularly clever bot that actually worked. Several students reported pride in their bots—they felt they had "made something" that would have life beyond the class, which they could share with friends and family, and which connected their work with a larger contemporary cultural phenomenon.

For humanities laboratories to truly be experimental, there must be space, both intellectual and administrative, for exploration and unexpected outcomes. Even failure can be generative in such an environment. For instance, in another laboratory in Cordell's class students worked with Amanda Rust, Northeastern's digital humanities librarian, to research important historical figures or social justice organizations from the Boston area that were unrepresented or underrepresented on Wikipedia. In preparation for this lab, students discussed the culture of Wikipedia, practiced navigating the site's history and talk pages, studied the guidelines for creating articles, learned the basic markup used to structure Wikipedia articles, researched their chosen topic using materials from Northeastern's special collections and other public sources, and worked in groups to draft and publish their articles on Wikipedia. One group focused on Community Resources for Justice, a 130-year-old social justice organization born when several nineteenth-century reform groups in the Boston area merged. The students' most polished revision was submitted on March 25, 2014; on April 1, an established Wikipedia editor, "John from Idegon," marked the page for deletion.[28] John cited Wikipedia's guidelines for "notability" of organizations and companies, writing that there was "no indication of notability beyond the local area" for Community Resources for Justice.[29]

Cordell's students were incensed. They could not believe that this important group, which they had researched so thoroughly, would be labeled as unremarkable by the Wikipedia community. This moment seemed, in some sense, to mark a failed experiment—they had been tasked with making their organization visible to the world's largest reference source, and their work might disappear. However, in the kaleidoscopic classroom such moments of failure constitute an opportunity for looking anew at the object of study, which in this case was as much Wikipedia as it was students' chosen historical subjects. The proposed deletion of the "Community Resources for Justice" page sparked a series of intense discussions about what *notability* means in practice for Wikipedia pages; who makes such decisions; and how dynamics of race, class, and gender contribute to what knowledge is and isn't represented on the site. Ultimately, Cordell's students worked with Rust to respond to John from Idegon's critiques, thicken the page's citations, and protest the proposed deletion. The revised site was retained and can be found in its current iteration.[30]

For such experimentation to be possible, however, students must know that risks within the spirit of a lab assignment will be rewarded, even when they do not lead to an ideal outcome. In the case above, had the "Community Resources for Justice" page been deleted, the group would not have been penalized. Their work in the lab assignment fully met its requirements and was in fact quite good. Indeed, the proposed deletion of this page offered an alternative view into the politics and silences of Wikipedia that benefited the entire class. Far from a failure, the students' exchange with a skeptical Wikipedia editor proved a welcome variable that clarified the goals and theoretical underpinnings of the assignment. However, the experimental nature of the assignment required both students and instructor to adapt to unpredictable circumstances. To build something that will persist beyond a given course—in this case, to build a Wikipedia article that will both persevere and be expanded by other users in the future—students and instructors must experiment with new technologies, platforms, and modes that will stretch the boundaries of the classroom into other scholarly and public venues.

Contribution

The Wikipedia lab assignment above highlights the productive challenges students can meet when they are able to share their research with interested publics beyond the classroom. Such contribution-based laboratory experiences foster students' mindfulness of the connections and possible tensions between their own and others' intellectual work. Helping students become more aware of the stakes of scholarly contribution speaks to an ethical imperative we see emerging from the event of the digital in literary studies: to better define and refine what student contribution means within a fuller ecology of scholarly practice and discourse. We mark student contribution as central to the learning goals and necessary outcomes of the literary studies classroom. Outside the laboratory site, traditional literary instruction locates forms of student contribution within what are typically more student-to-student contributions (e.g., classroom discourse or group presentations). We seek to include our students as participants in the meaning-making practices of not just the classroom but also the field.

We also hope to unsettle a troubling characterization of students as *not yet* scholars. As the digital ushers in new modes of scholarly research and analysis, it presents new models of knowledge contribution that can include a more diverse community of practitioners and participants. Such shifts compel us to reconsider the role of students in advancing the field and to make clear(er) the available means of students' contributions in the *now*. We see this not as a facile provocation for student agency, and we would not suggest that all student work should be valued as scholarly. Rather, we see that the means (and media) through which students might apply their developing expertise have significantly altered such that their, our, and others' sense of the value of their work may extend beyond the traditional literary studies course or classroom. There are very real ways our students can creatively and confidently assert claims on the field, even as they hone their own scholarly practice. Emerging digital tools, resources, and projects offer increased opportunities for students to not only adopt but also *adapt* more responsible attitudes toward their own and others' intellectual contributions.

A kaleidoscopic pedagogy takes full advantage of such developments by prioritizing the concepts and practices of student contribution. One example of this contributive pedagogy has been our work with students on *The Early Caribbean Digital Archive* (*ECDA*).[31] A key component of the *ECDA* is to integrate digital research technologies and learning models that can better facilitate junior scholars' contributions to the ongoing study of the early Caribbean. In an early experiment in kaleidoscopic pedagogy, Hopwood and Doyle, at the time project managers of the *ECDA*, began to clarify a student-centered model of archival scholarship while working with three undergraduate students who had been given the opportunity to construct an alternative research project for their nineteenth-century African American literature course (taught by Professor Nicole N. Aljoe). In helping the students design their project, Hopwood and Doyle realized that the students needed to approach their research not only as a collaborative learning experience but also as a contributory process, where they could self-assess and assert the value of their work for both the course and the community of researchers engaging the *ECDA*. Because this digital project took shape outside of their primary seminar, students had to show their instructor how their research fit the learning goals of the course, even as their research asked them to identify and engage problematics and impacts related to their research that went beyond the expectations of the course.

Building on their readings and discussions during the semester, the students proposed a research project that explored the concept of *embeddedness* in early Caribbean slave narratives.[32] We worked with the students to clarify the aims of their project and to assign each colleague a role in building. The initial concept proposed to create a broad overview of the history of embedded publication practices in the Caribbean that would then move toward a more focused discussion of an understudied embedded narrative, "The Narrative of Louis Asa-Asa, a Captured African."[33] With the aim of highlighting the significance of the primary source and related concepts of *embeddedness* to early Caribbean scholarship, their project combined practices in visual argumentation through mapping; research of historical, bibliographic record through metadata; and composition of scholarly narrative and analysis through editorial headnotes. Initially we were excited by the opportunity for the students to offer a way for researchers to visualize the print histories of the Caribbean. However, we became equally interested in how, during the implementation and necessary redesign stages of the project, their individual and collaborative investments shifted from a curiosity about the digital to an appreciation for its limitations in uncovering a history of embedded slave narratives in nineteenth-century literature. They moved between concerns about the challenges of the digital tools they were using (in this case, working with Google Maps Engine) and the ability of those tools to effectively represent the ideas and arguments they hoped to offer. In fact, it was in those moments when they realized the tool, while vital, *required*, rather than replaced, their scholarly intervention. In other words, the map couldn't argue persuasively or meaningfully on its own. Moreover, actively acknowledging and responding to the limits of the digital brought back into focus for the entire team those critical, familiar humanistic questions regarding the nature of texts, publication data, and the function of authorship. The students' conversations about their research began to consider, for example, the gaps in the historical record and how such gaps impact scholarly research. They were forced to contend with absences of metadata available for tracing the publication history of Louis Asa-Asa's narrative, for example, which has historically and currently been packaged and studied as an appendix to Mary Prince's more well-known and well-researched narrative, *The History of Mary Prince* (1831). In response, they implemented a more nuanced research practice that employed alternative methods for locating the data they desired (e.g., searching other archive repositories, thumbing through footnotes and bibliographies of scholarly articles and book projects), and actively negotiated those moments where such absences could not be overcome to keep the project going and to establish future lines of inquiry. Relatedly, the frustrations they shared when they could not locate bibliographic information about their texts created opportunities for the group to discuss the importance of micromoments of scholarly contribution; in other words, the function and import of metadata in primary source research and argumentation took on new and necessary significance that both pushed on and responded to the legacy of the archival record in the knowledge work of the field. Where the practice of metadata research in the building of their project seemed a lower-order concern for them in earlier conversations with the students, it had become, by the end, a central component to their shared work.

Across all stages of the students' project building (its design, production, and publication), we were thrilled at how they repositioned their relationship to nineteenth-century materials, moving from passive to active participants in knowledge making by locating new and notable points of contribution. This process of generative repositioning was made possible due to practices in defamiliarization and experimentation that the digital—in both its possibilities and limitations—necessitated. The creative and mindful strategies for building that our students employed throughout this project underscore for us the value of a kaleidoscopic perspective within the humanities digital laboratory. Our students located areas of critical need that gave their project immediate value to the field, placed their own interests and investments into dialogue with those of their audience(s), maintained an openness to revising their approach and outcomes throughout the building process, and sought out new lines of analysis that would ensure others might continue to learn from and build on their knowledge work.

Positioning students and their intellectual practices as contributory opens opportunities for them to claim not just agency but ownership over their research, to assess the significance of their work beyond the top-down evaluation hierarchies of the institution, and to strive toward (pro)active and ethical relationships to the making and doing of nineteenth-century American literature. By integrating occasions for contribution within laboratory exercises, we have seen how students' scholarly labor can have immediate and measurable value as responses to problems in and outside the field. We have seen too that when students begin not only to sense but also to advocate for and track the direct influence their research can have, they begin to develop a sense of care for the quality of their intellectual output. Promoting students' intellectual labor as scholarship is more than an attempt by instructors to inspire students toward successfully doing the work of the classroom. The aim is to underscore how microforms of contribution (e.g., metadata and bibliographic research, headnotes, annotation) are as essential as macroforms (e.g., curated exhibits, scholarly articles, book projects) in the scholarly process, and to assert that students can and should be involved directly in this process. When students witness and participate in these modes of contribution, they begin to take seriously their own scholarly roles. They develop confidence, creativity, and thoughtfulness in their approaches to literary research and textual analysis.

We aim not only to unsettle students' familiar systems of meaning, models of knowledge, and modes of intellectual practice but also to provide them the means to respond with a deeper sense of care for their own and others' experiences of unsettlement. As the word *unsettlement* indicates, however, a kaleidoscopic laboratory is not without its difficulties. We have seen the ways each component of our pedagogical practice (defamiliarization, experimentation, and contribution) can create situations that stifle rather than motivate some students. In a learning environment that values risk, unease, public engagement, and the application of often unfamiliar digital tools and methods into students' study of nineteenth-century American literature, students should be able to rely on more traditional pedagogical support mechanisms (e.g., one-to-one conferencing, group conversation sessions at strategic points in laboratory assignments, clear learning goals, assessment rubrics) to help them be successful contributors. In any kaleidoscopic laboratory, we maintain open dialogues with our students about not only the effectiveness of their own practices but also of ours. A kaleidoscopic pedagogy is necessarily always in the making. It must adapt to shifting patterns of instruction and learning if it is to effectively and ethically guide students toward participation in the knowledge work of nineteenth-century American literary studies.

Conclusion

In the kaleidoscopic classroom laboratory, students pursue a fuller under-standing of the nineteenth century through a sustained laboratory practice spanning analog and digital technologies. Here the nineteenth century is both the subject and object of their experiments. They "creat[e] and exhibit . . . beautiful forms" of knowledge using nineteenth-century technologies, such as the printing press, and twenty-first-century scholarly technologies, such as TEI. Practices of making or in the classroom prove uniquely suited to bridging the analog and the digital, revealing the historical contingencies of technology, and enriching students' own sense of how they might respond to the textual and material objects of the nineteenth century.

N. Katherine Hayles and Jessica Pressman argue in *Comparative Textual Media* that "conceptual understandings" in the classroom "are deepened and enriched by practices of production, a conjunction that puts critique into dynamic interplay with productive knowledges."[34] Hayles and Pressman ad-vocate for Comparative Textual Media (CTM) as a mode of engagement in literary studies focused on media and its effects, a "way to analyze literature that emphasizes its connections to the real world and to other fields of intel-lectual inquiry." Critique does not dominate in CTM but instead "is put into productive tension and interplay with what may be called an ethic of making." Such an ethic emerges, for us and our students, at this intersection between an operation of critique and a process of building: the countless moments of overlap between theory and praxis, the series of events that call on us to acknowledge how we take ownership over our ideas by not only employing them but by demonstrating their significance and responsiveness within and across learning contexts and for our available audiences.

In framing an ethic of making for our students, we emphasize a multidirec-tional perspective—a kaleidoscopic method, a prism of resources and resource-fulness—for how they might develop their own "practice-based research."[35] In adopting the phrase *ethic of making* to characterize our pedagogy, we mean that students must be guided toward a responsibility to their own intellectual practices and labor, where they simultaneously value and evaluate themselves as scholars and their work as scholarly. We see this not only as a complement to the theorizing and discursive practices that take place within a literature classroom, but as a vital component of such practices. The incorporation of digital work in the classroom can lead students toward adopting and adapt-ing a self-reflexive stance to their own intellectual labor and potential. By (re) forming a novel with TEI, mapping the movements of an enslaved person within their narrative, writing and revising entries for Wikipedia, or design-ing letterpress-ready type in a 3D printing studio, students are called upon to consider and reconsider the meaning and meaningfulness of the materials and material conditions of their objects of study.

The appendix for this chapter, an assignment by Elizabeth Hopwood on TEI as interpretive close reading, can be found at www.press.uillinois.edu/books /TeachingWithDH.

Notes

1. Scholars have increasingly been interested in developing digital laboratories and curriculum. For a discussion of how this might be accomplished on a macro level, see Cathy N. Davidson, "What If Scholars in the Humanities Worked Together, in a Lab?," *Chronicle of Higher Education* 45, no. 38 (May 28, 1999): B4.

2. For an introduction to this conversation see Neal Lerner, *The Idea of a Writing Laboratory* (Carbondale: Southern Illinois University Press, 2009).

3. David Brewster, *The Kaleidoscope: Its History, Theory, and Construction*, 2nd ed. (London: John Murray, 1858), 1.

4. Paul Fyfe, "Digital Humanities Unplugged," *Digital Humanities Quarterly* 5, no. 3 (2011), http://www.digitalhumanities.org/dhq/vol/5/3/000106/000106.html.

5. Amy E. Earhart, "The Digital Humanities as a Laboratory," in *Between the Humanities and the Digital*, ed. Patrik Svensson and David Theo Goldberg (Cambridge, Mass.: MIT Press, 2015), 393.

6. Jason Farman, "Kaleidoscopes and a Distracted Public," from an unpublished book in progress. For a popular press piece by Farman on the same subject, see "The Forgotten Kaleidoscope Craze in Victorian England," *Atlas Obscura* (blog), November 9, 2015, http://www.atlasobscura.com/articles/the-forgotten-kaleidoscope-craze-in -victorian-england.

7. Earhart, "Digital Humanities," 399.

8. Lauren Smith granted us permission via email to republish this lab report.

9. Jerome McGann, "The Rationale of HyperText" (1995), *Institute for Advanced Topics in the Humanities*, University of Virginia, May 6, 1995, accessed May 25, 2015, http://www2.iath.virginia.edu/public/jjm2f/rationale.html.

10. Stephen Ramsay, "On Building," *Stephen Ramsay* (blog), January 11, 2011, originally at http://stephenramsay.us/text/2011/01/11/on-building/; accessed April 19, 2018, via the Internet Archive Wayback Machine, https://web.archive.org/web/20170704144620 /http://stephenramsay.us/text/2011/01/11/on-building/.

11. Most importantly, we would point to Alan Liu's "Where Is Cultural Criticism in the Digital Humanities?" and Tara McPherson's "Why Are the Digital Humanities So White? or Thinking the Histories of Race and Computation" in *Debates in Digital Humanities*, ed. Matthew K. Gold (Minneapolis: University of Minnesota Press, 2012), http://dhdebates.gc.cuny.edu/debates, as well as the work of the #transformDH (http:// transformdh.org) and #dhpoco (http://dhpoco.org) collectives.

12. Jentery Sayers, "Tinker-Centric Pedagogy in Literature and Language Classrooms," in *Collaborative Approaches to the Digital in English Studies*, ed. Laura McGrath

(Logan: Utah State University Press / Computers and Composition Digital Press, 2011), 27, http://ccdigitalpress.org/cad/index2.html.

13. N. Katherine Hayles and Jessica Pressman, "Making, Critique: A Media Framework," in *Comparative Textual Media*, ed. Hayles and Pressman (Minneapolis: University of Minnesota Press, 2013), 232.

14. Michael S. Mahoney, "The Histories of Computing(s)," *Interdisciplinary Science Reviews* 30, no. 2 (2005): 129–130.

15. Mark Sample, "Building and Sharing (When You're Supposed to Be Teaching), *Journal of Digital Humanities* 1, no. 1 (Winter 2011), http://journalofdigitalhumanities .org/1-1/building-and-sharing-when-youre-supposed-to-be-teaching-by-mark -sample/.

16. Julia Flanders, "The Productive Unease of 21st-Century Digital Scholarship," *Digital Humanities Quarterly* 3, no. 3 (2009), http://www.digitalhumanities.org/dhq/ vol/3/3/000055/000055.html.

17. Jerome McGann and Lisa Samuels, "Deformance and Interpretation," *New Literary History* 30, no. 1 (1999), https://muse.jhu.edu/journals/new_literary_history /v030/30.1mcgann.html.

18. See *TEI: Text Encoding Initiative*, accessed March 26, 2017, http://www.tei-c.org.

19. Despite the learning curve, we've seen increased interest in developing literature courses around TEI and markup. See, for instance, Kate Singer, "Digital Close Reading: TEI for Teaching Poetic Vocabularies," *Journal of Interactive Technology & Pedagogy* no. 3 (May 15, 2014), http://jitp.commons.gc.cuny.edu/digital-close-reading-tei-for -teaching-poetic-vocabularies/.

20. WYSIWYG stands for "What You See Is What You Get." These are editors, like Microsoft Word, that visually represent the stylistic choices of the user while they are composing a document.

21. oXygen is a standard editor for xml markup. It includes an error checker that flags any issues in well-formedness of the markup (such as a missing angle bracket or including a paragraph element where it doesn't belong) as well as a way to check that the document is valid against TEI schemas. The students accessed oXygen through computers in Northeastern University's Digital Scholarship Group and also downloaded a free trial license for their own machines.

22. A note about the structure and scope of the assignment: because this was a literature course, students were not expected to gain a complete grasp of TEI to do the intellectual work they set out to do. Rather than requiring them to develop a comprehensive knowledge of TEI, which might include customized schema development, working with ODD files, or building prosopographies and gazeteers, the work they did was meant to hone their close reading and analytical skills by building upon course themes and making a critical argument about one or more texts. Because this was a small self-selected group (the students of the course were given the option to write a traditional paper or to work with TEI), the students who chose to undertake this assignment did so with a high level of curiosity and enthusiasm. Over the course of several weeks, the students met outside class to familiarize themselves with TEI. They were given an overview of common elements used to mark texts (such as struc-

tural elements like <p> for paragraph or <div> for divisions) and were asked to think about the interpretative categories in which they were interested. They chose texts they had read in the course and transcribed a short section to mark up. Their interpretive categories echoed larger course themes and included *race, gender, exclusive language, inclusive language,* and *religion,* among others. After the end of the course, one student (Lizzie Seaburg) who was particularly interested in and adept at the markup language was even hired as a TEI encoder for the *Early Caribbean Digital Archive.*

23. Lizzie Seaburg granted us permission via email to discuss her experiences with the TEI assignment and to republish excerpts of her final reflection essay.

24. Material enclosed using the "comment out" tag in XML, <!— Comment —>, is visible only when viewing the source code but is not rendered in a web browser.

25. The students used TEI Boilerplate to visualize and publish their work; see http://dcl.ils.indiana.edu/teibp/.

26. Singer, "Digital Close Reading."

27. See Cordell's full assignment, "Lab #12: Script(ing)," November 12, 2014, http://f14tot.ryancordell.org/2014/11/12/lab-12-scripting/.

28. For the students' final draft see "Community Resources for Justice," Wikipedia, accessed March 26, 2017, http://en.wikipedia.org/w/index.php?title=Community _Resources_for_Justice&oldid=601243763. Students' Wikipedia assignments were published, as per Wikipedia's guidelines, under a Creative Commons Attribution-ShareAlike 3.0 Unported License (CC BY-SA). Students were given the option to publish under their own names or pseudonyms, depending on their comfort with public writing.

29. Per Wikipedia's guidelines for notability, "If a topic has received significant coverage in reliable sources that are independent of the subject, it is presumed to be suitable for a stand-alone article or list." "Notability," Wikipedia, accessed March 26, 2017, http://en.wikipedia.org/wiki/Wikipedia:Notability.

30. See "Community Resources for Justice," Wikipedia, accessed March 2, 2016, http://en.wikipedia.org/wiki/Community_Resources_for_Justice.

31. Elizabeth Maddock Dillon et al., the *Early Caribbean Digital Archive,* Northeastern University, accessed March 3, 2015, http://ecdaproject.org.

32. Adopted from Nicole N. Aljoe's discussion of the Atlantic world slave narrative genre, *embeddedness* refers to the various ways in which the life narratives of enslaved and formally enslaved Africans of the Caribbean entered into print, often through highly mediated and fragmented textual forms. For a more detailed discussion of how Aljoe describes and uses this concept, see Nicole N. Aljoe, *Creole Testimonies: Slave Narratives from the British West Indies, 1709–1838* (New York: Palgrave Macmillan, 2012).

33. The "Narrative of Louis Asa-Asa, a Captured African" was first published in 1831 as an appendix to Thomas Pringle's publication *The History of Mary Prince, A West Indian Slave.*

34. Hayles and Pressman, "Making, Critique," xv.

35. Ibid., xviii.

2. The Trials and Errors of Building *Prudence Person's Scrapbook: An Annotated Digital Edition*

Ashley Reed

THIS ESSAY RECOUNTS my work with students on a collaborative digital project: an online, annotated edition of Prudence Person's scrapbook.[1] *Prudence Person's Scrapbook: An Annotated Digital Edition* was inspired by Ellen Gruber Garvey's exhaustive work on nineteenth-century scrapbooking practices. Intrigued by Garvey's thesis in *Writing with Scissors: American Scrapbooks from the Civil War to the Harlem Renaissance* that scrapbooking is itself a form of writing—one that reflects both the interests of the scrapbook's compiler and the "culture of reprinting" (as Meredith McGill has famously termed it) that characterized the nineteenth-century public sphere—I began looking for ways that I might use the scrapbooks preserved in the Southern Historical Collection at the University of North Carolina at Chapel Hill to introduce students to nineteenth-century literary and popular culture while also challenging them to think about our own current textual environment.

I began *Prudence Person's Scrapbook* as a collaborative endeavor with a class of nineteen students in a general education course called Writing about Literature. I expected my students and me, working together over the course of a semester, to complete an annotated digital edition of a scrapbook produced between 1860 and 1920 by Prudence Person, a (rather obscure) member of a prominent North Carolina family. We failed to meet that goal for several reasons. Some were technical: Scalar, the scholarly publishing platform we used, had a major data loss a few weeks into the project. Others were pedagogical: I had conceived the project as an addition to a sophomore-level literature course, when in fact the amount of time required to learn both the skills and the content to complete the project would have justified an entire semester of an upper-level course. The result was a half-finished project that offered students an introduction to nineteenth-century print culture and to the skill of scholarly annotation but did not produce a publishable project. I have come to think of this semester, with its frustrations and failures, as "Phase One," most useful, perhaps, for its negative lessons on how *not* to launch a digital project.

Unwilling to abandon the project, I then pursued it as an independent study with two of the students from the earlier course. Together we identified which of the scholarly annotations produced by their classmates needed revision and made a plan for performing those revisions, for adding contextual essays to the site, and for customizing the interface. Because we were such a small group—and because our class time was devoted entirely to the project—we were also able to plan and participate in other activities related to the scrapbook, including trips to the Person home and to an undergraduate research conference. We completed the project together by the end of the fall semester of 2014, and it is my hope that it will become the prototype for future editions that can be undertaken with larger groups of students.

I began conceptualizing *Prudence Person's Scrapbook* as a collaborative digital project in fall 2013. Like many people in the field of nineteenth-century U.S. literary and cultural studies, I had been reading Garvey's *Writing with Scissors* and marveling at the trove of materials she had unearthed and studied. I wanted to introduce students to nineteenth-century literary and popular culture while challenging them to think critically about writing and reading as practices with histories and genealogies all their own. Fortunately for me, the UNC Libraries own a large number of historical scrapbooks, and when I approached the rare books librarians at UNC they responded to my simple query—"Do you have any nineteenth-century scrapbooks you can show me?"—in characteristic librarian fashion: with a shower of resources. Dr. Emily Kader, rare book research librarian, pulled a selection of the many scrapbooks held in the North Carolina Collection and the Southern Historical Collection and invited me to come and peruse them. Several were compilations of articles and mementos from the Civil War and the Spanish-American War; others contained pamphlets or records of political activity; one included an Arabic transcription of the twenty-third Psalm as recorded by the Muslim slave Omar ibn Said.[2] While I gave my students the opportunity to examine each of these scrapbooks in class, the one I chose for the course project was by an unknown female resident of Louisburg, North Carolina. Many scholars, I imagine, have had the experience of falling in love with a holding in an archival collection; Prudence Person's scrapbook became the object of my affection.[3]

Prudence's scrapbook is large, a professionally manufactured one rather than one repurposed from used paper, as scrapbooks (particularly during and after the Civil War) often were. It includes one hundred pages (fifty leaves), nearly all of them covered to their edges with newspaper and magazine articles carefully clipped and pasted in by Prudence over a sixty-year period, from the 1860s to the early years of World War I. "Prude," as her family called her, decorated the front of the scrapbook with die-cut images of girls in flowing locks and fashionable bonnets; the first page shows the remains of a flower or fern leaf she pressed into it. The book contains very little of Prudence's own writing, aside from the occasional handwritten date, including the date of her wedding near the front. (She married at forty-one but had begun the scrapbook long before.)[4] Some of the pages are thematically arranged, with articles and images about Christmas, farming, or preparing for heaven; a number are filled entirely with obituary columns. Nearly every page contains a poem, ranging from dubious ditties by local bards to Tennyson's famed "The May Queen" and Rose Hartwick Thorpe's blockbuster "Curfew Shall Not Ring Tonight." Other pages showcase what Ryan Cordell (a contributor to this collection) has called "information literature": "lists, tables, recipes, scientific reports, trivia columns, and so forth."[5] Rarely does an item include information about the source from which Prudence clipped it (though some articles contain, in a byline or at the end of the piece, a reference to the editors' source or the notation "from Exchange"). In short, the scrapbook offers both a window into the concerns of an educated middle-class southern woman in a small but established North Carolina town and a detailed snapshot of postbellum American print culture.[6]

Aside from the "scissor-writing" represented in her scrapbook, Prudence left few other written records behind. The Person Family Papers at Duke University include a few of the formal compositions she wrote while at Louisburg Female College—including one on "Woman's Rights" and one on the hardships that test faith—and her handwritten copy of the college's rules.[7] The papers also contain her diploma and the holograph will in which she bequeathed the Person Place home and land—which she had inherited from her mother Abiah—jointly to her husband and nephew. How her scrapbook came to reside in UNC's Special Collections rather than among the Person Papers at Duke is unclear.

When I spoke to Emily about the possibility of creating a digital edition of the scrapbook, she was, again, all helpfulness and excellent suggestions. She consulted with the libraries' Scholarly Communications Office to make sure there were no copyright or intellectual property restrictions to prevent the publishing of digital images of the scrapbook online. She then placed the scrapbook in the queue for UNC's Scribe scanning machine.[8] The scanned object was provided to me as a single PDF rather than the individual pages students would need to complete their annotations, so I downloaded the PDF, saved each page image as a JPEG, and uploaded those JPEGs one by one to Scalar's hosted media server, where the students and I would create the digital "book" that would become *Prudence Person's Scrapbook: An Annotated Digital Edition*.

I chose the Scalar platform for the project because it is designed for multimedia publishing, because its editing interface functions similarly to many popular blogging platforms with which students might already be familiar, and because it offers users the ability to annotate images in dynamic and flexible ways. I considered building the project using Omeka, which has rightly become a standard for digital exhibits, but I had not used it before and was unfamiliar with its annotation capabilities; furthermore, at the time UNC-CH did not offer on-campus support for Omeka. I had also used WordPress for class projects involving archival materials, but WordPress's built-in organizational structure, which divides publications into "Posts" and "Pages," was unsuitable for the project, and UNC's on-campus WordPress instance did not include plug-ins for image annotation. So I chose a platform with which I was already familiar that offers the annotation capabilities my students and I would need and that supports a rich array of visual and textual materials. Scalar was designed by media studies scholars at the Alliance for Networking Visual Culture (ANVC) at the University of Southern California for the purpose of creating multimedia online textbooks, and one of its hallmarks is that "anything can annotate anything else." Scalar's content management system treats all input agnostically, without drawing distinctions between images, video, pages, or posts. This interface design allows for a flexible and segmented editing process as Scalar's designers intended: instead of deciding what the site will look like to users and then building pages accordingly, authors can concentrate on gathering images and video, annotating them, and writing explanatory or analytical text, and then decide how to assemble these various pieces of content in an order that makes sense to both editors and potential users. Media can be reused in different portions of a work without having to be uploaded separately and given unique names. And users can be offered different "paths" through a published work, so the author isn't forced to choose only one order of presentation.

Creating an annotated digital edition of Prudence's scrapbook would, I reasoned, offer the perfect opportunity to introduce my students to a wide array of concepts related to the study of literature: nineteenth-century print culture, the history of copyright, the conventions of newspaper publication versus novel publication, the changing cultural influence of poetry, and differences in the popularity and circulation of male and female authors. The project would also enable them to practice a number of critical reading and writing skills: primary and secondary source research, scholarly annotation, citation and scholarly integrity, digital publishing, and writing for the web. Perhaps most importantly, the project would help historicize students' own experience of reading and interacting with texts. The nineteenth-century print public sphere, which was characterized by a "wild west" mentality that reigned among newspaper editors after the rise of inexpensive printing and the "penny paper" but before the codification of international copyright law, shows striking parallels with our own digital media environment. I expected *Prudence Person's Scrapbook*, in combination with the self-referential texts we read together, to challenge students' assumptions about their relationships with text (see Appendix 2.1).

Phase One

Prudence Person's Scrapbook was originally designed to complement a 100-level English course called Writing about Literature that was populated mostly by freshman- and sophomore-level nonmajors. I designed the course to be conceptual rather than project driven: I wanted students to think about books as material and imaginative artifacts and to consider the collaboration between author and reader that happens at the level of the page. For course texts I chose novels that are explicitly about their own novel-ness—Jane Austen's *Northanger Abbey*, Vladimir Nabokov's *Pale Fire*, Ruth Ozeki's *A Tale for the Time Being*, and Italo Calvino's *If on a Winter's Night a Traveler*—and a few shorter pieces and films (Jorge Luis Borges's "Tlön Uqbar, Orbis Tertius," the preface to William Goldman's *The Princess Bride*, and director Marc Forster's *Stranger than Fiction*) that play with the relationship between creator, audience, and text.[9] To reinforce the lesson that all readers interact with texts in multiple ways—that texts change us as we absorb them—I designed writing and project assignments, including journal entries and *Prudence Person's Scrapbook*, that asked students not only to consume but also to actively contribute to and become part of the texts and artifacts we encountered together (see Appendix 2.2).

Over the course of the semester, students kept online reading journals using the WordPress blogging platform. These journals were not free form; instead, students could choose from a set of response questions or creative assignments I provided. Sometimes these assignments were straightforward blog entries (write a "reading memoir" about a book you read as a child; assess the relative strengths and weaknesses of the Scalar and WordPress platforms), but others required students to use web-based tools to analyze the literature we read together: during our reading of *Pale Fire*, for instance, we used the Poetry Genius online annotation site to collaboratively close-read a passage from the fictional writer John Shade's final poem.[10]

To complement this syllabus about the interaction between readers and texts, Emily arranged a small exhibit in the Grand Reading Room at UNC's Wilson Library, with artifacts ranging from medieval manuscripts to twentieth-century paperbacks. Emily selected texts in which readers had made their own contributions to the books they owned: a fifteenth-century incunable edition of Dante's *Divine Comedy* with annotations in two distinct hands; an eighteenth-century travel guide with one sightseer's notes about sites visited; a nineteenth-century printing of Tennyson's poetry with meticulous pencil and watercolor illustrations added by the book's owner; and C. S. Lewis's personally annotated copy of *Beowulf.* I wanted students to be comfortable with the idea of writing back to the texts they read and to understand that the intimate relationship between readers and texts stretches back for centuries.

While Prudence obviously never achieved the stature of Dante or C. S. Lewis, she too formed intimate relationships with the texts that populated her life. Prudence used her scrapbook to speak back to the culture in which she lived; she "wrote with scissors," as Garvey would say, about many of the most important social issues of her time. For instance, the scrapbook contains several clippings about women's rights and responsibilities; these selections embrace the idea of woman's privileged place in domestic affairs while decrying their involvement in ostensibly male pursuits like politics.[11] Prudence also participated in the culture of remembrance that animated southern self-identity after the Civil War: she clipped and saved poems and circulating stories about fallen Confederate soldiers. (Four of her five brothers fought in the war; two were killed, one at Gettysburg and one in Warrenton, Virginia.) And the scrapbook may offer clues to her own family life: early pages contain poems about the joys of marriage and instructions for how to be a good wife, while later pages counsel contentment in the face of disappointment and preserve popular poems and engravings dedicated to children dead and living.[12]

Annotating Prudence Person's scrapbook would, I reasoned, complement the texts we were reading by giving students an opportunity to write back to Prudence's scissor-writing—to resituate her editorial choices in their nineteenth-century context by tracing the clippings' origins and reflecting on the larger culture that produced them (and her). Students would become part of Prudence's text in a way analogous (but not, one hopes, similar) to Charles Kinbote's intimate relationship with John Shade's "Pale Fire" in Nabokov's novel, and they would engage in what Mark Sample has called "collaborative construction":

> A key point of collaborative construction is that the students are not merely making something for themselves or for their professor. They are making it for each other, and, in the best scenarios, for the outside world. Collaborative construction obliterates that insular sense of audience inherent in more conventional student assignments.[13]

Making the students' annotations public as part of a digital edition would invite readers on the web to become part of this cross-temporal cultural conversation, and *Prudence Person's Scrapbook* would enable the newspaper and magazine texts that Prudence so carefully preserved to reenter the maelstrom of circulation in yet another form.

Technologically speaking, incorporating the project into the course was neither difficult nor time-consuming. As I've mentioned, I chose the Scalar platform in part because its editing interface is similar to digital publishing platforms like WordPress, which my students were using to keep their reading blogs and which many of them had used before. Annotating an image in Scalar is easy: students can open an image file, "draw" a box around the newspaper clipping, die-cut illustration, or postcard they want to annotate (by feeding Scalar the page coordinates for the item), and write the annotation. The annotation is then attached to the media file (the JPEG image) rather than to a particular page on the site, and each annotation also becomes its own separate piece of the project, so that students can quickly edit and proofread their finished annotations without having to reopen the attached image files.

When I demonstrated this annotating technique in class, the students mastered it in about twenty minutes; while a few needed review during individual conferences, most found the Scalar platform intuitive and the image annotation function simple to use. One of the advantages of Scalar is that tasks like image annotation are largely independent of questions of interface design, so students could complete their annotations without being concerned about how the entire project would eventually look. This made it easy to distribute the technology learning process across the semester: students did not need to master the entire platform to begin completing their annotation assignments.

Because scholarly annotation is a skill unto itself, I offered students plenty of examples and opportunities to write their own annotations before they began working with the scrapbook. For the first reading assignment in the course I had chosen David M. Shapard's extensively annotated edition of *Northanger Abbey*, and in addition to our discussions of the book's content, the students and I identified the different types of annotations included in Shapard's text. Students then demonstrated their mastery of these different types in their online annotations to *Pale Fire*.

In theory, then, the course was well framed. As Ryan Cordell notes in a blog post helpfully titled "How Not to Teach Digital Humanities," often the best way to integrate DH work and concepts into the undergraduate curriculum is to interweave digital projects with more traditional course activities and to help students intellectually and materially situate recent technologies (like digital publishing) in the context of earlier ones (like the steam printing press and the newspaper exchange).[14] This is precisely the pattern I had laid out for my students in the design of my Writing about Literature course.

But in the execution the project proved untenable because *Prudence Person's Scrapbook* was a much larger undertaking than I had realized. Because Scalar is fairly user-friendly and because the internet (and particularly Google Books) has made it so much easier to trace historical sources than it used to be, I had imagined students could complete most of their annotation work outside of class, after which we would spend a few class days designing the site interface, and the project would be done.

But I underestimated the amount of contextual and conceptual work this would entail; students simply didn't have the historical-cultural knowledge that would allow them to correctly situate these texts in their nineteenth-century milieu and to write about them in a way that would be meaningful to general readers on the web. This was in large part because I had chosen to situate the project in a 100-level course not otherwise focused on nineteenth-century American culture;[15] many of the students in the class, while sharp and hard working, were first- and second-year students, and few of them were English, history, or American studies majors. While I spent time in class introducing students to general resources like the *American National Biography*, *American Periodicals Series Online*, and *Chronicling America*, students made their best headway in researching the materials Prudence clipped when they met individually with me, where I could help direct them to the particular resource they needed. Without my guidance, some of the less tenacious of them fell into bad habits: they searched for a poem or article in Google and accepted the first result as the correct one, leading to odd assertions like "Prudence clipped this article from the *Ottawa (Ill.) Free Trader*," which gave little thought to why a woman in Louisburg, North Carolina, with limited income would be ordering newspapers from thousands of miles away. I could correct some of these missteps in class, but others required one-on-one time with students, when I could demonstrate more sophisticated methods of research using subject-, region-, or period-specific databases—a teaching model better suited to a small, upper-level seminar than a general education course.

In retrospect, it strikes me now as somewhat ludicrous that I expected a class of undergraduate non-English majors in a 100-level course to

- read, absorb, and respond intelligently (in class discussion and on their blogs) to five very difficult novels, none of which was written during the period covered by the scrapbook;
- learn two different web-based publishing platforms (WordPress and Scalar);
- keep their own online journals;
- understand the intricacies of nineteenth-century print culture (including the absence of copyright law, the prevalence of newspaper exchanges, and the ubiquity of poetry, aphorism, and religious meditation in the popular press);

- familiarize themselves with an artifact in the North Carolina Collection and understand the historical and material conditions under which it was produced;
- learn the purpose and form of scholarly annotations;
- write scholarly annotations for a 150-year-old scrapbook;
- and research and compose a ten- to twelve-page paper on an aspect of that scrapbook or one of the novels.

It is a testament to how ambitious, curious, and downright game UNC undergraduates are that my students were willing to give this convoluted course design the benefit of the doubt.

Unrealistic course design notwithstanding, the project would likely have progressed further than it did during this first phase had we not experienced a major technology failure. A few weeks into the semester the server on which Scalar's creators hosted outside media (including the 104 JPEGs I had painstakingly uploaded) crashed, rendering those media inaccessible to students. The process of retrieving the lost media took longer than expected, so Scalar eventually provided a new (and consistently backed-up) external media server.[16]

Paradoxically, at this point the problem of an overpacked syllabus helped mitigate the problem of data loss. If I had built my entire Writing about Literature course around *Prudence Person's Scrapbook*, then the server crash would have brought the course crashing down with it, forcing me to reboot the semester altogether. But because the scrapbook project was only one of many balls we had in the air, dropping it (at least until it became clear that the data would not be recovered quickly) left the rest of the course largely intact. I was eventually able to re-upload the images to the new server the ANVC put in place, but by then there was little time left in the semester for the students to do more than annotate their four or five assigned pages; interface design and contextual elements fell by the wayside.

Meanwhile, students were quite content to focus on the reading and on their own digital journals and to put off the scrapbook annotations until our technical difficulties were surmounted—a circumstance that confirmed that I had not done enough to cultivate their interest and investment in the project and to integrate the digital edition with the course's other assignments. Course evaluations for the semester, while positive, commented primarily on the novels and stories we read together and on our class discussions rather than on the scrapbook project. Students did not feel the loss of the project particularly acutely, suggesting that they did not, in fact, consider themselves to be engaged in an act of "collaborative construction," and that I had integrated neither the project nor the concept of collaborative learning fully into the course. The work that students managed to complete by the end of the semester was mostly solitary: they researched and wrote their annotations and added them to our Scalar site. Because of technical and other difficulties, we ran out of time for those aspects of the project that would have been more collaborative, including reviewing and editing their peers' annotations and making decisions as a class about the user interface. By the end of the semester students had some experience conducting primary source research and writing scholarly annotations, but they did not have a finished digital project to call their own.

While this first phase of *Prudence Person's Scrapbook* didn't result in a publishable product, it still led to useful pedagogical outcomes. The project helped to historicize and denaturalize for students the practices of information retrieval, absorption, and circulation they now perform moment by moment on their mobile devices. "In the twenty-first century," Garvey writes, "we are so accustomed to the cut-and-paste terminology of our digital devices that these terms are nearly extinct metaphors. Instead of reading a paper newspaper with shears or penknife in hand to clip articles of interest, we read online news sources saved and organized by digitized place marking and cut-and-paste functions."[17] My students and I examined the similarities between the nineteenth-century "culture of reprinting" that made scrapbook collections possible and our current web-based culture, in which it is difficult and sometimes impossible to correctly trace the source of a joke, image, or quotation as it propagates across social media sites.

We also considered the historical lag between changing print and distribution technologies and the legal structures meant to protect copyright and intellectual property. As students used Google Books and large primary-source databases to try to track down the origins of the texts Prudence clipped, it became increasingly clear to them that the nineteenth-century editors of the *Southern Planter* were no more concerned with authorial attribution than are the modern-day editors of Buzzfeed. The major difference, of course, is that in the early to mid-nineteenth century "the republication of foreign works and particular kinds of domestic texts was perfectly legal; it was not a violation of law or custom but a cultural norm."[18] In our twenty-first-century digital milieu, the laws that govern information and creative works have not caught up with the technologies that help people produce and distribute them, and the laws that *are* in place are often ignored by uninformed or content-hungry editors.[19] Learning the history of copyright and intellectual property not only reinforced for students the importance of proper attribution and scholarly integrity but also paved the way for discussions about open-access publication and freedom of information.

These lessons learned from the *Prudence Person's Scrapbook* project not only gave students a point of entry into an otherwise foreign nineteenth-century culture but also enhanced our analyses of the fictional texts we read together.

When Jane Austen uses the tale of Catherine Morland to train her audience in the skill of critical reading, she is advocating for a thoughtful interaction with text that may or may not be modeled in Prudence's scrapbook. When Italo Calvino depicts the novelist Silas Flannery mechanistically churning out his "endless verbal production of thrills, crimes, and embraces," he is commenting on the interpenetration of artistic endeavor with capitalist forces such as the mass market publisher and the newspaper exchange. When Ruth Ozeki crafts scenes in which a humiliating video of her teenage protagonist Nao goes viral on the internet, she depicts how the public's hunger for novelty and sensation makes private individuals into unwilling celebrities. These themes resonated for my students, many of whom have spent their lives documenting their actions on Snapchat and Instagram and being subjected to anonymous taunting on platforms like Yik Yak. Though they weren't always able to identify with the themes of Prudence Person's scrapbook—questions such as "Why are there so many poems about dead people?" and "Why was she so sad?" prompted several discussions about pre-penicillin medical science and postbellum southern poverty—students had no trouble identifying with a woman who immersed herself in all available media and collected her favorite information, gossip, jokes, and poetry.

Thus, though the first phase of *Prudence Person's Scrapbook* did not result in a publishable edition, it did serve many of the pedagogical purposes for which it was designed. For this first group of students, the scrapbook project became very much about process rather than product: they learned how to write scholarly annotations, how to conduct basic primary source research on the internet, how to interrogate the results of that research, and how to work with two different digital scholarly publishing platforms. And they practiced (and saw me demonstrate) an increasingly essential skill in our computer-assisted world: the art of dealing with unexpected technological breakdown.

I had expected my students and myself, working together over the course of a semester, to complete an edition of the scrapbook that could be made public at the end of the course. What we wound up with instead was a partially finished project that offered students an introduction to nineteenth-century print culture and to the skill of scholarly annotation.

While I had been the manager of an important digital humanities project (the *William Blake Archive*) for seven years, *Prudence Person's Scrapbook* brought to my attention the many differences between managing a digital project outside of the classroom and leading one inside it. Collaborating with students to produce a public project alters the instructor-student relationship by raising the stakes of failure: I had expected my English 127 students to have something public to show for their work at the end of the semester, and when they didn't, I had to question my efficacy as an instructor. When the platform for creating the project is new to both instructor and student (I had worked with Scalar but was no expert), the hierarchical model of information transfer does not apply: the instructor must be willing to admit how much he or she doesn't know. When the end of the semester presents an inexorable deadline, scheduling and task management become paramount: there is no asking an editor for an extension.

Fortunately, scholars who work in the digital humanities generally and digital pedagogy in particular quickly learn to anticipate, if not to expect, failure and even to welcome it as an opportunity for learning. As Lisa Spiro notes in her detailed discussion of the values that animate the digital humanities, "the digital humanities community recognizes the value of failure in the pursuit of innovation. . . . Failure is accepted as a useful result in the digital humanities, since it indicates that the experiment was likely high risk and means that we collectively learn from failure rather than reproducing it."[20] John Unsworth recommends that digital humanities projects "produce new ignorance" if they are to be worth pursuing at all.[21]

But anticipating and welcoming difficulties can be particularly stressful in the case of digital pedagogy: the willingness to look less than perfectly competent in front of our students can be an uncomfortable posture to inhabit. Some instructors never manage it, preferring to remain the "sage on the stage" for their entire careers. This posture can be particularly difficult for early career instructors, especially those who do not yet feel at home in the classroom.[22] And there is, of course, the not unimportant fact that pedagogy, digital or otherwise, should primarily be about what the students learn and not what the instructor learns. In the case of *Prudence Person's Scrapbook*, I can confidently say that the difficulties we experienced were pedagogically useful, or at least not insurmountable, for both the students and myself. But as Spiro notes, failure is only productive if it is documented for the benefit of oneself and others, so this essay stands as evidence of the periodic failures and ultimate success of *Prudence Person's Scrapbook*.

Phase Two

Having thus snatched pedagogical victory from the jaws of defeat, I was nevertheless still eager to see *Prudence Person's Scrapbook* completed and made available to the public. So I chose two of the strongest students from the spring course, Meagan Keziah and Jimmy Zhang, and invited them to join an independent study to take place in fall 2014. Meagan was majoring in English and taking advantage of UNC's new minor program in composition, rhetoric, and digital literacy; her experience (and patience) with Scalar was invaluable. Jimmy Zhang was a chemistry major planning to attend dental school after graduation; he became our resident expert on Prudence and her family. I was fortunate that Meagan and Jimmy had room in their academic schedules for independent study, and we met regularly on Monday and Wednesday afternoons to continue work on the digital edition.

We began our work by determining precisely what needed to be done to complete the edition and then setting deadlines for these tasks. Because one of the skills I wanted Meagan and Jimmy to gain from the independent study was project and task management (an underrated and essential skill in almost any career, and certainly in digital humanities work), we tracked our progress using a free, web-based application called Trello, which UNC's Digital Innovation Lab (of which I was a member at the time) uses for its internal project tracking.

We determined that our first act should be to write annotations for pages that had no commentary at all (usually because a student had withdrawn from the previous class after pages were assigned). Jimmy and Meagan divided up the blank pages and composed new annotations based on their own research. While doing so, they also wrote short contextual essays to accompany the digital edition; Jimmy wrote a history of the Person family and their Louisburg, North Carolina, home, while Meagan learned the basics of descriptive bibliography and composed a short piece about the scrapbook to alert readers to the materiality of the physical source. Jimmy also wrote a formal research paper on the Civil War experiences of North Carolina cavalry and home guard regiments. To document our progress and give us an outlet for commenting on some of the scrapbook's odder inclusions, Meagan, Jimmy, and I kept a project blog on Tumblr.[23]

Affectionately titled *The Dancing Tomato* after one of Prude's selected poems and its accompanying illustration, the blog includes, among other posts, an account of our visit to the Person Place Historic Site in Louisburg, North Carolina, where we were given a guided tour by Joe Elmore, official historian of the Person Place Preservation Society. On the same trip we also visited Louisburg College, where Maury York, director of the Tar River Center for History and Culture, explained the college's origins in the Franklin Male Academy and the Louisburg Female College, which Prudence attended as a teen.[24]

Between annotations, contextual essays, research papers, and blog posts, Meagan and Jimmy each completed at least forty pages of formal and informal writing over the course of the semester. They also practiced the skill of editorial revision as they corrected the annotations written by their former classmates. Once the writing and editing were complete, it was time to make choices about interface design and information presentation. While Scalar (like many blogging and entry-level website design platforms) uses a combination of PHP (hypertext preprocessor) and CSS (cascading style sheets) to offer users themes that standardize page layout, colors, and fonts, it is up to the user to determine exactly how information is presented.[25] Scalar, as aforementioned, treats all media (including images, videos, annotations, and body text) equally, so the creators of a Scalar "book" choose how and in what order to present those media to readers. Meagan and Jimmy opted to give visitors to *Prudence Person's Scrapbook* two different paths: a front-to-back path, in which users encounter each page in the order it appears in the physical artifact, and a thematic path that groups pages by subject matter or content type. Themes include poetry (by far the largest group), education (including a long newspaper article about commencement exercises for Prudence's graduating class at the Louisburg Female College), obituaries, religion, illustrations (whether picture postcards or popular engravings reproduced in local newspapers), and racial and ethnic "jokes."[26]

By mid-November the project was far enough along that Meagan and Jimmy felt prepared to present the results of their work at the State of North Carolina Undergraduate Research and Creativity Symposium in Raleigh.[27] Our project lent itself to a "digital poster presentation" format, so at the event Meagan and Jimmy found themselves, laptops at the ready, surrounded by posters about mold spores, old-growth trees, chemical reagents, and pharmaceutical interventions. When approached by symposium visitors they fielded questions about the scrapbook's origins, about Prudence Person's life and family, and about the Scalar platform.

The independent study thus served as a capstone experience: an intensive research and writing project that helps to prepare students for advanced study. By the time we made *Prudence Person's Scrapbook* public in March 2015, Jimmy and Meagan had become minor experts on nineteenth-century newspaper and scrapbooking culture, on Prudence, the Person family and the Person Place Historic Site, and on using Scalar to build a digital edition. And they had practiced valuable skills in formal and informal writing for a public audience, in project and task management, and in public speaking and presentation. They also formed strong professional relationships with me and with each other. Their sense of ownership over the digital edition is evidenced by their willingness to continue working on it well into the spring semester, after the official end of the independent study period.

Lessons Learned and Plans for the Future

The story of *Prudence Person's Scrapbook* is about the need for extreme flexibility when designing and pursuing digital pedagogy projects. But it is also about the immense rewards such projects can offer, whether pursued with a large group of students or a small one. Though the first phase of the project sputtered, having Meagan and Jimmy on board for another semester made it possible to salvage the preliminary work students in my Writing about Literature course had done and to finish the digital edition. Indeed, Meagan and Jimmy are the heroes of this twice-told pedagogical tale.

I originally envisioned *Prudence Person's Scrapbook* as a pilot for other student-created digital editions, and I now feel confident I can design a better course next time.[28] In this next iteration, the scrapbook project will serve as the centerpiece of an intensive upper-level course on nineteenth-century print culture. In this redesigned course the readings, both primary and secondary, will directly (not just conceptually) complement the students' work on annotations and contextual essays, and more in-class time will be devoted to both the intricacies of nineteenth-century newspaper culture and twenty-first-century methodologies for responsible online research. To cultivate students' investment in the project, I will likely allow them to choose a scrapbook to work on (perhaps from a small assortment I have prescreened with university librarians) rather than handing them an already selected one, and to counter the isolation and difficulty of working on one's own I will ask them to research, write, and edit their annotations in pairs or small groups. Finally, I will adapt the model of project planning with Trello that Meagan, Jimmy, and I developed to a classroom setting so that students learn to guide and manage a project as they are creating it. Sharing project planning and management duties with a large group of undergraduate students may be similar to herding cats, but an endeavor cannot honestly be called collaborative if the majority of its participants are simply following instructions. The next scrapbook digital edition my students and I make together will involve students more directly in every aspect of the project so that it becomes less of an assignment and more of a shared endeavor.

The choice of whether to build future scrapbook projects on the Scalar platform involves, as technical decisions always do, a weighing of considerations.[29] None of Scalar's existing themes offers quite the balance of image and text that Meagan, Jimmy, and I were hoping for; the applet that displays the JPEG images, for instance, tends to hide the annotations my students worked so painstakingly to complete. So while the Scalar platform has provided nearly all of the features we need, and has done so in a relatively simple and user-friendly manner, it currently does not provide an ideal display environment for *Prudence Person's Scrapbook: An Annotated Digital Edition*. But one of the features built into Scalar is a customizable front end; users can alter a theme's CSS template to produce the user interface best suited to their materials. As I repeat the scrapbook project with other artifacts and other students, I may apply for a small grant to pay for the design of such a customized interface.[30]

The *Prudence Person's Scrapbook* project may be scalable and extensible as well. As Garvey details, there are hundreds, if not thousands, of nineteenth-century scrapbooks preserved in archives around the country, each of them providing a unique window into the life and interests of a local (though perhaps not typical) resident of that archive's environs. Instructors of American literature and culture could seek out their campuses' holdings or those available through local historical societies and design editions around them; together these projects could form a trove of online source materials for scholars and students alike. And depending on the particular holdings of a library or archive, the project could be useful in other disciplines as well; the North Carolina Collection contains a number of French-language scrapbooks, for instance, that would provide fascinating projects for Romance languages or immigration history classes.[31] And as Garvey notes, scrapbooks often provide the only detailed records of communities whose histories have not been officially preserved, making them, when available, ideal objects of study for classes on minority histories. Despite the difficulties my students and I encountered while planning and executing *Prudence Person's Scrapbook*, I remain convinced of the pedagogical usefulness of such projects and hope that other scholars will pursue them as well.

The appendixes for this chapter, assignments by Ashley Reed on creating an annotated digital edition and journaling encounters with a text, can be found at www.press.uillinois.edu/books/TeachingWithDH.

Notes

1. Meagan Keziah, Jimmy Zhang, and Ashley Reed, *Prudence Person's Scrapbook: An Annotated Digital Edition*, accessed March 26, 2017, http://scalar.usc.edu/works/prudence-persons-scrapbook/index. For their help with the project and with this article, I wish to thank Emily Kader and Fred Stipe of the UNC Libraries and the curators of UNC's North Carolina Collection; Sharon Billings, Michelle Brough, Joseph Elmore, and the other members of the Person Place Preservation Society; Maury York and the Tar River Center for History and Culture; Jentery Sayers and the Alliance for Networking Visual Culture; and, of course, Jessica DeSpain, Jennifer Travis, and my fellow contributors to this volume. I owe my greatest debt of gratitude, naturally, to my students in English 127: Writing about Literature (spring 2014) and to the coauthors of the project, Meagan Keziah and Jimmy Zhang.

2. See Omar ibn Said, *A Muslim American Slave: The Life of Omar Ibn Said*, ed. Ala Alryyes (Madison: University of Wisconsin Press, 2011), and "Omar ibn Said, b. 1770? and J. Franklin Jameson (John Franklin), 1859–1937," *Documenting the American South*, University of North Carolina at Chapel Hill, accessed March 26, 2017, http://docsouth.unc.edu/nc/omarsaid/menu.html.

3. Images of the scrapbook are available at *archive.org*, accessed March 26, 2017, https://archive.org/details/scrapbook00pers.

4. For this and other biographical information about the Persons that appears in this essay, I am indebted to Joseph Elmore, the official historian of the Person Place Historic Site, who has performed extensive research on the property and its residents. He kindly provided me with copies of the various reports he has compiled on behalf of the Person Place Preservation Society. He is also the author of a series of articles on the Persons that have appeared in the *Franklin Times* (Louisburg, N.C.) over the past thirty years, for which he also generously provided copies.

5. Ryan Cordell, "'Many Facts in Small Compass': Information Literature in C19 Newspapers (MLA15 Talk)," *ryancordell.org* (blog), January 9, 2015, http://ryancordell.org/research/mla/many-facts-in-small-compass-information-literature-in-c19-newspapers-mla15-talk/.

6. Items included in the scrapbook are rarely dated, but Prudence seems to have added to it from before the Civil War until shortly before her death in 1922. Some of the last items in the volume pertain to World War I. There appears to be no shortage of clippings from the Reconstruction era; as Ted Curtis Smythe notes, the postwar North Carolina press was comparatively healthy because editors had established their papers on a cash-subscription basis and thus were not dependent on the occupying Northern forces to provide revenue through the purchase of advertising space. Ted Curtis Smythe, *The Gilded Age Press, 1865–1900* (Westport, Conn.: Praeger, 2003), 3.

7. "Guide to the Person Family Papers, 1754–1971," Duke University Libraries, accessed March 26, 2016, http://library.duke.edu/rubenstein/findingaids/personfamily/.

8. UNC is one of over a thousand institutions that participate in the Internet Archive's Open Content Alliance. The UNC Libraries' Digital Production Center operates a Scribe scanning station, which enables libraries to produce high-quality scans of even rare and fragile materials for their own institutional purposes and for inclusion in the open-source Internet Archive.

9. I had originally included David Mitchell's *Cloud Atlas* as the final text in the course, but it became clear halfway through the semester that students would not be able to finish both the novel and their various research and writing projects.

10. Poetry Genius is a subsection of Genius, a site that allows users to easily annotate and discuss song lyrics as well as texts related to news, history, and literature. See Genius, Genius Media Group, accessed March 26, 2017, http://genius.com.

11. In this she was typical of many Southern women who, as Elizabeth Fox-Genovese notes, "were known to rail against the injustices that women endured at the hands of men. But their discontents . . . rested on the conviction that the system of southern civilization 'obeys and displays the great law of nature—series, gradation, order.'" Elizabeth Fox-Genovese, *Within the Plantation Household: Black and White Women of the Old South* (Chapel Hill: University of North Carolina Press, 1988), 338.

12. There has been no detailed written history of the Person family, and there is no evidence that Prudence ever had—or lost—a child. Joe Elmore, historian for the Person Place Preservation Society, has no knowledge of any pregnancies. Poems about dead children were staples of nineteenth-century popular culture, so the fact that Prudence included them need not be a clue to her own experiences. According to Elmore, how-

ever, Person family members were surprised when Prudence married Wile Mangum Person (her first cousin); Wile had a reputation for rambling and wild behavior. It is possible that Wile and Prudence had a rocky marriage and that the scrapbook's apparent shift from optimism to self-soothing reflects this.

13. Mark Sample, "Building and Sharing (When You're Supposed to Be Teaching)," *Journal of Digital Humanities* 1, no. 1 (2011), http://journalofdigitalhumanities.org/1-1 /building-and-sharing-when-youre-supposed-to-be-teaching-by-mark-sample/.

14. Ryan Cordell, "How Not to Teach Digital Humanities," *RyanCordell.org* (blog), February 1, 2015, http://ryancordell.org/teaching/how-not-to-teach-digital -humanities/.

15. This choice was brought about in part by my status as a graduate student with little control over my teaching assignments. I had a vision for *Prudence Person's Scrapbook* and I had been assigned to teach Writing about Literature, so I found a way to incorporate the project into that course.

16. The creators of Scalar are not primarily in the business of hosting media; they much prefer that projects created in Scalar link to media hosted elsewhere, including YouTube, Internet Archive, Critical Commons, or the Metropolitan Museum of Art's online digital repository. And as I mentioned above, the ANVC has since replaced their media server with a new one with robust data preservation protocols. I had, and still have, no qualms about continuing the *Prudence Person's Scrapbook* project on the platform.

17. Ellen Gruber Garvey, *Writing with Scissors: American Scrapbooks from the Civil War to the Harlem Renaissance* (New York: Oxford University Press, 2013), 21–22.

18. Meredith L. McGill, *American Literature and the Culture of Reprinting, 1834–1853* (Philadelphia: University of Pennsylvania Press, 2007), 3.

19. See, for instance, the example of a magazine editor who lifts articles whole cloth from blogs because she mistakenly thinks that anything published on the internet is in the public domain. Linda Holmes, "The Day the Internet Threw a Righteous Hissyfit about Copyright and Pie," *Monkey See*, November 5, 2010, accessed March 26, 2017, http://www.npr.org/sections/monkeysee/2010/11/05/131091599/the-day-the-internet -threw-a-righteous-hissyfit-about-copyright-and-pie.

20. Lisa Spiro, "This Is Why We Fight: Defining the Values of the Digital Humanities," *Debates in the Digital Humanities*, ed. Matthew K. Gold (Minneapolis: University of Minnesota Press, 2012), http://dhdebates.gc.cuny.edu/debates/text/13.

21. John Unsworth, "Documenting the Reinvention of Text: The Importance of Failure," *Journal of Electronic Publishing* 3, no. 2 (1997), http://quod.lib.umich.edu/j /jep/3336451.0003.201?view=text;rgn=main.

22. This is one of the ways the digital humanities, a field that should (and does) attract innovative young scholars, can also repel the population that might otherwise be best suited to it.

23. The blog can be found at http://prudeperson-blog-blog.tumblr.com/. I encouraged Meagan and Jimmy to tweet about the project as well, but since they use their Twitter accounts primarily for personal purposes, most of the tweets that appeared under the #prudeperson hashtag were mine.

24. Both Joe and Maury are graduates of UNC Chapel Hill, and during our visit Meagan, Jimmy, and I discussed the important role North Carolina's public university

system plays in educating the historians and cultural heritage professionals one meets throughout the state.

25. As an open-source digital humanities tool, Scalar's source code is publicly available for viewing and download at https://github.com/anvc/scalar.

26. Prudence clipped stories that mined "humor" from stereotypes about Irish immigrants and African Americans. One of the items she included in its entirety was "Cousin Sally Dillard," a courtroom sketch that was ubiquitous in nineteenth-century newspapers and magazines—probably because it confirmed white readers' prejudices about the unreliability of black witnesses—but that has received little scholarly attention since. As a prosperous farming family, the Persons owned several slaves. Prudence's father, Thomas A. Person, inherited around 1,100 acres of land in Sand Creek, N.C., from his own father in 1847; in 1850 he owned thirty-five slaves and farmed wheat, corn, and oats. He used the profits from the farm to buy the Person Place in Louisburg, which Prudence would eventually inherit. Historian Michael R. Hill records that "most of the 28 slaves which Thomas A. Person owned in 1864 did leave [after emancipation]. A few did, however, stay with the family. Record exists of several former slaves being paid for their work." Hill goes on to enumerate the names and wages of these former slaves and those of their descendants who remained with the Persons. Michael R. Hill, *The Person Place of Louisburg, N.C.* (Raleigh: North Carolina Division of Archives and History, 1985), 70–80.

27. Attending this event was their suggestion. Meagan, who held a part-time job at North Carolina State University, heard about the symposium and alerted Jimmy and me to it a few weeks before abstracts were due.

28. The riches Emily brought me from UNC's North Carolina Collection and Southern Historical Collection would take many semesters to exhaust, but I left UNC in July 2015 to take up a position at Virginia Tech. Fortunately, the law of amazing librarians applies there as well, and Marc Brodsky, public services and reference archivist at the Carol M. Newman Library, has already earmarked for me several fascinating scrapbooks in Virginia Tech Special Collections.

29. Scalar currently has only seven themes for users to choose from. While an eighth, Cantaloupe, is under development, it was not released in time for the launch of our digital edition (much to my students' disappointment).

30. The most customizable solution, of course, would be to mark up the scrapbook and annotations using XML-TEI and to build XSLT and CSS style sheets for display. But a custom-built project (as opposed to a customized interface integrated into an open-source platform) can be difficult to maintain and upgrade over the long term, and the XML markup language can be off-putting to students and educators new to digital humanities work. In the interest of collaboration and sustainability, it seems best to continue the project in Scalar (though the future of the Scalar platform itself is an open question).

31. Not every campus has extensive archives, of course, and not every library has access to a high-end scanner. But for scholars who wish to pursue scrapbook editions but do not have either the source materials or the necessary scanning facilities, partnerships could be formed between large campuses and regional schools or small

liberal arts colleges; universities that take part in the Scribe program (see note 8 above) could scan their materials and make them available online to smaller schools, whose students could then edit their editions on the free, open-access Scalar platform. One of the concerns that animates scholars working in the digital humanities is the question of how DH can be pursued outside the walls of large, research-intensive universities. As William Pannapacker notes, while DH often can seem like the exclusive purview of large universities, in its embrace of "teachers and students as co-researchers, collaborating across disciplines and cohorts, attempting to build projects that can serve a wide range of needs, seeking support for those projects, and presenting that work at conferences and now, increasingly, online," it should actually be seen as "an enhancement of the core methods of an ideal liberal-arts education." "Stop Calling It 'Digital Humanities,'" *Chronicle of Higher Education*, February 18, 2013, http://chronicle.com/article/Stop-Calling-It-Digital/137325/.

3. Nineteenth-Century Literary History in a Web 2.0 World

Augusta Rohrbach

With Adam Heidebrink, Kellie Herson, Aaron Moe, Charlie Potter, David Tagnani, and Stacey Wittstock

IN "THE AMERICAN SCHOLAR," Ralph Waldo Emerson adjured that "one must be an inventor to read well."[1] In the fall of 2011, I, along with a group of graduate students at Washington State University, took him at his word. The expanding menu of digital tools offered us an opportunity to put Emerson's assertion into action in a graduate seminar called Literary History Becoming Digital. The class promised prospective students the chance to propose, design, build, and assess a semester-long digital communications project arising out of our study of Ralph Waldo Emerson's writings. Over the course of the semester, we came to appreciate the serendipity of that selection: Emerson's arguments for the necessity of self-reliance in the building and sharing of knowledge helped us break down pedagogical barriers using twenty-first century technologies. As this essay explores, the focus on building provided by the website project offered a rich opportunity to engage in metacritical conversations about the vital relationship between the material we were studying and the pedagogical principles that aligned most closely with it. The dual emphasis on content expertise (Emerson's work) and presentation (building the website) highlights how integral field proficiencies are to the formation of professional skill sets that extend beyond the field itself.

As we moved more deeply into Emerson's thinking and brought it to bear on our study of the digital space, it became clear that the relationship between teaching and research was inherently reciprocal. Emerson's preference for the gerundive form—thinking rather than thought—was replicated by our focus on building the website, heightening our attention to the process elements of knowledge production.[2] Showcasing our research on the web inextricably linked research with teaching and teaching with research. In turn, those pedagogical practices confirmed the relevance and role Emerson played in bringing into view the very issues that most need attention as we prepare students to enter an ever-changing workforce. This is not as far-fetched as it might seem. As scholars and educators, we need not limit the impact of our scholarly endeavors to traditional classrooms—or online learning management systems for that matter. The openings created by new media allow writers (and readers) to blow by the gatekeepers that shape education through the control of publication outlets, creating a whole generation who simultaneously occupy the roles of student and teacher, creating the ethos of mutual inquiry Emerson encouraged. This essay explores how we can use our knowledge to inform broader engagements with the world around us by focusing on the theoretical underpinnings of Web 2.0 technologies in terms of the pedagogical stance called for by Emerson.

We built *Digital Emerson: A Collective Archive* by bringing Web 2.0 capabilities into contact with content-rich study rooted in the field-specific priorities of literary studies.[3] We subtitled our course site "A Collective Archive" after Walter Benjamin's article "Theses on History," in which he describes the reciprocal action of the archive as a place that simultaneously contains and commits history. The archive, according to Benjamin, is as much a record as it is an argument. So, too, this website records our efforts to understand and share our knowledge of Emerson's work, while it also makes an argument for the value we add to the study of Emerson in a Web 2.0 context. In other words, as an archive and an argument, it expresses a pedagogical approach that is as participatory as the work that went into making it. Adhering closely to Emerson's principle that "each generation must write its own books," our website and this essay use student work to explore the scholarly, ethical, aesthetic, technical, and cultural problems that arose as the seminar members worked to expand the limits of our classroom.[4] We found that our reading of Emerson resonated deeply with the shift in educational philosophy voiced in the work of Paulo Freire, author of the revolutionary book *Pedagogy of the Oppressed*.[5] In that work, Freire advocated for a pedagogy that would flip the power dynamics of the traditional classroom, an ethos that resonated deeply with Emerson's commitment to active learning. By linking Emerson's charge that "the only sin is limitation" with the fluidity of the web, we could mobilize not just our thinking, but also the thinking of those who might encounter our site.[6]

The seminar's engagement with Emerson produced a distinct set of pedagogical practices—beginning with the early teachings of thinkers like Paulo Freire and carried forward by Paul Lauter, Cary Nelson, Michael Bérubé, and Chandra Talpade Mohanty, among others[7]—which can be substantially enhanced by digital tools. Emerson's insistence in "American Scholar" that "each generation must write its own books" suggests a dynamic relationship to knowledge production that resonated as much with our class as it does with today's DIY digital culture. As seminar member Charlie Potter observes, "Emerson is a perfect specimen for digital tinkering" (CP 1).[8] As Jentery Sayers explains, "tinkering not only enables critical engagements with technologies but also affords an opportunity for students and instructors to step away from the screen and collaborate around and through physical objects."[9] Yet, our experience takes this assertion one step further: digital tools helped us gain a new sense of textual materialism in which reading and writing take shape and form in the digital space. Indeed, our class felt strongly that if Emerson were alive today, he would likely urge us to engage in as many of the opportunities to spread our ideas offered by Web 2.0 technologies and the internet as possible.

What seemed clear to us was that Emerson's notion of "creative reading" accords with the kind of mental agility required by twenty-first-century workplaces, an agility fostered by active learning and peer-to-peer engagement.[10] This notion also meshed well with our Freirian model of education: to reduce the power differential between us and our students/users.[11] Following our understanding of Emerson, the class was committed to exploring and even privileging the linkages between process and product, method and content. In so doing, we did not "bracket," to use Brett D. Hirsch's term, the importance of pedagogy in our scholarly endeavors.[12] In the context of training graduate students to go forward into their careers as educators and active citizens, it would be counterproductive to sideline or underplay the process by which we came to understand the relationship between our critical analysis of Emerson's work and the role digital tools serve in sharing that knowledge. Our work on the website and our jobs as educators came together under the heading *curation*, as defined in the recent MLA volume on *Digital Pedagogy in the Humanities*.[13] What we did in/with Digital Emerson was to curate a space for thinking about Emerson. One of our essential functions as curators was to create angles or vectors of access to Emerson's thought and thus bring others into contact with his ideas. As a focus in the graduate student classroom, curation is a more embodied, less tactical form of teaching. By asking students to handle materials with a view toward reception, we emphasized a continuum of experiential knowledge that only began with us. Our work had an end that was to be more dynamic and more fluid than the final paper and the final grade. Our ambition was to introduce Emerson to those beyond our classroom by offering the tools for their own "liberation"—in the Freirian sense—from the text as static and/or authoritative.

With Emerson as our literary/historical/philosophical focus, we also used metacritical sources to help us theorize digital technology's transformative role.[14] During each unit, we divided our attention between understanding key (predigital) samples from Emerson's oeuvre and the study of digital archives that feature nineteenth-century literature and culture.[15] In addition to close readings and learning about the scholarly reception of the text in historical context, we also addressed issues of interface design and online communities by looking at text-based presentations versus multimedia sites.[16] In the end, we decided that our goal was not to reproduce text as archive-oriented sites tend to, but rather to provoke interpretive acts by offering viewers a collection of materials that included text, context, and the tools we used to frame them.

Lastly, we scrutinized the tools we would be using. After testing several other content management systems, we decided to use Omeka.[17] Omeka seemed best suited for our goal to build a multimedia, group-authored website leveraging what we'd learned about web design from the scholarly world and Ralph Waldo Emerson, our focal figure and intellectual champion. As Charlie Potter, one of the seminar participants, put it: "thinking about Emerson within the context of the digital humanities offered many new ways of considering the material" (CP 3). Part of what Potter was pointing to was the fact that context and presentation, shape and form were crucial factors.[18] Our awareness of just how crucial the design elements are to the intended learning outcomes began during our content management selection process and remained ongoing throughout the course.

From Theory to Practice

We began with several readings that focused on ideas about collective intelligence and expertise. Peter Walsh's "That Withered Paradigm: The Web, the Expert, and the Information Hegemony" became a kind of urtext for the class.[19] Students found the essay not just subversive—Walsh argues that the advent of the internet has also brought an end to experts as such—but liberating. Walsh's essay argues Web 2.0 technology is instrumental in leveling the barriers between teacher and student, knowledge and power. The essay opened the way for students to reconsider the social purpose of knowledge and to imagine a different role for themselves in the world—one that aligned in a purposeful way with contemporary approaches to teaching and learning that had not yet been brought into contact with field-specific content.

Dave Tagnani, the most advanced graduate student in the group, recognized and charted the ways in which building the website departed dramatically and productively from the research process whetted for writing the scholarly essay. A major goal students took up was to "avoid the overt argumentation that is at the heart of most scholarly activity" (DT 3). Working through Walsh's reflections on the end of the expert paradigm gave students a new way to understand the goals of expertise—to share knowledge rather than control it. As Dave realized that the usual place of scholarship—in footnotes and direct references—only preserved the expert paradigm we were working to subvert, he had to grapple with the real place of scholarship in his work. Rather than use the routine steps he had been trained to take, he had to develop a more utilitarian relationship to the work of others. He had to determine not just what they said, but why it might be useful to share that information with others. The biggest question all of us had to contend with was how to share information without making an argument.[20] The degree of dislocation was palpable. As Dave put it: "not only was I out of my element regarding medium, I was also working outside my usual mode: argumentation" (DT 13).[21]

After our introductory sessions around syllabus and project planning, the course unfolded in three segments, each corresponding to a major theoretical shift prompted by the interaction of our study of Emerson and the digital context into which we wanted to position him. During the "Rethinking Matter" unit, we extended our investigations that focused on design elements to thinking more about how active engagement with form and content create meaning and understanding. Leveraging the power of collective knowledge, we began by editing a Wikipedia entry on Walter Benjamin, whose "Theses on History" we used to launch our collective theorizing. As Charlie Potter noted, "the experience of doing this [entry] as a class helped me understand the power of collective knowledge, which became a concept central to our overall course project" (CP 7). Working on the Wikipedia entry also helped students better understand how the communication of knowledge on the internet has begun to break down what Peter Walsh calls the "Expert Paradigm." Students elected to use their expertise as researchers to foreground and amend what they thought was important for others to know about Benjamin's essay. For instance, the original entry did not mention the Paul Klee painting referred to in Benjamin's essay. The Klee painting is a linchpin in Benjamin's conception of history and historical materialism. Benjamin argues against the notion that history is a continuum of progress. He uses the pose depicted in the Klee painting he dubs "the angel of history," with its back to the future, to distinguish the idea of history from the event of history: "Where we see the appearance of a chain of events, he sees one single catastrophe, which unceasingly piles rubble on top of rubble and hurls it before his feet. . . . That which we call progress, is this storm."[22] Students found it impossible to interpret Benjamin's insight without Klee's image of a figure startled by what it sees. The Klee image helped students visualize the difference between the ordered narrative sequence history takes and the experience of history as random events, so the class decided to augment their discussion of the Klee painting by uploading its image to the entry. By adding the image, the class meant to combine the impact of textual literacy with its visual counterpart and thus invite readers/viewers to interpret the painting and its function along with them. Now, more than five years later, that section of their revision of the Wikipedia entry remains virtually intact. The philosophical commitment to provide as much contextual information carried through as a major theme in all that we did when building the website. Indeed, much like the inclusion of the Klee painting, our overall design favored "contextual information present[ed as] primarily practical knowledge." This emphasis, as Tagnani notes, "subverts the expert paradigm by presenting some tools by which users might create their own abstract knowledge. The same can be said for most of our website: the "Parlor," "Library," and "Abroad" sections all present information devoid of interpretation to facilitate the creation of knowledge by our users" (DT 2–3).

The readings and activities in our second unit, "Rethinking Agency," helped focus our attention on how our roles as curators impacted the agency of the materials we were interested in presenting, working in what seminar member Adam Heidebrink called the "intersection between the technological and the historical" (AH 3). As we studied the idea of the archive—on- and offline— we used existing sites devoted to major figures of literary history and digital culture. Our approach to these sites was infused with a DIY ethos because we approached the work of others with the goal of making a site for ourselves. Linking the practical focus of website development with the disciplinary demands of literary studies, we saw these examples, therefore, through a double lens. As a result, we could recognize design decisions according to the basic requirements of the medium, but we could also view them as an aid (or barrier) to knowledge production. For instance, *The Ambrose Bierce Project* uses several images of the author on its landing page as clickable navigation icons.

In our discussion of this design decision, however, we wondered how those images functioned as signifiers. We concluded that they succeeded in reinforcing the subject of the site but failed to help the user navigate the site. From a design perspective, our class believed the choice should have been driven by the content on the other end of the tab. When it came time to build our own site, we took a lesson from this example, selecting images that resonated with the intended impact of the material users would discover upon their click. The image we chose for the "Context" tab, for instance, shows the ripple effect of a drop of water—a visual analogy for how we hoped contextual elements would affect our readers/users.

Approaching author sites with a view toward making our own provoked us to think differently about the material we encountered by taking its presentation as seriously as the content. On a certain level, formal choices like the use of the author's image on the Bierce site become content and thus require site designers to read images both functionally (will the image guide users?) and metaphorically (how will the image shape the content it is meant to label?). Activities like these helped us fine-tune our visual literacy while also grappling with how the medium's requirements structure (or at least inform) knowledge. It also sharpened our sense of the intertwined roles of reader and writer, user and maker—principles that were enhanced by further engagements with the world beyond the text and our classroom.

The "New Materialisms" unit kept the theoretical issues of web-based media in the foreground when we dug into the practical decisions of selection and composition. As important as the content-rich engagement with Emerson and digital humanities was, students also understood that they were learning higher-order organizational skills that required a degree of fluidity that is not typically required by the conventional instruments of scholarly production— the essay, the book, even the edited collection do not require attention from their makers once the project is complete. But does the fact that authors are no longer active participants in their texts make their texts longer lasting? Surely, they are archived and indexed, discoverable by search engines, and preserved on library shelves and in digitally available resources. Yet, questions about the mortality of texts are even more trenchant when we turn our attention to web productions. Scholars Diana Coole and Samantha Frost encouraged students to rethink this idea through the lens of New Materialism, which includes

> rediscovering a materiality that materializes, evincing immanent modes of self-transformation that compel us to think of causation in far more complex terms; to recognize that phenomena are caught in a multitude of interlocking systems and forces and to consider anew the location and nature of capacities for agency.[23]

The class noted that our attention to design features and the digital tinkering required to build the website primed us to understand the "multitude of interlocking systems and forces" in a dramatically tactile way. Each choice we made—from using Omeka to creating sections and tabs—reinforced our awareness of how tethered our production was to schedules, skill sets, licensing, and all sorts of other contingencies.

Still, web-based design offers a fluidity that mirrors language itself. We made use of Xtranormal, a now-unavailable platform for creating animated movies, to manifest the transformative power of motion in knowledge production. We liked the idea that anyone could script and create an animated short and that the freely available software might encourage others to experiment with it. As Adam Heidlbrink explained, the web is "a dynamic, formative space, we the designers have the convenient ability to assess, reassess, and redevelop the site as our audience sees fit" (AH 5). He described the overall shift from a print-based model to a web-based model as going from a "Stasis-Normative" to a "Motion-Normative" ontology (AH 5). Using the software offered a visceral lesson on how "the variety of characters, scenes, camera angles, and artificial voices allow for depth of performance and delivery" (AH 11). Experimentation with Xtranormal "served a dual purpose of testing out the potential of this technology as well as providing a more concrete example of the things discussed in class" (AH 11). Students used the platform to set up dialogues between major thinkers and explore important concepts. For instance, one student created an Emerson character who explained transcendentalism to another character. As our culture moves more into video delivery of information and argument, a clear understanding about how these formal choices shape content is essential. The platform forced the students to think differently about reception: camera angles, tone of voice, accent, and gender were all components of the presentation. As Stacey Wittstock explained, the software gave students a way to explore "the expression of textual content in a medium beyond pure text" (SW). Putting the idea of "usability" first and foremost is an important emphasis going forward into the twenty-first century. We all need to think as critically as possible about the use value of our work for multiple constituencies—not just for ourselves as scholars. This approach stresses training students to value expertise and to use it judiciously to spread knowledge and create an expanded intellectual community.

At the same time, as scholars, our discipline requires that we retain a degree of skepticism—even as we remain exuberant about the possibilities offered by the digital world. Kellie Herson observed, "The digital humanities, like Emerson himself, have been the subject of numerous essentialized claims of democratization which do not always hold up against scrutiny—and these are the intellectual tensions I found most relevant to our collective work and the subject matter of it while moving through the theoretical and creative processes" needed in the class (KH 2). Class members remained cautious about the risk of overselling the digital as a tool for democratizing knowledge production. We understood the importance of scholarship and its practices—not just as a tool for the expert but as necessary controls over the integrity of sources. This became especially interesting when we were working on how we would provide appropriate scholarly citations for those who wished to further explore the content we offered. Part of why we choose Omeka was for the Dublin Core feature. By using this standardized format for metadata, Omeka gave students a new appreciation for provenance and how it figures in structuring information. Kellie Herson "essentially conceptualized metadata as both the citation of Omeka and the searchability quota of our particular Omeka-hosted archive, and since one would never skimp on generating an accurate works cited page on a piece of written scholarship that one hopes will be taken seriously," she "took my metadata seriously" (KH 14). Using Dublin Core allowed students to be freewheeling with the composition, association, and remixing of information, without sacrificing the power attribution accords. Citing our sources was just as important as being able to successfully blend and synthesize them. Though we did not use Tumblr, we might well have since, as Kellie notes, "Tumblr, as a platform, is totally in line with remix culture—it's the place we could post pictures of Emerson tattoos or men in transparent eyeball costumes and see where other people take it through re-blogging and conversation, and it's yet another way we could bring our work to audiences who might not encounter it otherwise and therefore keep expanding our collective and drawing connections between Emerson and other cultural trends and artifacts" (KH 16).

Literary History 2.0

Throughout the composition process, we took note of how transient websites can be, so we did our best to preserve our site. We partnered with our library to sustain the site by hosting it on their server. Though this partnership ensures that the site is preserved, it could not prevent the incursion of change. The contributions that used Xtranormal are no longer available; in their place is a "page not found" message. Even though we thought we had protected the project from the fragility of the web by partnering with the library, using a tool that was free and unsupported by an institution subverted those plans. The project, like a modern-day Oxymandias, has degraded over time, reminding us that the tools we use and the work we do are subject to the vicissitudes of capital and technology, not just the ravages of time and natural forces.

Nonetheless, DH-focused pedagogy grants graduate students greater agency—both in terms of what they are studying and the reasons for study. We all left the course ready to take a more action-oriented approach to our roles as educators and a robust interest in future encounters. The class's engagement with theories of meaning, publication, and pedagogy from the point of view of *making* awakens students in a radical way to the transient nature of meaning beyond the most rigorous engagements of Derrida or other poststructuralists. As a result, students came to appreciate how radicalizing digital humanities can be to the enterprise of literary studies.[24] Our approach encouraged us to reckon with the tensions and ambiguities of Emerson's texts without forcing ourselves or our users to resolve them. Indeed, a major emphasis in the design of the site was to retain these tensions and provoke additional exploration, fully leveraging the power of skepticism to move the user to click through as a way to satisfy curiosity. As highfalutin as this goal might sound, an examination of the website and the student's work on it confirm how closely students came to bearing it out.

Notes

1. Ralph Waldo Emerson, "The American Scholar," in *The Essential Writings of Ralph Waldo Emerson*, ed. Brooks Atkinson (New York: Modern Library, 2000), 48. All references to Emerson's writings are drawn from this edition.

2. Ibid., 44.

3. Aaron M. Moe, Adam Heidebrink , Charlie Potter, David Tagnani, Juan Carlos Flores, Jennifer Kiehne, Kellie Herson, Rachel Sanchez, and Stacy Wittstock, *Digital Emerson: A Collective Archive*, accessed March 26, 2017, http://digitalemerson.wsulibs. wsu.edu/. For a broad engagement with how the field of American literature produces specific pedagogical practices, see Carol Batker, Eden Osucha, and Augusta Rohrbach, "Critical Pedagogies for a Changing World," special issue, *American Literature* 89, no. 2 (2017).

4. Emerson, "American Scholar," 46.

5. Paulo Friere, *Pedagogy of the Oppressed* (New York: Seabury Press, 1968).

6. Emerson, "Circles," 255.

7. Michael Bérubé and Cary Nelson, eds., *Higher Education under Fire: Politics, Economics, and the Crisis of the Humanities* (New York: Routledge, 1994); Chandra Talpade Mohanty, *Feminism without Borders: Decolonizing Theory, Practicing Solidarity* (Durham, N.C.: Duke University Press, 2003).

8. In addition to the material featured on the website, students produced a lengthy end-of-semester reflection. Throughout this essay, I quote and refer to these reflections papers. Students granted permission for the use of their work via email.

9. See Jentery Sayers's discussion of tinkering in "Tinker-Centric Pedagogy in Literature and Language Classrooms," *Collaborative Approaches to the Digital in English Studies*, ed. Laura McGrath (Logan: Utah State University Press / Computers and Composition Digital Press, 2011), http://ccdigitalpress.org/cad/index2.html.

10. Emerson, "American Scholar," 48.

11. Freire believed that good classroom practices empowered students to be "critical co-investigators in dialogue with the teacher" rather than "docile listeners." Freire, *Pedagogy of the Oppressed*, 81.

12. My commitment to forefront the linkages between content and method are at the heart of this course's design; for a deep engagement with the inherent connection between form and content as manifest in the digital humanities, see Brett D. Hirsch, "<Parentheses>: Digital Humanities and the Place of Pedagogy," in *Digital Humanities Pedagogy: Practices, Principles and Politics*, ed. Brett D. Hirsch (Cambridge: Open Book, 2012).

13. As Julia Flanders explains, for the site to be "a working system rather than a static object: maintaining its viability means endowing it with ongoing relevance rather than simply preserving it in its original state." Julia Flanders, "Curation," in *Digital Pedagogy in the Humanities: Concepts, Models, and Experiments*, ed. Rebecca Frost Davis, Matthew K. Gold, Katherine D. Harris, and Jentery Sayers, MLA Commons, Modern Language Association, accessed March 26, 2017, https://digitalpedagogy.mla .hcommons.org/keywords/.

14. The complete reading schedule is available at Literary History Becoming Digital Syllabus, *Digital Emerson: A Collective Archive*, http://digitalemerson.wsulibs.wsu.edu /exhibits/show/about/syllabus.

15. We studied websites featuring or focusing on major nineteenth-century authors, including Herman Melville, Emily Dickinson, and Walt Whitman.

16. Readers interested in exploring the differences between text-based and multimedia authoring please see Debra Journet, Cheryl E. Ball, and Ryan Trauman, eds., *The New Work of Composing* (Logan: Utah State University Press / Computers and Composition Digital Press, 2012).

17. We experimented with Collex, a platform designed for displaying and manipulating texts. We also considered starting from scratch, but few seminar members had coding skill or background in web development.

18. Readers might enjoy Meredith McGill's discussion of this topic through the lens of nineteenth-century poetry in "What Is a Ballad? Reading for Genre, Format, and Medium," *Nineteenth-Century Literature* 71, no. 2 (2016): 156–175.

19. Peter Walsh, "That Withered Paradigm: The Web, the Expert, and the Information Hegemony," accessed April 27, 2018, http://web.mit.edu/m-i-t/articles/index_walsh .html.

20. Jerome McGann, *A Critique of Modern Textual Criticism* (Charlottesville: University of Virginia Press, 1983). McGann was among the first to give due consideration to these issues.

21. Were I to teach this course again, I would certainly assign Jennifer Travis's essay "Wikipedia and American Women Writers" for the ways in which it helps both map the intellectual project and guide readers through the practical steps of editing a Wikipedia entry. Jennifer Travis, "Wikipedia and American Women Writers: Closing the Gender Gap through Collaborative Learning," *Polymath: An Interdisciplinary Arts and Sciences Journal* 3, no. 3 (2013): 35–42, https://ojcs.siue.edu/ojs/index.php /polymath/article/view/2841.

22. Walter Benjamin, "On the Concept of History," chapter IX in *Illuminations: Essays and Reflections*, edited by Hannah Arendt (New York: Knopf, 1969), 257–258.

23. Diana Coole and Samantha Frost, "Introducing the New Materialisms," in *New Materialism: Ontology, Agency, and Politics*, ed. Diana Coole and Samantha Frost (Durham, N.C.: Duke University Press, 2010), 9.

24. As George P. Landow writes, "Derrida, more than any other major theorist, understands that electronic computing and other changes in media have eroded the power of the linear model and the book as related culturally dominant paradigms." George P. Landow, *Hypertext 3.0: Critical Theory and New Media in an Era of Globalization* (Baltimore: Johns Hopkins University Press, 2006), 67.

PART TWO

Read

4. Melville by Design

Wyn Kelley

WHY READ HERMAN MELVILLE for a whole semester? Here is an official answer. In MIT's literature department, an advanced undergraduate seminar devoted to a single author can introduce students to literary texts and to historical and theoretical contexts as well as research and writing skills used by scholars in the field. But since few MIT students major in literature, and only a small number seek graduate degrees in the humanities, we offer seminars to familiarize students with the distinctive discourses of the field. Students themselves also give "official" reasons for taking a literature seminar: to learn more about a writer and his or her works, improve communication skills, complete a concentration, minor, or major, experience the pleasures of a small discussion class, or come away with new insights about human knowledge and social behavior. Increasingly aware of how much humanities scholars depend on digital tools, I have included them in my teaching over the years. Students in my seminar Mapping Melville learned something about digital resources and significantly, how to implement these tools themselves. In several iterations of the Melville seminar, I have seen striking results in terms of students' greater appreciation for a complex, nineteenth-century white male author viewed in contexts made accessible through experiments in digital pedagogy.

Recently, I learned another answer to the question of why students might study Melville for an entire semester, an unanticipated one contained in a single word: *design*. After reading Melville's works and using digital tools to map place-names, annotate text and sources, and code manuscript revisions, one student noted at the end of the semester that she had begun to consider literary study "in the context of engineering and 'design thinking.'"[1] In fact, most of the tools we used were still in design and testing phases, and students found that working with them experimentally freed them to read, discuss, write, and think critically in new ways. We drew on numerous perspectives. John Bryant's theory of fluid-text editing and the resources of the *Melville Electronic Library*, including TextLab (a tool for coding and analyzing manuscript revisions), provided a primary foundation.[2] Reading practices grounded in research by Henry Jenkins et al. informed classroom discussion and assignments. Annotation Studio, developed in MIT's HyperStudio, expanded students' power to track verbal patterns, share comments, and build reports and essays. And a geo-mapping tool, Locast, from MIT's Mobile Experience Lab, offered ways to visualize Melville's global imagination.[3] This blend of tools apparently showed my student that she might encounter design thinking in a humanities classroom; and that discovery led me to speculate on what makes nineteenth-century American literature especially hospitable to such an approach.

Design thinking is, like digital humanities, a broad abstraction that has inspired strong criticism even as it has been adopted more widely throughout academic and popular culture. Developed in part as a model for creative practices in product design (with considerable impetus from the d.school or Hasso Plattner Institute of Design at Stanford University, partnering with Silicon Valley companies), design thinking suggests what engineers have adapted from humanities methods to release creative and aesthetic potential in their own fields. With Steve Jobs and Google, the open floor plan, and a mandate to ideate, test, and create, a flourishing design culture produces elegant tools that touch people's lives across the globe. It seems ironic that humanities fields may be taking design thinking *back* in serious ways, even as outside the academy the term can become fuzzy and silly.[4]

In a field as broad as design thinking, Johanna Drucker provides a useful starting point for thinking critically about digital pedagogy in particular. Technically she devotes her work to "designing digital humanities" (as the title of her 2012 lecture at MIT implies), not applying design thinking *to* the humanities, as my student's comment suggests. But her method, drawing from graphic design and book history, illuminates the issue of design in humanities classrooms. In her MIT lecture, she identifies a blind spot in humanities studies: "Most humanists . . . remain convinced that this [digital humanities] is the work of professional librarians and archivists . . . that humanists have everything to gain by using these materials in various ways, but they don't necessarily see it as their responsibility to engage in the process of design."[5] She sees design, however, as social behavior that creates new models of research and learning: "What does it mean to show interpretation? We wanted to create a space in which all reading activity, all annotation activity, all interventions in a text [*Ivanhoe*, in this case], through collaboration and a social space of exchange around that process, could be recorded and rendered visible, . . . [to] show interpretation as a collaborative social behavior."[6] In the "collaborative social behavior" that likewise produced her coauthored book *Digital_Humanities*, a similar argument appears in the section "Designing Digital Humanities," which speaks of "design as a method of thinking-through-practice": "Digital Humanities is a production-based endeavor in which theoretical issues get tested in the design of implementation, and implementations are loci of theoretical reflection and elaboration."[7] Drucker and her collaborators call not so much for coding expertise as for "understanding the *rhetoric* of design" (emphasis mine) in a collaborative space, a "space to iterate and test," where "process is favored over product; versioning and extensibility are favored over definite editions and research silos," and students can be "active participants and stakeholders in the creation and preservation of cultural materials."[8]

In this emphasis on the social dimensions of the classroom as learning lab or design space, Drucker's work dovetails nicely with Henry Jenkins's focus on participatory culture in his MacArthur white paper. Recognizing fan cultures as models of robust social learning, Jenkins proposes a classroom structure that draws on participatory practices found in digital communities. These communities, he argues, can be recognized as ones

1. With relatively low barriers to artistic expression and civic engagement
2. With strong support for creating and sharing one's creations with others
3. With some type of informal mentorship whereby what is known by the most experienced is passed along to novices
4. Where members believe that their contributions matter
5. Where members feel some degree of social connection with one another[9]

Such principles, also underlying his *Reading in a Participatory Culture: Remixing* Moby-Dick *in the English Classroom*, redefine traditional models of literacy and textual interpretation, redistribute expertise in the classroom, and give students larger, more dynamic communities within which to share creative and critical work.[10]

John Bryant's theory of fluid-text editing establishes a significant context for digital pedagogy as well. First, his book stresses the historical role of social communities around multiple versions of a text, thereby breaking down the "definite editions and research silos" Drucker mentions. Second, he creates a thick description of editing as an inclusive function that, as much as preserving textual artifacts from the past, also records the many acts of interpretation—including censorship, remixing, bowdlerization, and multimedia adaptation—that speak to diverse strategies of meaning making and storytelling over time.[11] In so doing, he has inspired me to develop pedagogy around the idea of "students as editors," as agents in the ongoing cultural work of texts, rather than as simply novice learners.[12]

My ideas about pedagogy design, however, also grow organically from the texts I work with most, and as the above review of resources suggests, Melville's writings have proven compatible with this effort. Especially in *Moby-Dick*, Melville seems preoccupied with design himself: Ishmael often wonders how to create a narrative that can encompass his vast subject, how to approach so difficult a task, what tools to use, what resources to borrow—where, even, to begin? In chapter 3, "The Spouter-Inn," for example, Ishmael puzzles for some time to understand the artist's "design" in a "boggy, soggy, squitchy picture" he observes hanging in a dim corner.[13] His analysis resembles the problem-solving methodology my student identified at the end of our seminar—a creative blend of traditional humanities methods and new user-oriented thinking.

Thus, Ishmael begins with classic research: "it was only by diligent study and a series of systematic visits to it, and careful inquiry of the neighbors, that you could any way arrive at an understanding of its purpose." Hence follows close reading and thick description: "But what most puzzled and confounded you was a long, limber, portentous, black mass of something hovering in the centre of the picture over three blue, dim, perpendicular lines floating in a nameless yeast." Finally, Ishmael throws out a series of hypotheses that show both creative imagination and practical ingenuity:

> Ever and anon a bright, but, alas, deceptive idea would dart you through.—It's the Black Sea in a midnight gale.—It's the unnatural combat of the four primal elements.—It's a blasted heath.—It's a Hyperborean winter scene.—It's the breaking-up of the icebound stream of Time. But at last all these fancies yielded to that one portentous something in the picture's midst. That once found out, and all the rest were plain. But stop; does it not bear a faint resemblance to a gigantic fish? even the great leviathan himself?

Ishmael's speculations and false starts bring him finally to a correct, or at least sustainable, identification of that "black mass of something" at the center of the picture, and at the center of his story as well.

But Ishmael's wild guesses suggest that he is thinking about not only what makes the picture meaningful but also for whom. For someone interested in maritime voyages, then, "the Black Sea in a midnight gale" would satisfy. For a romantically minded reader, "the breaking-up of the icebound stream of Time" makes the most sense. Finally, however, because Ishmael has some inkling of his reader's expectations, he recognizes "the great leviathan himself" as the likeliest possibility. Specifying not just what but for whom suggests that the reading process has a design beyond satisfying an individual's desire for a certain kind of meaning. It opens the process to experimentation, trial and error, visualization, collaboration, and perhaps the "breaking-up" of meaning itself.

I wanted to make my seminar, Mapping Melville, a place where students could engineer—hack and redesign—the reading process for themselves and their peers.[14] The tools I describe in the assignments that follow focus on reading itself, *close* reading, and it might be fair to ask if I am simply adopting new devices to serve old paradigms, close reading being by now one of the oldest and most controversial of them all. As several essays in this volume suggest and as debates in participatory-culture and literacy studies also imply, mid-twentieth-century models of close reading have often proven themselves arcane, exclusionary if not racist, ahistorical, and outmoded. Students strenuously resist what appears to them as literary vivisection. Critics of the humanities certainly make a compelling case against a form of exceptionalism that would claim the particular value of close reading of literature and culture. And yet, what else do humanities classrooms provide and students seek there but the satisfaction of close study and understanding of a text that might seem alien on first reading? With only a dim sense of exactly how it happened, I had seen in the projects described below that students' reading became sharper, cannier, more social, and more productive. In Mapping Melville, digital tools proved indispensable to the design of new learning outcomes.

As much as possible, I tried to share the design of the class and its use of digital tools with students. I set up three projects, each one exploring a different mapping strategy, each focused on a different digital tool, and each addressing different Melville texts. For their part, students provided materials from their research, shared their annotations and reports on work-in-progress and final essays, and tested the tools critically, giving feedback on functionality, drawbacks, and discoveries. With an eye to this project-oriented learning, I also tried to break down assessment into component parts. Each report was graded separately from the final essay. When grading the essay, I made reference to annotations and other preliminary stages (annotated bibliography, reports, workshop discussion) as a way to emphasize process as well as product. No assessment strategy works perfectly, as we are constrained by conventional grading rubrics, but I tried in my feedback to acknowledge the students' creative use of tools, their generous support of each other's work, and their spontaneous contributions to class discussion and annotation as well as their formal written essays. I hope that this approach lent itself, at least in part, to the idea that we were designing the class together. (All three assignment prompts are available in Appendix 4.1.)

We began with Locast and an attempt to map *Moby-Dick* using geographical references. Locast was an open-source mapping tool developed by Federico Casalegno of MIT's Mobile Experience Lab (a research group in the Department of Comparative Media Studies/Writing). Designed originally for Italian tourism and for Android or computer, Locast allowed users to upload images, video clips, and text to a "cast" or enriched site on a Google map. Casalegno's Open Locast Project collected digital narratives, media-rich guides, and community development initiatives, to which Locast technology lent coherence by gathering different kinds of geographical, visual, and textual information. Together we adapted it for a literary studies classroom and as a basis for class discussion, student reports, and essays.

The *Moby-Dick* site at Locast built on the efforts of a team of *Melville Electronic Library* (*MEL*) researchers: Dawn Coleman, Elyse Graham, Peter Riley, Haskell Springer, Brian Yothers, and myself. Using the Longman Critical Edition (LCE) of *Moby-Dick* edited by John Bryant and Haskell Springer, we created a spreadsheet of place-names in the novel, labeling them as mappable (Tahiti, for example) or unmappable (Tartarus), supplying modern names for old (Mosul for Nineveh), providing geographical coordinates and brief quotations, and identifying quotations by page and line numbers. We included names explicitly identified with a particular place (Greenland), as well as adjectives clearly betokening locations as well (Parisian). Working from our approximately 1,500 entries, Locast developer Amar Boghani created the Melville Locast site and with Pelin Arslan conducted a study of students' uses of Locast in several of my classes.

I began our discussions of *Moby-Dick* by explaining that as both sailor and reader, Melville had traveled widely before writing the book and that knowing his geographical context would help us make sense of this global narrative. Although we would engage with Melville's themes and ideas, students' reports and essays for this first mapping assignment would build on what they learned about places mentioned in the text. As well as researching what I called Melville's "geographical imagination" and sharing their findings with other students, they would be enriching the Locast *Moby-Dick* site by adding their images, clips, and comments for other students (current and future) to see.

As a side benefit, all this work would also be distracting them from the terrifying discovery that they were reading and taking apart the Great American Novel in wholly unconventional ways. In a most remarkable development, students chose locations that had meaning to them. One student noted Melville's references to an old Manxman and was delighted to discover that her father, whose family came from the Isle of Man, might have inherited a culture of fisheries along with his genes. A student who played the pipe organ got interested in Haarlem's "pipes" (mentioned in a description of the whale's baleen in chapter 75), and another student, fascinated by Melville's giant wine cask in chapter 77, researched the Heidelburgh Tun. One student was surprised to find so many references to Africa in a book more generally concerned with Pacific whaling grounds. Another stayed close to Melville's home by exploring the many moments when Nantucket appears in the text. In every case, their reports and essays took them to neglected corners in the book, offered unexpected readings of passages they might have considered from more conventional perspectives, and gave them a sense of connection with a novel that had intimidated them at the start. The essays, in particular, gave them an opportunity to develop beyond their Locast map reading and to analyze Melville's language in greater detail.

A second assignment considered mapping as a metaphor for literary source study. I asked students to locate literary references in Melville's short fiction and to annotate them using Annotation Studio, an open-source MIT instance of the Annotator.[15] Built in MIT's HyperStudio, Annotation Studio provides a workspace where users can upload texts, search and select passages, add comments, share or not as desired, import links and images, and tag for themes, versions, or a classroom folksonomy.

I used Annotation Studio previously in writing classes to make visible students' reading process, to open the layers of private or shared encounters with the text that a finished product, the essay submitted for a grade, cannot reveal. In the Melville seminar, we relied on Annotation Studio for each assignment, but the literary source-study project focused on combining traditional humanities research with the special affordances of an annotation tool of considerable flexibility and range.

Students first chose a source for one of Melville's mid-1850s works—say, Dante's *Inferno* in "The Paradise of Bachelors and The Tartarus of Maids" or Spenser's *The Faerie Queene* in "The Encantadas." Their process involved both collaborative exercises—sharing their digital annotations, reporting on their findings, and presenting their final work to the class—as well as working alone to research and write their essays. Similarly, they blended print and digital resources. Research in books and literary databases established that Melville borrowed from literary sources, and as the assignment was designed to exercise their research skills, students learned to search databases and library shelves, employing traditional tools. But in using Annotation Studio to chart exact passages where Melville quotes from or adapts a text, students made new discoveries of their own. Furthermore, when they reported on their findings and wrote their essays, they had a precise record of their close readings of the text to share with the class and draw on for their own writing.

The clear, detailed annotation that Annotation Studio enables supported their research and writing in manifold ways. Given specific passages to consider and compare, students tended to proceed more confidently and to choose more arcane projects than I would expect of undergraduates. Essays included such topics as melodrama in Frederick Douglass's *The Heroic Slave* and Melville's

"Benito Cereno"; slavery, technology, and the story of Jael and Sisera in "The Bell-Tower"; the presence of Poe in "Bartleby" and "The Bell-Tower"; *The Confidence-Man* and *Paradise Lost*; or, in an unusual historical topic, the reference to reformer Elizabeth Fry in *The Confidence-Man*. I have included here the topics that most strikingly went beyond the norm. All, however, showed remarkable initiative and willingness to venture widely afield.

I cannot attribute these developments solely to the use of Annotation Studio. In their comments on the tool, however, students mentioned how it helped them locate precisely the points of interest they wanted to consider in a text. I may have led them to literary sources and scholarship, but their experiments with Annotation Studio sharpened close reading, made their writing more detailed, and allowed them to learn from each other by sharing their work. For example, those who researched Melville's English antecedents—Shakespeare, Spenser, Milton—clearly took pride in what they learned about these (to them) remote authors and began to recognize that, as a group, they were providing a sort of literary history for the rest of the class. A student who gravitated toward the Bible found that other students' work challenged—and refined—his own. The workshops where students presented their reports—one on research-in-progress, then another on the final essays—produced genuine arguments about specific passages the students had annotated and interpreted. I had not expected such a level of engagement in the texts themselves. Students seemed to appreciate the idea that just as literary antecedents of *Moby-Dick* had shaped the novel, those earlier authors could also speak to twenty-first-century readers in unanticipated ways.

The third assignment engaged students in perhaps the most complex "mapping" of all, reading *Billy Budd* and tracking Melville's writing process by studying revisions in his manuscript text. TextLab, housed at the *Melville Electronic Library* and developed by John Bryant at Hofstra University and Nick Laiacona at Performant Software, digitally displays the *Billy Budd* manuscript (as does the Houghton Library, which generously gave *MEL* access to the digitized text) and furthermore allows users to transcribe it in TEI (Text Encoding Initiative) format. I have found TEI difficult and time-consuming for undergraduates to learn, but it has considerable advantages in rendering their editorial work searchable, shareable, and plastic in other ways.

TextLab's first stage of engagement, called Primary Editing, allows users to make their own decisions about Melville's revisions as recorded on the page, hence putting them in the same position as Melville's early-twentieth-century editors Raymond Weaver, Barron Freeman, Harrison Hayford, and Merton M. Sealts Jr., none of whom had a print text of *Billy Budd* to consult.

TextLab then enables users to construct the "revision sequences" and "revision narratives" (at the Secondary Editing stage) that provide a foundation for interpreting Melville's revisions throughout the manuscript. A student could go from noting Melville's addition or deletion of a significant word in the Primary Editing stage to creating a step-by-step model of Melville's likely choices (for example, to write and delete a word and then substitute another), and finally to advancing an editorial argument for the causes and effects of certain changes. It sounds gritty, and it is. No other device I've tried gets students so involved in the precise workings of a text under construction.

For students with technical skills, it turns out, this kind of work is tremendously appealing. It also uncovers sophisticated issues in Melville's prose, fine-grained matters of word choice and sentence structure that open significant thematic complexities and philosophical questions. Students quickly feel themselves experts on a particular section, character, or even word in *Billy Budd* and devise innovative theories for the effects of Melville's changes.

The essays responded creatively to what these TextLab exercises made visible. One student, for example, looked at Melville's change from "oakum" to "pretty silk-lined" to describe the basket in which orphan infant Billy is found; her essay probed the story's gender politics as revealed in that telling phrase, while another student, examining the same wording, took it to refer to equally significant class differences. In an early description of Billy, Melville's narrator compares him to a "grand sculptured Bull." Melville initially wrote "deified Bull"; a student explored the other references that suggest Billy's godlike— though often heathen—character. Another student followed John Bryant's suggestion that Melville's revision of "white . . . forecastle-magnate" to "handsome sailor" opens up the possibility that Melville initially envisioned Billy as black, like the Liverpool Handsome Sailor of the opening pages; she expanded this insight to speculate on possible connections between Billy and the African mutineer Babo in "Benito Cereno."[16] A student's study of the changes in language describing Captain Vere led to speculation that Melville began with a "sketch" but developed his narrative unexpectedly into something that probed human character more deeply. Melville's late addition of "that great heart" to his dedication to Jack Chase struck one student as indicating the increasing role of the *heart* in the story as it developed. A subtle reading of "conscientiousness" as a term applied to the minor character Captain Graveling appeared to another student as evidence that conscience likewise grew in importance as the story proceeded, and as Vere wrestled with his own. A different essay located the workings of conscience in Melville's tinkering with the word "disquietude" to draw attention to the difficulty characters face in squaring moral training with martial duty. In chapter 1 Melville's narrator changes his reference to "important variations that will evolve themselves as the story proceeds" to read "important variations made apparent as the story proceeds"; did Melville mean to make the reader a passive spectator of events "made apparent" throughout the text rather than "evolving" according to some logic or intention? One student was curious to find out.

I have been teaching *Billy Budd* to students at various levels for many years. In my other classes, students have used Annotation Studio to focus and develop their close readings of the text. The seminar students' use of TextLab opened up even more dazzling feats of close reading, but these amplified themselves further through the social momentum of the class, which by the final weeks of the semester had developed enormous esprit de corps. I should not then have been surprised when one of the students asked when I would take them to see Melville's manuscripts at the Houghton Library at Harvard University. We had been studying his works, including poems, marginalia, and letters, in various media and at different stages of composition and reception history. It apparently seemed natural to students that they would take the next step of consulting Harvard's collections for themselves. But I have never received such a request before, and the students could not have known how much I rejoiced in it. I could well remember speaking on digital tools many years ago and having the renowned scholar Walter Bezanson ask me if I were not just replacing the reading process with a set of games and distractions. I have often returned to that question since. At least with this class, the outcome of using digital resources was to *return* them to the texts in their material forms.

Obviously, my students enjoy extraordinary privileges, among which the least might appear to be proximity and access to rare Melvilleana at Harvard. But that is just my point. The fact that they would *desire* this access—arising, apparently, from my offhand comment one day, "You know, you can just go down the street and see these things for yourself!"—seems an unexpected outcome of their use of digital technology. Yet their mapping of Melville's geographical and global imagination, his capacious embrace of literary sources, and his complex writing process as revealed in unpublished manuscripts, provided them with, well, a map to an author they might otherwise have found impenetrable.

But how did this famous but still somewhat fearsome nineteenth-century author, with or without the twenty-first century technology we explored, inspire such excitement in students who are heading into nonhumanities fields? They do tell me jokingly that their thoughts on *Moby-Dick* have consumed at least ten minutes of a medical school interview. But you cannot sell a class on the fact that many doctors, engineers, and other professionals cherish a nostalgic love for their college English texts. If my students began the class thinking of Melville as a trophy author, they did not expect to experience as much satisfaction as they apparently did—one student even going so far as to say that her reading of *Moby-Dick* had produced an intense existential crisis and was keeping her up at night more than her problem sets. No, I have come to think that the study of nineteenth-century literature resonates in particular ways with twenty-first-century students, and that we can design pedagogy to capture that resonance in our classes.

Without oversimplifying this problem, I would suggest that students experience their learning as meaningful when given the power to choose and investigate for themselves. At MIT their science and engineering classes stress the importance of failure, and even in as competitive an environment as theirs, they can experience the lessons of crashed experiments. In a literature class, however, they often imagine that their only choice is to find out what the instructor wants to hear or thinks is embedded in the text and dig it out. If literary study is a treasure hunt, then the prizes go only to the best equipped, and I find students often lack the confidence even to begin.

But in the Mapping Melville seminar, students seemed compelled to make judgments for themselves because they found that Melville's characters, even fictional and incomprehensible figures like Ahab, Hunilla, Babo, and Captain Vere, were wrestling with "real" problems of serious consequence. They seemed too to see in Melville someone engaging with social, intellectual, and literary issues of great weight. Their reading of Melville had led them, even without the digital tools we explored, to global geographies, deep histories, and broad social concerns—abolition, gender rights, labor issues, to name just a few. Through Melville they found a Bible they did not recognize and a Shakespeare they had never seen before. Previously taught to appreciate characters for being "relatable," they found themselves in an intellectual landscape they could not easily navigate—until they created a map of their own design, one fashioned from their own studies and discoveries.

Although I chose Melville by default, knowing both the subject and digital resources best, I would not hesitate to take a similar approach with authors like Phillis Wheatley, Frederick Douglass, Emily Dickinson, or Mark Twain, whose work offers students the opportunity to make choices about what they are reading, even what version they are reading, and what it means. I would characterize their choices in several ways. The most common one is thematic and still structures much of literary discussion in the classroom: what do we think of the dilemmas this character faces? How would we act in this situation? What does the author expect us to think or make of this problem? How does the author complicate and then resolve it? Such questions, I have found, engage students powerfully but do not ultimately lead to choices they find meaningful. They are not, after all, having to choose for themselves. The choice remains in a hypothetical or fictional world and is one I would associate with "students as readers," that is, deciding what they respond to or do not respond to in a text, what moves them, what reading reveals about themselves.

When students can study multiple versions of a fluid text, however, or revisions of a text they thought was stable, or histories of a text that has changed its impact over time, then they are making the decisions editors have to make. What in the history of this text has survived and what was dropped? How does this text read its sources, and how has it been read by later readers, fans, and adaptors? What do those readings say about reading cultures over time? What does the choice of a particular word say about the author's historical or ideological context, about his or her readers and circuits of communication? These choices position "students as editors," as having to decide if a previously admired text will survive into the next generation, and in what version.

Another set of choices faces "students as designers." They can choose not only what they think of a literary work or shape its meaning in different versions or for different audiences but also map and thereby create a learning experience for themselves. Here I would argue that although digital pedagogy enables certain possibilities, technology is not the only answer. Distance is at least one important dimension. That is, to be aware of oneself as designing the experiment by which he or she reads a text, the student must have some depth of resources to draw on—histories, scholarship, reception studies, fans, multimedia adaptations. Such textual complexity calls for finding aids, annotation strategies, and analytical tools.

America's long nineteenth century provides a comfortable amount of distance for many of our students. The language, if occasionally verbose or unfamiliar, is not foreign. The issues are recognizable in a current context but also stand at a historical remove. Whereas students may find current global conflicts frightening or complex, they may more easily grapple with problems from another era. More than that, they can sift the language of another time, their eyes and ears trained by attention-getting devices like Annotation Studio and TextLab to test and fine-tune their assumptions.

The case of Melville suggests not just the exceptional advantages of reading, mapping, annotating, or deconstructing his texts but also the manifold possibilities of encountering authors who seem *just* far enough away.

The appendix for this chapter, an assignment by Wyn Kelley on mapping and analyzing locations mentioned in a text, can be found at www.press.uillinois .edu/books/TeachingWithDH.

Notes

1. I distributed questionnaires at the end of the semester; students' comments from the questionnaires appear here anonymously. I have drawn on three different occa-

sions when I taught Melville's texts using these tools and am presenting them here as one semester.

2. John Bryant, dir., *Melville Electronic Library*, Hofstra University, accessed March 24, 2017, http://mel.hofstra.edu/.

3. Although the Locast *Moby-Dick* map was once available online at http://locast .mit.edu/melville#!home, the project is no longer supported, and I have looked for other alternatives. The *Melville Electronic Library* has developed a program called Itinerary that makes it possible to map and edit routes from an author's life and works. See http://hofstra.github.io/itinerary/melville-in-rome/ or http://hofstra.github.io /itinerary/melville-in-london/ for models.

4. For taking design thinking back, see, for example, Steven Henry Madoff, ed., *Art School (Propositions for the 21st Century)* (Cambridge, Mass.: MIT Press, 2009), and Michael Shanks and Jeffrey Schnapp, "Design Thinking as Arteriality: A Manifesto for the Arts and Humanities" (Palo Alto: Stanford University, 2011), accessed March 26, 2017, http://jeffreyschnapp.com/wp-content/uploads/2011/06/Design-thinking-as -artereality.pdf. For outside the academy, see Adam Kirsch, "Technology Is Taking Over English Departments: The False Promise of the Digital Humanities," *New Republic*, May 2, 2014, https://newrepublic.com/article/117428/limits-digital-humanities-adam-kirsch; and Tara Parker-Pope, "'Design Thinking' for a Better You," *New York Times*, January 4, 2016, http://well.blogs.nytimes.com/2016/01/04/design-thinking-for-a-better-you/.

5. Johanna Drucker, "Designing Digital Humanities" (lecture presented in the Comparative Media Studies/Writing Colloquium, Massachusetts Institute of Technology, Cambridge, MA, April 23, 2013), podcast at http://cmsw.mit.edu/podcast-johanna -drucker-design/.

6. Ibid.

7. Johanna Drucker, "Designing the Digital Humanities," in *Digital_Humanities*, ed. Anne Burdick, Johanna Drucker, Peter Lunenfeld, Todd Presner, and Jeffrey Schnapp (Cambridge, Mass.: MIT Press, 2013), 13.

8. Ibid., 21–23.

9. Henry Jenkins, with Katie Clinton, Ravi Purushotma, Alice J. Robison, and Margaret Weigel, "Confronting the Challenges of Participatory Culture: Media Education for the 21st Century," occasional paper, John D. and Catherine T. MacArthur Foundation, 2006, 9, http://www.macfound.org/media/article_pdfs/JENKINS_WHITE_PAPER .PDF.

10. Henry Jenkins and Wyn Kelley, eds., *Reading in a Participatory Culture: Remixing* Moby-Dick *in the English Classroom* (New York: Teachers College Press, 2013).

11. John Bryant, *The Fluid Text: A Theory of Revision and Editing for Book and Screen* (Ann Arbor: University of Michigan Press, 2002).

12. See Jim Paradis, Kurt Fendt, Wyn Kelley, Jamie Folsom, Julia Pankow, Elyse Graham, and Lakshmi Subbaraj, "Annotation Studio: Bringing a Time-Honored Learning Practice into the Digital Age" (white paper), MIT Comparative Media Studies/Writing, 2013, http://cmsw.mit.edu/annotation-studio-whitepaper/.

13. Herman Melville, *Moby-Dick*, ed. John Bryant and Haskell Springer (1851; New York: Pearson/Longman, 2007), 30.

14. While trite, the term *hack* has resonance for my enterprise. It is an ancient and

honorable word going back to the thirteenth century; I work in an institution where students celebrate a history of "hacking" as playful and ethical pranks; and I want my students' hacking to exhibit creative skill, not hackneyed drudgery. See *Interesting Hacks to Fascinate People: The MIT Gallery of Hacks*, accessed March 26, 2017, http://hacks .mit.edu/Hacks/.

15. Annotator, accessed March 26, 2017, http://annotatorjs.org/.

16. See John Bryant, "How Billy Budd Grew Black and Beautiful: Versions of Melville in the Digital Age," *Leviathan* 16, no. 1 (March 2014): 60–86.

5. Data Approaches to Emily Dickinson and Eliza R. Snow

Cynthia L. Hallen

THIS CHAPTER DISCUSSES some of the benefits of bringing a digital approach into courses on nineteenth-century language and literature. In a recent discussion of distant reading, Ted Underwood identified a problematic divide between literary studies and the social sciences.[1] English instructors who are drawn to words, authors, genres, periods, and theories of literary criticism may feel alienated from the numbers, tools, graphs, programs, and algorithms of digital text analysis. In other words, doctors of philosophy may not automatically relate well to wizards of technology. Quantitative approaches that rely on statistical correlations may alienate scholars in the traditional humanities fields who are accustomed to qualitative approaches that rely mainly on establishing logical causations.

However, problems with applying digital research to literary studies may lie closer to home than the tension between humanities and computer science or between literary criticism and the social sciences. Within the discipline of humanities itself, a more immediate problem may be the division between literary studies and language studies that came about with the gradual retirement of philology in the late 1800s. By the end of the nineteenth century, the field of philology had separated into several new fields such as ethnography, art history, structural linguistics, and literary criticism. In the humanities, language studies became more mathematical, and literary studies became more dependent on philosophy than philology.

Because of the turn away from traditional philology in the humanities, today's typical literature instructor may find it hard to identify with the nuts and bolts of detailed language analysis, in spite of the advent of digitized literary corpora. For example, in a recent discussion group on "Emily Dickinson and Other New England Writers," the session moderator seemed astonished when I included corpus data on high-frequency content words in my presentation. "Nouns!" she wondered aloud, "nouns?" She was not dismissive, but she did not seem to realize that nouns convey the most semantic content in a text, that other content words help carry the meaning of discourse, and that content-word frequencies can help provide concrete evidence for identifying an author's main themes. In sum, digital data as a foundation for language-based literary interpretation may be alien to some Dickinson scholars.

The potential for alienation can likewise be a problem for teaching literary database analysis to undergraduate students in the humanities. Throughout the twentieth century, literature courses dominated English departments in the United States, and English language courses were often relegated to service classes for native-speaker instructor training or international student remediation. Ted Underwood, for example, expressed a reluctance to share much of his data-based "distant reading" of British Romantic period texts in the college classroom because his literature-loving students might be put off by a digital approach.

This essay begins with an overview of how I collaborated with students to create a dictionary for all of the words in Emily Dickinson's poems.[2] I then present a case study that demonstrates the use of digital philology in a senior seminar course. My experience suggests that instructors and students can transcend any potential alienation between digital and traditional approaches by making a return to philology, which is "the love of words" according to Noah Webster's nineteenth-century definition:

> PHI-LOL'O-GY, n. [Gr. φιλολογια; φιλεω, to love, and λογος, a word.]
>
> 1. Primarily, a love of words, or a desire to know the origin and construction of language. In a more general sense,
> 2. That branch of literature which comprehends a knowledge of the etymology or origin and combination of words; grammar, the construction of sentences or use of words in language; criticism, the interpretation of authors, the affinities of different languages, and whatever relates to the history or present state of languages. It sometimes includes rhetoric, poetry, history and antiquities.[3]

I suggest that digital philology may be the bridge that we need to link language studies and literary studies in our humanities courses. This is not a new call to action. In 1803, Vicesimus Knox recommended that literary humanists turn to science to refresh their studies:

> STUDENTS who have been most attached to classical literature, and who consequently have succeeded best in it, have often been grossly ignorant of those pleasing parts of science, the laws and operations of nature. . . . Poetry, history,

moral philosophy, and philology, though truly delightful of themselves, will become more so when the sameness of the ideas which they represent is relieved by the delightful and diversified scenes of natural philosophy. . . . A knowledge of nature and of arts, as well as sciences, supplies a copious force of new ideas to the writer.[4]

Digital approaches to pedagogy are valuable because they provide tools for students to participate in meaningful, real-life, hands-on learning activities, blending the disciplines in the refreshing ways that Knox encouraged over two hundred years ago. During my time at Brigham Young University (BYU), I have witnessed and participated in a digital renaissance that has become the main platform for my classroom teaching as well as my academic research on the language of Emily Dickinson. Hundreds of students became my collaborators when I used digital resources to author the *Emily Dickinson Lexicon (EDL)*, a dictionary of all the words in the poet's collected verse, now available as a component of the *Emily Dickinson Archive (EDA)* of Harvard's Houghton Library.[5]

My original goal was to produce and publish a print edition of the *Emily Dickinson Lexicon* in three years, but that deadline was not realistic for a collaborative dictionary project entailing complex definitions for words with numerous possibilities for interpretation. Therefore, I decided to make internet publication my primary focus and print publication a secondary priority. As if by prescient intuition, Emily Dickinson also bypassed the selective auction of formal publication in commercial forums, preferring the productive option of personal publication in social media forums: notes to friends, poems to mentors, letters to family members, and hand-sewn fascicle packets faithfully hidden away in a dresser drawer for unidentified future readers. This homemade distribution of her prolific writings makes the poet a perfect candidate for big-data literary studies in a universe of digital discourse.

As my student Russell Ahlstrom was pursuing a master's degree in linguistics, he realized that his real career interest was in web design. We discussed possible thesis-worthy web projects with a linguistic basis, and Russell expressed interest in creating a state-of-the-art, professional-quality website for the *Emily Dickinson Lexicon*. With my input, Russell created a schema for our XML code that would enable me to upload, download, upgrade, and reload files for each letter of the *EDL* dictionary. He built a host of features for the *EDL* project, including an attractive layout, a home page, a registration page, an introduction, a contributor's list, an interactive suggestions monitor, a supplementary essays tab, a FAQ page, an email interface, reference lists, and search functionality.

When it was time to launch the beta version of the *EDL* website, we made two important decisions: (1) to publish all of the *EDL* letter files, not just the ones that had already been thoroughly revised, and (2) to add another corpus to the website: a digital renovation of the 1844 Webster's "Lexicon" that Dickinson had referred to as her "only companion."[6] The first decision was a turning point for both *EDL* and me. I had intended to upload the letters of the dictionary one at a time as they were polished, but I made an executive decision to "go live" and to upload all of the *EDL* letter files at once, notwithstanding typos, scanning glitches, content errors, HTML problems, and incomplete entries.

Miraculously, uploading the entire set of *EDL* files into an online digital database expedited my editing in ways that I never could have anticipated. Scores of scholars, translators, and students using the *EDL* were able to identify miscues and report them to me for immediate resolution. Russell and I decided that the *EDL* website should include a searchable database for Webster's 1844 dictionary, using the same XML process that he had developed for the Dickinson files. I had learned that a large academic corpus does not have to be perfect to be useful: our decision to let the *EDL* files go online before perfection gave us courage to upload the whole scanned version of the Noah Webster 1844 *American Dictionary of the English Language* (*ADEL*). The online editions expedited the editing and proofreading of the *EDL* and the *ADEL* substantially. Our "go-live" decision was later confirmed when I read the book *Big Data* by Viktor Mayer-Schönberger and Kenneth Cukier: "We don't give up on exactitude entirely; we only give up our devotion to it. What we lose in accuracy at the micro level we gain in insight at the macro level."[7] I realized that we do not have to be perfect to do something worthwhile, and I pass that thought on to my students whenever they feel discouraged about their works in progress.

Now that the Dickinson lexicon and Webster dictionary corpora are available in the *EDL* and the *EDA* websites, I continue to find ways to introduce these tools to students in my classes. In a big data approach, we do not have to limit ourselves to philosophy-based theories that are "fixated on causality; instead we can discover patterns and correlations in the data that offer us novel and invaluable insights."[8] Technological advances for computational corpora and digital databases have greatly facilitated our ability to examine language features within authors in the same cultural context and beyond to other people, places, times, and circumstances. Digital tools enable us to discover new dimensions of the author's craft, culture, and circumference.

Thus, early in 2014, when I was assigned to teach a senior seminar open to both English language majors and linguistics majors, I designed a course in which students would compare the language choices of two nineteenth-century American poets from Massachusetts: Emily Dickinson and the lesser known Eliza R. Snow. Eliza R. Snow and Emily E. Dickinson were parallel pioneers in the development of New England poetics and nineteenth-century American literature. Both poets were born in western Massachusetts, both left behind traditional church denominations, and both created a large corpus of rhymed metrical lyric verse that honored but transcended local and national considerations.[9] In addition to the *Emily Dickinson Lexicon*, students would use a newly created database of Snow's poems in order to compare and contrast word choices of the two authors, focusing on common themes as represented by the most frequent nouns in the poetry.[10] By fall 2014, eighteen people had registered for the seminar, a perfect number of students for a collaborative, research-oriented, and writing-heavy course. Each student was to write a capstone paper that would include language approaches, corpus data, and linguistic modes (see Appendix 5.1). The course format also incorporated elements from the Emily Dickinson International Society (EDIS) symposium on "Dickinson and Other New England Writers" in which I had recently participated. Required textbooks included *Emily Dickinson: A Poet's Grammar* by Cristanne Miller and a brand-new biography, *Eliza: The Life and Faith of Eliza R. Snow* by Karen Lynn Davidson and Jill Mulvay Derr.[11] In addition, students would use Dickinson's collected poems.[12]

To facilitate the coursework, I provided students with a digital copy of the complete poems of Eliza R. Snow and introduced them to the *EDL* website with its online lexicon for Emily Dickinson poems and its renovated edition of Noah Webster's 1844 dictionary. Throughout the semester we used a variety of digital tools to compare and contrast the language of Snow and Dickinson, and we took a field trip to Salt Lake City for a photo shoot of Snow's dwelling place at the Lion House and related sites, which would complement my photos of Dickinson's home in Amherst and Snow's birthplace in Becket. In addition to eighteen capstone research papers, students produced eighteen diction-analysis PowerPoint presentations, a prototype lexicon website for high-frequency words in Snow's poems, five exhibit boards for BYU's "Education in Zion" gallery, and several social media contributions for Twitter, Facebook, Instagram, and YouTube. Our digital-philological examination of the two poets' works revealed a complementary interplay of historical, spiritual, and textual connections.

In preparation for the capstone paper, I invited each member of the class to adopt one of the shared high-frequency Dickinson/Snow nouns, reading through every poem in which the word occurred. Each student explored the semantic, morphological, and syntactic aspects of a key noun in the corpora for Snow and Dickinson. Students read all of the poems containing that noun as well as the entry for that word in the *Emily Dickinson Lexicon*, Webster's 1844 *American Dictionary of the English Language*, and the *Oxford English Dictionary*. Then they wrote a dictionary entry for Snow's use of that noun throughout her poems.

Senior Malena Eads worked on the word *nature* and included an outline of Webster's definitions in her PowerPoint presentation to the class. She then selected definitions of *nature* from the noun entry in the *Oxford English Dictionary* database. Using the *Webster* and the *OED* definitions as a nineteenth-century standard, Malena drafted definitions for Eliza R. Snow's usage of the word "nature" in her collected poems:

- All creations of God; universe.
  D&D 5:4 And Nature sprung to light / Vast in extent—no finite bound

- Creator.
  D&D 5:18 No less ordains for man to grace / The sphere by nature given

- Laws of universe.
  D&D 285:7 Announce to Congress that the moon / Will yield obedience / To Nature

- Earth; physical world.
  D&D 387:10 This, then was but a wild retreat, / Where nature had no charms

- Physical body.
  D&D 4:27 Their souls . . . infirm with age, Yet venerable! Nature's fabric fell!

- Birth; family.
  D&D 145:21 And these the ties of nature, / Will constitute a chain

- Mortality, mortal life, life cycle.
  D&D 68:4 Where the Patriarch is sleeping. / Nature's sleep—the sleep of years

- Character, makeup, disposition; condition.
  D&D 384:7 We lov'd her noble heart—/ We lov'd her truthful nature

- Soul.
  D&D 198:1 A deep love in our nature for nature's own self

Finally, Malena compared her Snow poem definitions with the definitions of *nature* compiled for the *Emily Dickinson Lexicon* website. Now she was ready to write a capstone paper on various concepts of *nature* in the poetic works of Eliza R. Snow and Emily Dickinson.

Using that kind of lexical research as a foundation, my students began to explore topics for a paper that would incorporate skills from previous English language and linguistics coursework. In the digital dialogue forum of our on-line "Learning Suite" course package, they posted an abstract for their paper proposals and then gave feedback to each other in order to refine the title, background, purpose, methodology, and anticipated results of their research. As their papers progressed (or failed to do so), students met with me during office hours to check for content, organization, expression, and documentation.

In seminar style, students in clusters posted paper previews in the digital dialogue and gave feedback to each other in preparation for the final examination mini-conference. By the end of the semester, the cluster groups were ready to present their research findings in four panels with the following line-up:

Lexical Studies: (Joshua Day) "What Is Life? Lexical Vitality in the Poems of Emily Dickinson and Eliza R. Snow"; (Catia Shattuck) "A Lexical Study of Eliza Snow's and Emily Dickinson's Perceptions of Death"; (Holly Hickman) "The Power of Love in Dickinson and Snow"; (Lizzie Camarillo) "The Worth of Souls in Emily Dickinson and Eliza R. Snow."

Religious Studies: (Marie Hunter) "Fossilized Latter-Day Saint Church Phrases in the Usage of Eliza R. Snow"; (Jacob Crump) "'A Surer Light': Metaphors for Deity in Emily Dickinson and Eliza Snow"; (Anton Langer) "Linguistic Variances between the Webster Bible and the King James Version"; (Malena Eads) "Metaphors of Nature and God in Emily Dickinson and Eliza R. Snow."

Linguistic Studies: (Robert Faulkner) "'Holy Habitation': Eliza R. Snow at Home" [photo essay]; (Braden Bolton) "The Poetess: 'God' in the Eyes of Eliza R. Snow"; (Jason Orme) "Concepts of Eternity: Polysemy in Emily Dickinson and Eliza R. Snow"; (Shanna Moyes) "Creative Works Project in Response to Dickinson and Snow"; (Ashley Holmes) "Understanding Rhymes in the 'Hand' Poems of Emily Dickinson and Eliza R. Snow."

Philological Studies: (Jessie Rose) "Gilbert and the Afterlife: A Lexical Analysis of Seven Dickinson Elegies"; (Paige Ashby) "The Lexis of American Transcendentalism in Emily Dickinson's Poems"; (Holly Astle) "Editing Emily Dickinson: *Primum non nocere*"; (Caroline Larsen) "The Syntactic Pair 'Heaven and Earth'; (Rogelio Bonilla) "Death in Emily Dickinson and the Japanese Man'Yoshu Poems."

Panelists had two minutes each to present insights and results from their research. Panel members then had about twenty minutes to discuss linguistic and language approaches to poetry; linguistic concepts, authoritative sources, digital databases, and philological methodologies that they had used; linguistic assumptions underlying the approaches and methods they had used; what they had learned about the writing process; what connections they could see between their research and that of others; and suggestions for further research.

For example, Jacob Crump's paper abstract described the results of using Mark Davies's *Corpus of Historical American English* (*COHA*) to study the metaphor of "light as deity" in nineteenth-century English usage:[13]

The purpose of this paper was to examine the use of this metaphor in the poetry of both Emily Dickinson and Eliza Snow in order to determine similar semantic patterning and also to discern where the two poets diverge in their metaphoric use of *light*. I then attempted to place the two poets' use of the metaphor in the greater context of nineteenth-century American English through collocate analysis of the term *light* using the *Corpus of Historical American English* (*COHA*) . . . in the period of 1820–1889, roughly the period during which the two women lived and wrote.

Analysis showed that while the majority of metaphoric uses of "light as deity" were similar between the two poets, Snow seemed to employ the metaphor more frequently and with more semantic detail than did Dickinson. Both poets' use of "light as deity" essentially aligned with its broader use in nineteenth-century American English.

Other digital database approaches included Marie Hunter's use of the *COHA* and the *LDS General Conference Corpus* to compare the phrases *brethren, still small voice*, and *tender mercies* in Snow's poems and in nineteenth-century New England usage.[14] Caroline Larsen consulted the *COHA* and literary citations in the *Oxford English Dictionary* to draft nine different definitions for the formulaic pair *heaven and earth* in its English language syntactic contexts.

One of the concerns about computational approaches to literature is a failure to combine numerical results with insightful interpretation and meaningful commentary.[15] Catia Shattuck's research paper exhibited an excellent balance of digital data and literary analysis. Catia used corpus evidence and a digital approach to explore attitudes about the high-frequency noun *death* throughout the collected poems of Snow and Dickinson. She enhanced her research by applying optimism cues that she had learned about in an introductory digital tools course for linguistic majors. Here is an excerpt from her paper:

> Linguistic optimism cues have been studied by a group of linguists using LIWC, or *Linguistic Inquiry and Word Count*. [Pennebaker and Persaud] stated, "People who are upbeat and optimistic tend to use present and future tense verbs, first person plural pronouns (we, our, us), simple words, and words that denote positive feelings and, at the same time, tend to avoid words that express negative feelings."
>
> Using these same specifications, I've gone through [Snow and Dickinson] poems where death is viewed as leading to heaven and have recorded optimism cues. Positive emotion words included words like *love, hope, content, bliss, friend, home*, and *tender*, while the negative emotion words included words like *pain, loss, despair, grief, fear, jealous*, and *doubt*. Big words were considered to be any words that were nine letters or longer . . . The results are very similar except for the use of present tense verbs and the use of positive emotion words. Dickinson uses almost twice as many present tense verbs as Snow does, and Snow uses twice as many positive emotion words as Dickinson does. . . . Both poets seem to consider death as a natural thing, and both wrote poems that describe death as leading to heaven, although Snow wrote more of these kinds of poems. Snow also seems more certain about the goodness of death and heaven than Dickinson does, but linguistic analysis reveals that they are equally optimistic in their poems about death leading to heaven. Their audiences and their aims when writing their poetry can explain the differences in their optimism cues.

Catia's successful use of digital data and her incorporation of knowledge acquired from other coursework fulfilled two of the learning outcomes for the senior seminar.

Encouraging students to create data-mining projects of this type requires a great deal of personal attention; I frequently conferenced with students one on one about the development of their ideas. Three students had to abandon their original abstracts and take a last-minute leap of faith into an approach that would better facilitate fluency and accommodate their real academic interests. In spite of his proven talent for generating original ideas, Robert Faulkner struggled with writer's block. I challenged Robert to abandon a traditional analysis of the word *home* and instead to create a photo essay on the homes of Dickinson and Snow with photographs that we had compiled for the course. The resulting paper was thoughtful, practical, and informative, but not digital.

Shanna Moyes wanted to write a detailed linguistic analysis of the word *name* as a metonymy in the poems of Snow and Dickinson, but after she stated her proposition, the thesis was at a dead end with no further insights forthcoming. As we discussed other avenues, Shanna revealed that she had independently been writing poetic compositions in response to class activities and assigned readings. I encouraged her to write a paper analyzing the language details of her own creative works, which included several hymns, poems, and meditations, as well as an English translation of a poem that she had composed in Japanese. When given permission to magnify her unique strengths, Shanna produced a detailed paper that was genuine, vibrant, and deep.

Jessie Rose wrote a solid paper about definitions of the word *heart* in Snow and Dickinson, but she was bored with her topic after completing the lexical analysis, so the resulting draft had lackluster prose. As we discussed the problem and possible solutions, Jessie expressed a keen interest in a subset of poems that Dickinson had written after the death of her nephew Gilbert that seemed to hint at the poet's hope for an afterlife. I mentioned that the American Literature Association had recently issued a call-for-papers on the topic of "Dickinson and the Afterlife" for a session of the May 2015 conference to be held in Boston. At my suggestion, Jessie completed the seminar requirements by drafting a new abstract and a new paper on "Gilbert and the Afterlife: An Analysis of Seven Dickinson Elegies." After grades were in, we prepared and submitted a revised abstract for a coauthored paper to be presented together at the ALA:

> There are traditionally three parts to an elegy: the lamentation for the loss, the praise and celebration of the deceased, and the consolation for the living (*Poets. org*). As a scholar of the classics, Emily Dickinson was familiar with the elegy as a poetic form, and she used it in seven poems written about the death of her nephew Gilbert Dickinson: Franklin 1623, 1624, 1625, 1626, 1628, 1662, and 1666.

... These elegy texts provide an interesting data set for a study of how the poet's lexis portrays various perceptions of life after death. . . . Using a philological approach, we will evaluate her range of metaphors for the afterlife, including bondage, compensation, heaven, infinity, light, mystery, scene, and world. . . . In references to the afterlife, the poet makes the point that Gilbert's death did not harm him. Death is merely a journey we make to learn the great "secret" of eternity.

To our delight, the abstract was selected for the conference, and we worked together on a ten-page paper that combined our lexical insights and research findings. Our paper used Webster's 1844 *American Dictionary of the English Language* (*ADEL*), the *Oxford English Dictionary* (*OED*), and the *Emily Dickinson Lexicon* (*EDL*) in digital formats to explore the semantic depths of repeated key words in the seven Gilbert poems. We concluded that, out of sensitivity, Dickinson used circumlocution, metonymy, and analogy to allude to death rather than mention it directly. Dickinson portrayed the afterlife as a secret to be learned and a new stage on which to act. To enhance our ALA presentation in Boston, we arrived a day early in order to see some of the Dickinson papers in the Bianchi archives of the Special Collections holdings in the John Hay Library at Brown University in Providence, Rhode Island. The conference and its related activities was the perfect venue for meaningful instructor-student research collaboration based on findings from digital research.

In conjunction with the *Emily Dickinson Lexicon* project, I have used digital resources to teach principles of philology as well as skills of lexicography, etymology, exegesis, rhetoric, style, translation, discourse analysis, and literary interpretation. I like to tell my students that we are living in a renaissance parallel to the period of the English language in England after the 1476 arrival of the printing press. We can logically examine language features as particles in a detailed description of composition. We can chronologically observe dynamic language aspects as waves in a linear evolution of causality. We can also philologically view holistic language patterns as fields in a spiraling galaxy of correlations.

The appendix for this chapter, an assignment by Cynthia L. Hallen on data approaches to texts, can be found at www.press.uillinois.edu/books/Teaching WithDH.

Notes

1. Ted Underwood, "The Problem with Distant Reading," guest lecture, Humanities Center and Office of Digital Humanities, Brigham Young University, March 5, 2015. See also Ted Underwood and Jordan Sellers, "The Emergence of Literary Diction," *Journal of Digital Humanities* 1, no. 2 (2012), accessed March 26, 2017, http://journalof

digitalhumanities.org/1–2/the-emergence-of-literary-diction-by-ted-underwood-and-jordan-sellers/.

2. Cynthia L. Hallen, ed., *Emily Dickinson Lexicon*, Brigham Young University, accessed March 26, 2017, http://edl.byu.edu/.

3. Noah Webster, *American Dictionary of the English Language* (New York: Harper Bros., 1844), s.v. "philology."

4. Vicesimus Knox, "On the Propriety of Extending Classical Studies to Natural and Experimental Philosophy, and Uniting Philology with Science," *Essays, Moral and Literary* (1793; London: Mawman, Walker, Nunn, 1803), 2: 64, Google Books, https://books.google.com/books?id=tqENAAAAYAAJ.

5. Leslie Morris, et al., eds., *Emily Dickinson Archive*, Houghton Library, Harvard University, accessed March 24, 2017, http://www.edickinson.org/.

6. Emily Dickinson, *Emily Dickinson's Selected Letters*, ed. Thomas H. Johnson (Cambridge, Mass.: Belknap Press of Harvard University Press, 1971), 172.

7. Viktor Mayer-Schönberger and Kenneth Cukier, *Big Data: A Revolution That Will Transform How We Live, Work, and Think* (Boston: Houghton Mifflin Harcourt, 2013), 13–14.

8. Ibid.

9. A comparison of Snow and Dickinson as New England poets has a precedent in a 2004 study by Edward K. Whitley (a contributor to this volume) of Snow alongside other American bards. Edward K. Whitley, *American Bards: Walt Whitman and Other Unlikely Candidates for National Poet* (Chapel Hill: University of North Carolina, 2011).

10. Marie Bourgerie Hunter et al., eds., *Eliza R. Snow Lexicon*, Brigham Young University, accessed March 26, 2017, https://erslexicon.wordpress.com/poems/.

11. Cristanne Miller, *Emily Dickinson: A Poet's Grammar* (Cambridge, Mass.: Harvard University Press, 1989); Karen Lynn Davidson and Jill Mulvay Derr, *Eliza: The Life and Faith of Eliza R. Snow* (Salt Lake City: Deseret Book, 2013).

12. Emily Dickinson, *Poems of Emily Dickinson*, ed. Ralph W. Franklin (Cambridge, Mass.: Belknap Press of Harvard University Press, 1999).

13. Mark Davies, *The Corpus of Historical American English*, Brigham Young University, accessed March 26, 2017, http://corpus.byu.edu/coha/.

14. Mark Davies, *LDS General Conference Corpus*, Brigham Young University, accessed March 26, 2017, http://www.lds-general-conference.org/.

15. David Hoover, "Quantitative Analysis and Literary Studies," in *A Companion to Digital Literary Studies*, ed. Ray Siemens and Susan Schreibman (Oxford: Blackwell, 2008), http://www.digitalhumanities.org/companionDLS/.

6. Reading Macro and Micro Trends in Nineteenth-Century Theater History

Blair Best, Madeleine G. Cella, Rati Choudhary,
Kayla C. Coleman, Robert Davis, Ella L. Gill,
Clayton Grimm, Malin Jörnvi, Philip Kenner,
Patrick Korkuch, Mahayla Laurence, Joanna Pisano,
Teagan Rabuano, Lawrence G. Richardson,
Haley Sakamoto, Victoria K. Sprowls

STUDYING NINETEENTH-CENTURY U.S. drama is complicated by a problematic critical heritage. The field has endured a long-running stigma associating pre-twentieth-century American theater with commerce and cheap melodrama. Advocates of so-called high culture bemoaned the lack of artistic integrity on the stage, and the prejudice continued well into the twentieth and, in some cases, twenty-first centuries.[1] With irregular scholarly and theatrical attention given to nineteenth-century American theater, the archive of plays and productions is frustratingly fragmented, with few reliable, centralized resources. Since digital scholarship often relies on building stable datasets, the relationship between reader and archive remains problematic for studying a century of theater that is almost nonexistent in the classroom or on the professional stage. This chapter documents the collaboratively authored effort of a digital nineteenth-century theater history class at New York University's Tisch School of the Arts as we tested how accessible nineteenth-century American theater was for an arts-based, digital humanities (DH) classroom. The class was composed of sophomore theater majors taking the course as an honors seminar. The majority of the class members were actors in training with minimal programming experience. This chapter details our effort, as well as our struggles and discoveries, to create a representative corpus of plays from the nineteenth century and to analyze them with text analysis, methods of distant reading, and mapping tools. The result, we hope, will be a roadmap outlining how theater history can be taught in the DH classroom, showing where it is both well suited and problematic in a wider theater curriculum. We hope that our work points a way to leverage digital tools to reconsider the critical heritage of the nineteenth-century American theater.

The seminar provided a survey of nineteenth-century U.S. theater history and some core aspects of digital scholarship: text analysis, mapping, and network visualization (see Appendix 6.1). Classes were conducted in a laboratory-like environment, with each session requiring students to apply a tool to a text or body of texts and collectively interpret findings in a Google Document. We extended this approach to this essay by collaboratively deciding on a broad topic and choosing a variety of tools and subjects to demonstrate our approaches to the material. We worked on this coauthored contribution alongside our regular class meetings over the second half of the semester. We think this work serves as a useful example of how free, open-source tools can invigorate the study of pre-twentieth-century theater in disciplines where digital humanities scholarship is not firmly established. This chapter was written collectively by the class with each member contributing to the conception and methodology of the work, while also conducting analysis, authoring a section, and collaborating on edits across the chapter.

Tools and Corpus

The class began this project by identifying challenges in working with nineteenth-century American theater. The most pressing difficulty that we identified was limited access to plays since many were lost, few were anthologized, and manuscripts are scattered across archives. In addition, there is also relatively scant contemporary descriptive criticism, especially from the antebellum period; therefore, there is little writing about the performances themselves, and the few primary sources that we found were not reliable.[2] In addition, there are well-established problems with writing about theater history since plays are meant to be performed rather than read. On a practical level, we found that digital scholarship requires skills that are not usually taught in a theater studies curriculum. As students with a background in close-reading individual works, it was an abrupt change to work with computational tools, which requires scrupulous data collection and curation skills (see Appendix 6.2).

When discussing possible topics for this contribution, we were all interested in the relationship between nineteenth-century theater and society. Following a class brainstorming session, we agreed that we wanted to look at how theater responded to ongoing historical struggles. In particular, we wanted to see how word usage associated with violence, race, or gender changed in the years before and after the Civil War. Since the Civil War is largely neglected in theater history, we hoped to find shifts in word usage or dramatic action from the antebellum and postbellum periods. It is easy to make connections between historical events and the art of the time in hindsight, but our goal was to use digital tools to see how contemporary audiences and artists responded to their historical conditions. Regardless of the result, we thought it would be interesting to know to what extent if any the Civil War changed the nature of theater in the United States. We broke down potential subquestions and tools among students and set about creating projects that addressed our historical questions.

Given the lack of an existing dataset of nineteenth-century American plays, our first task was to find and prepare a workable corpus. We assembled a small test corpus of twenty-three plays that we agreed were representative of well-known or well-produced original American plays.[3] Most of our selection came from class reading and a previous "dramatic text roundtable" assignment in which each of the fifteen students read a different play from across the century and, coming together, shared and discussed the theatrical elements of each text and genre. In subsequent class meetings, we used this collection of texts to cut our teeth on digital tools by making maps, network diagrams, and other visualizations from many of these scripts. In following our interest across the century, we chose twelve plays by vote from before the Civil War, three from during the war, and eight from after the war, spanning the years 1845–1876. We strove for an even diffusion among genres including drama, comedy, and melodrama.[4] Sources included Google Books, HathiTrust, the ProQuest Literature Online Database, and the print holdings of NYU's Bobst Library.

We immediately found that working with dramatic literature has its own set of roadblocks. In contrast to most prose, a playtext features multiple types of writing, including dialogue, scenic description, and stage directions, often by multiple authors. For example, playtexts list a speaker's name by every line, so any digital program counting words will count every time a speaker's name appears, conflating how many times a name is used as direct address with how many times they speak. Secondly, there is little certainty that the published text reflects the original performance script. Stage directions are particularly difficult to remove from the texts, confusing what is part of the dialogue and what, as pointed out below, might have been added later by a prompter.[5] We began with an in-depth "cleaning" process of selecting plays and removing some of the nondialogic material with Microsoft Word's find/replace function. This process, which was rarely straightforward, had implications on our final data as full character names were not always cleaned from the plaintext files. In Dion Boucicault's *Poor of New York*, for example, *Bloodgood* did not get removed from the text because it had been shortened to *Blood.* to indicate the

TABLE 6.1. Our Collection of Representative Plays

Play	Author	Genre	Date (of first performance)
Fashion	Anna Cora Mowatt	Comedy	1845
Putnam, the Iron Son of '76	Nathanial Bannister	Melodrama	1845
A Glance at New York	Benjamin Baker	Comedy	1848
Uncle Tom's Cabin	George Aiken	Melodrama	1852
Madelaine, the Belle of the Faubourg	Virginia Cunningham	Drama	1853
A Gentleman from Ireland	Fitz-James O'Brien	Comedy	1854
The Bankrupt	George Boker	Comedy	1855
The Poor of New York	Dion Boucicault	Melodrama	1857
Medea	Matilda Heron	Tragedy	1857
Rights of Man	Oliver Shephard	Comedy	1857
Fast Folks	Joseph Nunnes	Comedy	1858
The Octoroon	Dion Boucicault	Melodrama	1859
Leah, the Forsaken	Augustin Daly	Drama	1862
Rosedale	Lester Wallack	Melodrama	1863
Taming a Butterfly	Augustin Daly	Drama	1864
Rip van Winkle	Dion Boucicault (and others)	Comedy	1866
The Black Crook	Charles Barras	Melodrama	1866
Under the Gaslight	Augustin Daly	Melodrama	1867
Humpty Dumpty	George Fox	Comedy	1868
A Flash of Lightning	Augustin Daly	Melodrama	1868
Davy Crockett	Frank Murdoch	Melodrama	1872
Two Orphans	N. Hart Jackson	Romance	1874
Two Men of Sandy Bar	Bret Harte	Frontier Drama	1876

speaker's lines. This skewed the results when that file was put into software, so it seemed like the word *blood* was used 194 times in the corpus, when in fact 79 of those times were in error. If we had not known that a character in the play was named Bloodgood, we might have completely overlooked this error. Throughout the project, we often had to practice both "distant" and "close" readings by beginning with a "macro" view of texts and then having to scrutinize them closely to verify patterns.

For our analysis, we chose to employ free, open-source or open-access tools as a test of what resources might be available for theater students doing digital research. Students were free to choose their own tools; the most popular by far was AntConc, a corpus analysis tool developed by Laurence Anthony at Waseda University, Japan, that allows for an easy and reliable analysis of word count, concordance plots, n-grams, and collocates.[6] Other software employed include Palladio, an online network visualization tool from Stanford's Humanities + Design Lab, Google Maps Engine Lite, Carto DB, Voyant Tools, as well as some specialized frameworks like the New York Public Library's Map Warper, which enables users to overlay historical maps on current Google Maps.

Over the process of two months, we built a dataset, with students either working alone or in small groups to prepare the data, select tools, and conduct analysis. At weekly meetings, we shared and critiqued our in-process findings with the instructor and each other. Because each student was allowed to conduct his or her own analysis on the dataset, we were concerned that the focus would be too diffuse. We considered narrowing our work to look at one playwright's body of work rather than a general collection of plays but deliberately chose a more decentralized approach. While most of the projects discussed here are separate case studies, we feel that they represent the diversity of our interests as well as open multiple potential uses for digital tools to analyze pre-twentieth-century drama and theater. This work reflects what Stephen Ramsay describes as "screwing around," stressing the importance of how digital tools allow us not to find *the* path but *a* path in the vast archive of texts and to view this as an invitation to create and play.[7] Play—improvising without expectations and goals, allowing failure to see what you might discover—is exactly what we have done together throughout this course.

This chapter includes the majority of our projects, with sections covering text analysis and visualization, mapping, and network analysis. Unfortunately, there was not space for everyone's historical research and digital findings, but these sections are representative of our combined efforts. In text analysis, we focused on finding the context of words associated with violence, as well as creating word clouds of dialogue broken down by gender and class in a selection of plays. We continued with a more experimental mapping section, looking at the locations of plays in our collection, and we created a heat map of a crowdsourced sentiment analysis of locations in New York City, an overwhelmingly popular setting for our plays. We conclude with network analysis of dialogue and branch out more into traditional theater history to show how actors' networks changed over a transitional period in the century.

Text Analysis

Beginning with a broad overview of our texts, we used AntConc to look at the most common words. Contrary to our expectations, we found initially that words associated with violence or war were not as common as words associated with more sentimental plots such as romance or family. A stoplist, or file of common English words for the software to skip counting, was applied. Additionally, we filtered out proper names and obvious errors in the

TABLE 6.2. Twenty Most Conspicuous Words in Our
Play Collection

Word	Occurrences	Occurrences (as stem)
Man	907	1277
Good	831	883
Dear	572	616
Love	566	796
Time	508	606
Hand[1]	501	912
House	452	498
Father[2]	448	461
Poor	440	445
Night	423	450
Child	419	662
Heart	413	497
Mother	372	378
Life	368	371
Woman	337	340
True	328	509
Friend	318	493
Hear	317	583
Speak	213	337
Heaven	299	334

[1] Although *hand* appears often, a sizable percentage of this is in stage directions, indicating what a person is carrying in their hand. *House* also includes some mention in stage directions.
[2] The position of *father* is in part due to the fact that there are priests in a few plays who are addressed with the term *father*; however, the word occurrence in regular conversation is still high.

Optical Character Recognition scans (OCR). The search with the stem shown in Table 6.2 indicates a truncated search, so, for example, *dear* will include *dearly* and *dearest*. The table indicates the twenty most conspicuous words in our play collection.

We agreed that even this straightforward layer of analysis was a potentially good point to start analyzing nineteenth-century drama. Although we never anticipated producing a complete analysis for this project, we could envision class projects that would break down these words by date and genre to search for a recognizable "generic fingerprint" over the period. We used AntConc to quantify the relationship between several keywords as they appeared before, during, and after the Civil War. Although we didn't find the exact results we were looking for, we identified patterns in how gender, class, and geographies were applied, suggesting that digital-based inquiry can complement a range of classroom assignments (see Appendix 6.3).

The collocate tool in AntConc finds words that are frequently used before and after a search term. Seeing how words are associated with each other can often tell us more about a word's context than the sheer number of times a term appears in a corpus. We looked for patterns in words related to gender, race, and violence by analyzing the collocates for the words *battle*, *blood*, *death*, *free*, *kill*, *man*, *slave*, *violence*, *war*, and *woman*.[8]

According to our analysis, dramatic writing shows a shift from an active, more positive association with violence to a passive, regretful stance. Before the Civil War, *death* was associated more with active verbs like *whipped* or *screamed*. After the Civil War, *death* also tended to have words associated with it that were less direct and more sorrowful, such as *threatened* or *starvation*. High on the list of collocates with the word *death* prewar was the word *brilliant*, which is not similar to any word on the post–Civil War collocates for *death*. Likewise, the most frequent collocate for *violence* postwar is *shameful*.

This shift is complicated when analyzing the word *war*. In the antebellum plays, *war* had collocates largely associated with Native Americans, such as *path*, *scalping*, and the interjection *whoop*. By contrast, the post–Civil War collocates showed more nuanced positive associations like *song* and *happiness*. With more texts to analyze, our results would be even richer, but already patterns like these point the way for deeper analysis of the texts and show that plays do not often respond to their time period in expected ways. The Civil War remained a topic in U.S. theater for the remainder of the century, and a collocational analysis can provide necessary data for situating plays like Augustin Daly's *Under the Gaslight* (1867), Bronson Howard's *Shenandoah* (1888), and William Gillette's *Secret Service* (1895) in a wider context of shifting cultural sensibilities.

We looked at words associated with *slave* in plays on either side of the Civil War. The most common collocates with the word *slave* before the Civil War were largely neutral or supportive of slavery as an institution. *Parental*, *dabbled*, *figuratively*, *forbids*, *trade*, and *life* ranked high in both the statistical and frequency analyses. The post–Civil War collocates are radically different, with *caprice*, *dungeon*, and *power* dominating the list. The shift shows a noticeable trend in acknowledging slavery in the plays. A fuller analysis of the words in context across a broader corpus might help measure a shift in attitudes toward the institution, as plays responded to the postbellum economic and social shifts of emancipation.

Since the class expressed a long-standing interest in gender dynamics across the century, we also looked at the collocates for *man* and *woman*. We found a drastic difference in gendered discourse, with postwar collocates containing more aggressive connotations. Pre–Civil War, the word *man* was associated with neutral-seeming words like *represented, shirt, withhold,* and *establish.* *Woman* was most commonly associated with adjectives such as *tenderness, supplications,* and *hypocrisy.* After the war, the number one statistical post-war collocate for the word *man* is *worshipped.* Likewise, the highest collocate for the word *woman* is *worshipful.* *Woman* was also associated closely with words like *upsetting, unwomanly,* and *domestic,* while *man* was associated with *laboured, wheeling,* and *trapper.* Again, the specific descriptive words linked to *woman* show a drastic shift in the representation of women and a directed hierarchical attitude to gender. Examining our findings alongside a history of gender might add insight into how theater responded to its wider historical context. To delve further into gender roles—and to apply another tool—we ran an analysis on gender and class through a smaller selection of plays that offer an easy way to connect plays to social history in the classroom.

Taking an overview of our plays' stage roles, we looked at the gender break-down among cast lists. Excluding ensemble roles such as *villagers* or *fairies,* we found a ratio of 221 male characters to 126 female characters. Since there is a well-documented shift in audience demographics as women began to attend the theater in increasing numbers at midcentury, we expected to find a more equitable cast balance.[9] In this period, we noticed more domestic-themed plays and an increase in star actresses, but only two plays had more female characters than male, and these were both adaptations of French originals—Matilda Heron's adaption of Ernest Legouvé's *Medea* and Augustin Daly's adaptation of Victorien Sardou's *Taming a Butterfly*—leading us to suspect that the gender composition of companies remained male dominated through the period.

In selecting a tool to visualize gender dynamics within plays, we agreed that word clouds would be a simple and straightforward mode of representation. Although basic in what they convey, word clouds provide a clear view of the types of language and topics employed by members of different classes and genders in our plays. The creative visualization allowed us to see all of the selected texts at once and compare two or more clouds side by side. This made it easier to contrast speakers of different groups and to quickly detect broad patterns in a visually appealing way. Word clouds represent the most frequently used words in a corpus. The size of the words in the word cloud depends on how often the word was used in comparison to the other frequently used words. For this reason, word clouds are not only useful in comparing different texts to one another but also in comparing words within the same text.

The word clouds pictured in the link below represent the spoken text of characters divided by class and gender. This research was originally inspired by an earlier class assignment analyzing Henry James Byron's 1880 international hit play *Our Boys*, centering on two father-son pairs of different social classes.

From this starting point, we selected other plays containing characters of distinct social classes to analyze, including *Robert Macaire* (Charles Selby, 1830s), *Tea at 4 O'Clock* (Mrs. Harrison Burton, 1886), *Under the Gaslight* (Augustin Daly, 1867), *The Elevator Farce* (W. D. Howells, 1885), *Mousetrap* (1886), and *Guy Domville* (Henry James, 1895). To prepare the text for analysis, the dialogue of each play was copied and pasted into four separate plaintext documents that were divided by gender and class. From there, each category was combined into a new document that ultimately became the analyzed text.[10] The documents were loaded onto Tagxedo, a website that generates word clouds.[11]

Looking at the word clouds, we immediately noticed that many of the larger (and therefore higher-frequency) words used when referring to men, such as *Mr.* and *sir*, are present in the higher-class word clouds, whereas *Miss* is more prevalent in the lower-class word clouds, particularly for females. This information can tell us that lower-class females are more likely to directly address higher-class females, rather than males, but both males and females of a higher class often address high-status males directly. Additionally, feminine exclamations, including *oh*, [*good*] *Heaven*, and *ah*, are of a high frequency for higher-class females. While *oh* is largely present in the lower-class female cloud, other exclamations occasionally are replaced by lower-class language such as "*em*" and "*regler*," indicating the distinction between the social classes. Other differences between the two seem to indicate their role, as many of the terms included in the lower-class cloud refer to work or seem to be addressing or answering a command (*yes, going, make*). There were, however, similarities between high- and low-status men, such as *yes*, *friend*, and *know*, perhaps indicating that for many playwrights at the time, a man's gender seemed to take precedence over his class. Although the process of preparing texts for this approach was prohibitively time-consuming, word clouds could be useful for introducing students to digital tools, as they quickly reveal patterns in a user-friendly environment. A word cloud is limited in its scope, but it introduces concepts of counting, visualization, and refinement, as students need to sift through the important and extraneous words in a text or corpus, which proved to be vital skills in our work.[12]

Though our early work had concerned the dialogue in dramatic texts, in seeking to reclaim nineteenth-century theater, we also wanted to investigate perhaps the most unstudied aspect of the period: stage directions. Although they are instrumental in play production, it is unclear who wrote them in any given script. Often, the playwright might write some stage direction to indicate their vision for significant events, but stage direction might also be the product of a prompter, producer, or publisher. Regardless, many of the scripts for our plays were the texts used for subsequent productions, so we felt that they represented a vast, untapped resource to study how theater actually played on stage.

Owing to the difficulty of separating dramatic text and stage direction, we chose twelve different plays from our collection—half were written before the Civil War and half after—to look for patterns indicating how stage directions changed over the period.[13] Using a combination of manual cleaning and regular expressions, we removed all dialogue to create plaintext files that only had stage directions, including notes directing actors to enter, exit, move on stage, or conduct business, as well as direction regarding lighting, sound, and scenic effects.

Stage direction language is specific and economical, typically noting action or effects for future productions. Although some specific action is mentioned at heightened moments, prompts are typically general. For example, texts often mention *music* without specifying the type, or *crosses* without discussing the way an actor should walk. Despite this laconic tendency, stage directions provide an unprecedented view of the physical experience of contemporary productions.

The stage directions of these twelve plays have a word count of 58,645 composed of 4,857 different types of words. Table 6.3 indicates the most used words. The most common words denoting movement of effects are *music, aside, exit,*

TABLE 6.3. Most Used Words in Our Play Collection

Frequency	Word
1755	To
628	it
516	enter (enters, entered, entering)
487	on
419	at
368	l
363	r
349	d (down)
306	exit(s)
303	h (or hand)
273	from
244	off
230	aside
186	music
168	c (center, central)
118	run (runs, running)
106	cross (crosses, crossed, crossing)
105	re

and *enter* and stage location such as *l*[eft], *c*[enter], and *r*[ight]. Being able to study these patterns in the collection allowed us to gain a glimpse at how actors were prompted to move through space across time, as well as see how the technical aspects of theater were integrated with stage action. Looking at the concordance for the term *music* in stage directions, for example, allows us to see how often and where music was called for in a script. In the case of our plays, it was often used in connection with the term *enter*, referring most commonly to an actor's entrance, perhaps to add dramatic emphasis to an ongoing scene.

Although most directions merely call for an actor to *enter*, the second most common phrase is *runs on* (or *running*), which is used ninety-two times, or variations of *rushes on*, which is used twenty-six times. By contrast, stage directions do not frequently note calm entrances, suggesting that nineteenth-century playscripts paid special attention to noting the highly dramatic moments of a play and possibly considered low- and medium-energy entrances and exits to be unworthy of note.

Looking for overall patterns in stage direction over time, we made a word cloud of pre- and post–Civil War examples. The most noticeable trend between the clouds is the increase in word variety and specificity. A new group of words appear, such as *Aside, Door, LH* [Left Hand], *RH* [Right Hand], and *goes*, indicating that postbellum playscripts either contained more action or recorded movement in greater detail.

One of the unexpected contrasts in the pre- and post–Civil War word clouds was the appearance of the word *door* in the postwar stage directions. Although it was used 144 times across the collection, *door* appeared on average 4 times per play in prewar stage directions and 22 times per play in postwar directions. This trend demonstrates a rise in functional, interior sets in the second half of the nineteenth century, a trend that is rarely noticed on the production level. Although we will never know for certain how many plays were staged, word counts and concordances have begun to show significant patterns in production, design, and staging, aspects that are generally ignored by conventional histories of nineteenth-century theater.

Approaching the period through word clouds, word count, and collocates provided us with the freedom to create our own relationship to the course content. For students who have no background in the period, we felt that it was more rewarding and informative to actively explore plays with digital tools rather than learning about them through a lecture. The tools were relatively easy to learn and apply. While the results could benefit from further analysis, our work revealed key issues in the period that informed subsequent class discussions and offered observations that set the stage for future scholarly work. At the same time, this process has taught us useful scholarly skills, including pattern finding, cross-checking, and the importance of validating one's own work.

Mapping Locations and Texts

Based on the complexities of our findings in the language of nineteenth-century drama, the class wanted to use maps to get a representative overview of where plays were set in our chosen period. We were curious to see whether there was a noticeable shift in locations between rural/urban, North/South, or exterior/interior spaces, so we made a Google Map based on the locations of texts. We also wanted to push the boundaries of what maps could do and to include an experimental map of words associated with places in New York City where we found most of our plays were set.

To bypass the laborious work of reading plays purely for settings, we attempted to use the Stanford Named Entity Recognizer to extract place-names from the plaintext files, but this tool required more time and programming knowledge to train it to recognize the types of places we were looking for.[14] We eventually combed through the texts and made a Google Sheet of the locations, which were easily imported into Google Maps Engine Lite for visualization.[15]

The actual map ended up spanning the globe, with locations in Greece (*Medea*, 1856) and Wales (*The Phantom*, 1856). We noticed that pre–Civil War plays largely take place in urban or fantasy locations such as ancient Greece. In contrast, more post–Civil War plays take place in rural areas, such as Greene County, Tennessee (*Davy Crockett*, 1872), and the Catskill Mountains in Shandaken, New York (*Rip Van Winkle*, 1866). Out of the twenty-three plays surveyed, there is roughly an even percentage of geographic distribution that is constant through our collection. The plays we looked at that were first produced during the Civil War largely took place in rural locations and had a distinctly greater concentration of exterior scenes, which, along with our analysis of stage directions, marks a clear trend toward representations of interior scenes as the century progressed. Ideally, if we were going to study this further, we would want to increase the number of Civil War–era plays to determine if these trends extend across the century or are an anomaly.

As a counterexample, a small group of us worked on creating a map based on a focused dataset composed of plays and adaptations by Augustin Daly. Since Daly was a highly successful playwright and producer, he provides a useful test case to see if a thirty-two-play selection of one author's plays ranging from 1862 to 1896 would agree with the same trends noted above. Overall, Daly's plays included more international locations, an expected result as adapting international plays were increasingly common in this period. There are several Daly plays that have multiple locations, which are always in two locations on the same continent. For example, *Man and Wife* (1870) has two setting locations, but they are relatively close to each other: South Lanarkshire and Windysgate, Scotland. In *Pique* (1875), there are three locations, but they are all in Massachusetts. Transcontinental location changes do not occur in his plays. Out of the twenty-five plays included in this map, there are only eight plays that have multiple locations. Most of his plays only have one location in terms of city or county area.

Instead of just using a Google Map, we used the New York Public Library's Map Warper application to create an interactive historical map.[16] The Warper site is a freely available digital collection of more than twenty thousand maps from 1544 to 1980. After selecting the map, a user must rectify it, which entails matching latitude/longitude points on both maps so that the computer can take the older map, which most likely has a different orientation than the current map, and overlay it on the contemporary map with accurate coordinates.

Since we only wanted the island of Manhattan to appear in the overlay, we cropped the map before rectifying. Afterward, the map was exported into a GeoJSON application, and we manually added geotags for the locations of our plays.[17] Eventually, we had a workable map with locations pinned to the 1869 city.

Since New York proved a popular location in Daly's plays, appearing sixteen times out of a total of forty-two separate locations, we mapped Manhattan locations only.[18] All the plays' locations are below Union Square. Although the city had moved far uptown by the end of our Daly collection, these plays indicate that the lower part of the island remained a more dramatic place. Despite knowing that there were a number of Manhattan locations, it took mapping it to see that they were highly clustered.

In addition to plotting locations, we were also interested in exploring Google Maps' ability to map words and concepts to locations. Such a map could be a useful tool for putting New York City locations into context in studying or producing these plays by showing how contemporaries viewed each location. Taking an experimental turn, we combined AntConc's toolkit and Google Maps to represent the words associated with nineteenth-century New York City neighborhoods. We quickly found that characters rarely talk about places in plays, possibly because the location is often represented in the scenery, removing the need for verbal description. Instead, we turned to New York City guidebooks as a source that could demonstrate how authors talked about location. To begin with, we assembled a collection of twenty-two guidebooks from the 1830s to the 1890s from Project Gutenberg, the Internet Archive, and HathiTrust. After choosing seventeen notable locations, we ran collocates for common New York place-names and used the Key Words In Context (KWIC) tool to select the top-ranked adjectives used in close proximity to these areas.[19]

The biggest challenge was that many of the texts were the products of inaccurate OCR (optical character recognition) scans. A large portion of the collocates were strings of words without spaces, such as "tohavebeenpeaceful."

After a process of filtering out similar terms, we built a spreadsheet of the places with the most-used adjectives to describe them in our collection. From this list, the class crowdsourced a rough sentiment analysis of the words. We created a Google Poll asking the class to rank eighty-five place-name adjectives on a scale from "Not Respectable" to "Respectable," based on our class readings of nineteenth-century culture.[20] Although the results were subjective, we hoped that they would be reliable in aggregate. Once the responses were collated, the results were translated to a CSV (comma-separated values) file with the latitude/longitude of the location and the rank for each category. We imported this into CartoDB, a professional mapping application with a free option (registration required).[21] We created a "heat map" of "Respectable," "Neutral," and "Not Respectable" locations, according to our interpretation of guidebook literature from the period. The larger and darker the circle around a location indicated a higher presence of words tagged by each category.

The results show some expected tropes of New York urban history: as the population grew, elites moved uptown, so "respectable" areas tend to be higher uptown, with chaotic and "not respectable" areas remaining downtown. However, the surprising finding in this heat map is that the infamous Five Points District, which was in close proximity to key theaters of the period, featured prominently on all of the crowdsourced categories and texts.[22] Instead of being shunned, this slum area, which was once considered the murder capital of the world, received near-equal attention from pedestrians, politicians, reformers, and tourists, suggesting that it was the site of much activity, despite being socially "unrespectable." Such a map could be a useful tool for putting New York City locations into context in studying or producing these plays by showing how contemporaries viewed each location.

While it took time to devise a reasonable workflow, we felt that the map was fairly commensurate with what we read about areas of the city in the period. Further work could include a wider dataset, more scrupulous OCR, and a wider corpus. Overall, we believe that mapping via Google Maps is a useful and user-friendly tool for almost any level of course. We could envision class assignments with a map that allows students to gain a greater understanding of theaters in an urban environment. For example, mapping theaters and other venues, shopping or dining sites, or, in a somewhat more advanced application, shifting demographics according to census data could reveal significant information about the social and cultural context of nineteenth-century drama.

Network Analysis

Inspired by the trends we discovered in the increase of violent language, more hierarchical gender discourse, a tendency toward more urban interiors in play settings, and a consistent preference for New York City as a popular dramatic location, we turned to network analysis to produce a visualization of shared dramatic language, as well as a snapshot of actors' professional lives. We had previously created graphs of individual plays by following the method Franco Moretti lays out in his article "Network Theory, Plot Analysis," which chiefly looks at connections between the characters in *Hamlet*.[23] While Moretti's network diagrams reveal fascinating patterns in *Hamlet*, it only treats the play as a literary text, not a performed event. Unlike Moretti's methodology, we began by looking for broad patterns of connections in word usage. In addition, we sought to include a more concrete historical analysis, so we created a small network of key actors in the period between the transitional years of 1857–1865 to examine who acted with Edwin Forrest, generally considered the most popular actor of the antebellum period, and Edwin Booth, Forrest's counterpart in the postbellum period.

We again turned to AntConc to test for collocates of *blood, war,* and *death*. Since network analysis is best when looking for connections between words, we used it to see what terms were popular among the various playwrights in connection to these key words. We created a CSV file with the playwrights, terms, and weights, and we imported it into Palladio. We found Palladio to be useful because it has a short initial learning curve and straightforward approach to representing modest-sized networks.[24]

As a result, we had graphs with two kinds of nodes, or points, for each key word. One class of nodes was for the authors in our corpus. The other was for collocates of the key word. When a word appeared in the collocates of an author's use of *death*, for example, Palladio would draw a line connecting the author's name and the collocate. If another author used that same word as a collocate of *death*, the two become connected in the graph. The nodes are sized according to how many connections they have, so if *frozen* is used with *death* often, it will appear bigger than *bore*, which is not used as much.

The two key graphs we studied closely were for collocates of *blood* and *death*. *War* was highly fragmented and inconclusive, suggesting that there was not as much linguistic variety devoted to the term over the period.[25] Among the most shared collocates of *blood* pre–Civil War were *flesh, human, thirst, slaughtered, rigged,* and *frozen*. Post–Civil War, the field changed to take on distinctly more violent terminology with *tremor, flesh, stained, spilling, raking, freely, superb,* and *trained*. The most populated networks are both the pre– and post–Civil-War usage of *death*. Pre–Civil War collocates for *death* include *screamed, hunter, pining, poor, ability, problem, mourn, romanced, brutes,* and *petrified*. Post-Civil War collocates include *freeze, spectre, hoarded, threatened, pining, frightening, lament, sake, barrier, worse,* and *father*.

While much of our effort has been rooted in texts, we wanted to get a broader view of the theatrical world of the period our plays cover. We created a graph linking actors in New York between the years of 1857 and 1865. The graph focuses on Edwin Forrest, Edwin Booth, and Mr. and Mrs. F. B. Conway. We collected the data by combing through George C. D. Odell's *Annals of the New York Stage*, volume 7: *1857–1865*, part of a fifteen-volume collection of New York City theater records from the earliest times to the end of the nineteenth century. Compiling the information in the first decades of the twentieth century, Odell synthesized older chronicles, newspaper advertisements, and extant playbills. His work is inconsistent, but it remains the most complete record of what was produced on the New York stage. Although the volumes are in print, we found it easier to search via the Alexander Street Press's *North American Theatre Online* database's digitized version. Going through Odell's (messy) chronicle, we made note of which actor worked with whom and how many times they worked with each other. In our data, the *source* is the major star (Booth or Forrest), the *target* column records Odell's notes of which actors they performed with, and *weight* is how many times the pair acted together. We noticed that Frederick and Sarah Conway were frequently performing in the period, so we expanded the dataset to include their performances.[26] Palladio then drew connections between each actor when they acted with one of the major stars, making the nodes, which represent actors, larger depending on the weight of their connection.

The initial graph in Palladio was too cluttered, so we decided to remove Mrs. Conway since her contacts were almost identical to Mr. Conway's. Nevertheless, we still had a cluttered field because Palladio, which is in development, lacks detailed filtering features. A high number of actors who only acted once remained visible, obscuring the data. In the case of collocates, Palladio worked well, since we preselected the network, but with over two hundred nodes, we had to turn to Gephi, a more robust open-source platform with more advanced features.[27] Although it has a steep initial learning curve, there is copious online documentation, and we could rather easily create a simplified graph that revealed significant patterns in this transitional period.

In the resulting graph, the nodes are sized according to their "Betweenness Centrality," which measures how connected they are to other nodes. The thickness of the lines denotes the number of contacts between the two. We were able to filter out everyone who only appeared with an actor once and thus had no connection between Booth, Forrest, and Conway. The years covered by the graph mark a period in which no single star actor dominated the New York stage, as Forrest had done in the 1830s and early 1840s and Booth would later do, starting in the late 1860s. The graph reflects both Forrest's decline and

Booth's ascent, but most noticeably they worked with few of the same actors. In other words, it was not only the rise of Booth and the fall of Forrest, but a shift in entire repertoires and companies that was happening, a fact that is nearly impossible to see in a close reading of Odell, as the sheer labor of sifting through so much detail is overwhelming.

From the graph, we can infer that Mr. Conway was a great contact to have in the theater industry, as he is connected to the most people on both Forrest's side and Booth's. Quite possibly, Conway was, in a way, more successful than either Forrest or Booth since he maintained his profession throughout the time period despite the changing theater scene. We can also begin to measure the relative position of other actors across the period. For example, we can see that Mme. Ponisi and Charles Fisher were prominent figures in the theater, having worked with both Forrest and Conway. It is also interesting to see that J. W. Collier, John Nunan, and Mary Wells, who all worked with Forrest many times, began to work with Booth too (comparing the thick line to Forrest and the thin line to Booth). B. T. Ringgold was also well connected, having a relatively strong tie to Forrest as well as ties to both Conway and Booth. Even though tools like Palladio and Gephi conduct analysis on a macro scale, they can reveal more information about the lives of forgotten actors than reading a chronicle.

Such data and visualization could be used to explore further topics in the social lives of American actors including whether an actor's success can be measured by how many actors they knew or by which actors they worked with. It also gives us a visual overview of the theater community at the time; however, it is only a snapshot. We can imagine a class project to build a more in-depth picture of the theatrical world of any time in the century with this same methodology. With the work we have done, it seems that network analysis has the potential to process massive chronicles like Odell's efficiently and to visualize them in ways that produce immediate results, allowing us to further expand our work to gain an unprecedented view of the acting profession.

Conclusion

This project has shown that distant reading and close reading shouldn't be thought of as opposite forces: both forms of analysis can draw upon the other. We would like to see a new type of learning emerge as a result of accessible digital tools, creating hybrid reading practices and enabling students to create their own relationships with texts and textual data. This work provided us with a richer experience than a typical term paper, as it allowed us to take greater ownership of the research, providing, as one student said, "a deeper connection and sense of dedication between the researcher and their work."

Overall, we felt that this work sparked a creative *and* scholarly interaction with nineteenth-century theater and culture.

This work was difficult, to say the least. The time required to learn tools, assemble a corpus, and prepare texts for analysis was daunting. Often, it required us to redo our work more than once, which can be frustrating for newcomers. We had a near-constant need to switch back and forth between our texts and our analysis, as several trends turned out to be textual errors or blips in our workflow.[28] One student noted that "these tools and even the subject of digital humanities can be intimidating." Another effectively summed up our work process by saying "there is always a struggle/mental breakdown/brain numbing period," and then "you start to form your own methodology for how you work with these tools and get results with your sanity still intact." Ultimately, we felt that for students with no formal computer science training, the hands-on and collaborative aspect of a seminar format was crucial. One student said that "guided learning and the discussion with others in the same boat has been really, really rewarding. It has allowed us to feel safe enough to go outside of our comfort zones and try out new things." Despite the Sturm und Drang of learning the tools and their applications, students responded positively to the assignments for their ability to provide, according to one participant, "a taste of what it is like being a historian, not having assignments but rather having to make new discoveries." And as another of us remarked after we finished collating our work, "even the most daunting tasks can be made into cool projects."

Although there is hardly a canon of nineteenth-century drama, by using multiple databases and online collections, we were able to assemble a working collection of scripts, which we would like to see augmented in future classes. Digital tools cannot repair the gaps in the century's theatrical archive, but working with our texts, we recognized tensions in the theatrical community of midcentury New York as a new generation of actors took the stage in the postbellum period, how word patterns shifted across the Civil War, and the ways in which the fictional worlds of plays coincided with geographic space. We hope that this initial exploration provides a convincing argument for future courses that the nineteenth century was as dynamic and robust as any other period in U.S. theater history.

In the classroom, our work demonstrated that digital tools merit a place in the theater studies curriculum by engaging students in novel ways to approach history and literary studies (see Appendix 6.4). Over a semester, we conducted in-depth literary analysis, learned about the lives of actors, and discovered the changing urban environment of major theaters, thus providing a broad *and* in-depth foundation for any further study in the period. Digital scholarship need not be confined solely to "digital" classes. For example, we employed low-barrier tools with short learning curves such as word clouds and Google

Maps, which might have a place in theater history classes of almost any variety. Despite their limitations, and even sometimes because of them, tools teach lessons in how to prepare, refine, and interpret data, valuable skills for any kind of scholarship.

We found unique benefits to practicing digital scholarship in our course. Most conspicuously, our tools allowed us to study large collections of texts and, within a few seconds, to display information and find patterns previously undetectable due to the immense human labor they would require. A key strength is that digital tools present us with new ways of processing and analyzing data, causing us to think outside the box and to view our material with a fresh pair of eyes (simply because of the innovative nature of this subject). We have learned that digital analysis of a textual corpus can add to artistic innovation as well. Analyzing a piece of dramatic literature digitally can give an actor or director insights that might otherwise not have been apparent. Despite their difficulty, we agree that digital tools have tremendous potential to empower us to create our own data and draw our own conclusions from historical practice.

The appendixes for this chapter, a syllabus and assignments for a course by Robert Davis on using digital tools and methodologies to study theater history and dramatic literature, can be found at www.press.uillinois.edu/books/Teaching WithDH.

Notes

1. See Mark Hodin, "Late Melodrama," in *The Oxford Handbook of American Drama*, ed. Jeffrey H. Richards and Heather S. Nathans (New York: Oxford University Press, 2014), 159–72. David Savran shows how critics chose to see a select few early twentieth-century playwrights as initiating a modern, "elevated" American drama, effectively discounting everything that had come before. David Savran, *Highbrow/Lowdown: Theater, Jazz, and the Making of the New Middle Class* (Ann Arbor: University of Michigan Press, 2009), 221–64. The idea of O'Neill as a "dramatic messiah" delivering audiences and critics from the commerce of the previous century has long persisted. For example, Bert Cardullo opens with "American drama, for all practical purposes, is twentieth-century American drama" and "The [pre-twentieth-century] theatre was a broadly popular light-entertainment form, then, much like television today," in *American Drama/Critics: Writings and Readings* (Newcastle: Cambridge Scholars, 2007), 1.

2. As one student described our relationship to the source material: "Digitally studying nineteenth-century theatre feels akin to walking into a dark cave with a flashlight that's running out of battery; you have a tool that can work magic, but the content you're putting in it does not always allow you to use it properly."

3. Once the period that we wanted to study was selected, we chose a workable body of available texts that we felt would represent the period. We did not choose plays that were transplanted from Europe or the works of Shakespeare that were frequently pro-

duced. We did include some adaptations, since adapting European hits was common in the second half of the nineteenth century.

4. Determining genre is a difficult task, as tragedy, comedy, and melodrama are fluid categories that have changed over time. As much as possible, we strove to assign the genre that contemporary audiences would have associated with the play, trusting to published playtexts and playbills for our sources.

5. For example, obvious stage direction terms appear frequently in our corpus: *aside* (812), *enter* (779), *exit* (577), *scene* (376), and *crosses* (170). Other words are less obvious. For example, *door* appears frequently (501) but is almost entirely in stage directions instead of dialogue.

6. "AntConc," Laurence Anthony's Website, accessed March 26, 2017, http://www .laurenceanthony.net/software/antconc/. A concordance plot shows where a search word appears in each text of a corpus, N-Grams show the words that appear close together in phrases across a corpus, and collocates show the words that statistically appear in a range near the search term. For an overview and guide to getting started with AntConc, see Heather Froehlich, "Corpus Analysis with Antconc," *Programming Historian*, accessed March 26, 2017, http://programminghistorian.org/lessons/corpus -analysis-with-antconc.

7. See Stephen Ramsay, ""The Hermeneutics of Screwing Around; or What You Do with a Million Books," in *Pastplay: Teaching and Learning History with Technology*, ed. Kevin Kee (Ann Arbor: University of Michigan Press, 2014), 111–20.

8. AntConc measures collocates with two methods: by frequency, which counts the number of times words fall within a certain range of each other, and by statistic, a metric that measures how probable it is that the two words will occur within the range across the corpus. For our analysis, we looked at both approaches to identify trends, which we ranked together. We did not include articles, such as *the*, *an*, or *a*, but instead focused on active words. We took the highest statistically ranked words and checked their frequency to ensure that they were not anomalous before including them in our work. For a fuller account of collocational analysis, see Tony McEnergy and Andrew Wilson, *Corpus Linguistics: An Introduction* (Edinburgh: Edinburgh University Press, 2001), 75–102.

9. See, for example, Richard Butsch, *The Making of American Audiences: From Stage to Television, 1750–1990* (New York: Cambridge University Press, 2000).

10. Due to the lengthy process of cutting and pasting every line of dialogue by charac-ters of different classes and genders, we used plays that had already been prepared in pre-vious classes rather than staying within the larger collection of texts used for this chapter.

11. Tagxedo, accessed March 26, 2017, http://tagxedo.com/.

12. For more on the usefulness and limitations of word clouds, see Shawn Graham, Ian Milligan, and Scott Weingart, *Exploring Big Historical Data: The Historian's Mac-roscope* (London: Imperial College Press, 2016), 74–79.

13. The plays selected were *Putnam, The Iron Son of '76* (1845), *Uncle Tom's Cabin* (1852), *The Phantom* (1856), *The Poor of New York* (1857), *The Octoroon* (1859), *Leah, the Forsaken* (1862), *The Black Crook* (1866), *Rip Van Winkle* (1866), *A Flash of Lighting* (1868), *Davy Crockett* (1872), *Tea at 4 O'clock* (1886).

14. "Stanford Named Entity Recognizer (NER)," Stanford Natural Language Pro-cessing Group, March 26, 2017, http://nlp.stanford.edu/software/CRF-NER.shtml.

15. "Pre/Post–Civil War Play Locations," *Google My Maps*, https://www.google.com/maps/d/edit?mid=z5Q5oiXjRCLM.kkLISV7vnYfg&usp=sharing.

16. "NYPL Map Warper," New York Public Library, accessed March 26, 2017, http://maps.nypl.org/warper/. The actual map rectified for this project is currently available at http://maps.nypl.org/warper/maps/16234#Preview_tab.

17. GeoJSON, accessed March 26, 2017, http://geojson.org/.

18. New York City appears as a location for thirteen plays, nine more than the second most frequent location, Massachusetts, which appears four times.

19. "KWIC (Keywords in Context) Output," eXist, accessed March 26, 2017, https://exist-db.org/exist/apps/doc/kwic.xml. Our locations were the Bowery, Park Row, Fifth Avenue, Madison Square, Union Square, Five Points, Bowery Theatre, Chatham Square, Park Theatre, Barnum's Museum, 42nd Street, University of New York, Astor Place, Broadway, Canal Street, Houston Street, and the Battery.

20. See, for example, Karen Halttunen, *Confidence Men and Painted Women: A Study of Middle-Class Culture in America, 1830–1870* (New Haven: Yale University Press, 1982).

21. CartoDB, is now called Carto. Carto, accessed March 27, 2017, https://carto.com.

22. For more on the history of Five Points, see Tyler Anbinder, *Five Points: The 19th-Century New York City Neighborhood That Invented Tap Dance, Stole Elections, and Became the World's Most Notorious Slum* (New York: Free Press, 2001). The Five Points serves as a backdrop in the Martin Scorsese film *Gangs of New York* and the BBC America television show *Copper*. Chatham Square and the Bowery were also in close proximity and can be seen nearly merging with the Five Points circle.

23. Franco Moretti, "Network Theory, Plot Analysis," *New Left Review* 68 (March–April 2011): 80–102; reproduced by Stanford Literary Lab, accessed March 26, 2017, https://litlab.stanford.edu/LiteraryLabPamphlet2.pdf.

24. Palladio, Stanford Humanities + Design, accessed March 26, 2017, http://hdlab.stanford.edu/palladio/.

25. Interestingly, the post–Civil War network contains only half the total collocates of its pre–Civil War network. This could be attributed to the destructive impact the Civil War had on the country.

26. Mr. and Mrs. Conway, as they were known, were a husband and wife team who acted through a range of genres. In 1864, Sarah Conway took over management of the Brooklyn Theatre, which she ran until her death in 1875, frequently performing with her husband.

27. Gephi, accessed March 26, 2017, https://gephi.org/.

28. For example, *hit* appears as a top term in the corpus. We though this confirmed an abundance of violence post–Civil War, but it turned out to be an HTML tag that was left over when uploading the text from an HTML file.

PART THREE

Recover

7. What We've Learned (about Recovery) through the *Just Teach One* Project

Duncan Faherty and Ed White

IF THE *JUST TEACH ONE (JTO)* PROJECT can be called a digital humanities initiative, in many ways this designation reflects the accidents of its birth and not original intentions. Truth be told, after several years of preparing and teaching lesser-known works of fiction, we had set out to compile a traditional print anthology that would consist of a handful of neglected early American novellas, judicious selections of serialized short fiction, and a range of period writings about the cultural functions of fiction. Our aim was to prepare a volume that might fruitfully complicate the structures of courses focused on early U.S. cultural production. We were motivated by a sense that early American literary studies had coalesced around the novel form and become dominated by a small constellation of texts, many of which were available for classroom use in multiple scholarly editions. We wanted to disrupt this calcified canon by making a wider range of texts readily accessible for course adoption; and, as a corollary ambition, we hoped to alter the kinds of pedagogical and critical conversations occurring in a field that had concretized around a set of texts that seemed, if not atypical, at least narrow in range. By expanding the pedagogical range of the field, we believed an expansion of scholarly practices would follow. Even though well over a hundred domestically authored novels and novellas were produced in the United States between 1787 and 1820, less than a dozen of these regularly receive any sustained critical attention. Even fewer regularly make their way into classrooms, and almost all of these—with the notable exception of Leonora Sansay's *Secret History* (1808), which was first made widely available in a Broadview edition by Michael Drexler in 2007—were originally published in the decade of the 1790s.[1] In essence, early U.S.

literature had become conflated with a thin slice of textual production from the 1790s, and it was a commonplace in the field that after this date textual production waned until the rise of historical fiction and sketches in the 1820s. The space between was unmapped, unexplored, and largely imagined as bereft of merit, and it was almost impossible to counter this narrative in a classroom unless one had access to such paywall-protected databases as those operated by Readex or Proquest.

As we debated the possibilities of what this traditional print anthology might contain, questions about canonicity, serialization, periodization, and form dominated our thinking. The idea of a digital platform remained remote to our discussions, and more than once we considered abandoning the enterprise before it even started, without seriously considering the possibilities of a digital home. Our failure to consider a web-based platform largely resulted from our lack of digital literacy: neither of us had ever been involved in any digital humanities work, nor did we possess any particular technological fluencies. Our turn toward the digital only occurred after we became frustrated by our efforts to pursue a traditional print format for the project. Across several months, we had reached out to multiple publishers to pitch the idea and had an extended conversation with one of them. In the end, these exploratory discussions yielded little. The publisher with whom we spoke maintained that while instructors might frequently signal they had an interest in teaching new texts, in reality, when it came time to order books for courses, they almost always returned to the familiar and the canonical.[2] For every successfully recovered text—that is, a text that proved to be financially sustainable for a traditional print-based press to keep in circulation—there were multiple abandoned editions that may have generated some initial interest but quickly fell back into obscurity.

In short, we were told that there was no measurable profit in recovering the unrecovered. Instead, this publisher offered us a counterproposal: if we prepared two or three editions of canonical standards (which would enable the publisher to market a "full" roster of early American texts), we could try to resurrect a solitary noncanonical text. Such an enterprise held no appeal for us. We had no vested scholarly interest in the texts we were asked to edit, and, moreover, we felt that having multiple editions of the same set of texts was in fact becoming an unacknowledged problem in the field. With our ambitions for this project continually frustrated, we maintained our independent course of producing personal editions (some transcriptions, some slightly corrected OCR versions) of neglected texts and using them in our own classrooms. We imagined that if we began to expose graduate students to a wider range of materials it might slowly begin to have an impact on scholarly production, and we did what we could to encourage doctoral candidates to think more broadly about the textual horizons of early American literary production. Additionally, we discussed our experiences teaching these texts and tried to reference them in our own scholarship, including organizing pertinent sessions and delivering related papers at field conferences. These efforts were aimed at amplifying attention to lesser-known texts by providing individual case studies and more broadly pointing out just how limited the operative canon was for the field. It was in the aftermath of one of these sessions, which also featured papers by Karen Weyler and Michelle Burnham, that the project began to coalesce around the idea of conjoining recovery and pedagogy.

The conference session, titled "Recovering Recovery; or, Canonical Speculations," took place at the Eighth Biennial Conference of the Charles Brockden Brown Society in 2012. Since this conference never schedules simultaneous sessions, the majority of the conference participants (approximately sixty specialists in post-Revolutionary U.S. literary studies) attended this panel.[3] The session foregrounded the necessity of expanding the canon of early U.S. literary studies, and the papers sought to demonstrate how the recovery of particular texts could shift longstanding assumptions within the field imaginary. In many ways, the session and the conversation that followed from it were inspired by the provocative arguments framed by Theresa Strouth Gaul in an essay titled "Recovering Recovery: Early American Women and *Legacy*'s Future." In this piece, Gaul advocates linking recovery efforts to the classroom to ensure their viability, and she does so in part by tracing how some of the recovery efforts, begun in the 1980s, had become stalled since relatively few instructors had used those texts in their classrooms. In short, Gaul argued, recovered texts that infrequently found their way into the hands of students seldom seemed to remain recovered for very long. This failure to make lasting canonical change created a hamster wheel–like need for scholars to recursively reissue the just previously recovered. In seeking to promote a wider adoption of early-nineteenth-century novels written by women that had just been reissued, Gaul argued that recent critical developments in what she called "Transnationalist approaches, whether framed as transatlantic, circumatlantic, Atlantic, inter-American, hemispheric, or even planetary," provided "teachers and scholars the tools to train a potentially transformative lens on works from this period."[4] Our canon, in other words, no longer needed to be constrained in order to serve "nationalist paradigms," and the possibilities inherent in such a critical turn marked for Gaul an opening for a generative communal return to recovery efforts. The practical challenge, as we understood Gaul to be framing it, was to make sure that recovered texts found their way into classrooms and into ongoing critical conversations. In many respects, she clarified the problem as a kind of chicken and egg puzzle: recovered texts that do not inspire a sustained critical conversation seldom manage to achieve regularized course adoption, and texts that are not often taught receive only fitful critical attention. Somehow both issues come first. The task at hand, we concluded, was to manufacture a way to have multiple scholars and instructors engage new texts simultaneously, to attempt to foster multiple engagements with a new text within the same semester to spark grounded conversations about canonicity and recovery.

In the aftermath of the conference session, we began to discuss more seriously the idea of trying to engage other field specialists in experimenting with neglected texts in their own classes. At first, we imagined this as a way to prove to publishers the viability of our idea for the print compilation outlined above. The conference allowed us a chance to speak with a range of other scholars about our ideas, and their collective enthusiasm and their pointed feedback were crucial to our thinking about possible next steps. At this juncture, we knew what we wanted to do was to conceptualize a sustainable recovery project untethered to precarious institutional support or subject to the currently narrow parameters of the academic publishing industry. We also simply wanted the chance to experiment without having to elaborate a lengthy justification for our efforts. We knew that to succeed, this would have to be a collective enterprise. Since we had already tested the texts that were to become the first few *JTO* editions in our own classrooms, we had some sense of what kinds of conversations these works might generate and how they might be positioned within and between canonical texts. In short, we knew how these texts worked to alter our students' perceptions about cultural production in the early republic, how they shifted questions about authorship, form, mobility, seriality, anonymity, geography, agency, slavery, abolition, and labor in productive ways. Or, perhaps more accurately, we had subjective assumptions about how these texts worked based on our own classroom experiences and informed by our sense that early American literary studies had become too attached to a small constellation of texts. So, with some encouraging conference conversations behind us, we decided to forge ahead.

Our simple starting assumption was that if instructors would commit to teaching one new text every semester, a text that might only take a single class session to consider, then larger collective conversations about pedagogy and canonicity might emerge. After selecting our first text, we contacted about twenty colleagues from around the country, asking them to teach the novella *Amelia; or The Faithless Briton* in fall 2012. As that initial solicitation made clear, we had no edition prepared, no platform by which to disseminate the text, and no clear selling point beyond our textual summary and our pleas for joining the endeavor. Literally—and remarkably—within minutes several people had signed on. A conversation with Paul Erickson of the American Antiquarian Society further propelled our efforts when he offered us a home at *Common-Place*, the on-line "journal of early American life" founded in 2000. This location and partnership with AAS has allowed *JTO* to dwell at the intersection between print and electronic media. Our freely available editions are lodged on a website but are prepared as accessible PDFs for easy printing. This multiuse format, as opposed to a strictly digital platform, was part of our effort to remove some of the obstacles and frustrations that often accompany teaching out-of-print texts: for example, cost, availability, and accessibility. At the same time, we did not want to invent new hurdles by assuming all instructors or student bodies had access to e-reading devices and digitized classrooms. Digitally, the *JTO* site was to be the place for short blog posts about classroom experiences from the volunteer instructors, and we envisioned a space in which discussions about teaching successes and failures (or even related research pursuits) might be explored. Ideally this discussion would spur further reflections and changed practices concerning pedagogy and canonicity, with people reconsidering how they assembled their syllabi.

The present moment offers a strange blend of opportunities and impediments for recovery work. Our ambition has been to fashion a practical laboratory for canonical and archival expansion predicated on using new texts in classrooms. Now, five years later, we have produced ten editions, mostly of short, neglected early U.S. novellas. We began with *Amelia; or The Faithless Briton* (1787), a magazine publication widely reprinted through the 1790s, much like our second text, *The Story of Constantius and Pulchera* (1789–1790). Our third text was the anonymous *Humanity in Algiers, or The Story of Azem* (1801), published by a Baptist-affiliated press in upstate New York. We then followed with Sarah Savage's anonymously published *The Factory Girl* (1814), which last was reprinted several times in the antebellum era. Next, we published the anonymous *St. Herbert—A Tale* (1796, attributed to "Anna"), another magazine serialization; the November 1786 issue of the *Columbian Magazine*; Susanna Rowson's serialized 1803–1804 novel *Sincerity* (published in 1813 as *Sarah, or The Exemplary Wife*); and the "Account of a Remarkable Conspiracy Formed by a Negro in the Island of St. Domingo," a work of French origin (1787) that circulated in Atlantic periodicals for years after. In fall 2017 we produced an edition of Herman Mann's *Female Review* (1797), a text that purports to be a memoir of Deborah Sampson, who, as "Robert Shurtliff," served in the Continental Army at the end of the American Revolution. Our most recent edition is *Equality–A Political Romance* (1802), a utopian travelogue first serialized in the Philadelphia deist journal *Temple of Reason*. As this short catalogue should indicate, we have been slowly working to diversify our materials.

We have also been moving to more collaborative work: our *Columbian Magazine* edition was prepared with the help of Jared Gardner; we worked with Toni Wall Jaudon in preparing "Account of a Remarkable Conspiracy," and we partnered with Jodi Schorb in preparing the *Female Review*. The project has always been a collaborative one between the two of us and has always been informed by our conversations with other scholars and instructors. As a public-facing scholarly project, its success is entirely dependent on a network of collaborators who inform what we do both during the editorial process and after the editions are complete. Moreover, as we have become more accustomed to the rhythms of working with each other in this way, it has become easier for us to formally partner with other scholars. We also have a kind of spiritual collaboration with our sister project, *Just Teach One: Early African American Print*, as we occasionally trade ideas in conversations with the editors of those editions (about such things as how to recruit volunteers or about the kinds of notes that undergraduates might find useful). As Nicole N. Aljoe, Eric Gardner, and Molly O'Hagan Hardy detail in their essay in this volume about *JTO: EAAP* (see chapter 8), that project has a more expansive sense of collaboration than we have enacted so far. The editorial collective for the *JTO: EAAP* project identifies itself as a "kind of loose collective, initially convened as a specific group but open to change," a vision of assemblage and collectivity that surpasses our comparatively more straightforward partnership. In reflecting on some of the foundational differences between the two projects, we have begun to think through what adopting some of their practices would mean for the original *JTO*. In some ways, the two projects are silo versions of a similar concept, and each iteration offers the companion the opportunity to learn, revise, reformat, and reflect. In recent months, we have begun to work with Molly O'Hagan Hardy to take what she has learned with *JTO: EEAP* and devise a plan to retroactively create TEI-coded companion editions to our original PDF editions, as well as think about trying to produce both versions of new texts as we move forward.

All told, the texts we have produced for the *JTO* project have been or are currently being taught by over 125 instructors from across the country in a wide range of courses. We have more to say about usage patterns and demographics below, but one thing we must underscore about recovery work in the twenty-first century is that it is best done as a do-it-together (to borrow a phrase from Cathy N. Davidson) project rather than a do-it-yourself endeavor.[5] None of what we have done would have been possible without our various partners and collaborators. Most importantly, none of it would have mattered very much if colleagues were not willing to test these texts out in their classrooms. We dwell on this inaugural moment to underscore the collective foundation of this project in its infancy and to highlight the willingness of our colleagues to experiment alongside us.

We want to conclude with some reflections about participation and practices during the four years of this project. We have not yet had the opportunity to pursue a formal survey of participants to assess the effect of *JTO* on academic understandings of canonicity, recovery, and pedagogy, or even to compile concrete information about how many students read or wrote about these texts, how many instructors have incorporated these texts into their scholarship, how texts have been shared, and so on. What we offer here are speculations based on what we know about the first five of the eight editions we have prepared.

Across our first two and half years, we had sixty-five distinct classroom uses of *JTO* texts, or roughly thirteen instructors for each new text. Of these sixty-five teachings, thirteen participants have taught *JTO* texts multiple times: one for three different texts, and twelve for two. So, of the sixty-five uses, we had fifty-two different instructors. Of these sixty-five classes, the instructors self-reported that twenty-five (39 percent) were surveys of American literature, that twenty-one (32 percent) were upper-level courses, that eight (12 percent) were graduate seminars, that six (9 percent) were courses for sophomore level nonmajors, and five (7 percent) were other kinds of courses (including composition). The vast majority of these courses, not surprisingly, were housed in English departments, although two were in history programs, and at least five were also cross-listed with women's studies programs.

As we look over these blog posts and think about where these texts were taught, it seems fair to suggest that the *JTO* project and the questions of recovery work that it hopes to foreground have most often been featured in survey courses (again about 39 percent of the time). Anecdotally, it seems that the *JTO* texts are often used to illustrate the problems attendant to constructing a survey to begin with and have been deployed to foster conversations about canonicity. Our choice of texts has been to some degree driven by some underlying assumptions that we have had about the early American canon, and these assumptions (especially at the start) caused us to think about texts that would work well when paired with canonical standards. So, for example, we selected *Amelia; or The Faithless Briton* as our first text since we imagined its very different notion of female agency would serve as a counterfoil to Charlotte Temple's infamous passivity. Many of the teaching posts about this text suggest how Amelia was deployed to initiate conversations about sentimentality and the cultural legacies of canonizing certain forms of behavior over and against other possibilities.

In more specialized courses, with either more narrow temporal ranges or thematic approaches, it seems fair to suggest that the *JTO* texts have often been incorporated as a kind of problem or test case used to highlight a particular pedagogical issue. Perhaps this speaks to the fact that both the survey and upper-level courses often have historical and/or critical orientations, so recovery work is a useful component; perhaps such work fits less well in many nonsurvey courses at the second-year level of the curriculum (many of which may not be focused on the early U.S. period on which we have built our recovery efforts). An excellent example of how courses emphasized questions of recovery lend themselves to this project can be found in Caroline Woidat's essay in this volume (see chapter 9), which details her fascinating course titled Women and Literature: The Politics and Practice of Textual Recovery. Within her essay, Woidat vividly describes how her course moved to both consider several digital recovery projects (including our *JTO* site) and require students to undertake their own nascent recovery efforts. Woidat's essay, and her course, move to underscore how the *JTO* project is but one island in an archipelago of recovery efforts, and her signposting of "the impact of the Society for the Study of Women Writers (SSAWW) for supporting literary recovery with the journal *Legacy* and for building a strong literary community" underscores our own indebtedness to those same networks for foundational inspiration.

One surprising trend that emerged from our analysis of the initial participants was that graduate courses were a relatively small part of our mix, just over 10 percent of our total number of courses so far. This may reflect the smaller number of instructors regularly teaching at the graduate level, or again it may reflect the smaller number of graduate seminars that are focused on this period in such a way as to make these texts central to a conversation. It is possible as well that there is a greater rigidity in the graduate curriculum, or less concern with making a point about recovery work in these courses. While we are aware that we have a small data sample size, the seeming lack of an embrace of questions about recovery at the graduate level concerns us since our own graduate teaching has so often been framed around issues of recovery. Indeed, we have consistently asked our own graduate students to undertake archival-based recovery assignments, using such open-access sites as *Documenting the American South* or *Internet Archive*, as well as paywall protected databases such as Readex and Proquest, to great success. Obviously, there are many ways beyond *JTO* by which graduate seminars might require or encourage students to consider recovery, but this low percentage of graduate level participation is puzzling.

Of the fifty-two different participants, thirty-five (or about two-thirds) teach at public schools; the rest teach at private schools. Of these private schools, they are mostly liberal arts colleges (most of these are Catholic institutions, and two of them are Ivy League schools), and one of them was an overseas school (Scottish). It is difficult to interpret this information, but it may indicate something about institutions in which surveys are open to a wider range of staff and taught with greater flexibility. Another possibility may be that many public schools do not subscribe to databases like Readex because they are so cost-prohibitive, and that the *JTO* project is providing access to materials that would otherwise not be possible for these instructors and students. We suggest this observation in part because at a workshop we ran at the Society of Early Americanists Conference in June 2015, several participants asked us to include pages from the original editions of texts on our webpage so that their students could have access to period-specific material they might not otherwise have. Alongside our edition of Rowson's *Sincerity* we reproduced (thanks to the generosity of the AAS staff) the June 4, 1803, edition of the *Boston Weekly Magazine* in which the first installment of that serialized novel appeared.

Finally, here are some observations about the demographics of the instructors who participated by teaching one of our first five editions. Of the fifty-two instructors, five were graduate students, one an adjunct, three were visiting professors or postdocs, two were full professors, fifteen were associate professors, twenty-six (half) were assistant professors. Of the thirteen instructors who taught multiple times, eight (or 62 percent) were assistant professors. Despite our concerns about the lower number of graduate classes accessing the edition, graduate students and junior faculty lead in the work of teaching these recovered texts in their classrooms: thirty-five junior people (graduate students, adjuncts, visiting faculty, and assistant professors) compared with seventeen more senior faculty, an overall ratio of 2:1. Perhaps this ratio reflects a generational gap in terms of comfort or facility with "digital" texts, or it might suggest something about the ways in which syllabi become ossified over time. It is also possible that this generational issue evinces something about the texts themselves and what kinds of new questions they might bring into relief for a newer generation of scholars. Since the project is focused on early American literature, this pattern may also reflect the relative youth of the field as compared to other subfields within American literary studies. Of the fifty-two people, thirty-two (61 percent) are women and twenty (38 percent) are men. We're not sure of the current breakdown of faculty and graduate students, but the 3:2 ratio is probably greater, with women more active participants in recovery work. Most of the graduate students were women; the two participants from history programs were women; the handful of courses cross-listed with women's studies were taught by women; nine of the thirteen (almost 70 percent) instructors who taught *JTO* texts multiple times were women. We have speculated between ourselves, based on anecdotal evidence but also corroborated by our own recent experiences as external evaluators, that some pre-tenure instructors are using their participation in the project to document that elusive evaluative category known as "teaching effectiveness." Participation in the project allows them to share published, public reflections about their own teaching as well as gesture toward involvement in a larger fieldwide conversation about pedagogy. If (and when) we can more routinely foster ways of publicly networking classes across institutional divides, this secondary function of the project might become even more generative. Happily, some of the texts that we have recovered have begun to find their way into conference presentations, a first step perhaps toward people publishing about them. This last step, the production of article-length scholarship about these texts, may be one important index of the success of the *JTO* project and in this area our grade remains incomplete.

Where do we go from here? As our earlier list of texts has indicated, we are trying to expand the range and scope of our texts, in part to see what works well for instructors, in part to see what meshes with new scholarship, in part to give a different inflection to the formulation of recovery work. Our recent texts have tried to pose different questions about recovery: the periodical issue to explore a different form, reprint culture, intertextuality, reading practices, and the like; *Sincerity* to think about the novel as a serial form but also to pose questions about an important writer who is often associated with a very different single text (Rowson's *Charlotte Temple*); and "Account of a Remarkable Conspiracy" to reflect on Atlanticity, reprint culture, translation, and discourses surrounding slavery. We have mentioned our collaborations with Jared Gardner and Toni Wall Jaudon, both of whom helped with prefatory materials. With our edition of Rowson's *Sincerity*, we prepared a special forum for an issue of *Legacy: A Journal of American Women Writers* featuring essays by five *JTO* instructors and scholars (Lisa West, Karen Weyler, Michelle Sizemore, Jennifer Desiderio, and Theresa Gaul).[6] We hope that this pedagogical and critical collaboration prompts a greater interest in Rowson and continues to move our critical gaze beyond *Charlotte Temple*. Collaborative opportunities will likely continue to shape our selection of materials in ways we cannot foresee.

We also continue to encourage discussion and perhaps even debate about recovery work. While we had hoped the *JTO* site would become a place for exchanges, it has instead become more a place of storage, like a syllabus exchange, in which people might survey others' teaching successes and failures. Perhaps the discussions we envisioned speak to a scholarly, as opposed to pedagogical, interest that has a slower tempo and more private or personal expressions, whereas teaching innovations have typically been viewed more as resources than as challenges to address. The posts have seldom been commented on, even as we know from the American Antiquarian Society's analysis of the site that people are consistently reading them, which may reflect the ways in which literary studies seldom sustains public debates about teaching practices. Rather than being spaces of debate and discussion, the teaching posts have almost exclusively remained siloed artifacts that may be (silently) shaping the work of other instructors but not in any way that we can measure. The promises and possibilities of a digital teaching commons have not yet overcome the ways in which the profession has habituated us to largely think of our own individual classes as enclosures. Participants have suggested that as the project unfolds they would like us to foster conversations between classes and between instructors during the semester, and we have begun to explore ways to address this. These extensions of the project might take the form of an additional blog space that would allow multiple classes to interact with one another around the issue of recovery, or a more private forum for instructors to exchange ideas about how to use a new text in their courses. In the fall 2015 semester, several instructors independently created a private WordPress site that connected undergraduate students from across the country, and the instructors who participated in that linked connection suggested that this is something that we should continue to foster and expand. Across the length of the project, many participants have told us, especially those who have taught a *JTO* text more than once, that their undergraduate students are enthusiastic about the experimental nature of the project. Some of these instructors have stressed that their students are particularly excited by the idea that they are among a larger collective from across the country interacting with a recovered text in the same semester. Our initial vision was to think about the ways in which the project might change course design and scholarly praxis by asking people to experiment and then reflect on their experiences after their courses were over. Increasingly our participants have underscored that perhaps the best way to undertake the work of linking recovery and teaching would be to foreground how the project might bring multiple classes and a wider range of students into conversation with one another virtually while the courses are still in process. Instead of being passive recipients of an anthologized canon, the experimental (and serial) nature of the project offers instructors and students the potential to break down the fourth wall that normatively separates them from editors and publishers. Moreover, the project offers instructors a potential hub of connection to experiment with connecting their students with students at other institutions by a joint adoption of the same experimental text in the same semester. Based on this feedback it seems clear to us that we need to do more to find new ways of creating connections for students across institutional and geographical divides. This issue of student connectivity is central to our thinking as we imagine *JTO* 2.0.

Notes

1. These novels are William Hill Brown's *The Power of Sympathy* (1789); Susanna Rowson's *Charlotte: A Tale of Truth* (aka Charlotte Temple) (1794); Hannah Foster's *The Coquette* (1797); Royall Tyler's *The Algerine Captive* (1797); Charles Brockden Brown's *Wieland* (1798), *Edgar Huntly* (1799), *Ormond* (1799), and *Arthur Mervyn* (1799); and occasionally Hugh Henry Brackenridge's *Modern Chivalry* (1792–1815).

2. In January 2014, Maurice S. Lee posted a request to the C19 listserv asking for instructors to send him syllabi for pre-1865 American literature survey courses. Lee

has compiled the data from all of the 131 sample syllabi he received, and his findings confirm the canonical devotion of these courses; for example, he reports that "white authors constituted 83.4 percent of class time" and that "male authors constituted 75.5 percent of total class time." While Lee's statistical analysis is in some ways based on a small sample size, his findings are revealing in relationship to pedagogy and canonicity. Maurice S. Lee, "Introduction: A Survey of Survey Courses," *J19: The Journal of Nineteenth-Century Americanists* 4, no. 1 (Spring 2016): 125–130.

3. "Speculations: Aesthetics, Risk, and Capital in the Circum-Atlantic World, 1790–1830," Eighth Biennial Conference of the Charles Brockden Brown Society, CUNY Grad Center, New York City, April 19–21, 3012, http://www.brockdenbrownsociety.ucf.edu/albums/CUNY/CBBSCUNYProgram.pdf.

4. Theresa Strouth Gaul, "Recovering Recovery: Early American Women and *Legacy*'s Future," *Legacy* 26, no. 2 (2009): 276.

5. Michelle Burnham uses this phrase to describe both the ethos of the *JTO* project and the kinds of "collaborative forms of teaching and learning" that Davidson advocates in her online Coursera MOOC, "History and Future of (Mostly) Higher Education." Michelle Burnham, "Literary Recovery in an Age of Austerity: A Review of *Early American Reprints* and *Just Teach One*," *Legacy: A Journal of American Women Writers* 32, no. 1 (2015): 128.

6. "Susan Rowson's *Sincerity* and the Just Teach One Project" (forum), *Legacy: A Journal of American Women Writers* 34, no. 1 (Spring 2017): 129–197.

8. The *Just Teach One: Early African American Print* Project

Nicole N. Aljoe, Eric Gardner, and Molly O'Hagan Hardy

THE *JUST TEACH ONE: Early African American Print* project (*JTO: EAAP*) began out of a momentary confluence of events that was part of a nexus of diverse and longstanding concerns about praxis in American and African American literary and cultural studies. This essay explores these concerns as they interface with questions tied to the design, production, content, contexts, and use of digital editions, with emphasis on questions of engagement with digital tools such as TEI (Text Encoding Initiative) and of centering recovery work in our classrooms. We frame this exploration specifically through our experiences and challenges with the first iteration of *JTO: EAAP*.

In 2012, generously supported by the American Antiquarian Society (AAS) and the online journal *Common-place*, Duncan Faherty and Ed White developed a digital early American literature recovery project aimed at "provid[ing] a body of publicly available scholarly pdf transcriptions of early texts, with basic editing and apparatus," with some emphasis on creating "a critical mass of teachers incorporating" the featured early American texts into their classrooms and asking that "these teachers provide reflections on the text, insights and reaction, [and] intertextual possibilities" to "provide guidance for other teachers" (see also chapter 7 in this volume).[1] The success of the project led Eric Gardner, in his contribution to the 2014 Modern Language Association (MLA) convention roundtable on "Early African American Print Culture" focused on "access" and called for an African Americanist *Just Teach One* program. Paul Erickson, AAS's director of academic programs, was at the MLA session and afterward offered to explore the possibility with Gardner. Joycelyn

Moody and John Ernest—also part of the MLA session—shared in valuable early brainstorming. Soon after the conference, Ernest and Moody, along with Nicole N. Aljoe, Lois Brown, and P. Gabrielle Foreman, agreed to join Gardner as the *Just Teach One: Early African American Print* initial organizing group. Project planning and discussion—mainly via email—took place over the first half of 2014, and the project moved toward a "soft launch" of its first text, the 1827 *Freedom's Journal* serialized short story "Theresa; a Haytien Tale," led by Aljoe in fall 2014.

The concerns about praxis that led to these events are more complex, and teasing them all out would take more space than we have. Still, a set of critical issues led to concrete acts in the planning and initial release of *JTO: EAAP*.

First, conveners sensed that *JTO: EAAP* had to be not simply collaborative but a living and ethical collaboration that was both fluid and growing. Certainly a key early step in this process has been acknowledging the landmark work of Faherty and White to, in their words, offer "a practical, long-term and cooperative, if still modest, approach to the problem of textual recovery."[2] But in part out of respect for that work and in part recognizing specific responsibilities in African American studies, we wanted to adapt and revise their original efforts to address questions key to African Americanist inquiry. P. Gabrielle Foreman's question was in our minds: "What are the rights and privileges, the *responsibilities*, of belonging to fields that study the culture and the concerns, the lives and the literary productions, the circulation and consumption of disempowered groups—as someone who belongs to relatively empowered groups, as all of us, in part, today do?"[3] We wanted to address this question both in terms of the recovery of texts that are central to the work of African Americanists studying the nineteenth century but also in terms of technology. In other words, best practices in digital humanities could, we hoped, lead to more accessible and preservable texts, so that the work of wide recovery could be meaningful to us in the present moment and also to future generations of scholars and students of early African American literature.

To date, such thinking has led not only to expanding the initial group of conveners to include other collaborators but also to a sense that one or two people would take the lead on each text, that the roster of participants would change over time, and that some engaged scholars who were not among the initial group might take the lead on preparing future texts. The goal was not simply to create a kind of editorial board but to engage in the possibility that diverse voices might want to convene conversations in dialogue with original project planners. This kind of loose collective, initially convened as a specific group but open to change, seems one way to begin to address what Foreman notes as "the depth of experience and intellectual and demographic breadth necessary to responsibly engage the questions . . . put on the table."[4]

In this vein, it was important from the beginning to think about how *JTO: EAAP* might reach out to other projects, digital and otherwise—including the *Early Caribbean Digital Archive*, for which Aljoe is codirector.[5] Future texts will likely also engage with efforts such as *Colored Conventions*, which archives the proceedings of African American conventions "from 1830 until well after the Civil War."[6] In early conversations, Lois Brown especially argued that we should also think about ways *JTO: EAAP* could encourage more hands-on archival work such as the collection and transcription of historical texts and that our outreach needed to build bridges both to well-known repositories such as the AAS and also to lesser-known collections ranging from smaller HBCU (historically black colleges and universities) repositories to church collections, to aid not only in text sharing but also in text identification, preservation, and engagement with various technologies. (*The Colored Conventions* "Transcribe Minutes" program, which worked with African Methodist Episcopal Church members to help prepare digitized black convention minutes for online display, embodies some of these ideas.) These are among the questions on which we hope to focus as the project matures.

For many of us, *JTO: EAAP* had to be about access, responsible use, and the technologies that enable this ethos. We'd all read Frances Smith Foster's guidance on recovering and studying women's literature: "First, I had to learn what women had actually written, what those women had written about and why, and what were the best methods by which we could best evaluate their writings," all the while addressing "the problem of how to make available to others the writing and the writers that I found inspirational, instructive, and absolutely necessary to understanding literature, history, and myself."[7] Some of us had come to recognize that *recovery* is a continuous, on-going project—in Foster's words, "a lifetime project." We understood that we are recovering pieces of American literature and history that have been stolen, dismissed, and abused by a culture that couldn't and wouldn't admit to deep African American engagement with texts. Our methodologies thus also had to start from the same spirit of dissemination, circulation, fluidity, and flexibility that Foster advocates.

In this, some of the conveners found themselves identifying with parts of Faherty and White's rationale for the initial *JTO* project:

> Digital versions of texts are available in ways they never before have been, yet access is uneven and subject to vulnerable library budgets. . . . Meanwhile, print editions face formidable challenges—publishers shy away from unknown texts; works with modest sales fall out of print; books become more and more expensive; and many institutions do not reward the labor of recovery, be that through graduate projects or scholarly editions, as they once did.[8]

We knew that some of these problems were even more pronounced with African American texts. Because *digital* is not synonymous with *accessible*, African American studies still suffers in specific ways from the lack of dissemination of lesser-known texts. Specifically, many students of pre-twentieth-century American and African American literature have been far too quick, after decades of neglecting pre-Harlem black literature all together, to lock that field into a specific genre (the slave narrative) and/or a small handful of specific figures (especially Frederick Douglass). Additionally, African American writers of the eighteenth and nineteenth centuries did not always have access to the mediums we most closely associate (however erroneously) with literary production. Early African American literature, we now know, did not always come in a codex between two boards but instead lived in the columns of newspapers such as *Freedom's Journal*, the *Weekly Anglo-African*, and the *Christian Recorder*. It appeared in the handwritten letters exchanged among friends and the texts circulated in a host of other modes, from Lucy Terry's commemorative 1746 poem "Bars Fight," which circulated orally until it was finally written down in 1855, to Belinda Royall's 1783 petition to the Commonwealth of Massachusetts requesting a pension, to "Makandal, a true story" that appeared in the French journal *Le Mercure de France* in 1787.[9] These unexpected places in the archive where we might "find" African American literature add another layer to the challenges we face remediating these works in digital environments.

The past few decades have seen a growing number of scholars—some working individually and some collaboratively—challenge such easy dismissals by exploring numerous early black serials, considering questions of black engagement with print (from composition to reception), excavating the remnants of various networks that included black writers, and placing such work in dialogue with a rich range of questions in literary studies. Still, projects like the "North American Slave Narratives" portion of *Documenting the American South*—a beacon of accessibility, thick contexting, and challenges to easy assumptions about genre, geography, and circulation—remain far too rare.[10] Even more rare are innovative print projects like West Virginia University Press's Regenerations series edited by Ernest and Moody, "devoted to reprinting editions of important African American texts that either have fallen out of print or have failed to receive the attention they deserve," and emphasizing affordable books for classroom use.[11] Most importantly, anthologies, syllabi, classrooms, and graduate training have not kept up. Scholars have recognized that one of today's central challenges is to create points of access to rediscoveries that appropriately frame and present these critical pieces of African American (and so American) literature and culture and that allow individuals to work in responsible, well-informed, dialogic ways to benefit teaching, learning, and scholarship. We wanted to create a site that would help address such challenges.

We thus, for example, set our definition of *early* capaciously—intending to treat texts published up to the end of Reconstruction in part to combat the sense that African American literature began with Jim Crow (or even after) and so to argue for a more diverse and inclusive approach to pre-twentieth-century American culture. We emphasize texts found outside of bound books, with heavy initial focus on black serials, as these are the texts often left out of critical and historical narratives of black literature.

In all of this, we were drawn to the original *JTO*'s model of sharing short texts or collection of texts (usually fewer than thirty pages) that could be taught in one course meeting. Some of the conveners sympathized with Faherty and White's rationale for this decision, which is worth quoting at length:

> In an effort to reduce the "risks" of adding new material to a pre-existing course, we have prepared editions of short texts, which can be taught in a single class session. In other words, this project initially aims to increase our objects of study while minimizing the labor involved in reconfiguring our syllabi. Our selection of texts is in part motivated by how these recovered artifacts might intersect or complicate our operant sense of familiar objects of study, thus expanding our praxis by thinking about new textual constellations. By providing a platform to foster an ongoing pedagogical conversation about these new materials, we hope the project can serve as a practical laboratory for canonical and archival expansion.[12]

That said, we hope to foreground some of these "risks," and some of the conveners are deeply aware of the ways in which African American literature and culture has sometimes been written about and taught by scholars who have not taken the time and energy to fully educate themselves about the contexts of such texts or about the rich field of African American studies. Kimberly Blockett's account of a graduate student who "successfully misrepresented herself as a job candidate trained to teach in the field" with "a token dissertation chapter on Harriet Jacobs as her calling card" but didn't even know the term *Middle Passage* rings frighteningly true to some of the conveners.[13]

Thus, even as *JTO: EAAP* asks participants "to take the next step in rethinking the American literary and cultural landscape by agreeing to 'just teach one' lesser-known early African American text," we want to think hard about the ways that the teaching of individual texts can serve as a gateway to a fuller understanding of a massive scholarly field and can be done responsibly.[14] In part to address such hopes, in addition to providing an easily accessible, high-quality digital (PDF) copy of the text and spaces for instructors to post about their work with the text, we hope to provide rich contextual information and expanded apparatus to aid individuals in meeting the challenge of incorporating new curricular materials and to recognize that just teaching one text should ultimately lead to much deeper study. We anticipate exploring diverse models for responsible engagement with the project—including the *Colored Conventions* project's Memo of Understanding (MOU) approach, wherein project participants sign an agreement that stipulates the exact nature and process of participation.[15] At the heart of this work will be an expanded set of possibilities for participants to share material tied to their teaching, learning, and scholarship to provide the foundation for a dynamic community of dialogue surrounding the shared texts. The pedagogical focus of *JTO*, with its emphasis on sharing new materials, offers a perfect avenue for bringing an understanding and appreciation of early black America to a wider community. The rest of this essay explores how the project's initial foray addresses these and other questions.

Critical Making in Special Collections Libraries

After the MLA session and initial conversations, AAS's Paul Erickson approached the recently appointed digital humanities curator Molly O'Hagan Hardy about liaising between the project conveners and *JTO/Common-place*, in addition to consulting on the technical components. Initially funded by ACLS (American Council of Learned Societies), the position of digital humanities curator was intended to provide AAS with an opportunity to think through and facilitate the relationships between emerging technologies and the humanities. Having used guidelines from the Textual Encoding Initiative for the creation of a digital edition of Absalom Jones and Richard Allen's *A Narrative of the Proceedings of the Late Awful Calamity in Philadelphia* (1794), Hardy thought the TEI standards could be usefully employed for the *JTO: EAAP* texts and provide a new model of digital textual editing for the AAS. The very nature of the work of archival recovery by *JTO: EAAP* seemed like an ideal time to introduce new digital practices to the institution.

For over two hundred years, the AAS has dedicated itself "to collecting, preserving, and making widely accessible the early historical record of our nation," and the digital age has demanded that it imagine the work of fulfilling its mission in new ways.[16] President Ellen S. Dunlap recently articulated the challenges faced by AAS:

> If the Society does not continue to move aggressively toward the replication and sharing of its collection in the form of digital surrogates, we run the risk of a form of cultural obsolescence when the advantage of having the largest collection of originals in one physical place is trumped by having once-disparate collections aggregated together virtually.[17]

What forms such "replication and sharing" will take remain constant questions at the AAS, and special collections libraries are not alone in asking such questions. New modes of preservation have arisen in the digital age, and librarians, writes Marilyn Deegan, "charged to acquire, deliver, and preserve this most important of scholarly tools are facing new challenges." Deegan argues that contrary to G. Thomas Tanselle's assertion that "the format in which books are delivered is irrelevant," electronic textual editing "involve[s] a complete rethink of the economics of producing and handling these works" for "publishers producing or libraries collecting and preserving electronic editions."[18] Such modes might be part of the "social domain," where, according to Matthew Kirschenbaum, "actions and agency can serve to trump purely technical considerations."[19] These new modes of preservation might be found on the back end of electronic editions in the ways in which they are marked up to best ensure their longevity. Technological considerations reign supreme because data stored in formats and software that become obsolete might well be lost. Due to her own training at several TEI seminars as well as her own use of the tool for a digital humanities project that emerged from her dissertation, Hardy saw *JTO: EAAP* as an opportunity to try a new mode of preservation and dissemination for the AAS.

TEI is an application of the Extensible Markup Language (XML)—a metalanguage, a language used to describe other languages like syntax describing a sentence. If XML is providing the syntax, then TEI is the specific language or vocabulary that we are using.[20] TEI is intended to facilitate a more dynamic interaction with the text and is "designed to make its underlying markup (rather than markup that results from a rendering process) available to the reader for examination."[21] Since 1994, the TEI Guidelines have been widely used by libraries, museums, publishers, and individual scholars to present texts for online research, teaching, and preservation. TEI allows for the deep encoding and annotation associated with scholarly editions. TEI encoding offers the possibility of more flexible interactions with the text than PDF formats, as well as more complex search functions. In addition to highlighting and collecting of words, TEI markup can look at structural and grammatical features within and across several texts simultaneously: for example, tracking the number and placement of specific words, names, figures, and passages in a series of texts. TEI markup also allows encoders to highlight specific properties of a text, such as the employment of literary techniques like chiasmus or phrasings endemic to literary movements like those of sentiment or liberation theology. It provides not only contextual information for the many references and allusions, but also bibliographic elements, such as bindings, *mise-en-page*, collation, and other physical characteristics of a text. Such rigorous and complex searching allows us to see these texts in compelling new ways.

Finally, as an open, nonproprietary file format, TEI is intended to be widely accessible. Indeed, in its "Guidelines for Editors of Scholarly Editions," the Modern Language Association stipulates that electronic files should be "encoded in an open, nonproprietary format (e.g., TEI XML rather than Microsoft Word or WordPerfect)" because community-oriented open formats are the best way to preserve and share not only text itself but also the editor's scholarly work (and in Kirschenbaum's formulation, the two are not mutually exclusive).[22] By providing the text in an extensible markup language, we offered it in a format that is operable as data, rather than as a PDF that is static.

In her edition of the anonymously published "Theresa" in *African American Review* (2006), where the story appeared for the first time in print since its initial publication in *Freedom's Journal* in 1827, Foster characterizes the work of recovery as one marked by change, by new knowledge, and by new information. In reflecting on her own work, she urges models of scholarship that embrace flexibility and openness by "making [the story's] existence known in a way that seems likely to enlarge our African American literary data set while also inviting and encouraging more scholarship."[23] The selection of the text for *JTO: EAAP* was a response to Foster's call, and as is chronicled in the next section of this essay, the project has engendered "more scholarship" on this fictionalized account of a family of free women of color during the Haitian Revolution between 1791 and 1803. Encoding the text in TEI also meant that we were adding to the "African American literary data set" in a way that could make AAS proud.

This work to which we had all dedicated ourselves required new institutional alignments as well. Although a couple of organizations had page images of *Freedom's Journal* available online, neither was easily accessible. Initially, we had hoped to present the story in its original context of this newspaper. Images of the journal had been copied, uploaded, and made freely available by the Wisconsin Historical Society (WHS). However, because the copies were made using earlier optical character recognition (OCR) software, by 2014 the images had become so degraded that they were unreadable, forcing the WHS to take the copies down. Although other online databases, such as Accessible Archives, also had digital copies of the journal, they were frequently behind a paywall. Late in the process, we became aware that a freely available digital edition of the newspaper could be found on the Internet Archive. In the absence of designated funds to recopy the microfilm images, we decided to provide a link to what appears to be a digitized microfilm of the newspaper.[24] Given pressures of time and resources, we transcribed the document ourselves to create the XML needed for the TEI markup to occur. Our desire for page images paired with transcription led to an innovative collaboration: *JTO: EAAP* worked with EBSCO to prepare our second text, "The Afric-American Picture Gallery," originally from the *Anglo African Magazine*; EBSCO provided us with high-resolution page images and XML files to mark up with TEI.

As noted earlier, nonprofit libraries like the AAS are seldom able to do the time-consuming work that TEI requires. Though TEI is a more flexible format and makes searching easier and more nuanced, the initial encoding poses challenges because it requires a schema of markup guidelines that comes at the start of an XML file. The practices are necessarily distinct for each text. Aljoe and her colleagues at Northeastern generously offered to do the markup according to the standards recently established for the *Early Caribbean Digital Archive (ECDA)*, as they too would make use of the text in their own collection. The result was an expertly encoded XML file created by Northeastern English graduate student Sarah Stanley that is now at the *JTO: EAAP* site. Because *ECDA* did the encoding of "Theresa," *JTO: EAAP* used their style sheet and schema that calls for extensive annotations for the people, places, and nationalities in the text. The *ECDA* schema also includes interpretive markup, so that references to food or drink, to flora, to fauna, and to materials, persons, and events specifically related to military action are all encoded. However, because a distinct *JTO: EAAP* style sheet was not initially created, many of the elements tagged are not necessarily relevant to *JTO: EAAP*. A goal for the years ahead is to continue to develop a style sheet and schema specific to *JTO: EAAP*.

This process of encoding also revealed one of the challenges of TEI. Successful encoding is reliant on the development of distinct style sheets or schemas, and, unfortunately, the people with the coding expertise are often not necessarily the same folks with content knowledge required for building such style sheets and schemas. Indeed, Stanley, who did the encoding of "Theresa," though a brilliant Medievalist, is not a specialist in Caribbean literature. Deciding which features to encode is an interpretive decision that draws on literary-critical analysis. And we can't help but wonder, if the graduate student had had an expertise in early African American literature, whether the encoding would have been different. *JTO: EAAP* published its second text during spring 2016, "Afric-American Picture Gallery" edited by Leif Eckstrom and Britt Rusert, using TEI Simple. The encoding of that text was guided by Elizabeth Hopwood, also a Northeastern University graduate student, but one who specializes in Early Caribbean and Transatlantic literatures (and a contributor to this volume). AAS has since developed a schema for early African American literature that can be used for *JTO: EAAP* and adopted for encoding other early American texts. A recent installment of *JTO: EAAP*, Frances Ellen Watkins (Harper)'s *Forest Leaves* (ca. 1846), is the first text to be encoded with this new schema.[25]

In all, in addition to the PDF edition of the text and the instructor reflections on teaching the text that provided the basis for the original *JTO*, the new site includes the TEI-encoded version of the text, contextual information and links, connections to items in AAS's current holdings, and a list of possible topics and lines of inquiry based on prior experiences some of the conveners had teaching "Theresa" in other classes. *JTO: EAAP* has provided a model for future editorial projects at AAS that will also include more robust contextual information.

"Theresa" in the Action

In moving from the conceptual to the development stage, our overarching goals have been to build on the success of the original *JTO* and to enhance engagements with early African American print culture by facilitating more scholarly interaction and pedagogical support. In what follows, Aljoe discusses our steps in bringing the project online, as well as how she specifically worked with the project's initial text of "Theresa" in her own class; she concludes by elaborating on some of challenges we encountered.

Because we started planning the project relatively late over summer 2014, we decided to begin with a soft launch. In addition to focusing on one text for the entire year rather than, as the original *JTO* did, highlighting a different text each semester, we also had two of the initial conveners, Aljoe and Gardner (the latter aided significantly by Alex Black), act as "project managers" for each semester, dividing up the work and ensuring an equitable distribution of labor. During the late summer and fall, we collected links, contextual information, instructor reflections, and other materials. After reading through and organizing the materials, these items were uploaded to the site in January and February of 2015. Uploading a small set of the materials "early" offered spring 2015 adopters several models for consideration both at the undergraduate and graduate levels. Reflections and assignments from the spring 2015 semester were uploaded in May and June. The result was a crowdsourced, deep yet broad collection of reflections and resources intended to facilitate scholarly and pedagogical engagement with a rare text.

This contextual aspect of the site has been very successful. As in the original *JTO*, it has been gratifying to see such large numbers of instructors at a wide range of institutions volunteer to work with the text in their classes. Reading about what instructors have done with the text and seeing other possibilities for engagement and assignments have been intellectually exciting. During the fall semester "Theresa" was taught in four very different environments: a graduate course in feminist studies, an introduction to literary studies course, a comparative literature course, and a charter high school.[26] This wonderfully connected to several of our ideas about the value of teaching and working with these texts. The text was taught in a variety of ways, not just as ethnographic or historical illustrations that "uncritically reflect" the experiences of African Americans, but as a dynamic text engaged with a range of discourses, including the aesthetics of nineteenth-century literary sentimentalism and the politics of gendered revolutionary action. The reflections highlighted the instructors' enthusiasm for these texts and offered specific steps for engaging with this and similar texts in the classroom.

We quote Aljoe's on-site reflection in full as an example of how *JTO: EAAP* might be used in the classroom (see Aljoe's syllabus in Appendix 8.1):

> I taught "Theresa" during the Fall semester of 2014 in my Introduction to Literary Studies course. It was a class of 11 students, and the course was intended to provide, as the title suggests, an introduction to some of the components, practices, techniques, strategies, and goals of literary studies. I'd taught the course or one very like it, mostly successfully many times over my career. We turned to "Theresa" during the middle of the semester, after the students had read *Gulliver's Travels* and had been introduced to several different schools of literary theory such as feminism, Marxism, Post-Structuralism, and New Criticism among others. I titled the unit "Literary History and the Archive" and my goal was to introduce students to debates about literary history and its relationship to our notions about the archive. In addition to reading "Theresa" and Foster's essay about the story, the students also read three additional essays by scholars offering varying perspectives on early African American literary history, print culture, and notions of the archive: Leon Jackson's "The Talking Book and the Talking Book Historian"; Lois Brown's "Death-Defying Testimony: Women's Private Lives and the Politics of Public Documents"; and Saidiya Hartman's "Venus in Two Acts."
>
> We spent two class periods, the first focused on the story and Foster's essay, the second exploring the ramifications of the arguments by Brown, Jackson, and Hartman on our readings of the text. In initial reading responses students, as usual, expressed chagrin at their relative lack of exposure to African American literature. What was surprising was the number of students who focused on, for lack of a better word, the "Haitian-ness" of the narrative and how it exposed them to a more diverse representation of nineteenth-century Black culture. As one student noted, "I was also pretty disappointed in realizing that in every discussion of African American literature I'd ever participated in, whether it be at home or in a classroom setting, I'd only really ever been given examples of African American literature. I'd never even really considered the highly nuanced versions of literature that would've been produced by any of the several other populations of African descent scattered around the globe" (Yancey-Bragg). And another asked, "What kind of literature did the world miss out on?" (Von Benschoten).
>
> Our initial conversation was wide ranging, moving from "noticing" the details of the story (building on our early semester introduction to Peter Rabinowitz's *Before Reading*), such as its vivid, often anthropomorphized descriptions of the landscape, to considering the language of sentiment and its representations of

republican femininity. We also talked about the various lenses/theories through which we could read the story and engaged in a fun and interactive group exercise where the groups chose a particular theory and offered readings from that school/perspective. Although our discussions on the first day were wide-ranging, we did touch on some of the focused aspects of literary history, notions of the canon, and archives when we considered questions such as "how does this text help us reconsider African American literature? American literature, more generally? Black Atlantic literature?" On the second day, we focused our discussion much more closely on these questions. Because students tend to have difficulty "applying" or culling useful insights from essays not specifically written about the chosen primary text, I took the focused points they had made in their reading posts about the secondary essays and used them to craft the questions that formed the catalysts for the day's class discussion. For example, drawing on the students' notation of Hartman's analysis of critical romanticism, I asked them, "What elements might a non-romantic recuperative reading of the story focus on?," which elicited responses that focused on the nuanced characterization of Madame Pauline and her daughters as simultaneously passive and assertive, as well as the ways in which the writer explicitly embraces multiple rather than singular perspectives throughout the text.

Our discussions focused on literary history and the canon and the archive as a series of processes rather than an inert and stable object. The students were able to shift their thinking about the archive and the canon towards a more dynamic and "realistic" understanding of the archive/canon. This also led to an engaging discussion about print culture and how texts become part of the canon/literary archive. As another student noted, "I've never thought about the process and research needed in order to solve the mystery of historical text before they even reach the reader. I often forget that what I'm holding in my hand is a finished product, and as I read I don't think about the steps taken between an author completing the book and it landing on my desk" (Wilhelm). This discussion also brought us back to Rabinowitz's argument about the inherently political nature of most literary texts.

The students then used the class discussions and readings as the basis for an essay assignment that explored one of the four main questions/issues that we had dealt with in class: how the story alters our notions of literary history; how it relates to Black Atlantic culture; the details, strategies, and techniques employed by the writer; and the literariness of the text. Part of my thinking in highlighting these particular questions, in addition to helping the students focus their writing on making synthetic analyses as opposed to summarizing, was also intended to accommodate the different levels of comfort expressed by some of the students with the more speculative aspects of our discussion about the canon.

The story worked incredibly well in this environment. Because the students were new to college and the major, they were not so jaded about literary studies and were willing to consider the text on its own terms. Unfortunately, my past experience working with more advanced classes with this text found that they are often more suspicious of the fact that the text is unsigned and doesn't come pre-associated (at least to them) with some recognizable framework. Indeed, hearing that scholars are currently engaged in debates about this and other texts made the intro students comprehend the inherent dynamism of literary studies and held out the possibility that they could contribute to that discussion themselves. All in all, it was an incredibly rewarding experience working with this text with this level class. Generally speaking, the students agreed that, "Overall I was really intrigued by 'Theresa' and the discussion it can inspire" (Hollingshead).[27]

The range of levels of students who worked with the text is also remarkable and further reflects the complexity of these "ephemeral" texts that lend themselves well to rigorous analysis. All in all, these aspects of the site were and continue to be incredibly successful and in keeping with our professed goals. However, although this project had great support, it also had its challenges, most specifically in terms of providing access to facsimiles of the issues of *Freedom's Journal* in which the story appeared, facilitating user interaction, and moving from PDF to TEI format. And there is still much potential for further growth. For example, although the students in Aljoe's class used the TEI-encoded text, none of the student engagements or assignments with the text was reliant on TEI encoding. The brevity of the *JTO* format—in which instructors are invited to spend one or two class periods engaging with the chosen text—prohibited time-intensive activities. However, if more time is allocated, students can actually work with and employ TEI themselves.[28]

The development of the interactive or commons component of the site was a surprising challenge. As is ever the case, although digital technology offers the promise of ease and accessibility, in practice there always seem to be more complications. For example, the *JTO* project has always included a comments section for each text. Despite its presence over several texts, no one has ever taken advantage of it. In our initial discussions as conveners, we emphasized the importance of the democratic ideals of dialogue and conversation; however, in practice we encountered silence on the site. Maybe the commons format wasn't suited to discussion of early American pedagogy? But then how could one explain that these types of conversations did seem to happen on listservs such as those hosted by C19: The Society of Nineteenth-Century Americanists, the Society of Early Americanists, and other early American studies email listservs? Maybe the more explicit question-and-answer format of the listserv was more amenable to dialogic engagement, and, in the future, if interaction is truly a desired outcome, it needs to be facilitated through the development of a more explicitly dialectical format. Another suggestion to facilitate more conversation among the reflective pieces—which are collected after the courses are completed—might be to focus or create a discussion forum during the initial planning of the courses.

Aljoe's sense is that such conversation and collaboration can also be enhanced in future projects by productively engaging with the communitarian ethos manifested by the *Colored Conventions* project's Memo of Understanding (MOU) process. Given a project of this size with many components and collaborators at different schools with differing levels of technological capabilities and support, issues of commitment and management of work flow may be alleviated by MOUs, which clearly articulate agreements and process. Future implementation of MOUs might also offer a way to facilitate greater dialogic interaction among participants. The development of MOUs for projects such as this can reach out to local and lay communities, as well as to help create democratic citizen archivists committed to "recognizing not a deafening institutional, cultural, or political silence but rather a riotous, symphonic, insistent national, international, pan-African noise."[29] Conversations about these questions will be crucial to the next iterations of the *JTO: EAAP* project.

Although one of the goals of this essay was to provide an overview of one particular experience, it is important not to forget that the catalyst for this project was a "momentary confluence." And while we have provided one possible model, other texts may necessarily require more dynamic and different working models. As such, the primary lesson we hope to impart is of the necessity and vitality of substantive and thoughtfully engaged scholarly collaborations.

The appendix for this chapter, a syllabus by Nicole N. Aljoe for a course introducing students to strategies and skills for reading, researching, interpreting, and theorizing about texts, can be found at www.press.uillinois.edu/books/TeachingWithDH.

Notes

1. Duncan Faherty and Ed White, "Welcome to *Just Teach One*," *Just Teach One, Common-place: The Journal of Early American Life*, American Antiquarian Society, accessed March 26, 2017, http://www.common-place.org/justteachone/.

2. Ibid.

3. P. Gabrielle Foreman, "A Riff, a Call, and a Response: Reframing the Problem That Led to Us Being Tokens in Ethnic and Gender Studies; or Where Are We Going Anyway and with Whom Will We Travel?," *Legacy: A Journal of American Women Writers* 30, no. 2 (2013): 316.

4. Ibid., 312.

5. Elizabeth Maddock Dillon and Nicole N. Aljoe, *The Early Caribbean Digital Archive*, Northeastern University, accessed March 26, 2017, http://omekasites.neu.edu/ECDA/.

6. "About the Colored Conventions," *Colored Conventions: Bringing Nineteenth-Century Black Organizing to Digital Life*, P. Gabrielle Foreman, dir., University of Delaware, accessed on March 26, 2017, http://coloredconventions.org/.

7. Frances Smith Foster, "The Personal Is Political, the Past Has Potential, and Other Thoughts on Studying Women's Literature—Then and Now," *Tulsa Studies in Women's Literature* 26, no. 1 (2007): 29.

8. Faherty and White, "Welcome."

9. For more on the relationship between African American literary production and the book, see Frances Smith Foster and Chantal Haywood, "Christian Recordings: Afro-Protestantism, Its Press, and the Production of African American Literature," *Religion & Literature* 27, no. 1 (Spring 1995): 15–33; Frances Smith Foster, "A Narrative of the Interesting Origins and (Somewhat) Surprising Developments of African American Print Culture," *American Literary History* 17, no. 4 (Winter 2005): 714–40; Joanna Brooks, "Our Phillis, Ourselves," *American Literature* 28, no. 1 (2010): 1–28; and Joseph Rezek, "The Print Atlantic: Phillis Wheatley, Ignatius Sancho, and the Cultural Significance of the Book," in *Early African American Print Culture*, ed. Lara Langer Cohen and Jordan Alexander Stein (Philadelphia: University of Pennsylvania Press, 2012).

10. "North American Slave Narratives," *Documenting the American South*, University of North Carolina at Chapel Hill, accessed March 26, 2017, http://docsouth.unc.edu/neh/.

11. John Ernest and Joycelyn K. Moody, eds., Regenerations: African American Literature and Culture (book series, West Virginia University Press), accessed March 26, 2017, http://wvupressonline.com/series/regenerations.

12. Faherty and White, "Welcome."

13. Kimberly Blockett, "Do You Have Any Skin in the Game?," *Legacy: A Journal of American Women Writers* 31, no. 1 (2014): 64.

14. Nicole N. Aljoeᵒ et al., "Just Teach One: Early African American Print," *Just Teach One: Early African American Print, Common-place: The Journal of Early American Life*, American Antiquarian Society, accessed March 26, 2017, http://jtoaa.common-place.org.

15. "Teaching," *Colored Conventions*, http://coloredconventions.org/teaching.

16. The AAS's mission is articulated in several places. We are quoting here from Ellen S. Dunlap, "Report of the Council," *Proceedings of the American Antiquarian Society* 113, no. 2 (October 2003): 11.

17. Ellen S. Dunlap qtd. in Philip Gura, *The American Antiquarian Society, 1812–2012: A Bicentennial History* (Worcester, Mass.: American Antiquarian Society, 2012), 315.

18. Marilyn Deegan, "Electronic Textual Editing: Collection and Preservation of an Electronic Edition," in *Electronic Textual Editing*, ed. Lou Burnard, John Unsworth, and Katherine O'Brien O'Keefe (New York: Modern Language Association of America, 2006), http://www.tei-c.org/About/Archive_new/ETE/Preview/mcgovern.xml.

19. Matthew Kirschenbaum, *Mechanisms: New Media and the Forensic Imagination* (Cambridge, Mass.: MIT Press, 2008), 218. Thanks to James J. Brown for reminding us of this important point.

20. This description borrows from Julia Flanders and Syd Bauman's explanation offered in their invaluable NEH-funded seminars on Scholarly Textual Encoding through the Women Writers Project. "What Is the TEI," *Women Writers Project*, accessed March 26, 2017, http://www.wwp.northeastern.edu/outreach/seminars/tei.html.

21. "Guidelines for Editors of Scholarly Editions," *Modern Language Association*, accessed March 26, 2017, https://www.mla.org/Resources/Research/Surveys-Reports -and-Other-Documents/Publishing-and-Scholarship/Reports-from-the-MLA -Committee-on-Scholarly-Editions/Guidelines-for-Editors-of-Scholarly-Editions.

22. Ibid.

23. Frances Smith Foster, "How Do You Solve a Problem like Theresa?" *African American Review* 40, no. 4 (2006): 633.

24. *Freedom's Journal*, vol. 1 (1827–29), available from Internet Archive, https://archive .org/details/FreedomsJournalVol.1.

25. This schema is available on the AAS's GitHub repository: https://github.com /AmerAntiquarian/Just-Teach-One-Early-African-American-Print.

26. For specific details of the assignments, please see Nicole N. Aljoe, "Theresa Lesson Plan," *Just Teach One: Early African American Print*, http://jtoaa.common-place .org/2015/04/.

27. Nicole N. Aljoe, "Theresa Reflection," *Just Teach One: Early African American Print*, http://jtoaa.common-place.org/2015/04/.

28. In an upper-level class, students were given a brief introduction to the TEI and then encoded excerpts from the text. The assignment, created by Northeastern University graduate student Elizabeth Hopwood, offered students a new way to engage in close reading, which she discusses in her contribution to this volume (see chapter 1).

29. Lois Brown, "Death-Defying Testimony: Women's Private Lives and the Politics of Public Documents," *Legacy: A Journal of American Women Writers* 27, no. 1 (2010): 133.

9. Teaching the Politics and Practice of Textual Recovery with DIY Critical Editions

Caroline M. Woidat

TEACHING NINETEENTH-CENTURY literature by women authors who have been marginalized presents the challenge of asking undergraduate students to rethink assumptions embedded in the grand narratives that have informed American literary studies. In the twenty-first century, students of American literature may not even be familiar with F. O. Matthiessen's conception of the "American Renaissance" and its writers, but they likely have a general sense of this story: once upon a time, the American literary canon consisted of white male authors until the development of theoretical approaches to gender, race, and power added a wider range of voices to the literary curriculum and generated academic departments such as African American studies, women's studies, and Native American studies on college campuses. This oversimplified story of the canon's expansion in some ways mirrors popular cultural narratives of American history: the foundation belongs to the white fathers, and the activism of dissenters on the margins gradually achieves a more inclusive, representative literary canon and political democracy. Such a narrative falls short of interrogating the foundations of American history and literature, however, and the ways that white male "founders" were not creating the nation or its literature on their own, but rather *within* an expansive network. Textual recovery does more than add or restore marginalized texts to the field of literary studies: it can illuminate our understanding of the contexts in which texts were produced, of the scholarly work editors perform and its impact, of literary genre and techniques, and of issues surrounding the evolution of print and digital cultures. The digital era invites us to rethink the past in relation to our current understanding of *networks, connectivity,* and the *web*; indeed, nineteenth-century literary production has much in common with the information age.

This essay focuses upon the use of digital archives as a tool for transforming the ways that students think about literary texts, American history, and their own role as scholars. I specifically discuss experiences teaching an upper-level undergraduate literature course devoted entirely to the study and practice of recovery of American women writers and envisioning a course design that itself emerges from a network of pedagogical collaboration using digital resources. The course, titled Women and Literature: The Politics and Practice of Textual Recovery, is one of many pedagogical experiments that are decentering the classroom and rethinking literary studies in the digital age. The following description from the syllabus offers an overview of the coursework:

> This course foregrounds the process, politics, and critical issues involved in the recovery of marginalized or forgotten texts by American women writers and by anonymous authors writing about women in America. In its examination of fundamental questions about why we read, what we read, and how we read, the course focuses in particular upon what is at stake in the project of recovery. We will study eighteenth- and nineteenth-century texts that have been recovered from various states of neglect—from once popular but later forgotten print texts to newly discovered unpublished manuscripts—with attention to the scholarly work and larger debates surrounding their recovery. Students will engage with a range of literary criticism—from the critical reception of texts in their era to later evaluations and reevaluations of their merit, from theoretical arguments for recovery to further questioning of what it means to move beyond recovery. The course texts will include modern editions of marginalized texts, and we will examine the construction of those texts—not only the editing and scholarship involved, but also the practical concerns of marketing and publishing. We will explore the role of digital technology in textual recovery by considering sites such as *Just Teach One* and *Just Teach One: Early African American Print*, twin projects that raise questions about the teaching of recovered texts and offer an opportunity for our class to join the conversation. Each student will take a hands-on approach to recovery with assignments involving archival exploration and the work of researching, editing, contextualizing, and analyzing texts.

With weekly assignments asking students to approach texts as part of a larger literary network—for example, to examine the full issue of a periodical in which a text was first published—daily class conversations focused upon both common course texts and the various topics that individual students discovered in their archival explorations (see Appendix 9.1). As they worked toward the goal of constructing their own "editions" of recovered texts for the course's final project, students assumed responsibilities and cultivated skills enabling them to tell their own stories about nineteenth-century women writers and the reasons that their texts matter.

This approach immerses students in ongoing conversations about why we read, what we read, and how we read, challenging them to get their hands dirty digging into these issues in the process of *making* a critical edition of their own. Here I allude to the fundamental questions David H. Richter uses to frame his introductory essays in *Falling into Theory: Conflicting Views on Reading Literature* (1994), an overview of the contextual debates in which the creation and study of literary texts have always been entangled. Students tend to possess little, if any, knowledge of the politics and practice of textual recovery, let alone the ways that this work is essential to but also bigger than the project of canon revision. My course aims to give students a keener awareness of context in their reading of texts—not merely as literary scholars, but also as citizens of a digital age who have much at stake in rethinking *recovery*. With wireless networks at the tap of their fingertips and data storage in the "cloud," students are discouraged by the very language of digital technology from thinking deeply about the infrastructure supporting the texts in their hands. The expeditionary process of literary recovery, however, invites students to engage in sustained reflection about a text's dependence upon larger material and social infrastructures, from the print culture of the nineteenth-century to today's digital archives. After examining a digital copy of an antebellum conduct manual for girls, for example, one student not only connected examples of gender policing then and now, but also the ghostly image of the book scanner's hand to the shadowy presence of slave labor. Archival research, whether in brick-and-mortar or digital archives, enables students to approach a literary work not merely as a disembodied *text*, but also as a cultural artifact produced and preserved in a social context. With this emphasis, the course aims to recover certain roles that literary editors, critics, and communities perform—the vital work that is often effaced or demeaned as "secondary" and peripheral—along with "primary" texts by women authors.

The content of the textual recovery course I taught in fall 2015 included both print and digital modern editions, as well as called upon students to navigate digital archives of American literature, including full issues of popular periodicals, and thus acquainted them with the "web" in which literary publications were entangled long before the invention of the internet. When assigned "archival explorations," students engaged in browsing (or "surfing") early American periodicals and were challenged by the quantity and variety of writing and images in just one issue of *Godey's* or *Graham's Magazine*. The contrast between negotiating this raw archival material and encountering a text in a modern edition with interpretative paratextual frameworks gave students a firsthand understanding of theoretical issues that had otherwise seemed abstract. They marveled, for example, at the influence an editor could exert with his or her interpretation of the value of a recovered text, whereas before they viewed the editor's introduction as extraneous material and gave little thought to the research and work involved in creating a critical edition. Given that students were all working on developing their own editions for the final project, we closely examined the *design* of print periodicals (in digital archives), of modern editions of recovered texts, and of digital projects like *Just Teach One* and *Just Teach One: Early African American Print* (whose editors are contributors to this volume).

In line with the emphasis upon *building* in digital humanities, students assumed the role of designers in putting together an edition, but the assignment did not require them to create a digital edition of the text, which would have required significantly more time, technical skills, and technical support. Instead, students focused on the process of finding a text, researching it, and making an argument for its recovery to produce (1) a hard copy edition—including a critical introduction, suggestions for further reading, the annotated text, and optional supplementary materials such as illustrations and appendixes—as their final paper, and (2) a slide presentation of their project for the class at the end of the semester. Students created their project with both the audience of the class in mind and also a wider readership they needed to define in their "pitch" to the class—that is, the same way an editor would craft a proposal for a publisher. This choice *not* to jump to posting web content deliberately emphasizes the creation and circulation of manuscripts—by nineteenth-century authors and editors of modern editions alike—as a significant but overlooked form of literary production and readership. Stephen Ramsay's blog "On Building" elaborates upon his comments at an MLA panel in 2011 that "Digital humanities is about building things. . . . If you are not making anything . . . you are not a digital humanist," an assertion that generated much controversy and raises the question of what exactly it means to *build*.[1] The choice of verb is one that emphasizes work traditionally performed by men as engineers and architects; to *knit* or to *sew*, however, is also to make something (as Emily Dickinson hand-stitched volumes of her poems). Among the material objects we considered in the recovery course were the handwritten magazine *The Muzzeniegun or Literary Voyager* in which Ojibwe writer Jane Johnston Schoolcraft's writings appear and the holograph of Hannah Crafts's *The Bondwoman's Narrative* that Henry Louis Gates Jr. subjected to forensic analysis or "decoding" (as detailed in an appendix to his edition of the novel). Digital archives can reveal to students the crafting and piecing together of texts in nineteenth-century print culture and the richness of intertextuality, enabling us to better conceptualize and analyze the web of nineteenth-century American literature. By examining the original construction of these texts and their place in larger networks, recovery work makes visible the ways that women—and African Americans, Native Americans, and other marginalized groups—have always participated in the process of "building things" as contributors to American culture and the humanities. Foregrounding the role of editors and publishers, in contrast to focusing more narrowly upon author and text as students have generally been taught to do, expands the view of writers and their words to show how they are entangled in a larger communal web. This attention to the participatory nature of literary publication effectively locates nineteenth-century women writers and contemporary scholars engaged in the recovery of their writing within an ongoing process of effecting social change—work that is now being performed and enhanced by digital humanities.

My approach to digital technology as part of a cyclical story of transformation in the humanities seeks to complicate the linear narrative of progress embodied in Enlightenment thinking and, in turn, the ideology of Manifest Destiny, as one that has always been in conversation with other ways of thinking in American culture. Rather than envisioning the crossing of a frontier, in other words, my use of digital pedagogy embraces Mary Louise Pratt's conception of *contact zones* as "social spaces where cultures meet, clash, and grapple with each other, often in contexts of highly asymmetrical relations of power, such as colonialism, slavery, or their aftermaths as they are lived out in many parts of the world today," a model of hybridity that other educators also have explored.[2] Textual recovery can be used to better understand and resist hierarchies that have created imbalances of power and uneven representation of American voices in the past and present. In "Digital Technology for Feminist Pedagogy: A Useful Method for Learning Key Concepts in a Changing Academic Landscape" (2012), Katie Bashore and Jigna Desai write:

> Technology has a complicated history in feminist studies. It has been critiqued as a tool of oppression and appropriated as a means to empowerment. New scholarship suggests a reality beyond this bifurcation. Technologies are not "bad" or "good," but become embedded within particular social, cultural, and political relations. The challenge is to pay attention to how technologies function in specific contexts while also exploring their potential to help create dynamic ways of thinking and interacting.[3]

In contemplating the objectives for Women and Literature: The Politics and Practice of Textual Recovery, I held these ideas in mind when designing a hybrid digital humanities course that did not set as its highest priority the creation of digital editions of recovered texts. For each student, the challenge of using digital resources to identify, research, and analyze a nineteenth-century text in order to produce a new literary edition was itself an all-immersive and transformative experience as students assumed new identities as public scholars creating work to be shared, and as new members of larger communities dedicated to textual recovery and to exploring the possibilities of digital humanities.

Joining Networks

The study and practice of textual recovery fosters critical thinking about the ways that voices can be lost and found, not only in American literary history but also in the digital age. A course dedicated to textual recovery necessarily draws attention to the writing of editors and scholars who perform work that has itself been marginalized given the tendency of academic institutions to place higher value upon book-length monographs and other forms of publication. As texts migrate from ivy-covered, brick-and-mortar archives to digital formats, it may seem less important to publish editions that make forgotten or overlooked texts *accessible*, but there are new imperatives for scholars to negotiate the vast abundance of texts and different versions of them. The navigational skills of editors have arguably become more and not less important, in other words, with the immense sea of digital texts available at our fingertips—texts that may be floating out of context, broken into pieces, or partly obscured. Critical editions place marginalized texts in sharper perspective and establish their claim upon contemporary audiences, reinvigorating ongoing conversations about what we read, how we read, and why we read. By asking students to sharpen their own digital research skills and interpretive frameworks for reading a nineteenth-century text, the course illuminates the shadowy work that editors perform—in both print and digital media—and its larger social value. The course is designed to model the various networks joining authors, scholars/editors, instructors, and students across time and space, and how critical the work of textual recovery has been to the study of women and minority writers.

At the start of the semester, I explain to students how my development of the recovery course is connected to a larger network beyond the *Just Teach One* project prominently featured on our syllabus. In particular, I draw attention to the significant impact of the Society for the Study of Women Writers (SSAWW) for supporting literary recovery with the journal *Legacy* and for building a strong literary community. SSAWW's ongoing facilitation of pedagogical collaboration and sharing has, for example, contributed positively to efforts (including my own) to engage students in archival research and recovery using digital resources. In addition to scheduling syllabus sharing sessions and numerous panels and roundtables on pedagogy at its conferences, SSAWW nurtures ongoing conversations between members with its listserv (including a digital humanities listserv), website, Facebook page, and Twitter account. The website's page titled "Using Archives: Resources and Assignments" reposts materials from the listserv by various instructors of nineteenth-century American literature who have engaged their own students in archival research and textual recovery projects: Sarah Robbins, Frances Smith Foster, Eric Gardner,

Barbara McCaskill, P. Gabrielle Foreman, DoVeanna Fulton, Ellen Gruber Garvey, Deborah Gussman, Timothy Scherman, Theresa Gaul, Jennifer Putzi, and Katharine Rodier.[4] The shared reflections, teaching materials, and digital links were an invaluable cache of ideas as I considered the shape the new textual recovery course and assignments might take.

My own course thus joins linked, larger pedagogical endeavors to teach students the skills and the stakes involved in the textual recovery of women writers. From the exchange of comments and materials, Gussman was inspired to offer a senior seminar titled Recovering 19th-Century American Women Writers in spring 2015 and to create a digital exhibition with pages students designed to give "a snapshot of their larger projects."[5] Gussman's syllabus, linked to the site, incorporates elements of the assignments shared by Scherman and Gaul, modifying and building upon them.[6] The syllabus gives students the option of creating the type of final project that Scherman assigns in American Women Writers of the Nineteenth Century, a paper that he explains should "investigate a lesser known work by a woman writer of the nineteenth century" and take the form of "an 'edition' of the literary work . . . comparable in treatment (if not in length) to the introductions we have read in many of the texts we've discussed this term."[7] Gussman also offers students the option to write an analytical essay focusing upon a recently recovered text by adapting Gaul's archival assignment, which asks students "to explore nineteenth-century magazines, newspapers, and other writings through electronic databases in order to enrich your understanding of one of the novels."[8] Gussman developed a scaffolded approach to the final project in which students use this research to develop a short paper exploring the historical context of their text: it is the second of four short papers, with the first identifying the text for recovery, the third examining genre, and the fourth focusing upon style and close reading.[9]

These combined pedagogical efforts and individual innovations call to mind the act of quilting, and the course I created pieced together versions of these instructors' assignments with the others I crafted as *archival explorations*. For their final project, all students prepared an "edition" similar to ones in the assigned course texts and in Scherman and Gussman's recovery assignments. Students can be intimidated by this project, and many would have likely chosen the second option on Gussman's syllabus to write a research paper "focus[ing] on a recovered text that has become more well-known and about which a critical discussion has emerged." Without this alternate assignment available to them, my students shared the common experience of stepping into unknown territory to perform recovery work by making—or "building"—a new edition of a text. This unfamiliar and difficult work needs to be broken into steps for undergraduates, and I adopted Gussman's scaffolding of assignments for the recovery project by requiring three preliminary papers (identification, histori-cal context, and genre), with "style/close reading" incorporated into each essay rather than treating it as a separate topic. The preliminary assignments were also shorter in length (two to three pages), given that my syllabus interlaced eight other five-hundred-word papers into the coursework, each designed to practice critical skills for literary recovery in connection with reading assign-ments. With students engaging in weekly writing assignments drawing from their own research and archival explorations, the classroom resembled a studio space where designers practice, train, and experiment. We critically discussed the construction of the syllabus itself and the course's intended outcomes, the successes and problems students were encountering with their individual projects, and the strengths and weaknesses of different modern editions as models for their own choices. This decentering of the classroom was consistent with the course's investment in feminist scholarship and pedagogy, concerns with the politics of canon formation, and investigation of forms of labor and collaboration that have traditionally been overlooked.

Duncan Faherty and Ed White's digital project *Just Teach One* (*JTO*), with its self-described "practical, long-term and cooperative, if still modest, approach to the problem of textual recovery," provided a perfect starting point for ex-ploring these issues and thus served as a cornerstone for the course syllabus.[10] Students were assigned not "just one" but four of the texts on *JTO* and its sister site, *Just Teach One: Early African American Print* along with introductory, contextual, and pedagogical materials on the sites, and Michelle Burnham's essay "Literary Recovery in an Age of Austerity: A Review of *Early American Imprints* and *Just Teach One*" (2015).[11] Faherty and White's introduction to *JTO* and Burnham's review clearly lay out the economic impediments to textual recovery along with other obstacles to teaching newly recovered texts in the classroom. They address the paradox that the vast increase in versions of digital texts has in many ways added to the difficulty of introducing new works into the classroom given shrinking library budgets, skittish publishers, and the practical challenges confronting academics. In this "age of austerity," Faherty and White creatively developed what Burnham describes as a "do-it-together (DIT) project," with the following goals outlined in their introduction to *JTO*:

> First, with the generous support of the American Antiquarian Society and *Common-place*, we hope to provide a body of publicly available scholarly tran-scriptions of early texts, with basic editing and apparatus. Second, we hope to provide a critical mass of teachers incorporating the new text into their classroom. And finally, and most importantly, these teachers provide reflections on the text, insights and reaction, intertextual possibilities, and so on, in ways that should provide guidance for other teachers.[12]

In the years since its pilot project in 2012, *JTO* has achieved rock-star status among scholars practicing literary recovery and instructors teaching American literature, with participation soaring and new PDF editions of texts regularly being added to the site for classroom use. This collection includes essays from both *JTO* and *JTO: EAAP* that discuss the two projects in more extensive detail. Beyond exemplifying a highly successful scholarly and pedagogical collaboration using digital technology, *JTO* makes palpable the connection between textual recovery and classroom teaching. My own students observed at the end of the semester that making a text available "does not in itself constitute recovery": "For a text to be recovered, scholarly engagement with that text is necessary," and *JTO*'s "classroom focus allows for writings on the text, which can bolster a text's ability to stay recovered."[13]

Students arrived at these insights after studying a longer history of literary recovery, examining its practice in both digital and print editions selected for the syllabus to offer a range of cases for comparison. Although the course focused primarily on nineteenth-century women's literature, we began by reading three *JTO* editions of eighteenth-century novels—*Amelia; or the Faithless Briton* (1787), *The Story of Constantius and Pulchera* (1789), and *St. Herbert—A Tale* (1796), all by anonymous authors—and Cathy N. Davidson's print edition of Susanna Rowson's 1794 American version of *Charlotte Temple*, an example of a novel that has achieved a firm place in the canon and classroom in the decades since its recovery and subsequent reprinting in other editions.[14] Students considered the current ubiquity of *Charlotte Temple* in American literature courses in the context of Burnham's argument that "despite scholars' easy access to such digital materials, affordable print editions continue to dominate syllabi and to drive text selections, particularly in introductory undergraduate courses where the inclusion of such works can make the most difference."[15] In this upper-level course, the specialized topic enabled us to escape the constraints of a survey course and explore comparisons between *Charlotte Temple* and not "just one" but three contemporaneous texts, which together offered more nuanced images of women in the early American republic. Many of the instructors teaching *JTO* texts alongside *Charlotte Temple* similarly note that the contrast between Rowson's passive heroine and characters like Amelia or Pulchera shattered some of their students' assumptions about the cultural ideologies and the literary conventions of the era, particularly with respect to gender roles. After reading the novels and Eve Tavor Bannet's essay "The Constantias of the 1790s: Tales of Constancy and Republican Daughters" (2014), my students gained a new vocabulary complicating the familiar concept of Republican Motherhood, as well as the association of women writers with sentimentality—an issue of greater concern to feminist scholarship and textual recovery that we examined in the influential arguments of Nina Baym in "Melodramas of Beset Manhood: How Theories of American Literature Exclude Women Authors" (1981) and Jane Tompkins in *Sensational Designs: The Cultural Work of American Fiction, 1790–1860* (1985).[16]

Charlotte Temple's rise to prominence in early American literature courses with the canon revision that has occurred since the 1980s has not changed many of the fundamental issues to which *JTO* responds, pointing to the need for larger curricular and pedagogical changes to accompany the work of literary recovery. The inclusion of new women and minority writers in the canon is not necessarily an end goal, in other words, because the work forces us to confront the hierarchies and values informing the very idea of a canon and its emphasis upon individual, major authors. The direct appeal to instructors to "just teach one" seems to encourage us to rethink our pedagogies beyond this starting point, and here I am reminded of the compelling argument bell hooks makes: in *Teaching to Transgress: Education as the Practice of Freedom* (1994), she asserts that "the classroom remains the most radical space of possibility in the academy" and calls for "renewal and rejuvenation in our teaching practices."[17] In designing the course, I was pressed to consider how it might—in its own modest way—approach the issues of textual recovery by rethinking the nature of the work that students do in the classroom and, like Faherty and White, to try to imagine new ways that digital texts and resources might be used to effect changes in our teaching and larger understanding of early American literature. Their recovery of anonymous texts disrupts an author-centric approach to literary studies emphasizing individual genius, talent, and personality, and *JTO*'s attention to the importance of periodicals in American literary history—and in African American print—likewise argues for rethinking the value of editorial, collaborative, and communal literary productions that have largely been overlooked in undergraduate classrooms. Guided by Frances Smith Foster's arguments in "A Narrative of the Interesting Origins and (Somewhat) Surprising Developments of African-American Print Culture" (2005) and "Forgotten Manuscripts: How Do You Solve a Problem Like Theresa?" (2006), students gained a new understanding of nineteenth-century African American literature *beyond* the individual slave narratives that have overshadowed other literary genres and collective endeavors.[18] The syllabus paired "Theresa: A Haytien Tale" (1828) with an archival exploration of contextual materials on the *JTO: EAAP* site and of the full issues of *Freedom's Journal* in which the story appeared, accessed via the Internet Archive. Rather than "just teach[ing] one" text, our course approached *JTO* and *JTO: EAAP* sites as models for the students' own projects to "just recover one" text through their own research in digital archives. The timing did not work out for my class to read and participate in the discussion forum for Rowson's

Sincerity (1803–1804), posted on *JTO* shortly before the beginning of the fall 2015 semester and the longest of its texts, but we did devote class time to examining response posts by participants who taught the four *JTO* texts on our syllabus and comparing our own experiences. In short, my students missed the opportunity to join the other classes reading and discussing *Sincerity* at the same time but found a new way to engage with the *JTO* project by taking responsibility for *finding* texts on their own that arguably deserve reading and teaching. *JTO*'s attention to literature in periodicals demonstrated the fertile field students might examine to discover unknown or little-known women writers and texts, and their research also turned to various marginalized genres.

By exploring *Freedom's Journal* and other nineteenth-century periodicals and digital collections, students gained a different perspective of the ways that the literature was produced and shared through various networks and within larger contact zones. These digital resources and projects can work in the classroom to collapse the distance between the nineteenth century and the present when students sift through artifacts to select a text for recovery and to tell a story of their own about its importance both then and now. Similar to the way that *JTO* invites instructors to participate in a "do-it-together" project, digital humanities enables instructors to involve students in new kinds of DIY and DIT projects, including the work of textual recovery. The *Colored Conventions Project* (*CCP*), directed by P. Gabrielle Foreman with an interdisciplinary team of faculty, librarians, and graduate and undergraduate students at the University of Delaware, uses crowdsourcing to open its recovery initiative to any individual interested in participating in the transcription of minutes from nineteenth-century meetings of black political organizers. The introduction to the *CCP* team states that they are "committed to generating an online hub that 'brings buried African American history to digital life' and attends to social justice activism in scholarship and research by offering an opportunity for deep engagement with 19th-century Black political organizing."[19] The *CCP*'s ambitious undertaking models on a large scale the ways that digital humanities and literary recovery can transform teaching and learning through DIY and DIT projects.

Finding Voices

Digital archives and resources enabled me to decenter the syllabus and the classroom by asking students to think of themselves as editors engaged in literary recovery: in this class, they were to assume the role of the scholars and editors whose work we were studying—to negotiate and participate in the politics and practices of textual recovery as distinct from merely learning *about* the work. Most reading assignments in literature courses ask students to read the same pages of a text, but the common readings in this class were combined with digital "archival explorations" guided by individual inquiry. All students would engage in a directed research activity, yet each student would arrive at different texts and topics, bringing various perspectives to class as "experts" who might have to explain archival material unfamiliar to the rest of the class. For each archival exploration, students would examine—that is, browse with a purpose in mind rather than reading in entirety—digital materials such as an issue of an early American periodical, a digital collection of documents on a specific topic, handwritten letters, different versions of a republished text, or one author's short story contributions to diverse periodicals. The syllabus frequently paired reading and archival assignments, as follows for one day of class: "[read] *Amelia; or the Faithless Briton (Just Teach One); Archival exploration*: examine *The Columbian Magazine* (1787), with special attention to October and the supplement to the first volume, the issues in which *Amelia* appears (*Internet Archive*)." In class, students discussed *Amelia* and its recovery by *JTO*, but individuals also performed their own small acts of recovery by pointing the group's attention to a particular text of interest in the *Columbian Magazine*, and to themes, issues, language, and so forth, that provided new perspectives of *Amelia* and the context in which it was produced.

While I performed the preliminary work of tracking down relevant archival material in such digital collections as the Internet Archive and HathiTrust, students gained experience searching within the repositories and within the periodicals—skills that astonishingly few of them had practiced. Even when students knew where and what to look for in an archival exploration, they would still have trouble locating the material in the digital collections and in the early periodicals. Students needed to first become better familiarized with digital archives and their holdings before embarking upon their search for a text to recover, as their literary research typically focuses upon finding secondary sources and not primary texts, let alone marginalized voices. They received guidance throughout the semester from me—in class, comments on papers, and office hours—and from individual research consultations with our college librarians. With eyes opened to a vast new world of nineteenth-century digital artifacts, students faced the challenge of choosing a path, initially within smaller archival assignments, and then by conducting independent research to identify a text for their final recovery project.

Archival explorations were thus often linked to short paper assignments to help students focus their inquiry, sharpen their ideas, and come to class prepared with formulated comments to contribute to the class discussion. For example, students encountered prompts such as this: "draw upon your archival exploration of *The New-York Weekly Magazine, or, Miscellaneous Repository* to contextualize *St. Herbert—A Tale*, explaining how the content of the magazine enhances your understanding of the novel." On class days when these short papers were due, students led the discussion by explaining their individual discoveries—the texts they selected for analysis and the epiphanies that they gained from their research. These exercises provided practice for the final recovery project not only by enabling students to develop stronger writing and digital research skills, but also by helping them find their own voices as critics and become more confident as "editors" recovering a text. The course's emphasis upon digital archival explorations shares what *JTO* describes as an interest in "how these recovered artifacts might intersect or complicate our operant sense of familiar objects of study, thus expanding our praxis by thinking about new textual constellations."[20] Students responded to this challenge as they created editions for the final project with introductions designed to locate the "recovered artifact" in literary history, and with suggestions for further reading modeled upon the ones Faherty and White provide for each of *JTO*'s texts.

By asking students to find and think critically about such artifacts on a weekly basis, the syllabus is not dominated by texts that are already in print and are already subjects of scholarly study. One student remarked about this difference as follows: "Usually students acquire the required readings for their courses and do not wonder how the work came to be or how the professor located it—the work has just always been there. . . . Part of the uniqueness to [this Women and Literature course] and a textual recovery class is the fact that most texts are original works, and students are doing original work." With independent research using digital sources driving the coursework, the classroom becomes a studio workshop in which individual students share the materials and designs they have discovered, with the assigned print texts serving as case studies and models to guide their inquiry. I included my own edition of Elizabeth Oakes Smith's *The Western Captive and Other Indian Stories* (2015) among our course texts because it would enable me to discuss the process of creating the text starting from scratch—to pull back the veil and reveal the challenges, discoveries, and choices leading to the book's final design. The stories I offered with this case study worked not only to make editorial labor more real for students, but also to build a sense of shared endeavor and convince them of their ability to join in recovery scholarship.

Whereas the curriculum in literary studies has traditionally been preoccupied with "coverage," I selected course texts to familiarize students with a range of editorial approaches, issues, and designs as they engaged in their own archival explorations and recovery projects. After reading *Charlotte Temple*, students wrote a short paper comparing Davidson's commentary on the novel to the historian Bonnie Laughlin Schultz's introduction to *How Did Susanna Rowson and Other Reformers Promote Higher Education as an Antidote to*

Women's Sexual Vulnerability, 1780–1820?—a document project compiling primary texts published in the database/journal *Women and Social Movements in the United States, 1600 to 2000*, edited by Kathryn Kish Sklar and Thomas Dublin.[21] Positive experiences co-teaching an American studies course with a history professor led me to adapt our use of this database to my own American women's literature courses as a tool for teaching students how to develop more sophisticated connections between texts and their contexts. English majors at my institution—unlike history majors—are not required to take a course training them to use archival materials, and this digital collection effectively models research using primary sources and works well as a hands-on tool for students. While the collection identifies its discipline as history, literary texts are included among the "documents" collected, showing students how literature participates in larger social debates. Of course many print editions and digital resources present primary texts contemporaneous with a literary work, but *Women and Social Movements* is organized into document projects focusing upon an issue rather than a single text, showing students how to re-think history as a broad "background" by asking specific *questions* about the contexts in which a text was produced and using archival research to explore its place among other artifacts. The digital collection provides both a model of inquiry-based, archival research and a valuable tool for investigating women's involvement in social reform. Exploring anti-slavery documents, for example, one student discovered a reference by Charlotte Forten Grimké to an article under the pen name Gail Hamilton and then tracked down the essay in the *North American Review* to examine it for her project.

Students relied upon digital archives in the undertaking of their recovery work, but they also developed a better understanding of the importance of archival research more broadly through our study of previously unpublished literary texts by such nineteenth-century authors as Jane Johnston Schoolcraft, Hannah Crafts, and Elizabeth Oakes Smith. To gain some sense of the work involved in Robert Dale Parker's edition, *The Sound the Stars Make Rushing through the Sky: The Writings of Jane Johnston Schoolcraft* (2007), students worked in small groups to transcribe, annotate, and interpret handwritten letters from the Library of Congress's collection of Henry Rowe Schoolcraft's papers.[22] While they were grateful to be working with digital reproductions that allowed them to zoom in and out, students still struggled with the nineteenth-century handwriting, historical references, and interpretation of language and tone. In Henry Louis Gates Jr.'s edition of Crafts's *The Bondwoman's Narrative* (2002), the introduction and appendix describing the forensic analysis of the holograph manuscript likewise turned their attention from print texts to nineteenth-century material culture.[23] With my edition of Oakes Smith's *The Western Captive and Other Indian Writings*, students examined archival materials that illuminated her relationship to the Schoolcrafts and considered the problematic "translation" of Indian stories by white writers.[24] The archival research that led me to contextualize Oakes Smith's work using such varied genres as Indian ethnography and political campaign biographies of William Henry Harrison modeled for students the ways that they might expand their thinking about literary forms and traditions beyond the broader, more familiar categories they know. In their own recovery projects, students worked with genres that they had not previously encountered in nineteenth-century literature, including these and others: gift books, epistolary conduct manuals, speeches from black women's clubs, children's literature, pedagogical texts, and various kinds of periodicals—religious, political, popular, literary.

Digital resources can—although it might seem paradoxical—give students a more palpable sense of the "real world" of the nineteenth century and thus help them develop more sophisticated critical perspectives. One student writes, "The days where we were assigned to explore newspapers and magazines, like the *Godey's Lady's Book*, I enjoyed the most because I was really able to get a view of the period. Within my research, in HathiTrust, I was able to find how-to books, recipes and short stories, which were all in one magazine. The digital technology helped me evaluate a text within a larger work [and] to interpret it alongside others like it." To give one example, archival explorations of the "blood and thunder" tales recovered by Madeleine Stern in *Behind a Mask: The Unknown Thrillers of Louisa May Alcott* (1975) led students to engage more critically with Stern's own interpretation of the tales.[25] Upon examining publications in which Alcott's stories originally appeared—in *Frank Leslie's Illustrated Weekly*, *The Flag of Our Union*, and the form of a "novelette"—students began rethinking their understanding of the stories' historical context and genre. Given the working-class readership of novelettes and moralistic editorial frameworks they discovered in the periodicals, Alcott's stories appeared more, not less, consistent with her other writing, published not "behind" but without the mask of a pseudonym. Students were asked to think about the *story* each editor tells, knowing that they would be responsible for crafting their own stories when introducing a recovered text to readers and making an argument for its value. In practicing textual recovery, they learned that the stories we tell about literature are ever evolving, and they thrived upon the opportunity to join the conversation. For example, one student with an avid interest in nineteenth-century Spiritualism created an edition of selected poems by Sarah Helen Whitman that seeks to complicate the ways Whitman's writing has been framed in terms of her relationship to Edgar Allan Poe.

Our study of modern editions continually questioned what was at stake in each editor's literary recovery, and for most students, the practice of recovering a text evolved with a personal and political investment in their topic of choice.

The range of their interests is too diverse to summarize, but here is a sample of the types of writing they recovered: Christian, Zionist, Nature-Study, free-love feminist, kindergarten movement, domestic education, health reform, missionary travel, antimiscegenation, mourning, and factory literature. While I provided necessary mentorship and structure with detailed feedback on the preliminary papers in which they developed the final projects in several stages, each student assumed the role of the "expert" on his or her author and text. All of the recovered texts were indeed ones that I had not encountered before, and so were many of the authors. To offer guidance to each student, I had to immerse myself in digital research on numerous topics and to learn even more about nineteenth-century literature, culture, and archival resources than before teaching the course. If the students were at first daunted by the expectation that they would create a critical edition of their own modeled upon the work being undertaken by scholars with PhDs, I was also slightly overwhelmed by the task of responding to each individual's project proposal and ongoing research. The consensus among students at the end of the semester was that the coursework was too heavy, and I would agree that the experimental first version of this course was perhaps overly ambitious. Some slight adjustments could improve the course's design: cutting down the number of five-hundred-word papers, frontloading the archival assignments and short papers so that they taper off earlier in the semester, arranging for a librarian to provide more digital research instruction (maybe during a full class period at the beginning of the term), and integrating individual conferences into the schedule.

On the whole, however, the course successfully provided a transformative learning experience that pushed the boundaries of what undergraduates might expect to accomplish in their studies of nineteenth-century literature. In the end, each student in the class succeeded in using digital archives to make an original contribution to the study of nineteenth-century literature. All students gained a new sense of their abilities as authors, editors, and scholars, and some were positively astonished by the significance of their discoveries. Some notable achievements by individual students include solving questions of a text's authorship, correcting errors in bibliographic records, and locating a trove of biographical material and letters collected by an author's family member. Moreover, their recovery work has already influenced my own teaching; in the following semester's course on women writers and nineteenth-century social reform, I assigned a story recovered by one student from an 1844 issue of *The Factory Girl's Garland* together with *JTO*'s edition of Sarah Savage's "The Factory Girl" (1814). The student visited as a guest lecturer, taking her place in the classroom as a scholar and editor among her peers to give them a new perspective of both factory literature and recovery work. A number of students from Women and Literature: The Politics and Practice of Textual Recovery also presented their projects in a session at the college's spring undergraduate conference showcasing exceptional work. Within the English 443 classroom community, students introduced readers to once marginalized voices and texts, and their editions are now finding wider audiences. What is more, the students all arrived at a much more complex understanding of issues in literary studies that did not fully resonate until they personally engaged in the politics and practice of textual recovery—that is, in the ongoing rethinking of what, why, and how we read.

The appendix for this chapter, a syllabus by Caroline M. Woidat for a course on archival explorations, can be found at www.press.uillinois.edu/books/Teaching WithDH.

Notes

1. Stephen Ramsay, "On Building," *Stephen Ramsay* (blog), January 11, 2011, http://stephenramsay.us/text/2011/01/11/on-building/.

2. Mary Louise Pratt, "Arts of the Contact Zone," *Profession 1991* (New York: Modern Language Association, 1991), 34; Patricia Bizzell, "'Contact Zones' and English Studies," *College English* 56, no. 2 (1994): 163–169; and Cynthia L. Selfe and Richard J. Selfe Jr., "The Politics of the Interface: Power and Its Exercise in Electronic Contact Zones," *College Composition and Communication* 45, no. 4 (1994): 480–504.

3. Katie Bashore and Jigna Desai, "Digital Technology for Feminist Pedagogy: A Useful Method for Learning Key Concepts in a Changing Academic Landscape," in *Cultivating Change in the Academy: 50+ Stories from the Digital Frontlines at the University of Minnesota in 2012*, ed. Ann Hill Duin, Farhad Anklesaria, and Edward A. Nater (Minneapolis: University of Minnesota, 2012), http://purl.umn.edu/125273.

4. "Using Archives: Resources and Assignments," *SSAWW: Society for the Study of American Women Writers*, accessed March 26, 2017, https://ssawwnew.wordpress.com /archives/archive-assignments/.

5. Deborah Gussman, et al., *Recovering 19th-Century American Women Writers: An Exhibition of Senior Projects in Literary Recovery at Stockton University*, Stockton University, accessed March 26, 2017, https://blogs.stockton.edu/litrecovery/sample-page/.

6. Deborah Gussman, "Senior Seminar: Recovering American Women Writers," *Recovering 19th-Century American Women Writers*, https://blogs.stockton.edu/lit recovery/files/2015/04/SeniorSemSP15-1.pdf.

7. See Timothy Scherman, assignment in "Using Archives."

8. Theresa Gaul, assignment in "Using Archives."

9. See Gussman, "Senior Seminar."

10. Duncan Faherty and Ed White, "Welcome to *Just Teach One*," *Just Teach One, Common-place: The Journal of Early American Life*, American Antiquarian Society, accessed March 26, 2017, http://www.common-place.org/justteachone/.

11. Michelle Burnham, "Literary Recovery in an Age of Austerity: A Review of *Early American Imprints* and *Just Teach One*," *Legacy* 32, no. 1 (2015): 122–132.

12. Ibid., 128; Faherty and White, "Welcome."

13. In this essay, I quote Women and Literature students from my fall 2015 course anonymously, drawing upon written reflections that they generated during the final exam period. I am grateful for their willingness to contribute their ideas to this essay and for their work, collaboration, and feedback throughout the debut semester of the course.

14. Susanna Rowson, *Charlotte Temple*, ed. Cathy N. Davidson (New York: Oxford University Press, 1986).

15. Burnham, "Literary Recovery," 122.

16. Eve Tavor Bannet, "The Constantias of the 1790s: Tales of Constancy and Republican Daughters," *Early American Literature* 49, no. 2 (2014): 435–466; Nina Baym, "Melodramas of Beset Manhood: How Theories of American Literature Exclude Women Authors," *American Quarterly* 33, no. 2 (1981): 123–139; Jane Tompkins, *Sensational Designs: The Cultural Work of American Fiction, 1790–1860* (New York: Oxford University Press, 1985).

17. bell hooks, *Teaching to Transgress: Education as the Practice of Freedom* (New York: Routledge, 1994), 12.

18. Frances Smith Foster, "A Narrative of the Interesting Origins and (Somewhat) Surprising Developments of African-American Print Culture," *American Literary History* 17, no. 4 (2005): 714–740; Foster, "Forgotten Manuscripts: How Do You Solve a Problem Like Theresa?" *African American Review* 40, no. 4 (2006): 631–645.

19. "About Us: Introducing the Colored Conventions Project Team," *Colored Conventions: Bringing Nineteenth-Century Black Organizing to Digital Life*, P. Gabrielle Foreman, dir., University of Delaware, accessed March 26, 2017, http://coloredconventions .org/about-us.

20. Faherty and White, "Welcome."

21. Davidson, introduction to Rowson, *Charlotte Temple*, xi–xxxiii; Bonnie Laughlin Schultz, "How Did Susanna Rowson and Other Reformers Promote Higher Education as an Antidote to Women's Sexual Vulnerability, 1780–1820?," in *Women and Social Movements in the United States, 1600–2000*, ed. Kathryn Kish Sklar and Thomas Dublin (Alexandria, Va.: Alexander Street Press; Binghamton: Center for the Historical Study of Women, State University of New York, Binghamton, 2007), http://womhist. alexanderstreet.com/schultz/abstract.htm.

22. Robert Dale Parker, ed., *The Sound the Stars Make Rushing through the Sky: The Writings of Jane Johnston Schoolcraft* (Philadelphia: University of Pennsylvania Press, 2007); Henry Rowe Schoolcraft Papers, Manuscript Division, Library of Congress, Washington D. C., accessed on microfilm.

23. See Henry Louis Gates Jr., introduction to *The Bondwoman's Narrative* by Hannah Crafts, ed. Henry Louis Gates Jr. (New York: Warner Books, 2002), xxi–xciii; Joe Nickell, "Appendix A: Authentication Report," in ibid., 303–337.

24. See Caroline M. Woidat, "Appendix D: Oakes Smith and the Schoolcrafts," in *The Western Captive and Other Indian Stories* by Elizabeth Oakes Smith (Peterborough, Ont.: Broadview Press, 2015), 303–319.

25. Madeleine Stern, introduction to *Behind a Mask: The Unknown Thrillers of Louisa May Alcott* (1975; New York: Perennial, 2004), vii–xxxiii.

PART FOUR

Archive

10. Putting Students "In Whitman's Hand"

Catherine Waitinas

AS A WHITMANIAN FIRST and foremost, I didn't come to digital manuscript projects to teach my students about the digital humanities. I came to this approach to teach Whitman more effectively and, in so doing, had the happy accident of discovering how digital humanities can help our students learn not just differently but better—and with less handholding than with some other methods of teaching. Digital literary study, as Megan Norcia has stated so well, "enables students to find new meanings in old texts; offers a model of scholarly intervention in ongoing critical discussions; engages students of different learning styles by reinvigorating the writing and research process; and causes them ultimately to question how history is represented, framed, and processed."[1] In the case of Whitman, I think that digital, archive-based manuscript projects bring us exactly, it seems, where he wants us. He repeatedly exhorted his readers to be present, active, and communicative with him. Rather than destroying this poet-reader connection, our ever-improving technologies can bring us closer to the Whitmanian ideal of communion, both with him and with each other, now via computer, tablet, and phone screens in addition to hard copies of his poetry.

In this essay, I discuss one approach to digital manuscript projects that attempts to connect students to Whitman and to the history of poetic composition. In these projects, I ask students to use only the online *Walt Whitman Archive* to examine one of Whitman's manuscripts alongside at least one published edition of the same poem, with the goal of the students presenting an original argument about the poem to the class.[2] The guiding principle is that the argument itself must be possible only because the students used the manuscript; in other words, they must ferret out the significance of the writerly emendations to the "story" of the poem in question. To drill down a bit deeper: what I here call a *manuscript project* basically means any assign-ment—individual or group, oral or written, formal or informal—that requires students to study literary manuscripts either in addition to or in lieu of the published version(s) of a text. In addition to working with individual students on manuscript-focused papers and projects for capstone degree requirements (senior projects), I've facilitated collaborative Whitman manuscript projects in sophomore general education classes (Introduction to American Literature), junior English major surveys (Transatlantic Romanticism), senior seminars devoted entirely to Whitman, and graduate courses in early American poetry. Whatever the level, I've found that manuscript projects invite students to see literature not only or even at all as the product of a burst of inspiration but, instead, as the result of recurring acts of creation and re-creation, in which the writing itself leads to the philosophies therein, and vice versa.[3] As *The Whit-man Archive*'s cofounder and coeditor Ed Folsom puts it, the Archive's vast manuscript holdings "give you a sense of the DNA of Whitman's poetry. . . . You can see the original codes of the poetry emerging from his own hands."[4] A further benefit of archive-based manuscript projects is that they allow in-structors and students to marry new and old technologies, analyzing big data alongside old-school penmanship as, for instance, with the TokenX technology and the Archive's handwriting tool, both discussed below. By putting students in touch with the pen and pencil marks of the author, these assignments de-mystify the creative writing process even as they remystify the literary arts. This experience of feeling a text simultaneously become both clearer and more opaque is one of the most viscerally satisfying readerly occurrences for literary scholars at all levels.

While I've heard some colleagues express anxiety that too much technology will turn students away from the deep humanity of literary study, I've found the opposite: students working on these digital manuscript projects report feeling an intimate ownership of the poems with which they tussle, not one offered up in a lecture or a reading assignment but, instead, one they fought to realize. One student who was surveyed anonymously noted, "this is what the [English] major is all about"; another wrote that the project "adds a layer of tangibility to the coursework: all of the authors we read seem very far away and distant, but being hands-on with the manuscript makes me feel like I know Whitman personally. I think manuscript study is the reason I have been an English major, but I didn't realize it until this project."[5] There may be no substitute for the *frisson* of physically holding a piece of Whitman's writing—or his hair, as I once did at the New York Public Library—but I can say this as one of the privileged, credentialed few who are allowed access to the "real deal," hard copy manuscripts. Most undergrads and even many graduate students, though, will never have the chance to touch the original manuscripts. It's fortunate, then, that the digital manuscripts housed on *The Whitman Archive* bring students very close to this hands-on archival experience; their classroom *frissons* are real, too. Perhaps because of this, these manuscript projects increase their investment in traditional humanities research as well as in the digital humanities.

It's important to note at this point that this classroom project is just that: a collaborative *classroom* project, with minimal homework involved and, at least at the sophomore and junior level, with rather modest aims (instructors can adjust these introductory projects in terms of difficulty and scale for advanced senior and graduate seminars).[6] Frankly, this is a mere introduction to the ways we might use digital texts for literary study, and I've attempted here to provide both general advice for beginners to digital manuscript projects and specific tips for use in the classroom. I've chosen to focus on a brief introductory lesson—the sort of project that an instructor could slip into any course, even if both instructor and students are new to digital manuscript study, because my goal is to get as many students and instructors as possible using the manuscripts on *The Walt Whitman Archive*. I offer my specific observations and experiences based on teaching with Whitman's online manuscripts in order to share best practices and principles for any literature lesson that could include manuscripts. With adjustments for the materials available on different literary sites, the approaches and activities outlined here would work with other nineteenth-century online manuscripts as well, such as those offered by the *Emily Dickinson Archive*.[7] Also, basic digital manuscript projects can work in any traditional face-to-face classroom, if the students have wireless access and devices with connectivity.[8]

Because the digital manuscript project described here requires only one instructor and one digital resource (*The Whitman Archive* or another literary archive), it's relatively easy to implement and, as such, it's ideal for instructors who would like to introduce literary archives and digital humanities into their classrooms without sacrificing literary content. For those (many) of us who feel the pressures of meeting course content objectives in already circumscribed quarters or semesters, this manuscript project keeps the literary content front and center and may not require any juggling of the course reading schedule, depending on your ambitions or limitations.

In addition to the availability of the superb *Whitman Archive*, another of the many reasons I focus on Whitman for this manuscript project is that he appreciated the power of handwriting, and he saved many of his own manuscripts. In a newspaper article written in 1855, the same year he published the first edition of *Leaves of Grass*, he reported on a fascinating historical phenomenon: "When Napoleon took his army into Egypt, he took a battalion of *savans* also. Paleography (deciphering ancient inscriptions or signs) became the rage. . . . They made literal copies of long strings of hieroglyphics, and had them engraved, and printed, and circulated, and offered prizes for translations and keys."[9] Many years and editions later, Whitman marked the title page of every copy of the final "deathbed" *Leaves of Grass* (1891–1892) with his own handwritten title and signature. I've found that, like the Napoleonic *savans* in their obsession with the dead ancient Egyptians and Whitman with his interest in the dead *savans*, our modern students, too, want to commune with the dead. Manuscript study in the literary classroom proves that, for all their technological savvy, budding twenty-first-century literary scholars still recognize the value of the handwritten word: they, too, want to *print* and *circulate* their *keys* to the words of their literary heroes (words that mean very different things now, in the age of laser printers and keyboards, than they did when Whitman first wrote them). These students want to be the first to discover something—anything—new about the authors they read for class, about whom it seems sometimes like everything already has been said. In my experience, despite the stereotype that they have no time for the past, these students are downright hungry for the old-fashioned, for physical marks of human hesitation and intention, for an encounter with the squiggles and ink blots and coffee stains that reveal an author's humanity alongside his or her writerly craft.

We can use the manuscripts and complementary materials on *The Whitman Archive* to help students of varying expertise begin to sate this hunger. These manuscript projects employ primarily the manuscript section titled "In His Hand," but I've written before about how student access to all of the discrete editions of *Leaves of Grass* is itself a boon made possible only because of the Archive.[10] Where previous generations of Whitman scholars were relegated to using only one edition of his work, usually the deathbed edition, current generations can read the poems as they appeared to readers in the nineteenth century, noting the changes he made throughout that century. By comparing the published editions, readers now can see, for instance, how a poem originally published in 1856 becomes parts of three separate poems published in 1860, or how the same lines change and change and change again, sometimes returning to the original phrasing, with each published iteration. The manuscripts add an additional layer of complexity to the trans-editional study of Whitman afforded by the Archive. Complementing its published editions, the Archive's "In His Hand" offerings are an ideal tool for collaborative classroom manuscript study. The Archive houses hundreds of manuscripts that are all open-access, easy to manipulate (zooming, etc.), clearly labeled, and connected within the Archive to extensive additional materials: biography, criticism, contemporary reviews, encyclopedia entries, and the like.

The projects are meant to pull students into the orbit of digital humanities, to pique their interest, and to invite them to explore how digital humanities can help us to learn more about nineteenth-century authors. Because of the manuscripts available on *The Whitman Archive*, my students in only two to three days of class activities have a much broader understanding of Whitman as a poet and a man than I did after a similar number of (wonderful) classes during my undergraduate years. What have come to be reified interpretations of Whitman because of the prevalence of a few of his oft-read published poems face challenges in a classroom with manuscripts at its center; for instance, students walk away from manuscript projects with a sense of Whitman as a writer who was constantly removing as well as adding words—exactly the opposite impression many students walk away from after reading only one version of "Song of Myself."

So, while we may have necessarily limited expectations for these classroom projects, they do push our students into different and often more advanced ways of engaging with texts. As Sarah Werner has pointed out, there is much to learn digitally about a manuscript beyond paleographical analysis, and there are many techniques of reading digital texts that require knowledge far beyond that available to students in two or three days of class; she lists the possibilities and problems, for instance, of using technology to closely read digitized ink—and dirt, actual dirt—on the page. But she also offers words of advice to scholars that work, too, I think, for the students we teach:

> If we could use digital tools to estrange ourselves from our books, to defamiliarize what we think we know, we might learn something new about how they were made and how they are used. People keep pointing out to me that we are in the incunabula age of digital texts. We are. And replicating the familiar makes sense in the cradle days of digital texts. But let's not limit ourselves to reading the digital in the same ways we've always been reading.[11]

Unlike the collective researchers Werner counts among her "we," our students have not "always been reading" these digital texts (or, for that matter, the hard copies), and they can thus benefit significantly from what might seem like rudimentary paleographical approaches. Introductory digital paleography is, indeed, usefully "estranging" for them.

Part of this estrangement is due to the beneficial limitations of short-term manuscript projects. Students simply can't consider every question or every nuance. They must work relatively quickly, with laser focus on things they might not normally notice at all. Therefore, when introducing digital manuscript assignments in my classes, I give the students at all levels one primary rule: they must use only *The Whitman Archive*'s resources—no other sources, hard copy or digital (I make an exception for the *OED*)—to come up with an original argument that is discoverable and possible only because of the available manuscript(s). To come up with this argument, they must compare the manuscript to at least one published version of the text in question. This comparative step allows students to see how language that seems solid in its published version was at one point flexible, slippery, tentative (see assignment directions in Appendix 10.1).

This, I think, is the most important guideline for short-term projects: for students to quickly appreciate what manuscripts offer beyond published texts, students absolutely must focus on Whitman's emendations or alterations when they study and form an argument about the manuscripts. It's not enough for them simply to read the poem and come up with an argument about it, as they might for another text they study. Instead, the whole point of digital manuscript study is to force students to notice how the manuscript alters our understanding of the published text. For example, if Whitman replaces some words with others, the students must study the denotative and connotative meanings of both the original words and their replacements (this is why they are allowed and sometimes required to use the *OED* for their manuscript projects), and they must come up with readings of both versions of the line(s). In this way, they can track tonal and epistemological moves, be they reinforcements or rejections of where the text originally seemed to be heading. This requirement provides invaluable insight into Whitman's processes and revisions, inviting students to focus on writerly craft and to resist the beginner's sense that Whitman, without poetic technique or editing, just "vomits words onto the page," a charge leveled by many a beginning student of Whitman. Students may not have read the many Whitman biographies; they may not even have read more than a few of his poems. Sometimes, in fact, their very first exposure to Whitman is via manuscripts. But none of them leave the room believing that the work wasn't carefully written, rewritten, and sometimes rewritten again (and again and again). For this reason, their arguments often end up being about the writing process itself, as it is revealed on the manuscript page.

Turning toward the practical advice I've gleaned from teaching manuscript projects many times, I now offer a few time-tested tips, followed by a sample plan for a four-hour (240-minute) manuscript project.

First, while it's not necessary for the project to succeed, I have found it useful to invite students to explore *The Whitman Archive* as homework before the first in-class project day. To facilitate this exploration, I've worked with students to develop video introductions to the Archive and to manuscript study, and I've assigned the videos as homework viewing before the project begins.[12]

Second, while I encourage advanced students to choose their own manuscripts, I recommend that instructors in lower-level classes choose the manuscripts for their students, because the Archive's manuscript holdings can be difficult to navigate for novices. I usually select up to eight total manuscripts, and then I invite the student groups to "claim" one. I prefer a first-come, first-served approach in which they cross off their chosen title on the class whiteboard, which gets them thinking quickly and working together as a group toward an easy goal.

When selecting manuscripts for these projects, I choose those that include key concepts and terms from Whitman's poetry, representing a cross-section of the different editions of *Leaves of Grass* and, thus, a broad swath of Whitman's life and career. One invaluable benefit of careful manuscript selection in the early stages of the project is that it eliminates the need for separate lectures at the later stages, because students come to many accurate conclusions on their own; of course, you can corroborate or challenge their findings during and after their presentations, as described below. I also use a limiter when choosing manuscripts, be it geographical (the archive in which they're housed); thematic (e.g., poems about democracy, or the body, or the Civil War); temporal (e.g., poems written for a certain edition or in a certain decade); or otherwise. Most recently, I've limited my students to manuscripts that are available in hard copy at the Huntington Library, Art Collections, and Botanical Gardens in San Marino, California. I use selections from the Huntington because of its geographical proximity to my campus: most of my students at least recognize the Huntington's name, and many have visited its gardens. However, as is the case at most rare book repositories, the Huntington's rare book room isn't available to undergraduate and beginning graduate students, so these online manuscripts draw their attention to the bricks-and-mortar library even as they demonstrate the (necessary) limitations of archival study the "old way." Without a digital archive, students simply wouldn't have access to these documents.[13]

Finally, if you keep the students busy enough, they will not use their devices to waste time during class (e.g., Facebook, Twitter, etc.). But, because the students do have access during and after class to the internet and thus can easily access online sources about Whitman, I recommend against assigning poems that are commonly discussed in various study sources, especially for beginning students who may feel comforted by the opinions of "experts." It's better to let them flail a bit with lesser-known texts, as there's a lot of learning to be done in the flailing.

Minutes 1–30: Introducing the Project

30 minutes may not seem like long enough to complete the tasks listed below, but I've found that overexplaining in the beginning of the project is not useful. Students want to jump right in, and the Archive makes this easy for them.

These tasks require a classroom with a computer and screen projection.

1. Explain the assignment's goal: to study a Whitman manuscript alongside at least one published version of the poem, in order to present an original

argument about the poem to the class. Explain that students can use any
resources offered by *The Walt Whitman Archive* and that their argument
must rely on the manuscript; that is, it must fundamentally be about *how
the manuscript shapes and/or alters our understanding of the text at hand.*

2. Spend a few (very few) minutes introducing Whitman himself. In less than
five minutes, I cover his major contributions to American literature, such
as the introduction of free verse poetry, and I offer a bare-bones biography.
I do not recommend introducing his major poetic themes at this time, as
it is much more satisfying when students come to these organically while
studying the manuscripts.

3. Briefly introduce *The Whitman Archive* with an overview of its contributions. For introductory students, I recommend that you quickly show them
how to find manuscripts, but that you also provide a direct link to the
poems you want them to use on an online "handout," as seen in Appendix
10.1. (There's no need to print this document out for them, as they'll be
online already to use the *Archive*.)

4. Teach the word "manuscript"—"manu" for hand, plus "script" for writing—and show them a few sample manuscripts. Even at the graduate level,
this step makes a big difference. I recommend briefly discussing the possible shortcomings of a digital manuscript at this point as well, as digital
reproductions aren't always perfect. For instance, the Archive's online version of the manuscript for "Come, said my Soul" excludes handwriting that
is visible on the Huntington's hard copy; in the online version, the letter *I*
has been cropped from the fifth (struck-through) line of the poem, rendering it impossible to confidently identify online what in the hard copy version is clearly the contraction *I'll*. This is a good reminder for students and
scholars that while digital archives are invaluable resources that can even
offer some data impossible to get from hard-copy manuscripts, they are
not authoritative manuscript copies. Because of discrepancies such as this,
Sue Hodson, the Huntington's Curator of Literary Manuscripts, suggests
that any scholars doing manuscript work should clarify in their conference
presentations and publications whether they've used hard copies or digital
copies of the manuscripts to reach their findings.

5. Encourage students to consider every single thing they see on a manuscript: the words themselves, of course, but also the handwriting (neat or
messy? tentative or bold? different pen or pencil colors?), the paper on
which it's written, additional information they might find (e.g., the address
of a letter's recipient on the back of a poem). At this point, I usually show
them a few more sample manuscripts to demonstrate what they might seek
and find. If you have these samples lined up in your browser before class
begins, it will take only seconds for you to click through them to show students what they can look for.

6. Briefly introduce the digital tools available on *The Whitman Archive*: the
handwriting key; TokenX—a search tool that allows them to find every
time a word appears in the Archive; basic search functions; the biography;

the encyclopedia;[14] and the like. This introduction doesn't need to take more than five minutes, but it's one kind of "hand-holding" that pays off in spades. The Archive is easy enough to navigate that once you introduce students to its home page, they should easily be able to return to any of these areas for further study.

Minutes 31–180: Collaborative Archival Research and Argumentation

7. While the students work, you should circulate often. They will have questions, and they will need your help. Perhaps the most important part of your job at this point is to encourage students to be brave researchers and thinkers; this isn't the time for "safe" or expected interpretations. To help, you might point them to another resource on the Archive (e.g., an encyclopedia entry or a critical article), or you might gently redirect them away from one argument and toward another, especially if time restrictions would make the first impossible to responsibly pursue. (This is often the case with biographical arguments, which are enticing to students but which are almost impossible to prove convincingly, especially with a project of short duration when students have little prior knowledge of the author.)

8. Don't micromanage, but do encourage students to work on different parts of the project within their groups. I don't tell students how to divvy up the work, but I do suggest that they work on different tasks simultaneously; for example, the whole group might begin by reading the poem together, and then individuals might work to decipher different hard-to-read words. Once the group has agreed on what the actual words are that they see in front of them—which can take awhile!—they can then divide up new tasks: comparing the manuscript to the published version, reviewing the relevant years of Whitman's biography, viewing photographs of Whitman from the relevant years, searching for articles about the poem in question, running TokenX searches on key words (all of these tasks can be performed on the Archive). After they've gathered their data, they can report back to each other.

    Note: I've found that the ideal group size is three or four students, meaning that each individual must always be working hard, sometimes alone and sometimes collaboratively, in order for the group to complete its assignment on time.

9. Don't tell the students much, if anything, about the poems they're studying. Especially for introductory students, it's more exciting to let them come to conclusions organically. (But, again, I think it's okay to direct them away from serious misreadings at this point, in the interests of time.)

10. Encourage students to realize that asking questions can be as important as coming to conclusions in a project such as this one. When they present their group's findings, it's acceptable for them to say, "We want you all to

consider why Whitman used this word/changed this line/made this move here," rather than asserting that they know with certainty why Whitman made his editorial moves. What you'll find is that as each group presents their work, the students will start to see the same questions asked—and often answered in different ways—throughout Whitman's career.

11. While all the explorations described above are invaluable, you should continually remind students that, at the end of the day, they need to offer up one argument as the product of their manuscript study. I encourage simple phrasing such as, "We think the manuscript shows that in this poem Whitman is refocusing to emphasize the reader more than the writer," or "We think that the manuscript proves Whitman's continuing investment in the soul, because he adds the word three times to the poem and deletes other lines that contradict the notion of soul."

12. I suggest that you encourage your students to make very simple Prezi or PowerPoint presentations of their findings, so they can easily show their classmates their best ideas. Groups can begin by creating a very basic Prezi or PowerPoint presentation when they first come together to work on the project, and then they can add information to it as they work. Emphasize that the presentation software is meant to highlight the manuscripts, and not the other way around.

Minutes 181–240: Presentations and Discussion

This plan assumes that students will have approximately an hour remaining after their manuscript study to share their work with classmates. The sharing and discussion are just as important as the manuscript study, in my opinion.

13. Have student groups present their work in the order of the chronological date of publication of the manuscripts you or they have chosen. This will allow the students to appreciate how Whitman's politics, sexuality, spirituality, and the like change throughout the editions. This will also allow the instructor to offer context, first to individual groups as they work during class time and then to the class overall during the postpresentation discussion. As noted earlier, this approach will allow you and your students to present what would have been lecture information.

14. *Strictly limit* each group's presentation time. I've found that four to five minutes is enough if students know ahead of time that they must limit themselves, but that approximately eight minutes is the best length. I use a timer, give a thirty-second warning in the final minute, and (gently but strictly) cut them off if they run over time. If you're strict about presentation times, you'll have (just) enough time remaining for discussion and for you to underscore the information they've deduced—information that you would otherwise have presented in a traditional lecture or discussion.

During the manuscript study and the presentations, I recommend that you keep an eye out for students who seem especially turned on by manuscript study. These are students who might wish to pursue digital manuscript study for senior projects, theses, graduate study in the digital humanities, and the like. It's helpful if you encourage these students to pursue further coursework in coding alongside their work with you on more advanced manuscript projects.

A quick note here about teaching nineteenth-century literature with technology: in my opinion, it's not MOOCs (massive open online courses), with thousands of students working in solitude across the nation, that best marry the technological with the literary. It's in good, old-fashioned, but tech-friendly face-to-face classrooms where students work closely with each other that we can see students using technology not to find easy answers (e.g., SparkNotes) or "right" answers (e.g., Quizlets) but, instead, to do the most invigorating work of the field—the literary archeology of digging and discovery. That's why digital manuscript projects are an excellent introduction to the digital humanities. These projects spark interest in the real work of the field. The students get to know themselves and each other as readers and thinkers, and they gain insight into the craft of poetic composition. They leave the room literally buzzing. "Class was too short today," several said the last time I ran this project. "We need another week," another added—even though we were heading into the long-awaited holiday season. And they do need another week, or a whole quarter or semester, or a whole academic year—and this is how I recruit students to advanced seminars and/or individual projects that make much deeper use of digital literary manuscripts.

Ultimately, my goal in this essay and in my classes is to encourage students—and their instructors—to muck around in the dirty documents on digital archives, the messy ones, the ones that can reveal the inner (and outer) workings, the visions and revisions, of known and unknown authors. With digital literary manuscripts, students do original, textually grounded, technologically savvy literary work that is deeply satisfying from a pedagogical perspective. As a teacher, I've observed that when they complete manuscript studies, students learn the text in front of them intimately. They voluntarily immerse themselves in the *Oxford English Dictionary*. Advanced students can't wait to scour the criticism on Whitman to see if they've come up with something new—and, frankly, they usually have, as most current scholarship doesn't use the manuscripts; this has led to conference presentations and longer essay projects for these students. Students of all levels, even the shy ones, can't wait to give these presentations. They make lots of mistakes—and I've made lots of mistakes, too, in figuring out how to structure these assignments—but they are less afraid to make bold arguments, perhaps because they have something concrete, the markings on the manuscript, to back up their more abstract ideas.

They are less likely to plead ignorance. And their own words speak to their engagement with the materials at hand. I recorded the following comments during a recent collaborative session, as students worked to parse Whitman's handwriting and meaning:

- "Is that a C or an L?"[15]
- "Why is he capitalizing that word in that line? It's not capitalized earlier."
- "What does that word mean here specifically? We need to find other places where he uses it. . . . No, not just in this poem. Look in other poems, too. Try TokenX."
- "This poem is so great! I didn't realize it until we looked at the manuscript."
- "Why doesn't the handwriting guide include numbers? It really needs numbers."
- "Where's the biography? What was he doing when he wrote this version of the poem?"
- "Take a screenshot of this. And that. And that. Zoom in."
- "That phrase is new in the published version. It's not in the manuscript! What does that mean?"
- "Hey, this word is *signing*, not *singing*. That changes everything."
- "He has, like, a million dashes, but this one looks different. Why?"
- "This is good stuff. I don't want to lose this momentum. Can any of you keep working right after class?"

I love witnessing this sort of student work, in part because it feels so old-school, even as it lights up the room with laptops and other devices. And students love it, too; when surveyed, they described the manuscript projects as *interesting, productive, freeing, incredibly cool, intellectually stimulating, amazing and encouraging*, and *an intimate experience between writer and reader*. As for the collaborative aspect of the work, while enjoyment per se isn't a goal of my courses, I do find it pedagogically useful when students are comfortable while working on group projects, and feedback is overwhelmingly positive on this score as well; one student remarked, "This was the most fun I've ever had working on a group project." These students are, in a nutshell, learning by doing.[16]

The appendix for this chapter, instructions for a group project on working with manuscript and published versions of poems, can be found at www.press.uillinois .edu/books/TeachingWithDH.

Notes

1. Megan Norcia, "Out of the Ivory Tower Endlessly Rocking: Collaborating across Disciplines and Professions to Promote Student Learning in the Digital Archive," *Pedagogy* 8, no. 1 (Winter 2008): 94.

2. Ed Folsom and Kenneth M. Price, eds., *The Walt Whitman Archive*, http://www .whitmanarchive.org.

3. Discussions about the nature of poetic composition are especially fruitful in the Transatlantic Romanticism class, in which students already have read theories of poetic composition by William Wordsworth, Samuel Taylor Coleridge, Percy Bysshe Shelley, Edgar Allan Poe, Margaret Fuller, and Ralph Waldo Emerson, among others. Along with Poe's "Philosophy of Composition" in particular, Whitman's manuscripts work sometimes with, and sometimes against, the model of sudden bursts of poetic inspiration or poetic "Eolian harps" often associated with Romanticism.

4. Ed Folsom quoted in Geoffrey Saunders Schramm, "Whitman's Lifelong Endeavor: *Leaves of Grass* at 150," *Humanities* 26, no. 4 (2005): 24–28.

5. A recent manuscript-study cohort, two classes of students in a third-year literary survey course, completed short (four-question) anonymous surveys before and after undertaking the manuscript project. All the student quotes in this essay, unless otherwise noted, come from this survey. The students in these classes also completed informed consent forms to indicate their willingness to be observed during their manuscript projects and to be written about anonymously after the projects' completion.

6. Advanced students can work on more open-ended collaborative projects. In my advanced classes, students already are quite familiar with Whitman. They choose their own manuscripts, and their arguments are situated within their extensive existing knowledge of the poet and his work. These more advanced manuscript projects allow students to make publishable arguments that reveal expertise and originality by employing their preexisting knowledge alongside other archive resources (history, biography, criticism, imagery, and text analysis resources such as the TokenX tool). My seniors and graduate students have used their Whitman manuscript projects as the foundations of multimedia projects including a video series, graduate student application papers, and conference papers.

7. Leslie Morris et al., eds., *Emily Dickinson Archive*, accessed March 26, 2017, http://www.edickinson.org.

8. In nonwired classrooms, instructors could provide hard copies of poetry manuscripts and their corresponding published texts printed from *The Walt Whitman Archive*'s collections. This means that even low-tech instructors and classrooms can benefit from the digitizing of literary manuscripts and the open-access *Whitman Archive*. With this model, during class time students would have to forego using the Archive's additional resources, but further research could be completed as a homework assignment either before or after students begin working with manuscripts during class.

9. Walt Whitman, "One of the Lessons Bordering Broadway: The Egyptian Museum," previously published in *Life Illustrated*, 1855, reprinted in *New York Dissected: A Sheaf of Recently Discovered Newspaper Articles by the Author of Leaves of Grass* (New York: Rufus Rockwell Wilson, 1936), 36.

10. What have been called the *sites of pedagogy*—the expanding physical and digital places where instructors teach and students learn—are, increasingly, the websites of pedagogy; see Jeffrey R. Di Leo, Walter Jacobs, and Amy Lee, "The Sites of Pedagogy," *Symploke* 10, nos. 1–2 (2002): 7–12. For instance, the only text I use in my face-to-face senior-level seminar on Whitman is the online *Whitman Archive*. The website is as real a place to us as our computer classroom. The website is, in a very real sense, the classroom proper, although our physical shared space is also essential. The online archive means

that students are in the classroom when they're on campus in the computer lab, but also when they're at home, or when they're on the bus with a tablet or a smartphone. See Catherine Waitinas, "'A Noiseless Patient Spider': Whitman, Wikis, and the Web," *Teaching American Literature: A Journal of Theory and Practice* 2, no. 4 (2009): 47–74. This being said, I reject the notion that online coursework can replace what we do in face-to-face literary classrooms, especially at the advanced level. In other words, the online archive is a classroom per se only when it is paired with the face-to-face classroom. For manuscript study, it's essential that students can physically point to, circle, zoom in and out, and the like while also making actual eye contact with each other and hearing each other's voices—the sort of oral communication necessary to tease out the poems' meanings as a team.

11. Sarah Werner, "Where Material Book Culture Meets Digital Humanities," *Journal of Digital Humanities* 1, no. 3 (Summer 2012), http://journalofdigitalhumanities.org/1-3/where-material-book-culture-meets-digital-humanities-by-sarah-werner/.

12. These students used the iPad app Explain Everything, which has a very quick learning curve, and which allows users to import and manipulate images, short videos, text, and other materials. Because *The Whitman Archive* is open access, its materials are available for educational use in videos such as these, with proper attribution. My students' videos averaged twelve to fifteen minutes in length, but I'd recommend asking students to create shorter videos—the creating students can finish them more quickly, and the viewing students can watch more videos and are more likely to watch them in their entirety.

13. To satisfy the curious, these are the poems I've most recently assigned, all followed by their Huntington access numbers: "To the Future, " ca. 1860 (HM 11205); "To Him that was Crucified," ca. 1860 (HM 11208); "Thoughts," ca. 1860 (HM 11201); "Come, said my Soul," ca. 1874 (HM 6713), "Fancies at Navesink: The Pilot in the Mist," ca. 1884 (HM 1190); "Soon Shall the Winter's Foil be Here," ca. 1888 (HM 1192); and "To my Seventieth Year," ca. 1889 (HM 11207). The listed manuscripts are all available on *The Whitman Archive*: http://www.whitmanarchive.org/manuscripts/finding_aids/Huntington_CA.html.

14. "About the Archive: Whitman Handwriting Tool," *The Walt Whitman Archive*, http://www.whitmanarchive.org/about/guidelines/references/main_whithand.html; "Resources: Tools," *The Walt Whitman Archive*, http://www.whitmanarchive.org/resources/tools/index.html; "Life & Letters: Biography," *The Walt Whitman Archive*, http://www.whitmanarchive.org/biography/walt_whitman/index.html; "Commentary: The Walt Whitman Encyclopedia," *The Walt Whitman Archive*, http://www.whitmanarchive.org/criticism/current/encyclopedia/index.html.

15. Thus far, I haven't encountered any students who simply don't know how to read cursive handwriting, but with changes to elementary school curricula, I'm sure this is on the horizon. In the future, we might need to teach students how to read handwriting before we can do any paleographical analyses, hard copy or digital.

16. "Learn by Doing" is my university's motto. For this reason, my students might be uniquely positioned to appreciate and dive into collaborative manuscript study.

11. Making Digital Humanities Tools More Culturally Specific and More Culturally Sensitive

Celeste Tường Vy Sharpe
and Timothy B. Powell

CRITICISMS OF EUROCENTRISM in the digital humanities (DH) are not new. From Alan Liu raising the question "Where Is Cultural Criticism in the Digital Humanities?" to Tara McPherson's query "Why Are the Digital Humanities So White?" to Amy E. Earhart's "The Classroom and the Canon" in this volume (chapter 13), these important works call out the centrality and persistence of whiteness and Eurocentric models.[1] In the hope of making a constructive contribution toward helping DH move beyond the limitations of Eurocentrism and become more intellectually and culturally diverse, this essay focuses on pedagogical practices both for recognizing the limitations of existing platforms and imagining solutions that will enable digital humanities tools to more accurately represent how Indigenous peoples tell their own histories.

Pedagogical and Cultural Issues

Introductions to digital humanities courses often utilize a coverage approach, where instructors introduce students to a wide range of tools and methods for different purposes. These courses explore the collection, cleaning, analysis, and visualization of various data and metadata: geospatial, material, textual, and visual.[2] What is often missing, however, is a sustained conversation about the social and cultural foundations for those tools and methods—underpinnings that can render tools unfit for representing non-Western knowledge systems. As Miriam Posner argues, DH relies "on tools and infrastructure built for industry—or, in the best cases, for scientists. Which makes a certain amount of sense; one doesn't want to reinvent the wheel. But it's had material effects on the kind of work we can produce, and the horizons of possibility our work can open."[3] The argument for data and metadata standards in industry centers on a valuation of interoperability and shareability over the culturally diverse and specific. To be sure, there is substantial merit to the notion of connecting systems of information across the globe. But as Bethany Nowviskie compellingly states, there remains a strong "need to find a way to step back from patriarchal, colonial, heteronormative, and white mediation, and from its sense of control over time, in order (as Afrofuturist thinkers would have it) to make a new space-time in which broader and more diverse publics can assert that agency."[4] Building on Nowviskie's hope for a "new space-time," this essay recounts the pedagogical challenges faced in a DH class designed to contest the kind of "control over time" implicit in platforms such as Omeka, where the lack of temporal alternatives to chronological timelines are deeply linked to the history of colonization on these continents (e.g., the march of manifest destiny and the arrogant assumption that Indigenous history prior to European arrival is *prehistorical*). In doing so, our goal was to build a more culturally specific and carefully nuanced model of Iroquois or Haudenosaunee temporality.[5]

Many of the tools and platforms used in the digital humanities are built on the international standards for data formats published by the International Organization for Standardization, which promises interoperability and the potential to connect technological systems. Web-publishing platforms such as Omeka and timeline tools such as Neatline and TimelineJS were created around these data standards and, as such, are of limited use for representing events, narratives, and histories that cannot be narrowed down to a recognized temporal data point. Student assignments using Omeka, for example, often include students finding and uploading items, filling out robust metadata, and creating exhibits that present an interpretation.[6] Cultural critiques of the platform and, more generally, how to represent artifacts and narratives ethically and respectfully are largely absent from course syllabi. Notable exceptions to this are *The History Harvest* project started at the University of Nebraska-Lincoln, *Gibagadinamaagoom: "To Bring to Life, to Sanction, to Give Permission"* at the University of Pennsylvania, and the *Religions in Minnesota* project started at Carleton College.[7] But without formal and wider curricular inclusion, issues regarding representation of cultural diversity within the digital humanities and the digital world writ large risk remaining unspoken and thus unchanged.

To address these issues, we teamed up to design a course entitled Cultural Diversity and Digital Humanities at the University of Pennsylvania to teach students new ways of representing Indigenous narratives and histories that recognize and empower Native intellectual sovereignty (see Appendix 11.1). The class project focused on creating a timeline of Haudenosaunee history.

Over the span of the project, students were asked to consider several key questions: How to represent Haudenosaunee spiritual history (e.g., historical events misidentified as "mythical") in relation to the chronological timeline of European colonization?[8] How to depict what Lisa Brooks calls Indigenous "sacred geography" characterized by "a multitude of stories that recount migrations, revelations, and historical . . . incidents" on maps where the imposition of national and international borders cut up what the stories cut across?[9] How to read wampum belts as an alternative organization and classification system to the Dublin Core metadata schema for artifacts and narratives?[10] In short, the class was designed to explore the relationship between cultural codes and digital codes.

Pedagogically, the class was designed to expose the problem of ethnocentrism built into some of the leading DH exhibit building platforms and tools, to study how these technological oversights distort and demean Haudenosaunee stories of their own history, and to begin a discussion of how to design more culturally sensitive models. Rather than condemning DH as culturally biased, we adopted the pedagogical strategy of what Gerald Graff, at the height of the culture wars in the 1990s, called "teaching the conflicts" in the hope that doing so can "revitalize American education" and, in this case, the teaching of the digital humanities.[11] Confronting and imagining a way around technical limitations is, after all, a fundamental principle and value of DH.[12] As Amy E. Earhart writes in "Can Information be Unfettered? Race and the New Digital Humanities Canon": "We need to reinvigorate the spirit of previous scholars . . . who saw the digital as a way to enact changes in the canon."[13] If, as Jerome McGann suggests, "the entirety of our cultural inheritance will be transformed and reedited in digital forms," then, Earhart continues, "we must ensure that our representation of culture does not exclude work by people of color."[14] We are confident that the digital humanities can do a better job of reflecting, in this case, Haudenosaunee cosmology, although it must be emphasized that success depends on serious engagement with community-based elders, teachers, librarians, and tribal historians, all of whom deserve recognition as "DH scholars."[15] If the development of digital tools and their embedded epistemological assumptions are to succeed in moving beyond Eurocentrism, then collaboration with non-Western cultures who do not see, in this case, chronological time as a "universal" value becomes imperative.

In keeping with this strategy, the essay begins by describing the "Timeline of Haudenosaunee History" project assigned in class. The pedagogical analysis includes the progression of assignments, students' collaborative efforts, and lessons learned by the students and instructors regarding the facility of extant digital tools to represent Indigenous culture, history, and literature (see Appendix 11.2). In the second half of the essay, we discuss a work in progress titled "Mapping Temporal Patterns in Haudenosaunee Oratory" that came about as a response to the technological and cultural limitations encountered by the class. Both projects were made possible through close cooperation with Richard (Rick) Hill (Tuscarora), director of the Deyohahá:ge:ge: Indigenous Knowledge Centre at Six Nations Polytechnic (SNP) on the Six Nations of the Grand River reserve in Ontario. By setting these two projects in dialogue, new questions arise about the relationship between space, time, and culture as we endeavor to imagine a more fluid model of time wherein ancestors from precolonial times manifest themselves, powerfully, in the present moment along with those seven generations in the future.[16]

This critique of the chronological timelines and metadata standards embedded into web-publishing platforms like Omeka offers no alternative temporal models. In keeping with the collection's goals of expanding and enriching field-specific questions, we present a case study of a class project designed to model Haudenosaunee (Iroquois) ritual use of nonlinear temporality. One of the important contributions Native American and Indigenous studies can make to the field of digital humanities is viewing the field from an alternate cultural subject position. More specifically, studying how history unfolds in Haudenosaunee formal oratory reveals chronological time is not a universal truth, but a cultural conceit of the dominant culture. The assumption that nineteenth-century history moves in a linear progression from Reconstruction to the Industrial Age should be carefully examined. Expanding received notions of nineteenth-century literary forms, the essay argues that Haudenosaunee wampum belts and the accompanying oratory richly deserve to be studied alongside James Fenimore Cooper's novels about "Mingos" or Haudenosaunee. By making a video recording of Rick Hill's contemporary oration, whose historical echoes can be traced back through the nineteenth to the mid-eighteenth century, we hope to make accessible to instructors and students a literary form that tells a very different story than Cooper's stereotypical inscription of the vanishing Indian myth. Chronological time deeply informs historical reasoning, particularly the idea that to be considered nineteenth-century literature the document had to be written between 1800 and 1899. The nonlinear storytelling of Haudenosaunee history suggests that the contemporary wampum belt and Rick Hill's oratory is a literary form empowered to invoke stories from the eighteenth and nineteenth centuries into the present, confounding chronological timelines and their attendant historical reasoning.

"Timeline of Haudenosaunee History" Class Project

One of the most centrally important, and delicate, questions that arose in creating the syllabus for Cultural Diversity and Digital Humanities was the strategy for teaching students to see the cultural codes that are largely invisible to the untrained eye. As Tara McPherson helpfully observes, "Much of the work in the digital humanities [proceeds] as if technologies from XML to databases [are] neutral tools."[17] McPherson's point is well taken, but we worried that the technical nature of her analysis might fly over the heads of the undergraduates enrolled in the course with no previous experience in the digital humanities.[18] So we adopted a more humanistic approach based on Powell's relationship to Rick Hill; together they are working to digitize archival materials and return them to the Deyohahá:ge:ge: Indigenous Knowledge Centre at Six Nations Polytechnic, where an extensive digital archive is being built with materials from the National Anthropological Archive at the Smithsonian Institution and the American Philosophical Society. These materials are being used in a highly innovative educational program, The Two Row Research Partnership (TRRP) between SNP and McMaster University. Rick Hill provided the data for the "Timeline of Haudenosaunee History" project, and students were told their target audience was the TRRP group. The TRRP program is based on the Two Row Wampum belt or *Kaswentah* that forms the historical basis for Haudenosaunee diplomacy with European colonizers—the two row imagery symbolizing a non-assimilative model recognizing the sovereignty of both partners, which dates back to the early seventeenth century. As Rick Hill and Daniel Coleman write, "the TRRP group of student, faculty, and community researchers will co-create written, audio-visual, and digital materials to inform twenty-first-century relationships *within* Indigenous communities as well as neighboring communities."[19] In this way, the students contributed to an ongoing collaborative project that gave their work immediate real-world stakes. Not only did this reinforce student participation in the public humanities, but it also proved to have positive pedagogical benefits in that it dispelled any notion that the project was culturally neutral (see Appendix 11.3).

Ironically, perhaps, the first part of the course was carefully designed to set the foundation for the eventual failure of the DH tools and methods in the context of Haudenosaunee history. The students were asked to add one event to the list of dates Rick Hill had provided: the Haudenosaunee origin story of Sky Woman. In the story, as told by the widely respected Faith Keeper Tom Porter (Sakokweniókwas), Sky Woman falls through a hole in the sky world, tumbling until a flock of blue herons cushion her fall and set her down gently on the back of a big turtle where, with the help of the animals, she creates the world.[20] The story of Sky Woman is a critical part of Haudenosaunee history that deserves to be depicted equally along with the events that can be described with standardized temporal data. By reminding the students that the project was designed for the Haudenosaunee people, our hope was that this connection created a more empathic bond that would enable the students to see how the erasure of the Sky Woman story from conventional timelines carried greater ramifications. Indeed, we hoped that students would feel that the erasure of Haudenosaunee history echoed the removal of the people from the land and the cultural genocide perpetrated upon the Haudenosaunee by the boarding school systems in both the United States and Canada.

To prepare the students for this moment three weeks into the class, we read the introduction to Jean O'Brien's *Firsting and Lasting: Writing Indians out of Existence in New England*, which convincingly demonstrates the uninterrupted continuity of colonization from Plymouth Rock to the present day. O'Brien (Ojibwe) writes:

> New Englanders embraced Indians because doing so enabled them to establish unambiguously their own modernity. Non-Indians narrated their own present against what they constructed as the backdrop of a past symbolized by Indian peoples and their cultures. The master narrative of New England was that it had made a stark break with the past, replacing 'uncivilized' peoples whose histories and cultures they represented as illogically rooted in nature, tradition, and superstition, whereas New Englanders symbolized the "civilized" order of culture, science, and reason.[21]

Translating back into the terms of the class project, the point on the timeline associated with 1492 instigates a "stark break" between the "prehistoric" and "historic" periods based on the "fact" that only European cultures possessed alphabetic writing and therefore actually had "history."[22] And while the Eurocentrism of such a conceit may appear almost blinding, the American studies theorist Wai Chee Dimock is absolutely correct when she writes, in "Non-Newtonian Time," that the cultural authority of "numerical chronology [is] probably the least examined dogma of modern thought."[23] Dimock points out that the Newtonian idea that time was a "universal value" was discredited by Albert Einstein more than a century ago, and yet our research shows that no DH exhibit building platform offers a suitable alternative to the chronological timeline.

Given the absence of DH tools designed to correlate history and culture, we also wanted to guard against the risk of students immediately losing faith in the digital humanities. The next section of the course, therefore, was devoted to strengthening the students' resolve that DH can play a meaningful role in suturing these historical ruptures in ways that might directly benefit Indigenous communities. Powell's article, "Digital Knowledge Sharing: Forging Partnerships between Scholars, Archives, and Indigenous Communities," recounts the digital knowledge sharing initiative he implemented at the American Philosophical Society, where he directed the Center for Native American and Indigenous Research (CNAIR) from 2008 to 2016, with senior archivist Brian Carpenter. The digital repatriation project shared stories, audio recordings, and photographs with more than 150 Indigenous communities across Central and North America, helping to preserve languages on the brink of extinction, to generate millions of dollars in grant funding for tribes to build digital archives in their communities, and to preserve more than thirty thousand square kilometers of Indigenous homelands.[24] Siobhan Senier's "Digitizing Indigenous History: Trends and Challenges" provides an excellent overview of new projects devoted to digitizing Indigenous history such as the *Yale Indian Papers Project*, *The Occum Circle* project at Dartmouth, and Kimberly Christen's *Mukurtu* project to develop a content management system specifically designed for culturally sensitive management of Indigenous collections, to name just a few.[25] The goal of this section, which came immediately after teaching the conflict between the Haudenosaunee oral tradition and embedded chronological timelines, was designed to instill confidence in students that the cultural limitations hidden beneath the assumption that the chronological timeline is a universal constant rather than a product of colonization must be contested and, hopefully, overcome.

In the second half of the semester, the class turned to the pragmatic lessons of building a digital exhibit in Omeka that would include some sort of timeline. In meetings prior to the beginning of the semester, we had several considerations to balance in the process of deciding on platforms and tools. First, we wanted to manage the technical learning curve for students. Since the class did not require coding proficiency or any prior technical knowledge, we wanted to use technologies that had easily navigable graphical user interfaces and substantial end-user documentation. Second, we wanted to expose students to digital humanities tools that were well established to highlight common approaches and practices in the field and to offer them opportunities to gain firsthand knowledge of how to work with the technologies. Lastly, we wanted to use tools that had institutional support and did not require students to pay for access. This allowed us to connect the course to the burgeoning DH infrastructure at the University of Pennsylvania, rather than take on the additional costs of facilitating access to the technology and ameliorating a potential "boom-and-bust" situation where the projects sunset at the end of the course.[26]

Given the large number of images and text provided by Hill, most of which could be plotted on a conventional chronological timeline, we decided that Omeka was the best choice for both collecting and describing the items given its robust metadata capabilities. In addition, Penn provides institutional support by subscribing to a hosted version of the platform. While Omeka lacks Native timeline functionality, it provided a useful wrapper for aggregating the digital artifacts, creating interpretive exhibits, and displaying externally created timeline content within the same digital space as the artifacts. Nick

Okrent, coordinator and librarian for the humanities collection at Penn, set up the course site and uploaded all the digital images of the materials prior to the start of the course.[27] With the Omeka site established, the team turned to considering available timeline tools. In the end, we selected TimelineJS—a standalone timeline generator tool—for its lower technical learning curve and clean visual design. Okrent also generated the Google Sheets that students would use to enter timeline information for use in TimelineJS, and added the embed code to an exhibit page in the Omeka site so that the timeline, once populated, would display.

During the section of class dedicated to teaching students the praxis of building an Omeka exhibit, students learned about metadata standards and practices and then applied their knowledge to describing the digital materials uploaded into Omeka. Sharpe and the students discussed how to select the most appropriate Dublin Core fields, how the fields could be defined for the purposes of this project, and how to consistently fill in the relevant information for their assigned digital objects. For the purposes of the assignment, Powell selected and provided guidance for the thirteen relevant fields for each object: title, subject, description, creator, source, publisher, date, contributor, relation, coverage, abstract, date created, and rights holder. Powell wrote the instructions for each field in a conversational tone to encourage quick understanding and engagement by the students and to encompass the wide range of materials and historical eras of the timeline. For example, the title field had the following guidance: "Begin with the date to which the item is assigned on the timeline. Do your best to briefly describe the entry (a few words). Remember that I will review the titles at a later date, so don't worry too much about getting it perfect."

In the second part of the assignment, students worked collaboratively using Google Sheets to compile the required elements for the timeline. Each entry on the timeline included a date, title, and description—images with captions were encouraged but not required. Students then exported their collaborative work into TimelineJS, creating a chronological timeline embedded in the course Omeka site. Reckoning with the imprecise and nonstandard temporal data of the Sky Woman story provided a point of constant frustration for the students. The class discussed ways to fit Sky Woman into the timeline, and brainstormed different "hacks," such as assigning the story an arbitrary date range that would make it visually appear before events denoted by chronological time. Each suggestion generated lively discussion, but none were deemed perfect solutions. The class settled on separating the story into five parts, based on the events described, and assigned each part a date range (50 CE to 1000 for part one, 51 CE to 1000 for part two, etc.). While this provided a solution of sorts, it fell short of the instructors' and students' standards for culturally sensitive digital humanities praxis, particularly in light of the goal of contributing this timeline work to the Two Row Research Project. In this way, the students gained the experience of populating a timeline with pre-eighteenth century content and a keener sense of cultural sensitivity that pointed to the challenges yet to come in DH design.

By way of conclusion, we set aside time at the end of the semester to look back on what we had learned. Pedagogically, in both cultural and technological terms, the project succeeded as a way to teach students about the cultural assumptions encoded in data and metadata standards and the effects of these limitations on Haudenosaunee history. What seemed to resonate most powerfully with the students was, once the timeline's cloak of cultural neutrality was torn away, the realization that we ourselves had perpetrated violence upon the Haudenosaunee people we thought we were helping. It was no longer a technical problem somebody else had to fix: we had erased the story of Sky Woman and the teachings of the Peacemaker, one of the most sophisticated, well-documented, and well-preserved Indigenous histories in North America. Every year, the Haudenosaunee recite orations lasting days, all in the language(s). Yet the most sophisticated digital tools available at an elite university like the University of Pennsylvania could not re-present the story as it is understood and conveyed. This erasure has historical echoes in the appropriation of Haudenosaunee land on the Six Nations of the Grand River reserve and, later, in the boarding schools that systematically attempted to strip Haudenosaunee children of their language and culture; this galvanized the class to work on new ways to correct the problem.[28] Humility is not a bad thing for Penn students to take away from a DH course, and, through discussion, they demonstrated a greater appreciation for the challenges present in DH and a stronger appreciation of the need to foster equitable and respectful collaboration among experts in Native communities and academia. Ironically, the course also demonstrated that the living oral and beaded archive of the Haudenosaunee, at the very least, deserves closer study as a sustainable knowledge system worthy of the attention of DH scholars.

We hope, therefore, the experiences of the class may offer a lesson for the digital humanities writ large. The lack of attention to cultural specificity in the design of widely used tools not only hurts underrepresented cultures such as the Haudenosaunee but also discredits our field in the eyes of humanists who successfully negotiated the cultural turn twenty-five years ago.[29] We have complete faith that DH scholars can make a meaningful contribution, but it will take a concerted effort. In the next section, we argue that DH would benefit from working directly with Indigenous communities, who themselves are doing very innovative work with digital technologies. Across the continent, these communities are facilitating the digital repatriation of songs, stories, and photographs at a moment of unprecedented cultural revitalization in Indian

Country.[30] In terms of DH scholarship, digital repatriation may be viewed as so simplistic that funds for digitization are now being restricted by granting agencies like the Mellon Foundation, even in the Diversity Program. We would ask that this subfield of DH not be dismissed or defunded because we are not using supercomputers, but that instead its value be measured by the impact that the digitization of archival materials is making in Indian Country—preserving severely endangered languages, creating economic opportunities in some of the poorest communities in the country, and preserving boreal forests along with traditional ecological knowledge that can help save the planet.[31] As we hope to show in the next section, new tools like Scalar make it possible to create more innovative designs. Coupled with the emergence of *Mukurtu*, a content management system designed specifically for Indigenous communities that allows them to utilize XML to encode protocols for cultural sensitivity, these tools now provide the opportunity to utilize these programs to teach our students that DH can play a leading role in supporting cultural diversity and working to benefit underserved communities.[32]

"Mapping Temporal Patterns of Haudenosaunee Oratory"

After a semester exploring the cultural limitations of chronological timelines, Sharpe and Powell set out to design an alternative form of temporal representation that better embodies Haudenosaunee culture and history. Rather than beginning with a series of chronological dates, as we did in the class project, we decided to begin with an instance from the Haudenosaunee oral tradition. More specifically, Rick Hill generously agreed to create a video recording in 2015 about a wampum belt; the video records a formal exchange with Tim Powell, who at the time was the director of CNAIR. In 2014, Hill presented a wampum belt to CNAIR's senior archivist Brian Carpenter as a gift to thank CNAIR for digitizing, free of charge, a large number of manuscripts, audio recordings, and photographs to help build the digital archive at SNP. Hill, in turn, informed the American Philosophical Society (APS) which archival materials in its extensive Haudenosaunee collections are culturally sensitive and advised it to establish a protocol to protect these materials from being digitized and placed on the web.[33] Wampum belts constitute a canonical form of literature for the Haudenosaunee.[34] The APS belt is thus new in the sense that it is made of glass beads, but the pattern woven in beads—two purple squares joined by a purple line on a white background—represents the iconic Haudenosaunee image of the Covenant Chain, a symbol that dates back to the early seventeenth century. In keeping with Haudenosaunee protocols, Powell brought the belt to Deyohahá:ge:ge: Indigenous Knowledge Centre the following year "to polish the Chain of Friendship." Rick Hill's formal oration and the wampum belt itself thus form the basis for the "Mapping Temporal Patterns of Haudenosaunee Oratory" project designed by Sharpe in Scalar, with Powell providing the cultural commentary.[35] On the backend, we observed that TimelineJS and other timeline tools require events and phenomena to conform to a linear progression from oldest to most recent. To complicate this model, we sought to imagine a temporal alternative that would represent chronological and Haudenosaunee history together. (A quick aside: One needs to be cautious when using phrases like *Haudenosaunee history*. Rick Hill and other Haudenosaunee traditional knowledge keepers such as Tom Porter, Bear Clan elder of the Mohawk Nation, would be the first to remind us that no one person can speak on behalf of all Six Nations that comprise the Haudenosaunee people; we are analyzing just one instance of the oral tradition with no claim to representing the vast complexity that is Haudenosaunee history).[36] Sharpe uploaded the video of Hill and Powell's meeting to YouTube, which, of course, introduces the representation of chronological time in the form of the counter embedded into the video's frame. To create a countertemporal narrative, Powell tagged the transcript to denote the temporal shifts in Hill's oratory, which Sharpe then annotated onto the YouTube video so that the temporal tag appears at the moment when Hill initiates a shift. To clarify, by *temporal shift* we are referring to references within the oratory to specific events such as the Lancaster Treaty of 1742 or the invocation of the Peacemaker story, which cannot be assigned a chronological date but are no less real and are thus treated equally in the annotated video.

Sharpe chose the web-publishing platform Scalar to provide further layers of cultural context and discussion to the annotated video. The Scalar project thus centers on the video of Hill and Powell and the tagged transcript and uses the platform's flexible configurability of media, pages, and tags to present an alternate representation of chronological and Haudenosaunee history that is interconnected and nonlinear. Using the annotation feature in Scalar—in addition to the YouTube annotations—adds another layer of contextual information related to each temporal reference. Each annotation is also its own "page" of content, which offers further discussion of the cultural and historical context. One section of the project lists the temporal references in the order spoken by Hill, and each reference is linked to the corresponding video annotation. In this way, the order in which Hill invokes each reference provides the chronology of the project in place of the standard sequential chronology.

Another section of the project features a visualization of the relationship between the temporal references that shows the video as the central node with each reference connected and equally spaced around the video. In this way, the visualization collapses some of the entrenched conventions for visually understanding the relationship between time and space: whereas on chronological timelines the space between points denotes distance between temporal moments, our Scalar visualization instead shows the temporal moments equally arrayed in relation to Hill's oratory to allude to the nonlinear Haudenosaunee notion of temporality.

To connect the references in the oratory to the temporal events represented in the annotations requires a good deal of historical knowledge about Haudenosaunee culture, since they are essentially fleeting invocations of much longer stories. Because the audience for this essay are not specialists in Haudenosaunee culture, it is worth taking the time to quickly sketch out the stories behind a few of the temporal tags, providing readers with a better sense of the scope and complexity of Rick Hill's masterful use of the temporal patterns encoded in the oratory (a fuller analysis is available on the Scalar site).

1. The video begins with Hill observing, "Wampum has a long history among our people." The origin of wampum, according to the Haudenosaunee oral tradition, dates back to the time of the Peacemaker, whose teachings form the basis of the canonical Great Law of Peace. (Here, perhaps, is a glimpse of the more diverse canon that Earhart calls for in this volume.) The Great Law constitutes the foundation of the Confederacy of the five (and later six) nations—the Onondaga, Seneca, Mohawk, Oneidea, Cayuga, and Tuscarora Nations. There is speculation this occurred perhaps as early as 1141, although anthropologists argue it came about much later. We rejected assigning a chronological date and instead opted to use the word *swaige:hah*, which in Cayuga means "further back than *swe'geh* ('long ago')"—we are indebted to Roronhiakehte Elijah Deer, a revitalization strategist for the Six Nations Language Commission at Grand River, for his help with the language.[37]

2. The oratory then shifts back to the present (the video was made in 2015) when Rick Hill explains that the belt signifies "an agreement with the APS."

3. When he says, "It's a Covenant Chain belt," the reference becomes more temporally complex, with different historical events layered atop one another.

   a. The uppermost level is, of course, the present moment in which the Covenant Chain metaphor is being applied to the APS belt. But the iconic image/story of the Covenant Chain is so powerful that it immediately brings forth much deeper registers of time.

   b. The eldest story is that of the *Aterihwihsón:sera Kaswentah* or Two Row Wampum belt that forms the basis of Haudenosaunee diplomacy with all European colonizers. Here again chronology is an unreliable, contested system for representing one of the most important moments in Haudenosaunee history. As the historian Jon Parmenter points out, the date associated with the first presentation of the belt, 1613, continues to be hotly debated by non-Native historians. And so here again we eschew chronological time and represent the temporal event as "The origins of *Kaswentah*."[38]

c. Rick Hill could name dozens, if not hundreds, of other instances of the metaphor of the Covenant Chain being used in diplomatic relations between the Haudenosaunee and the American colonies. Here we focus on one particularly significant instance, the Lancaster Treaty of 1744. Hill is perfectly aware that Powell knows this text well, since it was published by Benjamin Franklin two years after he founded the American Philosophical Society. Hill reminds Powell of "the old Covenant Chain idea" and then shifts into a formal, very old style of oratory that draws on metaphors used by the great Onondaga orator Canasatego at the Treaty of Lancaster (and many other orators both before and after). Hill, for example, explains the significance of the line on the wampum belt (e.g., the Covenant Chain) as symbolizing a "pathway" that connects "the two parties making an agreement" and the "commitment to have open, honest communications between us [and] safe passage as we go from your fire or your home to our fire and our home. . . . We have to make sure that path is always clear." Canasatego similarly reminded the governor of Pennsylvania, George Thomas: "You then came nearer Home, and told us, 'You had left your House, and were come thus far on Behalf of the whole People of *Pennsylvania* to see us; to renew your Treaties; to brighten the Covenant Chain, and to confirm your Friendship with us.' Interestingly, Governor Thomas welcomed his "Friends and Brethren of the Six Nations" to Lancaster by acknowledging "we are mutually engaged to keep the Road between us clear and open."[39]

It is fascinating to speculate on how Rick Hill's use of the wampum belt and oratorical metaphors, working in concert, powerfully shape Powell's understanding of what the partnership between the APS and SNP entails. Again, Powell can only speak to what it means to him personally at this time. The goal here is to develop a more empathetic form of scholarship and pedagogy by focusing on how it felt to be in the presence of two of the most powerful stories—the Peacemaker condoling Hiawatha with the first wampum belt and the meanings encoded in the Two Row Wampum belt—in the Haudenosaunee canon.

Deeply unsure if he could or should connect himself to the sacred story of the Peacemaker, Powell at first distanced himself out of respect for the Haudenosaunee culture of the Longhouse, where such stories are told. This cultural/temporal distance, once established, immediately gives way to the Covenant Chain story, which calls Powell closer. This is accomplished through the artful use of metaphors. The linked metaphors of *Covenant Chain*, *Home*, and *Friendship* in the oratories of Hill, Canasatego, and Thomas work to foreshorten what, on a timeline, would visually appear to be a great temporal distance between 1744 and 2015. The "affect" of this temporal shifting serves to make Powell acutely aware of how this agreement between the APS and

SNP, sealed by the presentation of wampum, seems to lie ever so lightly over the space-time of the meeting between the Haudenosaunee and the colony of Pennsylvania in 1744. Powell found the compression of time that brings these events into the present to be at once strangely disconcerting and immensely comforting. The "irrationality" (read nonlinear logic) of this creative patterning of time reminds Powell of his connection to Benjamin Franklin, both as the founder of the APS and as an attendant to the Lancaster Treaty proceedings, thus greatly magnifying the gravitas of the agreement and deepening Powell's commitment. The effect/affect of bringing these two temporal events into close contact also serves to strengthen the sense of commitment of the APS to continue sharing its extensive holdings through digitization with the Six Nations to restore their sovereign right to be the keepers of their own history and of SNP's commitment to guide the APS in protecting culturally sensitive materials from Haudenosaunee communities. As Rick Hill explains in the video, this alternative form of temporality, can perhaps best be explained as a form of "living memory" in which the Covenant Chain is not a distant relic of the early seventeenth century but a metaphor with the power to shape events in the present and future such as the Two Row Research Partnership or the ongoing relationship between the APS and the Deyohahá:ge:ge: Indigenous Knowledge Centre.

Although this relationship—an agreement to digitize some archival materials and not to digitize culturally sensitive materials on behalf of the communities of origin—is not the way the digital humanities is usually perceived by scholars in the field, such partnerships between Indigenous communities, scholars, and archives can, we hope, benefit the field. This is the hope for a "new space-time" of which Bethany Nowviskie dreams. "Mapping Temporal Patterns of Haudenosaunee Oratory" and the work being done with Indigenous partners answer Alan Liu's admonishment that "digital humanists should create technologies that fundamentally reimagine humanities advocacy . . . in the form of publicly meaningful representations of the humanities."[40] Additionally, prototyping the Mapping Temporal Patterns project in Scalar opens up new avenues for critical student engagement with digital tools in future classes: Powell intends to incorporate Scalar as a platform for a series of digital exhibits that will be developed for a new program he is directing at the University of Pennsylvania titled Educational Partnerships with Indigenous Communities (EPIC). Scalar's flexibility is crucial for more imaginative engagements with non-Western cultures that deconstruct the notion that chronological time is a universal value and that allow for the creation of culturally specific interfaces for digital archives like the *Gibagadinamaagoom: "To Bring to Life, to Sanction, to Give Permission,"* which is based on the seven directions of Ojibwe cosmology.[41]

There is enormous potential for further scholarship in this field. The American Philosophical Society, the Archive of Traditional Music at Indiana University, the National Anthropological Archives at the Smithsonian Institute, and the California Language Archive at the University of California, Berkeley have digitized or are in the process of digitizing hundreds of thousands of manuscripts, audio recordings, and photographs related to Indigenous history. Perhaps less well known to scholars outside of anthropology, Native nations across North America are in the midst of an extraordinary period of cultural revitalization that can benefit enormously from digital repatriation efforts. It is our greatest hope, therefore, that these small projects will encourage other DH scholars to incorporate culture into the design of new tools that can be used to establish the field's growing commitment to the public humanities.

The appendixes for this chapter, assignments for a course by Timothy B. Powell and Celeste Tường Vy Sharpe on cultural diversity and the digital humanities, can be found at www.press.uillinois.edu/books/TeachingWithDH.

Notes

1. Alan Liu, "Where Is Cultural Criticism in the Digital Humanities?," in *Debates in the Digital Humanities*, ed. Matthew K. Gold (Minneapolis: University of Minnesota Press, 2012), http://dhdebates.gc.cuny.edu/debates/; Tara McPherson, "Why Are the Digital Humanities So White? or Thinking the Histories of Race and Computation," in Gold, *Debates in the Digital Humanities*.

2. Brett D. Hirsch, ed., *Digital Humanities Pedagogy: Practices, Principles and Politics* (Cambridge: Open Book, 2012); Eileen Gardiner and Ronald G. Musto, *The Digital Humanities: A Primer for Students and Scholars* (New York: Cambridge University Press, 2015).

3. Miriam Posner, "Money and Time," *Miriam Posner's Blog*, March 14, 2016, http://miriamposner.com/blog/money-and-time/.

4. Bethany Nowviskie, "alternate futures/usable pasts," *Bethany Nowviskie* (blog), October 24, 2016, http://nowviskie.org/2016/alternate-futures-usable-pasts/.

5. For more on the relationship between time and colonization, especially in the Haudenosaunee context, see Audra Simpson, *Mohawk Interruptus: Political Life across the Borders of Settler States* (Durham, N.C.: Duke University Press, 2014), 72–73; Tom Porter (Sakokweniónkwas), *And Grandma Said . . . Iroquois Teachings as Passed Down through the Oral Tradition* (Bloomington, Ind.: Xlibris, 2008), 308–309; Rick Monture, *We Share Our Matters: Two Centuries of Writing and Resistance at Six Nations of the Grand River* (Winnipeg: University of Manitoba Press, 2014), 3, 18; John Mohawk, "Racism: An American Ideology," in *Thinking in Indian: A John Mohawk Reader*, ed. José Barreiro (Golden, Colo.: Fulcram, 2010), 224–225; and Linda Tuhiwai Smith, *Decolonizing Methodologies: Research and Indigenous Peoples* (London: Zed Books, 1999), 30–31.

6. Alison Marsh, "Omeka in the Classroom: The Challenges of Teaching Material Culture in a Digital World," *Literary and Linguistic Computing* 28, no. 2 (2013): 279–282; Jeffrey W. McClurken, "Teaching with Omeka," *ProfHacker: Teaching, Tech, and Productivity* (blog), August 9, 2010, http://www.chronicle.com/blogs/profhacker/teaching-with-omeka/26078.

7. *The History Harvest*, University of Nebraska-Lincoln, accessed March 26, 2017, http://historyharvest.unl.edu/; *Gibagadinamaagoom: "To Bring to Life, to Sanction, to Give Permission,"* accessed March 26, 2017, http://ojibwearchive.sas.upenn.edu/; *Religions in Minnesota*, Carleton College, accessed March 26, 2017, https://religionsmn.carleton.edu/.

8. As explained below, the class never did solve the problem of how to plot the origin story of Sky Woman on the chronological timeline. The students read the version told by Tom Porter, *And Grandma Said*, 40–90.

9. Lisa Brooks, *The Common Pot: The Recovery of Native Space in the Northeast* (Minneapolis: University of Minnesota Press, 2008); Michel de Certeau, *The Practice of Everyday Life* (Berkeley: University of California Press, 1984), 129.

10. Several scholars have been exploring the idea that wampum belts served as a kind of Indigenous archiving system. See, for example, Ellen Cushman, "Wampum, Sequoyan, and Story: Decolonizing the Digital Archive," *College English* 76, no. 2 (2013): 116. Rick Hill, in his video with Tim Powell discussed later in the essay, states that the quahog shells that were used in older Haudenosaunee wampum belts had the power to remember the words spoken over them. The belts are considered to be diplomatic records and continue to be used as such in Haudenosaunee communities today. An excellent example of this is the Two Row Research Partnership, developed by Richard Hill and Daniel Coleman, which is discussed and cited later in the essay.

11. Gerald Graff, *Beyond the Culture Wars: How Teaching the Conflicts Can Revitalize American Education* (New York: W.W. Norton, 1993).

12. Anne Burdick, Johanna Drucker, Peter Lunenfeld, Todd Presner, and Jeffrey Schnapp, *Digital_Humanities* (Cambridge, Mass.: MIT Press, 2013).

13. Amy E. Earhart, "Can Information Be Unfettered? Race and the New Digital Humanities Canon," in Gold, *Debates in the Digital Humanities*.

14. Jerome McGann, "Culture and Technology: The Way We Live Now, What Is to Be Done?," *New Literary History* 36, no. 1 (2005): 71–82.

15. Timothy B. Powell, "Digital Knowledge Sharing: Forging Partnerships between Scholars, Archives, and Indigenous Communities," *Museum Anthropology Review*, 10, no. 2 (2016), https://scholarworks.iu.edu/journals/index.php/mar/article/view/20269.

16. A core value of Haudenosaunee teachings is the idea that "the Seventh Generation value takes into consideration those who are not yet born but who will inherit the earth." "Values," *Haudenosaunee Confederacy*, accessed March 26, 2017, http://www.haudenosauneeconfederacy.com/values.html. For a powerful critique of *objectivist history*, see Simpson, *Mohawk Interruptus*, 74–75.

17. McPherson, "Why Are the Digital Humanities," 142.

18. The Price Lab for the Digital Humanities at the University of Pennsylvania had just opened in the fall of 2016; up to this point there were few curricular opportunities for students to learn digital humanities tools and methods.

19. Richard Hill and Daniel Coleman, "Two Row Research Partnership," Six Nation Polytechnic, accessed March 26, 2017, http://www.snpolytechnic.com/indigenous-knowledge-centre.

20. Porter, *And Grandma Said*, 40–53.

21. Jean O'Brien, *Firsting and Lasting: Writing Indians out of Existence in New England*, (Minneapolis: University of Minnesota Press, 2010), xxi.

22. Walter Mignolo, *The Darker Side of the Renaissance: Literacy, Territoriality & Colonization* (Ann Arbor: University of Michigan Press, 2003), 412.

23. Wai Chee Dimock, "Non-Newtonian Time: Robert Lowell, Roman History, Vietnam War," *American Literature* 74, no. 4 (2002): 916.

24. Powell, "Digital Knowledge Sharing."

25. Siobhan Senier, "Digitizing Indigenous History: Trends and Challenges," *Journal of Victorian Culture* 19, no. 3 (2014): 396–402.

26. Posner, "Money and Time."

27. Nick Okrent's assistance setting up the site and uploading the images saved us one to two hours of technical work. Whereas some courses include in-class time for the students to upload images through the Omeka dashboard to learn the interface, thanks to Nick's help, we were able to avoid the inevitable in-class technical hiccups that come with uploading files simultaneously on spotty Wi-Fi.

28. For more on land claims and boarding schools on the Six Nations of the Grand River reserve in Ontario, see Theresa McCarthy, *In Divided Unity: Haudenosaunee Reclamation at Grand River* (Tucson: University of Arizona Press, 2016); and Susan M. Hill, "Conducting Haudenosaunee Historical Research from Home: In the Shadow of the Six Nations-Caledonia Reclamation," *American Indian Quarterly*, 33, no. 4 (2009): 479–497.

29. Liu, "Where Is Cultural Criticism?"

30. Examples include, but are not limited to, Lyz Jaakola and Timothy Powell, "'The Songs Are Alive': Bringing Frances Densmore's Recordings Back Home to Fond du Lac Tribal and Community College," *Oxford Handbook of Musical Repatriation*, ed. Frank Gunderson, forthcoming from Oxford University Press in 2018; Powell, "Anthropology of Revitalization: Digitizing the American Philosophical Society's Native American Collections," *The Franz Boas Papers*, vol. 1: *Franz Boas as Public Intellectual—Theory, Ethnography, Activism*, ed. Regna Darnell, Michelle Hamilton, Robert L. A. Hancock, and Joshua Smith (Lincoln: University of Nebraska Press, 2015); Powell, "Encoding Culture: Building a Digital Archive Based on Traditional Ojibwe Codes of Conduct," in *The American Literature Scholar in the Digital Age*, ed. Amy E. Earhart and Andrew Jewell (Ann Arbor: University of Michigan Press, 2011); Jason Baird Jackson, "Ethnography and Ethnographers in Museum-Community Partnerships," *Practicing Anthropology* 22, no. 4 (2000): 29–32; Paul Grant-Costa, Tobias Glazaand, and Michael Sletcher, "The Common Pot: Editing Native American Materials," *Scholarly Editing: The Annual of the Association for Documentary Editing* 33 (2012), http://scholarlyediting.org/2012/essays/essay.commonpot.html; Kimberly Christen, "Opening Archives: Respectful Repatriation," *American Archivist* 74, no. 1 (2011): 185–210; and Sonya Atalay, *Community-Based Archaeology: Research with, by, and for Indigenous and Local Communities* (Berkeley: University of California, 2012).

31. Powell, "Digital Knowledge Sharing."

32. Kimberly Christen, dir., *Mukurtu*, Washington State University, accessed March 26, 2017, http://mukurtu.org/about/.

33. Establishing protocols for the protection of culturally sensitive Indigenous materials in archives has been an ongoing struggle. While he was the director of the Center for Native American and Indigenous Research at the American Philosophical Society, Powell was part of a Native American advisory board that succeeded in getting the APS to adopt protocols, which can be found at https://www.amphilsoc.org/sites/default/files/2017–11/attachments/APS%20Protocols.pdf. For more on the national struggle to get the Society of American Archivists to adopt protocols see Jennifer O'Neal, "Respect, Recognition, and Reciprocity: *The Protocols for Native American Archival Materials*," in *Identity Palimpsests: Archiving Ethnicity in the U.S. and Canada*, ed. Dominique Daniel and Amalia Levi (Sacramento: Litwin Books, 2014), 125–142.

34. Powell's understanding of wampum has been deeply informed by Margaret Bruchac, who curates *On the Wampum Trail*, accessed March 26, 2017, https://wampumtrail.wordpress.com/. See also Rebecca Lush, "Wampum, Bibles, Treaties, and American Letters: Native American and Anglo-American Communications in Early America," *Early American Literature* 49, no. 3 (2014): 771–785.

35. The video and the Scalar project, *Temporal Patterns in Haudenosaunee History*, can be viewed at http://scalar.usc.edu/works/haudenosaunee-oratory/. The video, housed at the American Philosophical Society, was created by Diana Marsh and Lynette Ragouby and edited by Timothy B. Powell.

36. Porter, *And Grandma Said*, 46–47.

37. Roronhiakehte Elijah Deer, personal communication with author, February 22, 2016. For more on the Great Law of Peace see John Mohawk, "Words of Peace—A Six Nations Tradition," in *Thinking in Indian*; *Oren Lyons the Faithkeeper*, directed by Betsy McCarthy (Princeton, N.J.: The Moyers Collection, Films for Humanities & Sciences, 2006); Chief Jacob Thomas and Terry Boyle, *Teachings from the Longhouse* (Toronto: Stoddart, 1994); and William Fenton, *The Great Law and the Longhouse: A Political History of the Iroquois Confederacy* (Norman: University of Oklahoma Press, 1998).

38. Jon Parmenter, "The Meaning of *Kaswentah* and the Two Row Wampum Belt in Haudenosaunee (Iroquois) History: Can Indigenous Oral Tradition Be Reconciled with the Documentary Record?," *Journal of Early American History* 3 (2013): 82–109. We have used the spelling *Kaswentah* based on Hill and Coleman, "Two Row Research Partnership."

39. Susan Kalter, ed., *Benjamin Franklin, Pennsylvania, and the First Nations: The Treaties of 1736–62* (Urbana: University of Illinois Press, 2006), 115, 89.

40. Liu, "Where Is Cultural Criticism?"

41. "7 Directions," *Gibagadinamaagoom: "To Bring to Life, to Sanction, to Give Permission*," http://ojibwearchive.sas.upenn.edu/seven-directions. See Powell, "Encoding Culture," for an analysis of how an Ojibwe archive based on the seven directions came into being.

12. Teaching Bioregionalism in a Digital Age

Ken Cooper and Elizabeth Argentieri

They told me southern land could boast
Charms richer than mine own:
Sun, moon, and stars of brighter glow,
And winds of gentler tone;
And parting from each golden haunt,
Familiar rock and tree,
From that sweet vale I wandered far—
Washed by the Genesee.
—William H. C. Hosmer, "My Own Dark Genesee" (1854)

WE BEGIN WITH A POEM, or rather the first of its five stanzas, all of them concluding with an incantation of the Genesee River. It was published by a well-regarded writer and yet is nearly invisible to us now, as the numerous works of William H. C. Hosmer are all out of print save in digital form. We offer this quandary as typical for any teacher of regional, "minor," or noncanonical nineteenth-century texts: problems of access that might appear to have been ameliorated by digital archives really are just the beginning. Locally Hosmer was praised as "The Bard of Avon"—New York, that is—where his grandfather had founded a resort village known for its mineral springs. Among local historians, his poetry still can evoke a flickering of hometown pride before it sinks once again beneath the Genesee's dark waters. And what of readers who never have heard of him? For students who have grown up in a digital age, the obstacles to such a text are not just formal (Hosmer's metered verse and elevated diction) but what might be termed *locational*: in a web of everywhere, the status of being unknown consigns that person to nowhere; Hosmer isn't simply from the past or a small town, but cognitively from off the grid.[1]

"My Own Dark Genesee" is distinguished neither by poetic innovation nor its sentiment of missing home after moving somewhere else. Really, what we are left with in reintroducing the text is the single repeated word *Genesee* and all that it signifies. A student attending SUNY Geneseo (where we teach) will, if nothing else, momentarily grapple with a poem about the western New York river our campus overlooks—perhaps not directly visible, but inferred as a crooked line of trees on the valley floor below. That experience is potentially meaningful not because of Hosmer's text alone; rather, so much depends upon a reader prepared for the Genesee to signify as a shared place, a common home across the span of many decades or even centuries. In this regard our situation may be familiar to colleagues at many other academic institutions absent a famous author or literary scene, such as Concord or Harlem; the density of cultural archives we associate with cities; or (national) recognition as a canonical place, such as "Vermont Fall Foliage" or "Amish Country." Amid these seeming constraints, teaching regional texts stands as a challenge to light out for the territory under our feet. Much of that potential knowledge is *out there* at locations and within institutions demanding a more exploratory role for our students; the expanding digital archive makes available many local materials but cannot substitute for emplaced, embodied knowledge.

Our essay explores the pedagogical implications of digital nineteenth-century archives, an important and increasingly the only published source of local texts, from a bioregional perspective. As described by Robert L. Thayer, a *bioregion* is "definable by natural (rather than political) boundaries with a geographic, climatic, hydrological, and ecological character capable of supporting unique human and nonhuman living communities."[2] Bioregionalism shares many assumptions with kindred methodologies such as environmental studies, ecocriticism, and sustainability studies; for our purposes, its place-specific conception of knowledge and the (bio)archival creates an important counterbalance to the seeming placelessness of digital archives. Bioregionalism's focus upon active reinhabitation—"in an area that has been disrupted and injured through past exploitation"[3]—also makes it a useful corrective to nostalgia and the uncritical celebration of local history. Yet the program of reinhabitation, relocalization, energy transition, "heirloom technologies," and so on is not in most respects a natural fit for the technology and culture of digital humanities. Stephanie Posthumus and Stéfan Sinclair explain the situation like this: "Often wary of digital technologies, ecocriticism has been slow to explore the tools made available by the digital humanities. At the same time, the digital humanities have not yet expressed much interest in questions about nature and environment that are at the heart of ecocriticism."[4]

The sardonic retronym *IRL* indicates some of the distance to be bridged: in contrast to students' growing (in)habitation of online spaces, their time *in real life* is not necessarily the default setting and subtly reshapes prior conceptions of place. Digital archives bring with them latent questions concerning environments that are important to address, such as the many ironies that might arise from unmindful harvesting of local materials for transformation into virtual exhibits. What would be the point of unrelenting screen time in the service of better understanding the Genesee Valley? With these and other as-yet undiscovered caveats, we offer our experiences thus far concerning a hybrid project called *Open Valley* that has involved students, faculty, and community partners.[5] The essay is divided into three parts: our considerations in navigating the digital and bioregional interface; some of the technological and logistical challenges we have faced; and a brief account of the specific projects we have undertaken with students (for the syllabus, see Appendix 12.1; for additional project resources, see Appendix 12.2).

Discovery and Recovery of a Bioregional Poetics

Our project's name derives from one of several translations of the Seneca word rendered as *Genesee* or *Geneseo*: "beautiful valley," "shining clear opening," "pleasant open valley."[6] Ken, a professor of English, and Elizabeth, a special collections librarian, began collaborating in the summer of 2014 as one component of an upper-level English course on bioregional literature whose roster has averaged around twenty-five students. In the interests of focus and brevity we do not discuss at length some of that course's more traditional activities—the close reading of texts, the use of critical essays to frame discussions, individual research papers—that were thematically related to our concerns here. Initially there was no intent to undertake a digital humanities project because neither of us had a background in that emerging field; as becomes clear throughout this essay, some of the consequential challenges with which we have grappled probably would be shared by academic colleagues beginning with goals like our own: to involve undergraduates in meaningful local research, nudging them intellectually and even physically beyond the traditional classroom. Given undergraduate course loads and what was practicable to accomplish in a single semester, it made sense to have groups of students work collaboratively. We recognized at the outset that a project-driven methodology comes up against unpleasant student experiences of "group presentations," ranging from disappearing team members to anxieties over collectively assigned grades. Beyond all these obstacles, moreover, there can be a sense that group work isn't real work because its results span only those few minutes of a guided discussion or PowerPoint presentation. The audience for such presentations usually is composed of other class members, reinforcing their status as students due to the absence of any public or scholarly engagement. A desire for some more lasting accomplishment probably is what led us to consider digital platforms.[7]

In counterbalance to the growing screen time of modern academic work (and culture generally), the original plan was to organize four hands-on projects that would invite students to connect with institutions beyond the college campus:

1. Using Wadsworth family commercial documents at SUNY–Geneseo's Milne Library to create a map of regional nineteenth-century food infrastructure and contrasting that to contemporary land use (future partner: Genesee Valley Conservancy)
2. Editing as-yet unpublished diaries from a local farming family, spanning the years 1849–1937, along with fieldwork to create an online spatial humanities exhibit (partner: Milne Library archives)
3. Helping to develop a gallery show and online exhibit of angler art, using local pisciculturalist Seth Green to address issues of watersheds, nonnative species, and Indigenous fishing practices (partner: John Wehle Gallery, Genesee Country Village & Museum)[8]
4. Creating an interactive "Blue Tour" through Livingston County historical objects that foreground the themes of agriculture, extractive industries, and conservation (partner: Livingston County Historical Society Museum).[9]

Each project was framed to emphasize sustainability and the recovery of local knowledge. As with any undertaking, some of the details have changed over time, particularly in the manner that internship-like activities gradually acquired an explicitly digital dimension.

Two colleagues at Geneseo, Paul Schacht and Edward Gillin, developed a model that has influenced our thinking in productive ways. Schacht's *Digital Thoreau* project uses TEI encoding and open-source software called the Versioning Machine to realize Ronald E. Clapper's 1967 vision of *Walden* as a "genetic text"—an evolving opus of seven draft versions now dynamically visualized and searchable by readers.[10] Along with this editorial work, Schacht and his students have created an online annotation space for contemporary readers to "exchange ideas about Thoreau's writings in small groups keyed to particular interests or teaching situations."[11] Gillin, meanwhile, has taken a very different approach to teaching Thoreau in a digital age by having students collaborate on building a replica of his cabin at Walden Pond, not just in terms of layout and dimensions, but in terms of the social context of modernity that had led to its construction in the first place. Students have learned how to source lumber locally, mortise a joint, and build a foundation—both literally and in *Walden*'s figurative sense. Each Thoreau project is innovative on its own terms, but we were most attracted by thinking of them in tandem; student anecdotes suggested that those who had taken both courses appreciated the frisson of digital and IRL cultures.[12]

Our undertaking in *Open Valley* differs from Schacht and Gillin's work with Thoreau in a couple of significant ways. First, it is a spatially defined project—roughly, the Genesee River watershed—and as such is dependent upon those writers who have inhabited its environs. The (bio)region's history is a rich one, but aside from Frederick Douglass (who lived in Rochester between 1847 and 1872), none of its authors remain solidly in the nineteenth-century literary canon. Longstanding cultural dynamics involving aesthetic merits and conceptions of the cultural periphery inflect student perceptions of whether anything literary really happened here. At the time of writing this essay most of the major nineteenth-century authors—Emerson, Thoreau, Hawthorne, Whitman, Twain, and Dickinson—are the subject of digital scholarship initiatives with solid institutional support, often an outgrowth of existing print archival collections. A more eclectic range of projects are bringing online lesser-known writers of the nineteenth century, sometimes by scholars or institutions not located in that author's region, and this raises some relevant questions. Can, or should, a digital project on local culture affirm the legacies of regionalism? To what extent must its researchers reside in that place? Is the primary readership for such an enterprise still local, and if so, does that diminish its merit? We would suggest that earlier spatial designations organizing American literature into national and "local color" levels still matter in the digital age, though this is not self-evident for any given text upon a student's laptop screen.

A second, related distinction is that the bioregional paradigm invites us to gather in one location different types of knowledge besides the literary: cultural, economic, biological, historical, anecdotal, and more. Our project, we came to see, was indebted to spatial humanities enterprises such as *Digital Harlem*, the *Hypercities* platform, and Stanford's *Spatial History Project*.[13] Its emphasis was somewhat different, however, in that much of our terrain is rural, and the writers or "events" are often unknown outside of local historical societies. So, in addition to the absence of identifiable literary figures, there is the broader challenge described by Willa Cather in setting her 1913 novel *O Pioneers!* amid the midwestern farms of thirty years previous. A New York critic, she writes, "voiced a very general opinion when he said: 'I simply don't care a damn what happens in Nebraska, no matter who writes about it.'"[14] This sort of disconnection from rural ecology—did the critic care a damn about the wheat used to make his morning scones?—has if anything accelerated in the decades since, with less than 2 percent of Americans still working in agriculture compared to perhaps a third during this critic's times. A couple of generations earlier, when the Genesee region was renowned as "America's Granary" during its Erie Canal heyday, that proportion of farmers nationally was more like two-thirds—an agricultural heritage worth remembering at a time of global climate change and yet deeply unfamiliar to our students. Discerning what might be called a *bioregional poetics* across many different types of disciplines, documents, and genres of writing becomes a necessary part of teaching bioregionally.[15]

But what sort of poetics? The work of making a case for once-renowned local writers—like William H. C. Hosmer, Mary Jane Holmes, Jane Marsh Parker, or Henry F. Keenan—did not appeal to us because literary canonicity often has emphasized formal innovation and a leveling up from regionality to universality. Like Hosmer's poem "My Own Dark Genesee," the distinctive qualities of these local writers were fleeting, making sense only as part of a fabric. Some of the most vivid writing from the Genesee Valley, moreover, grows out of sensibilities that are not strictly literary: James E. Seaver's as-told-to captivity narrative by and about Mary Jemison, "The White Woman of the Genesee" (1824, with many subsequent anthropological emendations); Luther Tucker's progressive agricultural journal *Genesee Farmer* (1831–1865, in various iterations); the caterwauling business writing associated with Rochester, "America's First Boomtown"; or the popular historical sketches of twentieth-century newspaperman Arch Merrill.

A bioregional rubric has enabled us to span disparate texts, albeit with several necessary disclosures up front. First, bioregionalism is an interdisciplinary mode of engagement that no definition ever will conclusively demarcate—or should. Second, its concerns are tacitly ecological, even for texts not appearing to directly address matters of sustainability. Third, it is radically "anachronous" in foregrounding the contemporary, first-person subject as an ecological participant. Fourth, at times its poetics may engage with the dominant cultural imaginary in the manner of an alternate history, a recovery of local "arkive" for postcarbon resilience.[16] Finally, its greatest insights may not be *in* things, but *between* them as palimpsestic layers: the way nearby Conesus Creek once had been an important site for water mills (and might be again), now draining phosphorus-laden Conesus Lake into the Genesee River, or the way this ten-mile creek passes through the historic Wadsworth family Ashantee estate (earlier the site of Seneca villages) and figures in William H. C. Hosmer's 1844 epic poem "Yonnondio, Or Warriors of the Genesee," about historical events occurring in 1687. Any psychic connection to such diverse information is difficult to accomplish without the orientation of their shared place.

 We have come to think of *Open Valley* as a map in search of its territory. What began as an aspirational metaphor—to use spatial boundaries as the catalyst for intensive exploration—gradually deepened into a realization that the practical technologies and community of so-called "deep mapping" have evolved radically over just the past few years. David J. Bodenhamer, John Corrigan, and Trevor M. Harris write that geographic information systems (GIS), which operate as a series of layers with spatially encoded data, are of interest to those in the humanities despite their steep technological learning curve:

A deep map is a finely detailed, multimedia depiction of a place and the people, animals, and objects that exist within it and are thus inseparable from the con-

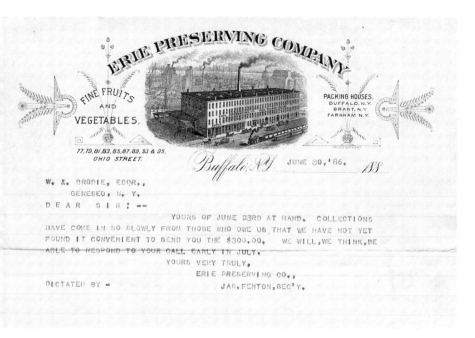

Commercial correspondence from the Wadsworth Family Papers. Image used by permission of Milne Library Special Collections, SUNY Geneseo. The correspondence is repurposed to envision western New York food infrastructure of the nineteenth century. The letterhead logo from 1886 serves two functions: as a web-friendly icon of the food processing company and as an object of analysis in its own right (an earlier version of the letterhead featured ships, not railroad engines, next to the factory).

tours and rhythms of everyday life. Deep maps are not confined to the tangible or material, but include the discursive and ideological dimensions of place, the dreams, hopes, and fears of residents—they are, in short, positioned between matter and meaning.[17]

Bodenhamer furthermore suggests that deep maps, while in many ways unthinkable without GIS technologies, depart from the goal of cartographic objectivity in favor of "inform[ing] the present more fully with the artifacts of social memory, the evidence of recall from various times and various perspectives." Their lineage encompasses humanistic, even radically avant-garde undertakings like William Least Heat Moon's *PrairyErth (A Deep Map)* and the 1950s French Situationist International that conceived of the map-territory portal "as a new creative space."[18] It's not a stretch to argue that Henry David Thoreau's *Walden*—with its spatially focused inquiry, interplay between objective cartography and subjective imagination, and its palimpsestic layers in "Former Inhabitants"—belongs in this genealogy of deep maps; yet Thoreau also returns us to the ecology of embodied experience, which is to say, as makers of maps. Although historically GIS applications have been used in the service of immediate functional, often infrastructural ends, the activity of palimpsestic "memories generated by intentional recall" sounded to us like a worthy goal for students investigating their bioregion.[19]

From Archival Groundwork to Digital Framework

Given a desire to foster student exploration spanning digital and embodied realms, our discussion pauses to consider logistical issues often beyond the purview of classroom teaching. How is "intentional recall" to be enacted, using what materials, through which applications? Technological opportunities and challenges are a given with digital enterprises; however, it's important not to overlook their IRL substratum. The success of the *OpenValley* project depends in large part on having access to relevant and important primary source materials, wherever they may reside. The Genesee Valley region is rich in libraries, archives, and museums (LAMs), ranging from large academic libraries' special collections (for example, at the University of Rochester) to the tiniest historical societies, and while efforts such as New York Heritage are bringing more of those materials online, much is still hidden—undigitized and often even uncataloged.[20] Websites and online catalogs, where they exist, are of limited value in ascertaining what these cultural organizations really have, so outreach and personal contact are required. And it is not only what they have, but what they're comfortable sharing with the wider world, especially through a digital humanities project that will digitize and likely repurpose content to create new knowledge.

We found ourselves returning to this basic question: what are the benefits to partnering in the *OpenValley* project? For regional LAMs, they include the opportunity to take advantage of a small but mighty workforce of college students possessing twenty-first-century skills that will help their collections and organizations become not only more visible and accessible to the public but also more meaningful, interesting, and relevant. Throughout the process of discovery and negotiation, it is important to remember that much of the bioregional archive has been preserved by volunteer organizations, even individuals, whose work has stubbornly resisted the online logic of placelessness. Academic institutions "harvesting" IRL materials will be less successful than the more patient work of exploring mutually beneficial alliances. An individual's or agency's reluctance may arise from a simple lack of resources, especially the time and staff available to work closely with even a small group of students. Additionally, some may be uncomfortable opening up unique primary materials to handling and scanning out of concern for the physical safety of the materials and at the perceived prospect of losing ownership or control through web publishing of what is uniquely theirs. These and other such concerns necessarily precede any matters of digital logistics or classroom pedagogy (for community partnership guidelines see Appendix 12.3).

It has helped us to think of student work taking place along parallel but distinct temporal tracks: the longer-term, cumulative activity of basic archival research and digitization extending beyond a single semester; and the shorter-term activity of using that research for critical writing that ends with the semester. These cycles of endeavor are less continuous than for institutions with graduate infrastructure, but still manageable. For most students, this is their first experience of using an inductive method. Learning to identify a nascent topic from unfamiliar archival sources, along with its ensuing questions and follow-up research, is an acquired skill. Perhaps the struggles to be overcome are holdovers from previously acquired research methods of first framing a topic then finding (online) sources to "prove" that thesis. In any event, although there seems to be little precedent for putting on cotton gloves to handle 150-year-old diaries or letters, students have risen to the challenge of imagining the lives implied by these objects. That material presence has grounded the digital aspects of their work, which entails introductory sessions on handling archival materials, best practices concerning scanning and file formats, and recording information using Dublin Core metadata fields (for a sample exam to test technical skills see Appendix 12.4).[21]

We would suggest *heavily* front-loading the long-term archival work with very clear expectations for each working group: digitizing half a dozen boxes of correspondence, for instance, with follow-up research as to geolocation using gazetteers and directories. During this phase of perhaps four weeks, while the semester is young and everything seems possible, it cannot be repeated too often that archival grunt work will be used in the service of imaginative brain work; otherwise some unexpected discovery might never occur because the procedure has become mechanistic. Another issue concerns the completeness of archival information and digitization that meets professional standards, which has been one of our greatest challenges (see Appendix 12.5 for a sample preservation and reformatting agreement). It seems to arise from various causes: the unfamiliarity of archival work to undergraduates; the frustrations of marshaling specific information (which often does not exist) upon a single local document, never mind an entire folder; the ease and casualness of using smartphones to photograph documents; and often what students may see as the tenuous link between past and present. Our most consistent output has come from work-study students and interns contemplating graduate study in library and information science (who become acclimated to these procedures), but we still think it's important that students in a semester-long course contribute in a meaningful way.

The familiar Omeka program upon which *OpenValley* is partially grounded uses an archival, museum-like logic: *items* are added to a database, thereafter to be incorporated into exhibits and collections.[22] The program has the virtue of a relatively simple interface, on-campus storage of data, and an open-source community; its page design is rudimentary but stable from a programming standpoint (i.e., updates not rendering old versions obsolete).[23] Omeka's work-flow is more familiar to history majors, perhaps, but still is congenial to a bioregional enterprise and prompts useful questions about what an *item* might be for our purposes. Certainly, an unpublished document or photograph is an item, along with oral histories, but what about information passed along informally from community members, or obscure nineteenth-century agricultural documents in other open-source archives? The scholarly process of grappling with source, categorization, attribution, and influence has a subtle ecological dimension in that students begin to recognize the place-specific fabric to which we have referred earlier. Creating an Omeka item is a concrete instance of intentional recall.

The most vexing technological issue we have faced arises from our desire to deep-map the students' research and writing for *OpenValley*. Omeka includes a geolocation plugin, but its engine—and user interface—is the ubiquitous Google Maps. Rebecca Solnit's critique of functionalist GPS (Global Positioning System) programs, their "cheerfully ugly aesthetic" and above all their presentism, speaks to our own frustrations in evoking historical alterity through such a contemporary window.[24] The other main Omeka option is its Neatline plugin and associated GeoServer hosting service, which is where the concepts of budgetary and staffing "back-end costs" made their way into our vocabulary.[25] SUNY Geneseo probably is at least average in terms of institutional support for digital projects but was hesitant to commit resources to even an open-source application that would require specialized IT support. At about this time a work study student—hearing us muttering about cartographic mysteries—asked us whether we ever had spoken with her geography professor, who, as it turned out, was teaming up with a biology professor to develop spatially defined research with the exact boundaries of our own: the Genesee Valley watershed. The four of us wrote a successful SUNY Innovative Instructional Technology Development (IITD) grant for the interdisciplinary use of GIS, and *OpenValley* began to grapple with deep maps as something more than a metaphor.

The many permutations of ArcGIS, which is the umbrella heading for a suite of programs developed by Esri (Environmental Systems Research Institute), is the subject for another essay.[26] It enters the discussion here because our college has an institutional subscription via the Geography Department, and so this schizophrenic program became the means through which we mapped archival information. We use this last adjective advisedly: ArcGIS Online has a simplified interface but severe limitations as to creating original map content; ArcMap for desktop is incredibly powerful, but its interface is reminiscent of mid-1980s MS-DOS.[27] Humanities instructors contemplating the use of ArcGIS should explore collaborations with others conversant in its use and brace themselves for a lengthy education. We're exploring which features of the programs (used in tandem) are realistic for undergraduates to use, and we sense that Esri is itself struggling to catch up with a growing interest in formerly specialized software. One of the benefits of ArcGIS discussed below is its Story Maps application, a recent and genuinely user-friendly interface that seems to acknowledge the possibilities of text and narrative in conjunction with geospatial information.[28]

A Multifaceted Pedagogical Approach

Student work on *OpenValley* now has spanned three academic semesters, with a fourth soon to commence. Rather than describe each of the individual projects involved, we approach this section of the narrative with an eye upon what we have learned through trial and error that might be of relevance to colleagues weighing similar projects. Above all, the trajectory of an academic semester is even *more* important to acknowledge than with traditional courses; for example, the ways in which collaboration can become a casualty of student triage amid midterm deadlines and must be protected via working-group time during class meetings toward the end of term. Conversely, the beginning of a semester is the best time to introduce unfamiliar practices. Given some of the archival and technical issues discussed in part two of our essay, it wouldn't be out of place to schedule an early practical exam to ensure that all class members are competent in the various skills that will be necessary throughout the semester. For *OpenValley*, that might involve (1) adding a couple of archival items into Omeka using Dublin Core metadata standards, (2) geocoding those items and incorporating them into an Excel spreadsheet, (3) using the spreadsheet to generate points on an ArcGIS map, and (4) configuring that skeletal map and its pop-up captions to link with Omeka for in-depth content. This sort of familiarity will ameliorate help-desk crises late in the term.

The first part of a semester, likewise, is the best time for fieldwork, not that it precludes targeted inquiry later on so much as it renders the project psychically tangible.[29] Just as it's now possible (via the web) to write an acceptable critical essay without ever having read the book, there are enough digital archives—textual sources like *HathiTrust* and the Internet Archive; historical maps at the

Library of Congress and David Rumsey Collection—to write about a local place without ever leaving one's computer.[30] Our experience has been that physically visiting a place changes students' relationship to it in their subsequent work. For instance, around 1890 a salt mine in nearby Retsof, NY built segregated housing for its workers that came to be called "Little Italy."[31] One student, who wrote that she had "been doing the majority of my learning for the past seventeen years in classrooms, from books," explained how her perspective was changed by a walk through the site led by a long-time resident: "Dave Nagel provided the perspective of a participant in the remnants of Little Italy. His community is made up, in part, of people who live there because their family moved to Little Italy generations ago." She recognized that her experience might "only be grasped in person, but . . . my ability to communicate the scene to an audience" had changed.[32] Similar awakenings by many other students have been among the most rewarding aspects of our project.

The exploratory methods implied by spatially defined inquiry have created some educational moments not possible online, or on a college campus for that matter. They also have made us better attuned to the issues faced by instructors overseeing vocational internships: availability of transportation, standards for professional communication with partner organizations, and lead times that are measured in weeks instead of hours. We would recommend that all such details be addressed with students explicitly, through discussion and a supplementary document. The long-term viability of *OpenValley* depends upon community partners who want to work with us again; students canceling an appointment or expecting unrealistic turnarounds at the end of a semester undermine that relationship. This need for a collective project to ensure minimum standards is different from a typical academic course—where individual students are freer to excel or fail—and Ken, as the classroom teacher, has not always been comfortable with a subtle change in his relation to students. There is a dimension of project management, supervision, and informing some students that their work is not (yet) up to acceptable standards that feels different even from feedback on graded essays: the challenge is to think of oneself as a mentor, not a boss. Conversely, there is a very real satisfaction in knowing that students' work in the course is preparing them for collaborative undertakings after graduation, whether academic or in the workplace.

We have learned through hard experience to create small working groups—no more than four or five students—to avoid the bystander effect with shared work and to facilitate the coordination of meetings or off-campus travel. To maintain some degree of long-term coherence with *OpenValley*, while still encouraging imaginative undergraduate writing in the short term, we think in terms of embedded "levels" of exhibits within the Omeka platform. To illustrate via one project, a group of nine students met early in the spring 2015 semester to brainstorm ideas for an exhibit based upon the diaries of Sheffield Peabody, a nineteenth-century farmer who lived in nearby Springwater, New York. A Voyant Tools word cloud revealed that he commonly began sentences with the phrase *I went*—"I went over to George Higgins' today," "I went to the valley"—and this led to the proposition that Peabody enacted in physical space those social functions we increasingly experience in webspace.[33] The exploratory essays for *Peabody Networks* came to be organized under three broad headings: *The Social Network*, which maps Sheffield's relations with various groups of people outside of his family; *Circuits*, which explores his farm as an economic node in relation to a circulation of mutual commerce and interdependency; and *The Safety Net*, focusing upon his later years and the need for medical, financial, and emotional support.[34] Within each of these subtopics, a working group of three students plus the course instructor collaborated to develop thematically linked essays reflecting individual interests. Any reader who has organized a conference panel session will be familiar with this interplay between rubric and individual projects, hopefully resulting in productive connections.

Another model for synthesizing individual scholarship and collaborative endeavor has been the atlas, described by Rebecca Solnit as "a collection of versions of a place, a compendium of perspectives, a snatching out of the infinite ether of potential versions a few that will be made concrete and visible."[35] Her two collections are recommended reading for any instructor who contemplates this approach. In the fall 2015 semester, students in an upper-level seminar brainstormed ideas for individual maps of the Genesee Valley—no topic out of bounds—and then a collaborative process of voting, winnowing, combining, and rubric-building led to a loose framework that became *Underground Atlas of the Genesee*.[36] The best individual maps in the collection were grounded in archival specifics (a midterm checkpoint of Omeka items is suggested) and multiple visits off campus: meeting with a community member, traveling to a small town alone, or creating a photo essay. Students more comfortable with reading assignments on a course syllabus and traditional academic essays struggled with this dimension of the course; perhaps one solution would be to have groups discuss their various roles. Once students created individual maps, accompanying text, and linked companion exhibits on Omeka, they were assembled into a single Story Map—whose embed code lets them be shared on the website of a partner organization.

We close this essay by differentiating between digital scholarship that remains within the parameters of an individual course and scholarship that is shared with the public. Our experiences regarding the latter is that it required many months before we felt ready to share it even with prospective organizations. At a certain point, however, it has become easier to "show, don't tell," and this upcoming semester will involve half a dozen collaborations in the area, whose subject matter ranges from a history of scenic viewpoints at Letchworth State Park to the spiritual geography of a nearby Cistercian monastery. Almost every organization with which we have spoken enumerates a long list of potential enterprises—there's no shortage of things to learn about the Genesee Valley, its rural locations notwithstanding. Having begun by conceiving of a digital archive as bioregional and palimpsestic, and having worked through logistical challenges to create a public website, we realize it becomes important to step back and reassess the purposes of *OpenValley*.

One outcome might entail seeking further resources and researchers in support of GIS-enabled programming to create what Bodenhamer calls "geographical context and depth to an expert interpretation of the past."[37] Another scenario that he envisions is perhaps less familiar to academic culture, one whose loosely collaborative nature creates "a fragmented, provisional, contingent understanding framed by multiple voices and multiple stories, mini-narratives of small events and practices, each conditioned by the unique experiences and local cultures that gave rise to them."[38] We confess that much of our own training has involved skills that result in expert narratives. More insidiously, so too has the training of our students and their educational expectations, with grades as the institutional arbiter. Yet, in other circumstances our students are makers, pinners, curators, collaborators, commenters, forwarders. Pedagogy recalls us to those important questions concerning what type(s) of person are being created by digital academic work; the bioregional imperative seems to imply collaboration because we are connected.

Our public college, although struggling like many others to chart its way in an era of privatized intellectual property and tax-free enterprise zones like START-UP NY, still retains a strong sense of contributing to the common good. The service-learning dimension of *OpenValley* allows students to get real-world experience while also contributing meaningfully to the IRL community in a manner that's distinct from online communities. The web of everywhere and its *potential* relation to the Genesee region recalls a piece of subtle advice given to Willa Cather: "One of the few really helpful words I ever heard from an older writer I had from Sarah Orne Jewett when she said to me: 'Of course, one day you will write about your own country. In the meantime, get all you can. One must know the world *so well* before one can know the parish.'"[39]

The appendixes for this chapter, a syllabus and assignments for a course by Ken Cooper and Elizabeth Argentieri on primary research related to knowledge of place, can be found at www.press.uillinois.edu/books/TeachingWithDH.

Notes

1. Our epigraph comes from William H. C. Hosmer, "My Own Dark Genesee," *The Poetical Works of William H. C. Hosmer*, vol. 2. (New York: Redfield, 1854), 355–356, http://catalog.hathitrust.org/Record/000117330. His collected works are available on archival sites like *HathiTrust* and the Internet Archive. An alternative model for reading Hosmer's poem might take its cue from Henry Wadsworth Longfellow's massive thirty-one volume anthology called *Poems of Places* (1876–1879)—where that lyric represents "Middle States: Genesee, the River, N.Y."—along with other locationally themed anthologies now available online. See John James Piatt, *The Union of American Poetry and Art: A Choice Collection of Poems by American Poets* (1882); Nathaniel Parker Willis, *Mountain, Lake, and River* (1884); Lucy Henderson Humphrey, *The Poetic New World* (1910).

2. Robert L. Thayer Jr., *Lifeplace: Bioregional Thought and Practice* (Berkeley: University of California Press, 2003), 3. For an introduction to bioregional thought see Kirkpatrick Sale, *Dwellers in the Land: The Bioregional Vision* (San Francisco: Sierra Club, 1985); Molly Scott Cato, *The Bioregional Economy: Land, Liberty, and the Pursuit of Happiness* (New York: Routledge, 2013); Tom Lynch, Cheryll Glotfelty, and Karla Armbruster, *The Bioregional Imagination: Literature, Ecology, and Place* (Athens: University of Georgia Press, 2012).

3. Peter Berg and Raymond Dasmann, "Reinhabiting California," in *Reinhabiting a Separate Country: A Bioregional Anthology of Northern California, San Francisco*, ed. Peter Berg (San Francisco: Planet Drum Foundation, 1978), 3.

4. Stephanie Posthumus and Stéfan Sinclair, "Reading Environment(s): Digital Humanities Meets Ecocriticism," *Green Letters* 18, no. 3 (2014): 254.

5. Ken Cooper and Elizabeth Argentieri, eds., *OpenValley*, accessed March 26, 2017, http://openvalley.org/.

6. George H. Harris, "Notes on the Aboriginal Terminology of the Genesee River," *Publications of the Rochester Historical Society* 1 (1892): 14, *HathiTrust*, http://catalog.hathitrust.org/Record/100556255.

7. Geneseo's Milne Library already began exploring the role of undergraduate institutions in digital scholarship and publishing. Its Genesee Valley Historical Reprints series, one of the library's first endeavors in this arena, preserved and made accessible online (and in print-on-demand format) thirty-three scarce monographs held in its regional history archives.

8. John Wehle Gallery, "Gone Fishin' Exhibit," Genesee Country Village & Museum, accessed March 26, 2017, https://www.gcv.org/explore/gallery/past-gallery-exhibits/.

9. Regina Carra, "Take the Blue Tour!" Livingston County Historical Society Museum, accessed March 26, 2017, http://www.livingstoncountyhistoricalsociety.com/blue-tour/ (no longer available).

10. Paul Schacht, *Digital Thoreau*, accessed March 26, 2017, http://www.digitalthoreau.org/; Susan Schreibman et al., *Versioning Machine 5.0: A Tool for Displaying & Comparing Different Versions of Literary Texts*, accessed March 26, 2017, http://v-machine.org/.

11. Paul Schacht, "The Readers' Thoreau," *Digital Thoreau*, http://commons.digital thoreau.org/.

12. Jennifer Howard, "Hammer, Nails, and Software Bring Thoreau Alive," *Chronicle of Higher Education*, November 17, 2014, A10-A11.

13. Shane White, Stephen Garton, Graham White, and Stephen Robertson, *Digital Harlem*, accessed March 26, 2017, http://digitalharlem.org/; Todd Presner, David Shepard, and Yoh Kawano, *HyperCities: Thick Mapping in the Digital Humanities*, accessed March 26, 2017, http://www.hypercities.com/; *Spatial History Project*, Center for Spatial and Textual Analysis, Stanford University, accessed March 26, 2017, http://web.stanford.edu/group/spatialhistory/cgi-bin/site/index.php.

14. Willa Cather, "My First Novels [There Were Two]," *Willa Cather on Writing: Critical Studies on Writing as an Art* (1931; Lincoln: University of Nebraska, 1988), 94.

15. In formulating a poetics that can encompass twenty-first-century digital culture and nineteenth-century agriculture, it also is important to confront what has been termed *temporocentrism* or *chronocentrism*—that is, the latent belief that we must be more intelligent than our ancestors, since our technologies appear to be more sophisticated. By the criteria of long-term sustainability, this assumption looks increasingly dubious.

16. See Arkive, a not-for-profit initiative that is using images and film to create a record of life, particularly endangered species. "Who We Are," Arkive, accessed March 26, 2017, http://www.arkive.org/about/.

17. David J. Bodenhamer, John Corrigan, and Trevor M. Harris, "Introduction: Deep Maps and the Spatial Humanities," in *Deep Maps and Spatial Narratives*, ed. Bodenhamer, Corrigan, and Harris (Bloomington: Indiana University Press, 2015), 3.

18. David J. Bodenhamer, "The Potential of Spatial Humanities," in *The Spatial Humanities: GIS and the Future of Humanities Scholarship*, ed. David J. Bodenhamer, John Corrigan, and Trevor M. Harris (Bloomington: Indiana University Press, 2010), 26–27.

19. Ibid., 28.

20. *New York Heritage*, Empire State Library Network, accessed March 26, 2017, http://www.newyorkheritage.org/.

21. Dublin Core refers to a set of fifteen metadata fields that were adopted in 1995 as capable of referencing a wide range of physical and digital materials amid the growth of web technologies; updated versions remain the standard protocol used by American libraries. For a more detailed introduction see Stefanie Rühle, Tom Baker, and Pete Johnston, "User Guide," *Dublin Core Metadata Initiative*, last modified September 6, 2011, accessed March 26, 2017, http://wiki.dublincore.org/index.php/User_Guide.

22. First released in 2008, Omeka combines elements of web content management, collections management, and archival digital collections systems for nonspecialist users.

23. See Lauren F. Klein, "Hacking the Field: Teaching Digital Humanities with Off-the-Shelf Tools," *Transformations* 22, no. 1 (2011): 37–52. Klein offers useful advice for those institutions with relatively modest budgets for dedicated programming: "Just as instructors and scholars must train themselves to harness the power of 'constraints-based approaches' and off-the-shelf tools, they must also acknowledge the limits of

tools, access, and knowledge itself" (49). Repeatedly, we have had to remind ourselves not to let digital logistics crowd out other important dimensions of the project.

24. Solnit and Snedeker write, "The problem with [GPS] technologies is that though they generally help get you where you're going, that's all they do." While *OpenValley* uses digital and nonprint technologies to geolocate bioregional history, we have been challenged by their argument that "what appears onscreen may not inspire contemplation the way [a paper] atlas can," which is to say that the aesthetics and navigation of digital maps are integral to their meaning. With regard to bioregionalism in an era of digital maps we need to remember how, "when you use the old-fashioned technology of paper maps, you build up the even more ancient resources of memory, mind, and spatial imagination." Rebecca Solnit and Rebecca Snedeker, *Unfathomable City: A New Orleans Atlas* (Berkeley: University of California Press, 2013), 5.

25. Neatline, Scholar's Lab, accessed March 26, 2017, http://neatline.org/; GeoServer, Open Source Geospatial Foundation, accessed Marc 26, 2017, http://geoserver.org/.

26. As of 2015, Esri controls an estimated 43 percent of the global GIS market worldwide, compared to just 11 percent for its nearest competitor. "Independent Report Highlights Esri as Leader in Global GIS Market," *GISuser*, March 2, 2015, http://gisuser .com/2015/03/independent-report-highlights-esri-as-leader-in-global-gis-market/. Published scholarly articles mentioning the (privately held) company originate almost exclusively from a user-group perspective: how to use a feature, apply the program to various fields of research, and so on. A sociology of GIS user culture, akin to Sherry Turkle's work on hackers, remains a tantalizing project. See Sherry Turkle, *Life on the Screen: Identity in the Age of the Internet* (New York: Simon & Schuster, 1995), and Turkle, *The Second Self: Computers and the Human Spirit* (New York: Simon & Schuster, 1984).

27. Esri, *ArcGIS Online*, accessed March 26, 2017, http://www.esri.com/software /arcgis/arcgisonline; *ArcGIS for Desktop*, accessed March 26, 2017, http://desktop.arcgis .com/en/.

28. Story Maps, Esri, accessed March 26, 2017, http://storymaps.arcgis.com/en/.

29. We use the term *fieldwork* in a very broad sense for a range of IRL activities that might include interviews, photography, GPS points generated by smartphones, or simply a walk and extended time spent in a given place in the tradition of nature writing. It also includes travel to local historical societies to consult archival materials whose physical place is so unfamiliar that it is experienced very differently than students' usual (online) research space.

30. *HathiTrust Digital Library*, accessed March 26, 2017, https://www.hathitrust. org/; Internet Archive, accessed March 26, 2017, https://archive.org/index.php; "Search Maps," Library of Congress, accessed March 26, 2017, https://www.loc.gov/maps/; and David Rumsey Map Collection, Cartography Associates, accessed March 26, 2017, http://www.davidrumsey.com/home.

31. Mary Auld, "Little Italy, Retsof NY," *OpenValley*, http://openvalley.org/exhibits /show/underground-atlas-of-the-genes/5—little-italy—retsof-ny.

32. Mary Auld, personal communication to authors, December 14, 2015.

33. Stéfan Sinclair and Geoffrey Rockwell, *Voyant Tools*, accessed March 26, 2017, http://voyant-tools.org/.

34. Noah Chauvin, Marisa Drpich, Jennifer Faes, Rebecca Gates, Devon Gawley, Brodie Guinan, Jessica Lolakas, Michelle Nitto, Courtney Yonce, Ken Cooper, Elizabeth Argentieri, and Joseph Easterly, "Peabody Networks," *Open Valley*, http://openvalley .org/exhibits/show/peabody-networks.

35. Rebecca Solnit, *Infinite City: A San Francisco Atlas* (Berkeley: University of California Press), vii.

36. Mary Auld, Noah Chauvin, Kristen Druse, Kevin Feeley, Jeremy Jackson, Danielle Kahn, Jordan Keane, Natalie Kelsey, Matthew Viglucci, Megan Wong, Elizabeth Argentieri, Ken Cooper, Colleen Garrity, Leah Root, and Stephen Tulowiecki, *Underground Atlas of the Genesee*, accessed March 4, 2016, http://arcg.is/21v0MVA.

37. Bodenhamer, "Potential of Spatial Humanities," 28.

38. Ibid., 29.

39. Willa Cather, preface to *Alexander's Bridge* (1912; Boston: Houghton Mifflin, 1922), vii.

PART FIVE

Act

13. DH and the American Literature Canon in Pedagogical Practice

Amy E. Earhart

DIGITAL HUMANITIES PEDAGOGY IS, by now, a well-established area of scholarly inquiry, with practitioners and theorists producing articles, journal issues, and books dedicated to its study.[1] This volume, though, is unique in its decision to examine digital pedagogy within the context of American literature scholarship. As I have argued in my recent monograph, *Traces of the Old, Uses of the New: The Emergence of Digital Literary Studies*, the practice of digital humanities is fluid, altered by the space and structure in which it is employed, whether in research or the classroom.[2] So too is the case with the application of digital pedagogies to American literature, where in the classroom we ask students to engage with concepts of nationhood, place, difference, genre, and historical, social, and cultural context. Perpetually evolving through critical debate, such ideas are reflected within the classroom by not only how we teach but by what we teach. While we might assign students tasks that use digital humanities techniques, such as simple data mining exercises or editing and archiving projects, the connection between digital humanities and American literature is not formed by practice alone but is intimately linked to the historical development of activist digital projects that expanded the American literature canon.

By the 1980s we were at the height of the canon wars, a battle over what counted as American literature. Feminist critics such as Judith Fetterley, Nina Baym, and Jane Tompkins rejected the assessment of "literary greatness [on] ahistorical, transcendental ground[s]," instead arguing for different ways of valuing American literary texts.[3] At the same time, scholars working within race and ethnic studies critiqued the whiteness of the canon, demanding a more complex understanding of difference and a broader literary tradition. The battle for control of the canon was not only occurring within scholarship but was being waged within the classroom. Scholars recognized that "the problem of the canon is a problem of syllabus and curriculum, the institutional forms by which works are preserved as *great* works."[4] Henry Louis Gates Jr. acknowledges, "the teaching of literature is the teaching of values; not inherently, no, but contingently, yes; it is—it has become—the teaching of an aesthetic and political order, in which no women or people of color were ever able to discover the reflection or representation of their images, or hear the resonances of their cultural voices."[5] The classroom, then, was a contested space in which instructional choices had interplay with scholarly representations of American literature.

The anthologies that shaped "American literature" during this period remained, to some engaged in the debate over the canon, limited, and instructors turned often to digital texts to resolve the limitations of print. With access to the internet and basic HTML markup skills, scholars could create texts for classroom use, reimagining what and who belonged within American literature. For example, Mitsuharu Matsuoka's *American Authors on the Web*, one of many "curated hyperlinked" sites, includes an extensive and broad list of American authors.[6] In the 1997 version of the project, Matsuoka compiled a list of 572 authors organized by birth and death dates and then subdivided his entries into chronological periods. The list resembles the table of contents of an anthology, yet an open-access and expansive anthology. In fact, Matsuoka's 1997 list of 572 American authors is far more diverse and expansive than that of the contemporary *Norton Anthology of American Literature* (1998), which included only 259 authors. Matsuoka's site also emphasized genres and authors not represented by the 1998 *Norton* such as children's literature author Susan Coolidge and Lizette Woodworth Reese, a prominent Baltimore poet championed by H. L. Mencken and often compared to Emily Dickinson. Like many scholars of the period, Matsuoka's project extended the limited American literature canon found in print anthologies.

Such projects form a crucial part of the history of Americanist digital pedagogical practice and foreshadow current digital practices. Curated hyperlinked projects were forerunners of contemporary crowdsourced digital projects. Matsuoka was only able to include works to which he could link, leaving more than half of his listed authors awaiting content. The quality of the texts was variable as well. Some were drawn from scholarly projects, others from Project Gutenberg, others from *The SUNET Archive* (Swedish University Computer Network), and still others from a hodgepodge of disparate sources.[7] The linked texts did not necessarily meet the standards of what we expect to find in a scholarly edition or even in a published anthology and were produced in a variety of ways, including the large-scale digitization of texts by etext centers, libraries, and consortiums and "small scale recovery efforts nurtured by an individual scholar who wanted to bring lost texts to scholarly and public attention," what I label *DIY activist projects*.[8]

The DIY activist projects played an important role in the shaping of an American literature canon as scholars began their digital work to correct what they believed to be missing in print anthologies.[9] For Donna M. Campbell, the lack of contextual social and historical information in the print anthology spurred the 1997 launch of the *American Literature* site.[10] Campbell wrote and digitized support materials, such as a definition of Calvinism in New England Puritan culture, timelines, bibliographies, and primary texts.

In an interview, Campbell calls the project a "political statement" that brought scholarly materials to a broad audience and published texts left out of anthologies.[11] For example, Campbell transcribed Maria Cristina Mena's "The Vine-Leaf" from its original publication in *The Century Magazine*.[12] The short story has since been anthologized, but Campbell's edition was the first to be republished and remains the only freely available version on the web. The important work conducted by Campbell and others was squarely positioned within a movement to rethink and expand the American literature canon, and scholars like Campbell saw the classroom as an important site in which to reform ideas about American literature.

So pervasive was the impulse to use the digital to expand American literature that scholarly organizations developed resources to encourage the creation and use of digital materials. The now defunct *American Studies Electronic Crossroads* website, a project of Randall Bass at Georgetown University, was heavily invested in supporting classroom applications related to such work.[13] Of the four sections of the website, two were dedicated to teaching: "Curriculum" and "Technology & Learning."

Bass's essay, "A Brief Guide to Interactive Multimedia and the Study of the United States," argues for the centrality of multimedia tools within the classroom:

> One of the most rapidly changing and exciting areas of education in the world today is the development of computer-based teaching materials, especially interactive multimedia programs that run on personal computers. These new technologies offer students and teachers access to materials as never before.[14]

To support classroom use, the site includes a remarkable number of resources for instructors including the "Directory of Dynamic Syllabi and Courses Online," pedagogical essays, and support materials from workshops including the "Crossroads Faculty Research and Study Project" and the "Technology & Learning Crossroads Workshop." These materials promote a broader view of American Studies, inclusive and interdisciplinary, and the site encourages instructors to develop pedagogical programs that would spread the word.

We might situate our current practice within this history, connecting our digital pedagogy to continued interrogations of the American literature canon. By doing so, we are positioning our work within a long tradition of Americanists dedicated to a teaching practice that shapes the field. While the canon doesn't attain the same critical attention as it did in the 1970s and 1980s, there are continual movements and reshapings occurring. My current work on American literature anthologies shows that authors continue to drop in and out of anthologies and, subsequently, classrooms. An analysis of the run of eight editions of the *Norton American Literature Anthology* reveals that anthologies have grown longer, but authors, texts, and even entire genres diminish and disappear over time as other texts and genres enter. For example, Paul Lawrence Dunbar, an African American poet commonly anthologized in the first half of the twentieth century, disappeared from anthologies during the canon wars, only to reappear in the 2007 and 2012 *Norton* anthologies. Other authors have been lost from the anthology over time, such as Norman Mailer, who was included in the 1979, 1985, 1989, and 1994 anthologies only to disappear from more current versions. To aid students in understanding an evolving concept of *American literature* and to encourage them to participate in discussions about canon formation, various approaches might be adopted, but digital pedagogies are particularly useful. Here I draw on research about educational practices within studio spaces, particularly design or library informatics studios. A well-developed mode of practice, "studio-based learning is rooted in the apprentice model of learning in which students study with master designers or artists to develop their craft. It emphasizes learning by doing, often through community-based design problems and is an integral pedagogy in architecture, urban planning and fine and applied arts."[15]

In my undergraduate courses, I have successfully used a blended model of the discussion class and the studio project. Such an approach is similar to the kaleidoscope pedagogy outlined in this volume's article titled "Kaleidoscopic Pedagogy in the Classroom Laboratory" by Ryan Cordell, Benjamin J. Doyle, and Elizabeth Hopwood (see chapter 1), which "adds building and experimentation to reading and interpretation, blends digital and analog media as tools and objects of our analyses, and repositions students as necessary and integral collaborators in the knowledge-making processes of the field." I teach a 300-level African American literature survey course, beginnings to 1930, which has a predominant population of non-English majors who take the class to meet core curriculum requirements (see Appendix 13.1 for the syllabus). As part of the course, we discuss the evolution of African American literature and how such literature is characterized, whether through time periods, genres, or themes. It is important for students to understand that the texts that they are reading are selected by editors and that each editor brings certain selection standards to the task. In their preface to the second edition of *The Norton Anthology of African American Literature* Henry Louis Gates Jr. and Nellie Y. McKay make plain that the editing of the anthology is a political act, "to make available in one representative anthology the major texts in the tradition and to construct a canon inductively, text by text, period by period, rather than deductively" and that the anthology will "give full voice to the key tropes and topoi that repeat—are echoed and riffed and signified upon—so strikingly across the African American literary tradition, thereby allowing formal linkages to be foregrounded in the classroom."[16] As Gates and McKay suggest, the choices made, whether in an anthology or in a syllabus, define the literature, the period, and the object of study, in a particular manner. The incorporation of digital pedagogy projects in the classroom that force students to select and curate primary materials is useful in teaching students that selection, editing, and collection are at play in every anthology and every canon.

In my class, students work with a digital archive project focused on a local race riot. The Millican "riot" occurred in 1868 in Millican, Texas, a small town on the Houston and Texas Central Railway. This was a troubled time in central Texas. Millican had been ravaged by yellow fever, a severe crop failure, and the railway's expansion north to Bryan, Texas, all of which diminished the Millican population. The black community was registering to vote at a rapid pace; blacks were elected to the Constitutional Convention, and all the local white politicians except the coroner had been removed from office and replaced by Republican unionists.[17] In June 1868 the Ku Klux Klan marched through Millican. Local blacks, participating in a church service led by Pastor George Brooks, a Methodist preacher and Union League organizer, led the parishioners into an armed attack on the Klan members, who promptly fled. This event started days of confrontations. By the third day, the local authorities called for a militia to be formed in Bryan and sent by train to put down the "mob." Newspapers describe the militia as being taken from the bars and brothels in the middle of the day. In the end an unknown number of black townspeople were injured and dead, including George Brooks, who was viciously beaten, mutilated, and lynched. The event was covered by newspapers from France to Panama, Edinburgh to San Francisco, and Hamburg to New York, suggesting the interest in and importance of the Millican confrontation.

Crucial to the incorporation of a digital project in the classroom is a careful match of subject to classroom materials. Course content and materials must lead to the digital project rather than the reverse. To understand the literature, students must grapple with the social, political, and historical context for the writing we examine, and a hands-on project where they sift through contemporary materials helps to illuminate the literature that they are reading. Much of the late nineteenth- and early twentieth-century literature that we read emphasizes African Americans' responses to white violence. Literature, such as Charles Chesnutt's *The Marrow of Tradition*, Ida B. Wells-Barnett's *The Red Record*, Pauline Hopkins's "As the Lord Lives, He Is One of Our Mother's Children," Claude McKay's "If We Must Die," films, such as *The Birth of the Nation*, and other visual and textual materials are considered within the context of student research and collection of Millican materials (for the full reading list, see Appendix 13.1). As students read this material they spend part of their week locating contemporary newspapers, political documents, and images. Instead of the instructor telling students about the contemporary resistance to voting rights, they read the editorials decrying voting rights or find news reports of lynchings that are directed against blacks who register to vote. The engagement with multiple forms of texts allows students, as Wesley Raabe explains, "to examine texts that have been domesticated for literary anthologies and editions, to enliven the classroom with alternate texts that show literary works to be more unruly than anthology publication forms may suggest."[18]

The contextualization of historical events in connection to creative production is reinforced by the course assignments. Students are responsible for researching the Millican riot, locating, editing, and curating primary materials related to the event, and repositing their items with Dublin Core metadata and a transcription in our course Omeka site.[19] In effect, students work together to build an open-source digital archive that collects materials related to the Millican riot. To support student learning, the project is stair-stepped across the semester with weekly lab days in which we work on pieces of the project. Lab days walk students through the project, teaching them basic research skills, copyright considerations, how to understand and construct metadata, and how to create entries in Omeka. I have written small assignments that build to our final project and teach important research, analysis, and writing skills. We begin by learning how to locate and select materials (see Appendix 13.2). To ensure that students navigate the complexities of digital databases and collections, they produce a research strategy, a paper that maps their research question and possible ways to locate information on that question, for my feedback. To facilitate students' historical and cultural understanding of not only the riot we are documenting but also the experiences to which African American writers are responding, students complete an assignment designed to contextualize the events they are exploring. Locating mentions of Millican in historical newspapers, students read the surrounding articles, research the politics of the newspaper in which Millican is reported, and write a short response paper analyzing the way in which such details inform the response to Millican. Students report that this assignment allows them to better understand what the writers they are reading are living with, responding to, and critiquing. As students conduct their research, they produce an annotated bibliography of primary and secondary materials, again allowing me to provide feedback during this crucial stage of the process (see Appendix 13.3). A visiting metadata librarian teaches students how to create the Dublin Core metadata necessary for their Omeka upload, and students add their materials to our class website (see Appendix 13.4). Finally, students write a traditional research paper based on their selected topic related to course readings using the historical and cultural materials located in the Omeka class website (see Appendix 13.5).

Further, students come to understand how lenses form the way that we view texts. African American literature scholars have recently argued for a recasting of literature written from Reconstruction through the end of the First World War. In a time period often characterized as "'The Dark Ages of Recent American History' or 'The Decades of Disappointment,' for the increased and de facto racial segregation," literature of the period paired with an investigation of the Millican incident reveals another narrative, a narrative of resistance.[20] Or, as Gebhard and McCaskill note, "Focusing exclusively on black victimization and de facto slavery gives us an incomplete picture of these critical years in America's history. In these decades, African Americans sustained and strengthened the vocal press and bedrock spiritual institutions they had organized during slavery, built new educational institutions, and created networks of political and social leadership to resist both the illegal and legal violence aimed at keeping them from full and equal participation in the nation's life."[21] While we might tell students that African American writers used literature as a political tool, they better understand its usage when they are immersed within period materials. Students come to understand how a body of knowledge about an event is shaped and misshaped. They begin to see the discrepancies in news stories, realize that the census did not record the names of slaves in Texas, and that newspaper accounts often didn't name black participants while using the full names of whites.

Teaching students to conduct digital research necessarily engages them in these political questions. In the essay "Less False Stories: Teaching Comparative Early American Literatures," Pattie Cowell argues that the classroom is a place in which we might focus on questions: "We ask what questions reveal about questioners, and whose questions these are anyway. We ask why some regions and groups have become the subject of extensive contemporary scrutiny and others have been neglected, why, for instance, we know so much of colonial New England and so little of the even earlier Spanish southwest settlements."[22] I add to these questions: What is an American text? And how do we understand literature's role in the formation of nationhood? Such questions center the current debates in American literature within the context of our turn toward hemispheric studies, continued explorations of nationhood, race, gender, class, and sexuality. Such questions help guide students to understand how canons are created. Amanda Gailey points to the use of digital approaches to emphasize the complex formations of American literature, noting,

> students tend to think of literature as a fixed field in which all the important decisions about what is included and what is excluded have already been made, usually on principled and objective grounds, by experts in the past. They sometimes know that the canon has undergone changes, mostly in response to the progressive movements of their parents' or grandparents' generation, but the work of deciding what is important or beautiful seems to strike them as now complete.[23]

At some point in the semester, a student will ask if a certain primary document might "count" for the assignment. This question will lead to a discussion about the purpose of the archive and what is in and what is out. As Leslie Bonds has noted, authentic learning through digital pedagogical applications forces students to deal with questions with which scholars might engage, in this case questions of inclusion and exclusion—of canon formation.[24] By grappling with these questions, students learn just how difficult such questions are to resolve. Further, the lack of firm answers sets up an opportunity for joint exploration. Paul Fyfe calls this "a terrific opportunity to join students in shared projects of inquiry and explore new aspects of the discipline."[25] It is also a moment to circle back to the basic question of what American literature is and how we define it.

Ultimately, an Americanist digital pedagogy is engaged with the same crucial questions that American literature scholars ask: What counts as American literature? What are the crucial questions that we must engage? The incorporation of digital projects focused on canon formation allow us to extend and deepen the questions that we have traditionally raised in the classroom. The self-referential creation and use of digital materials, especially those that extend the American canon, place the instructor within the long history of those who have practiced Americanist digital pedagogies, and it reengages students with crucial issues in the field.

The appendixes for this chapter, a syllabus and assignments for a course by Amy E. Earhart on African American literature from the early Americas to 1930, can be found at www.press.uillinois.edu/books/TeachingWithDH.

Notes

1. See Brett D. Hirsch, ed., *Digital Humanities Pedagogy: Practices, Principles and Politics* (Cambridge: Open Book, 2012); Ann Hawkins, ed. "Special Issue: Digital Humanities Pedagogy," *CEA Critic*, 76, no. 2 (2014); Diane Jakacki, "Digital Pedagogy: Select Readings," *Diane Jakacki* (blog), http://dianejakacki.net/digital-pedagogy-select -readings/.

2. Amy E. Earhart, *Traces of the Old, Uses of the New: The Emergence of Digital Literary Studies*, Digital Culture Books (Ann Arbor: University of Michigan Press, 2015).

3. Jane Tompkins, *Sensational Designs: The Cultural Work of American Fiction, 1790–1860* (New York: Oxford University Press, 1985), 5.

4. John Guillory, "Canon," in *Critical Terms for Literary Study*, ed. Frank Lentricchia and Thomas McLaughlin, 2nd ed. (Chicago: University of Chicago Press, 1995), 240.

5. Henry Louis Gates Jr., "The Master's Pieces," in *The Henry Louis Gates, Jr. Reader*, ed. Henry Louis Gates Jr. and Abby Wolf (New York: Basic Civitas Books, 2012), 163.

6. Earhart, *Traces of the Old*, 99. Mitsuharu Matsuoka's project remains in effect today; for the 1997 version, see *American Authors on the Web*, updated January 7, 1997, archived on the Internet Archive, accessed March 3, 2016, https://web.archive .org/web/19970109020526/http://www.lang.nagoya-u.ac.jp/~matsuoka/AmeLit .html#Authors.

7. Peter Shillingsburg, for example, calls *Project Gutenberg* "the product of abysmal ignorance of the textual condition" and a "textual junkyard." Peter Shillingsburg, *Scholarly Editing in the Computer Age: Theory and Practice* (Ann Arbor: University of Michigan Press), 161.

8. Amy E. Earhart, "Can Information Be Unfettered?: Race and the New Digital Humanities Canon," in *Debates in Digital Humanities*, ed. Matthew K. Gold (Minneapolis: University of Minnesota Press, 2012), 313, http://dhdebates.gc.cuny.edu/debates/.

9. Donna Campbell, "Brief Timeline of American Literature and Events: Pre-1620–1920," *American Literature*, archived on the Internet Archive, accessed March 4, 2016, https://web.archive.org/web/20050929191902/http://www.wsu.edu/%7Ecampbelld /amlit/timefram.html.

10. Donna Campbell, phone interview with author, September 2, 2011.

11. Campbell, interview, September 2, 2011.

12. Campbell, interview, September 2, 2011.

13. *The American Studies Crossroads* site is no longer being actively updated. The site materials are unevenly archived on the original Georgetown site and on the Virtual Knowledge project site, making the Internet Archive the most complete archive available.

14. Randall Bass, "A Brief Guide to Interactive Multimedia and the Study of the United States," Georgetown University, last updated 1997, archived on the Internet Archive, accessed on March 2, 2016, https://web.archive.org/web/19970614171001/http:// www.georgetown.edu/crossroads/mltmedia.html.

15. Martin Wolske, Colin Rhinesmith, and Beth Kumar, "Community Informatics Studio: Designing Experiential Learning to Support Teaching, Research, and Practice," *Journal of Education for Library & Information Science* 55, no. 2 (2014): 168.

16. Henry Louis Gates Jr. and Nellie Y. McKay, preface to the 2nd ed. of *The Norton Anthology of African American Literature* (New York: W. W. Norton, 2004), 184.

17. Cynthia Skove Nevels, *Lynching to Belong* (College Station: Texas A&M University Press, 2007), 19.

18. Wesley Raabe, "Estranging Anthology Texts of American Literature: Digital Humanities Resources for Harriet Beecher Stowe, Walt Whitman, and Emily Dickinson," *CEA Critic* 76, no. 2 (July 2014): 170–171.

19. Amy E. Earhart, ed., *Millican "Riot," 1868*, accessed March 3, 2016, http://millican .omeka.net.

20. Caroline Gebhard and Barbara McCaskill, *Post-Bellum, Pre-Harlem: African American Literature and Culture, 1877–1919* (New York: New York University Press, 2006), 1.

21. Ibid., 2.

22. Pattie Cowell, "Less False Stories: Teaching Comparative Early American Literatures," *Early American Literature* 33, no. 1 (1998): 89.

23. Amanda Gailey, "Teaching Attentive Reading and Motivated Writing through Digital Editing," *CEA Critic* 76, no. 2 (July 2014): 196.

24. Leslie Bonds, "Listening In on the Conversations: An Overview of Digital Humanities Pedagogy," *CEA Critic* 76, no. 2 (July 2014): 153.

25. Paul Fyfe, "How to Not Read a Victorian Novel," *Journal of Victorian Culture* 16, no. 1 (2011): 85.

14. *Uncle Tom's Cabin* and Archives of Injustice

Edward Whitley

IN 1853 HARRIET BEECHER STOWE gathered together many of the texts she had used as source material for writing *Uncle Tom's Cabin*—along with other documents she could point to as evidence that her fictional account of slavery in the United States was grounded in recent historical fact—and published them as *A Key to "Uncle Tom's Cabin."* She had the phrase *Facts for the People* printed on the title page of the book to underscore that her novel was not merely the product of her fertile imagination but was instead what we could call an *archive of injustice*: a curated collection of documents organized to mobilize action against unjust social formations. Several digital resources have become available in the past twenty years that allow students of nineteenth-century American literature to explore the texts and images that Stowe sifted through as she wrote *Uncle Tom's Cabin* and asked herself the questions that any collector or archivist must ask. Which documents will I include, which will I exclude, and why? How will I organize and display the information that I gather? How will my criteria for exclusion and inclusion, as well as for organization and display, serve to present my collection of documents not as ideologically motivated or idiosyncratically gathered, but as "facts for the people"? Finally, how will my archive determine not only what counts as a "fact," but who counts as "the people"?[1] Bringing such questions into an American literature classroom can give students the opportunity to think critically about how texts are structured and organized in a variety of genres and media forms (novels and political tracts printed on paper, digital archives published online), as well as reflect on the continuities and discontinuities between different historical moments: the antebellum years that saw the rise of print-circulated abolitionist texts and our current digital era where students can read from an electronic archive of nineteenth-century texts in one browser tab while keeping up-to-date on the curatorial work of social media activists in another.

In this essay, I describe a two-part assignment that gives students the opportunity, first, to reverse engineer the composition of *Uncle Tom's Cabin* by searching through digital archives of abolitionist texts and images to explore how Stowe's inclusion of some materials (and exclusion of others) shaped her resulting novel (see Appendix 14.1). The second part of this assignment asks students to consider how social activists today are sorting, cataloging, organizing, selecting, rejecting—in a word, *archiving*—the documentary record of social injustice appearing online in real time every day. The basic premise linking the two parts of this assignment should be obvious to most students: just as there was injustice in the nineteenth century there is injustice today, and studying the activism of the past helps us understand the activism of the present.[2] What is often less intuitive to students is the proposition that *Uncle Tom's Cabin* could be thought of not just as a novel but as an archive. A number of scholars and information professionals have recently begun to define the archive as, in Rodrigo Lazo's formulation, both "a place with research materials and reading desks and . . . a metonym for the organization of information."[3] In this more capacious definition of the archive that Lazo and others have embraced, "the archive as a concept of knowledge organization" has emerged as a compelling way to describe a variety of practices that seek to shape a culture through a process of gathering and organizing its texts.[4] The fact that Stowe could so quickly reimagine her novel as a collection of documents in *A Key to "Uncle Tom's Cabin"* points to the archiving impulse at the heart of her fictional narrative.

Following closely on this notion of the novel-as-archive is the idea that many of the digital activities that our students are already familiar with—blogging, tweeting, creating memes, building websites, sharing images—can also be thought of as archival practices with activist agendas similar to Stowe's. Given the amount of information available online, it has become increasingly important for activists to find ways to use digital media to sort through, keep track of, and promote the texts, images, audio files, and videos that can then be used to raise consciousness and mobilize action. For example, the micro-blogging platform Twitter was recently described on the popular news and entertainment website BuzzFeed as "a social network that is increasingly coming to influence the way we communicate, argue, and organize."[5] That last word—*organize*—carries a double relevance for activists as tweeted information can be organized on the fly into virtual archival spaces through the use of hashtags such as the anti-police brutality #blacklivesmatter and the feminist #yesallwomen, which can then in turn serve to organize protests, unify campaigns, and bring together the supporters of a cause. As my students have shown me, the path from *Uncle Tom's Cabin* to a Twitter hashtag is a remarkably short one, with campaigns for social justice from the nineteenth and twenty-first centuries linked by a common commitment to archival practice and experimentation with media forms.

I taught this assignment for the first time in an upper-division course on antebellum American literature, a class that focuses on the aesthetic practices of sentimentalism and the sublime, and how those aesthetics emerge from and potentially transform their cultural contexts.[6] (The other literary texts that students read in addition to *Uncle Tom's Cabin* include *The Narrative of Arthur Gordon Pym, Hobomok, Moby-Dick, Incidents in the Life of a Slave Girl, The Narrative of the Life of Frederick Douglass*, and poetry by Walt Whitman and Emily Dickinson.) I dedicated two seventy-five-minute class periods to discussing the different stages of the assignment, both in small groups and as a full class. This extended discussion period was critical given that the primary goal of the assignment is to trigger moments of self-reflection as students are asked to think across historical periods and media forms; its goal is to contribute to the kind of historically informed media literacy that should be central to the educational mission of the humanities in the early twenty-first century. To create the kind of disorientation that precedes self-reflection, the assignment has, by design, a lot of moving parts: Stowe's novel, the *Key to "Uncle Tom's Cabin*," online archives of abolitionist texts, twenty-first-century digital activism, questions of social justice, and an expanded definition of the archive as a method of selecting and organizing the records that define a culture. I asked my students to write two short essays, the drafts of which were due during two separate class periods: one on the roots of *Uncle Tom's Cabin* in antebellum abolitionist texts and the other on twenty-first-century digital activism. On the days that paper drafts were due we held both full-class and small-group discussions about what students had discovered online and how they had written about those discoveries. Final drafts of both papers were due one week later. I based my grading on the quality of the research and writing in the papers, with particular emphasis given to students' ability to compare historical periods and media forms, to use *the archive* as a conceptual link between disparate periods and forms, and to reflect on the processes through which texts are created, disseminated, structured, stored, and used to change the world.

When I introduced the assignment to my class on antebellum American literature, we discussed the archive as both a brick-and-mortar research space and as a metaphor for gathering and organizing information. We also discussed the ideological frameworks that motivate archivists to include and exclude objects their collections. There is a growing body of scholarship—much of it accessible to undergraduates—that helps explain the political implications of archival practice. To wrap their minds around the politics of the archive, students need to understand that while all archives are inherently political, not all archivists are political activists. I relied heavily on Ann Laura Stoler's description of the archive to generate discussion about the relationship between collecting information and shaping political reality. Stoler calls the archive "a force field that animates political energies and expertise, that pulls on some 'social facts' and converts them into qualified knowledge, that attends to some ways of knowing while repelling and refusing others."[7] In preparing to teach this class again, I have put together a collection of similar undergraduate-friendly snippets from scholarly works on archival theory—such as the following by Joan M. Schwartz and Terry Cook—that help to explain the politically motivated nature of archives that "are not passive storehouses of old stuff, but active sites where social power is negotiated, contested, confirmed."[8] Similarly, the series of questions that Rodrigo Lazo asks about the politics of the archive lay the foundation for an excellent classroom discussion:

> If archives do indeed "constitute" memory rather than just contain it or record it and if they are crucial in disseminating information, a variety of questions emerge. How do archives develop procedures for the inclusion and exclusion of materials, for the preservation and even inadvertent destruction of information? How do archives wield authority over what is considered important in public institutions and educational settings? Who has access to archives and what types of identity claims are made by the people who control and disperse that information?[9]

I have also begun to think about how such questions could have added impact if coupled with a trip to a library's special collections, particularly if an acquisitions librarian could talk with students about the guidelines that determine the library's holdings. Students tend to have only a vague notion about *what* material is held in their institutional libraries and even less consideration of *why* that material has been chosen. Talking directly with a librarian about the process of choosing, rejecting, and preserving texts can help foreground the assumptions that underlie the creation and maintenance of archives.

Following this introduction to the politics of archival practice, we turned our attention to the process by which the fictional narrative of *Uncle Tom's Cabin* emerged from Stowe's strategic selection and rejection of texts. At this point in the discussion many student assumptions came to the foreground: the first was that *Uncle Tom's Cabin* is a near-complete record of the experience of American slavery; and the second, related, assumption was that nineteenth-century Americans were living in a culture of media scarcity that gave them relatively few options for learning about current events. Because *Uncle Tom's Cabin* is such an exemplary work of activist literature—James Baldwin called it "everybody's protest novel"[10]—it can be difficult for students to see it as anything less than comprehensive. A better understanding of the abundance of printed texts available in the 1850s not only provided a useful corrective to this notion but also put students in a position to see Stowe as dealing with a problem of information overload rather than scarcity. Given this climate of textual excess, Stowe's project to write a novel in support of the abolitionist cause necessarily began with deciding what to include and what to exclude. By working with digital resources such as the *Black Abolitionist Archive*, the *Colored Conventions* project, the *American Abolitionism Project*, and *Documenting the American South* (see Appendix 14.1 for a longer list of resources), students began to see firsthand both the amount and quality of information that was available to nineteenth-century Americans.[11]

Before sending students to explore the rich holdings of these digital resources, I discussed with them a specific example from *Uncle Tom's Cabin* that illustrates the decision-making process Stowe went through as she chose to include certain segments of abolitionist discourse at the expense of others.[12] The goal of this discussion was to help them learn to identify absences in the text, to look for traces of what has been left out rather than taking for granted that Stowe has made her novel a comprehensive archive of abolitionist thought. About halfway through the novel, one of the characters predicts an uprising of African American slaves similar to what took place during the Haitian Revolution, noting, in particular, that slaves who are the children of white fathers would lead this conflict:

> "Well, there is a pretty fair infusion of Anglo Saxon blood among our slaves, now," said Augustine [St. Clare]. "There are plenty among them who have only enough of the African to give a sort of tropical warmth and fervor to our calculating firmness and foresight. If ever the San Domingo hour comes [a reference to the Haitian Revolution], Anglo Saxon blood will lead on the day. Sons of white fathers, with all our haughty feelings burning in their veins, will not always be bought and sold and traded. They will rise, and raise with them their mother's race."[13]

Students who had come to think of Harriet Beecher Stowe as, in Abraham Lincoln's apocryphal phrase, "the little woman who wrote the book that started this great war" invariably paused at the idea that *Uncle Tom's Cabin* predicted a race war rather than a civil war.[14] This potentially disorienting realization, however, led to a productive discussion on how fear of racial conflict made its way into Stowe's novel while talk of secession did not. Why did Stowe choose to highlight this fear of racial uprising? How prevalent was this fear in the discourses of abolitionism? Was it a central tenet? An outlier? What else did abolitionists predict as possible outcomes for the continuation of slavery in the United States? And how common was the belief that "Anglo Saxon blood" in slaves with white fathers would motivate rebellion? Such questions highlight the fact that Stowe's novel was neither inevitable in its argument nor complete in its presentation of abolitionist tenets; instead, it was a selective account drawn from a much larger, more diverse body of texts. With these questions in mind, students began to explore the documentary record of abolitionist thought available online.

One of my students decided to search for alternatives to the racialist account of slave revolt that Stowe presents through the character of Augustine St. Clare. This student took issue with the assumption that African Americans with white fathers "are enslaved because their African blood keeps them docile, whereas if they rebel, it will be because of a white lineage that yearns for freedom." After searching through a number of online repositories of abolitionist periodicals, this student found an article by African American antislavery activist Abner H. Francis that offers an alternative to St. Clare's essentialist argument about race and emancipation. Rather than assume that some races are hardwired for freedom while others are destined for servitude, Francis proposes that all people in bondage, regardless of race, respond to their oppression with similar desires for freedom: "All nations have been slaves in their turn. . . . But after long oppression has goaded them on to resistance, they have overthrown their oppressors, and continued on in the march of human progress."[15] This stunning counter-example published in Frederick Douglass's *North Star* throws into sharp relief the pattern of inclusion and exclusion by which Stowe crafted her archive of injustice, with some voices taking center stage and others being minimized or excluded entirely. Similarly, another student who learned about organizations for educating free African Americans, such as the Institute for Colored Youth in Philadelphia, noted that the decision not to highlight educational opportunities in the United States for former slaves was also tied to fears of racial conflict: "Stowe ignored institutions like these in her advocacy for abolition because they still left the possibility of the race war that she feared so much."[16]

In addition to identifying Stowe's exclusions from the historical record, my students also found moments where Stowe not only included important documentary evidence but also presented it in ways that amplified its potential impact. One student who researched the sexual abuse of African American women by white slaveholders praised Stowe for finding a way to address the issue within the confines of social mores forbidding the open discussion of sexuality. This student's first discovery was that finding the right material through keyword searches in an electronic database requires thinking in nineteenth-century terms: "when scouring the various archives devoted to news articles regarding slavery and the abolitionist movement, there exist no stories that address issues of 'sexual abuse' (as this is an anachronistic term)." After searching for the terms *mulatto* and *licentious* in Readex's *America's*

Historical Newspapers database, this student found an article in the abolition-ist periodical the *Liberator* denouncing the "cruelty to unprotected colored females, the branding with dishonor of innocent children, the deprivation of the inheritance of their parents, the desertion of wives and children."[17] Noting that the language in the *Liberator* echoed language in *Uncle Tom's Cabin*, this student argued further that Stowe's presentation of the same issue "strategi-cally recreates the atrocities of which the author of the article speaks; however, Stowe drives the narrative further when Cassy [an African American slave kept as a concubine by her white master] suffers additional abuse from her owner when he takes away her children." In other words, Stowe's inclusion of stories such as these are amplified by their narrative presentation because the novel's form allows for an account of sexual abuse to be combined with an account of family separation through the organizing principle of the fictional character. Different cultural texts can sit side by side in Stowe's archive of injustice when filed under the single heading of *Cassy*.

After exploring these digital resources of primary source documents and writing up their findings as short papers, my students came back to class ready to discuss their experiences and reflect on what they had learned. These discussions—which took place both in small groups and with the class as a whole—were essential moments for developing critical media literacy and for understanding the relationship between literary texts and historical context. The examples I've cited above demonstrate how some students are very adept at pointing out what *Uncle Tom's Cabin* excludes, while others are able to dis-cern the nuanced ways that Stowe brings pieces of her culture into the fabric of her literary text. Having students share their findings with one another in a supportive environment creates opportunities for self-reflection and critical thinking. For example, one of my students described how the events in *Uncle Tom's Cabin* compare unfavorably with "the historical reality made available through online archives," while another wrote that "Stowe crafted her story to reflect the truth of slavery as it really was." Each student located *truth* and *reality* in a different place: for one it was the novel, and for another it was the digital archives. The discussion that followed allowed us to reflect on the often unstable foundation of historical truth claims and to reorient ourselves to investigating the process by which truth is constructed—the selection, presen-tation, and dissemination of textual evidence—rather than the relative value of one truth claim over another.

Such comments created opportunities to reflect on the work that literature can and cannot do both to describe and to influence the culture from which it emerges; they also created a space for discussing the assumptions we hold about the content of archives (both digital and analog) and the access these archives grant us to "historical reality." David Greetham reminds us that despite our "desire for a totalised archive that reaches beyond the happenstance of actual documentary survival," what we are actually left with is considerably less comprehensive: "we have cultural scraps, garbage, leftovers, selections, bits of memory . . . [and] we feel uncomfortable about this because we probably still retain a desire for a structuralist sense of comprehension, of a grid on which all perfected works could be plotted."[18] For students who have never had the opportunity to engage in primary source research, either in digital archives or elsewhere, it can be disorienting to go from feeling that archives provide tremendous access to the historical record to being told that seemingly bottomless collections of digitized texts are partial, incomplete, and even at times untrue. First-time student researchers are not alone in this. Randolph Starn has written that, as a culture at large, we "remain committed to archives as a source of historical truth, despite having good reason to know that their truth-value is questionable."[19] The goal of this exercise and its follow-up discussion is pedagogical whiplash: to have students turn one direction to see how plentiful the historical archive is and how easily they can access it through digital resources, and then to turn the other direction to see how partial, fragmentary, and suspicious the archive can be as well. Students should emerge from this experience as more savvy consumers of the historical narratives with which they are presented, whether in fictional or archival form.

The second part of the assignment returned students to the familiar ground of online spaces such as social media, but with that ground somewhat defamiliarized by their experiences with Stowe's novel and its archival contexts. For the first part of the assignment, students were asked to find documents related to the social justice mission of *Uncle Tom's Cabin*; for the second part, they explored a contemporary social issue—such as police brutality, sex trafficking, or modern slavery—but instead of trying to find documents buried in a digital archive, they made simple Google searches online to see what found them. One of the goals of this part of the assignment was to identify the work that had already been done to make information about social injustice available to internet users, and then to reflect on that work as a species of archival practice. I asked my students to answer the following questions: What have individuals or institutions done to curate information about social injustice online? What digital methods are used to create improvised archives of online information (blogs, Facebook pages, hashtags, etc.)? What digital objects are being curated (tweets, articles, images, videos, memes, etc.)? And how do the chosen methods of curation shape, distort, or promote the information in question? I encouraged my students to think critically about how information is gathered and structured online and to see parallels between the nineteenth-century archives of abolitionist thought and the archives that are currently being built around contemporary social issues.

One student asked during this part of the assignment, "Am I writing about sex trafficking, or just about how hashtags work?" The answer: both. Information is never delivered in a pure, unmediated form. Whether in a nineteenth-century novel or abolitionist newspaper, or through tweets, blogs, and Facebook groups, the message and its medium always travel hand in hand. With a little help, most students are able to make the conceptual leap required to think about medium and message as interrelated concepts, though some struggle to see information as necessarily enmeshed in the medium of its transmission. Students tend to have the easiest time conceptualizing the hashtag as a source of information, a medium of transmission, and a method for organizing ideas into informal archival spaces. One of my students wrote, "The method through which people now archive issues of racial stereotyping and mass incarceration is primarily done though social media such as hashtags, which effectively act as a method for categorization of different issues." Every post made to a social media platform such as Twitter or Instagram that includes a hashtag—be it something innocuous like #puppies or #disneyland, or something politically charged like #ferguson or #bengazhi—will immediately be grouped with every other post carrying the same hashtag. Not only can social media users keep track of the conversations taking place around a topic of interest by following the hashtag as new content is added, but content can also be organized and preserved for later reference through websites such as paper.li and Wakelet, which aspire to be the successors to the popular but now defunct Storify service for both *storing* and *telling a story* through social media. The archival function of the hashtag can be instantaneous as information is gathered and structured in real time; with the help of third-party websites, hashtags can also serve to capture a fleeting moment for posterity. I would add here that our discussion of sustainability was more limited than I would have liked it to be. An archivist's interest in the long-term sustainability of a collection's documents and an activist's concern with immediate social change may suggest a divergence between activists' and archivists' agendas. Recent work on feminism and the archive (such as Kate Eichhorn's 2013 book *The Archival Turn in Feminism: Outrage in Order*), for example, points to ways that archivists and activists can share common ground.

Given the recent attention that high-profile movements such as #blacklivesmatter and #occupywallstreet have received for using social media platforms to advocate for social change, it is unsurprising that students gravitate toward hashtag activism as a method for organizing both people and information.[20] My students identified tremendous benefits to hashtag activism, as well as potential downsides, with the nineteenth-century abolitionist movement and *Uncle Tom's Cabin* providing them with useful frames of reference. For example, one student noted that activists who include additional hashtags alongside a

more prominent one can refocus the discussion in meaningful ways: by adding feminist hashtags such as #yesallwomen or #blackwomenslivesmatter to a
trending hashtag such as #blacklivesmatter, feminist activists can ensure that
issues of gender become part of the larger effort to end state-sponsored violence
against African Americans and other people of color. The reception history of
Uncle Tom's Cabin provides its own examples of activists yoking their efforts
to the prominent work that Stowe's novel accomplished, as Solomon Northup
wrote that his 1853 narrative *Twelve Years a Slave* could be read as "affording
another Key to *Uncle Tom's Cabin*," while the African American activists who
discussed the merits of *Uncle Tom's Cabin* in the pages of *Frederick Douglass's
Paper* put Stowe in conversation with abolitionist texts that argued both with
and against the claims of her novel.[21] In contrast to the success that hashtag
activism has in immediately directing the discourse surrounding issues of social
injustice, one of my students noted that the novel form of a text such as *Uncle
Tom's Cabin* has the ability to synthesize a variety of different factual accounts
into composite fictional characters who can then influence public opinion on
the injustice of slavery: "With retweets and reposts, a source can go viral in just
under a day. Though this modern strategy works tremendously well, there is a
failure to successfully synthesize the issue of racial profiling and police brutality.
What *Uncle Tom* did was present the nation with true stories of violence that
they could then incorporate into their view of slavery as a whole. Ultimately,
the current movement needs an *Uncle Tom's Cabin* that it does not have."

This same student argued that the distance between nineteenth-century
abolitionism and online activism is much shorter than we might initially think.
In researching the effort to end the global trafficking of minors, this student
found an organization called Operation Underground Railroad, which "works
to end the sex trafficking of children in large part by retracing the link back
to slavery in the United States." In addition to using Twitter, Instagram, and
Facebook "to archive the statistics regarding the number of children suffering
in the sex trafficking industry," Operation Underground Railroad uses language
drawn directly from the antebellum abolition movement in every aspect of
its campaign: its website encourages visitors to "Become an Abolitionist" and
asks for five-dollar donations to "Give a Lincoln, Save a Slave"; its social media
content carries the hashtag #iamanabolitionist; its email newsletter, the *Lan-
tern*, invokes the lights placed in the homes of conductors on the Underground
Railroad; and its YouTube channel provides "videos that condense both the
current information regarding the sex trafficking industry as well as historical background on slavery in the United States." This student concluded that
Operation Underground Railroad "wants to bring Stowe's very archive into
the twenty-first century. . . . The message: this is the *same* issue that was supposedly resolved."

Discovering such continuities between disparate historical moments can have a meaningful impact on students, particularly as these continuities inform the accounts of social injustice that they have grown accustomed to experiencing through social media and other outlets. Sarah Jane Cervenak has recently written on the pedagogical opportunities (and challenges) of classroom discussions about slavery that "quickly move from the mid-nineteenth century into our present" as antebellum accounts of violence against slaves and viral videos of police brutality "collapse into each other."[22] Early Americanist scholars have, in the last decade, begun to question with increasing urgency how both research and pedagogy can articulate a nuanced relationship between the historical legacy of slavery and the challenges of our present moment. Joanna Brooks, for one, encourages us to ask whether "the stories we tell about the past have the power to call us into a new relationship with the present," while Simon Gikandi similarly urges scholars and teachers to consider how "the archive of enslavement" can "speak to the politics of the present."[23]

Gikandi's call to perform the "recuperative work . . . needed to animate this archive so that it could be read not as an antiquarian project but as a living principle of American life and writing" comes with a set of cautions that are instructive for any attempt to draw parallels between the present and the past.[24] The cautions that Gikandi offers center on our relationship to the archive—specifically, whether we go to historical archives looking for a "response to the politics of the present," or whether we treat the archive as containing its own guidelines for interpretation and discovery independent of the demands that the crises of our current moment may make of it. Gikandi ultimately concludes that despite such "anxieties about the relation of historical texts and interpretative contexts," any "reading of the early American archive [cannot] escape the mandate of the present."[25] Our students' ability to analyze different species of archival practice and the various media forms these practices assume will prove invaluable to them as they work toward their own conclusions about the relationship between the present and the past, not to mention their own sense of what needs to be done to build for the future.

The appendix for this chapter, an assignment by Edward Whitley on collecting and synthesizing texts about social issues, can be found at www.press.uillinois .edu/books/TeachingWithDH.

Notes

1. Scholarship on the archive has blossomed in recent decades, following foundational work by Michel Foucault, *The Archaeology of Knowledge and the Discourse on Language*, trans. A. M. Sheridan Smith (New York: Pantheon Books, 1972), and Jacques Derrida, *Archive Fever: A Freudian Impression*, trans. Eric Prenowitz (Chicago:

University of Chicago Press, 1995). Notable contributions to the field include Carolyn Steedman, *Dust: The Archive and Cultural History* (New Brunswick, N.J.: Rutgers University Press, 2002); Diana Taylor, *The Archive and the Repertoire* (Durham, N.C.: Duke University Press, 2003); Marlene Manoff, "Theories of the Archive from across the Disciplines," *Portal: Libraries and the Academy* 4, no. 1 (2004): 9–25; and Antoinette Burton, ed., *Archive Stories: Facts, Fictions, and the Writing of History* (Durham, N.C.: Duke University Press, 2005). Since 2011 *Archive Journal* (http://www.archivejournal. net) has nurtured academic discussion on the place of archives in research, teaching, and institutional practice. My thanks to Lauren Coats for guiding my understanding of archive theory.

2. For other pedagogical guidelines for teaching *Uncle Tom's Cabin* across historical periods see Mark Bracher, "How to Teach for Social Justice: Lessons from *Uncle Tom's Cabin* and Cognitive Science," *College English* 71, no. 4 (2009): 363–88, and Erica D. Galioto, "Stowe's Suspicious Sentimentalism: Teaching *Uncle Tom's Cabin* in the 21st Century," *Teaching American Literature: A Journal of Theory and Practice* 4, no. 3 (2011): 12–28.

3. Rodrigo Lazo, "Migrant Archives," in *States of Emergency: The Object of American Studies*, ed. Russ Castronovo and Susan Gillman (Chapel Hill: University of North Carolina Press, 2009), 42.

4. Rodrigo Lazo, "The Invention of America Again: On the Impossibility of an Archive," *American Literary History* 25, no. 4 (2013): 764. For critiques of this capacious definition of the archive see Kate Theimer, "Archives in Context and as Context," *Journal of Digital Humanities* 1, no. 2 (2012); William J. Maher, "Archives, Archivists, and Society," *American Archivist* 61, no. 2 (1998) ; and Kate Eichhorn's description of "the archive's semantic drift" in the last twenty years in *The Archival Turn in Feminism: Outrage in Order* (Philadelphia: Temple University Press, 2013), 18.

5. Charlie Warzel, "Twitter Just Trademarked 'Tweetstorm'; This Is Why They Matter," April 18, 2015, BuzzFeed, accessed March 26, 2017, http://www.buzzfeed.com /charliewarzel/yep-im-still-writing-about-tweetstorms.

6. Our discussion of the sublime is grounded in selections from Edmund Burke's 1757 treatise *A Philosophical Enquiry in the Origin of Our Ideas on the Sublime and Beautiful*, and our discussion of sentimentalism comes from Joanne Dobson's seminal essay "Reclaiming Sentimental Literature," *American Literature* 69 no. 2 (1997): 236–88.

7. Ann Laura Stoler, *Along the Archival Grain: Epistemic Anxieties and Colonial Common Sense* (Princeton, N.J.: Princeton University Press, 2009), 22.

8. Joan M. Schwartz and Terry Cook, "Archives, Records, and Power: The Making of Modern Memory," *Archival Science* 2, nos. 1–2 (2002): 1.

9. Lazo, "Migrant Archives," 36.

10. James Baldwin, "Everybody's Protest Novel," *Partisan Review* 16 (June 1949): 578–85.

11. My thanks to Jordan Alexander Stein, Melissa White, and Martha Schoolman for helping me assemble this list of digital resources.

12. See also Susan M. Nuernberg, "Stowe, the Abolition Movement, and Prevailing Theories of Race in Nineteenth-Century America," in *Approaches to Teaching Stowe's*

"Uncle Tom's Cabin," ed. Elizabeth Ammons and Susan Belasco (New York: Modern Language Association of America, 2000), 37–45.

13. Harriet Beecher Stowe, *Uncle Tom's Cabin*, ed. Elizabeth Ammons (1852; New York: W. W. Norton, 1994), 234.

14. See Daniel R. Vollaro, "Lincoln, Stowe, and the 'Little Woman/Great War' Story: The Making, and Breaking, of a Great American Anecdote," *Journal of the Abraham Lincoln Association* 30, no. 1 (2009): 18–34, http://hdl.handle.net/2027/spo.2629860.0030.104.

15. Abner H. Francis, "Friends and Fellow Countrymen," *North Star* (Rochester, N.Y.), August 17, 1849, *Accessible Archives: African American Newspapers*, http://www.accessible-archives.com.

16. This student's source was Fanny Jackson Coppin, *Reminiscences of School Life, and Hints on Teaching* (Philadelphia: A.M.M. Book Concern, 1913), *Documenting the American South*, http://docsouth.unc.edu.

17. "The Intermarriage Law," *Liberator*, February 25, 1841, *America's Historical Newspapers*, http://www.infoweb.newsbank.com.

18. David Greetham, "'Who's In, Who's Out': The Cultural Poetics of Archival Exclusion," *Studies in the Literary Imagination* 32, no. 1 (1999): 16–17.

19. Randolph Starn, "Truths in the Archives," *Common Knowledge* 8, no. 2 (Spring 2002): 388.

20. See Manuel Castelles, *Networks of Outrage and Hope: Social Movements in the Internet Age* (Malden, Mass.: Polity Press, 2012); Paolo Gerbaudo, *Tweets and the Streets: Social Media and Contemporary Activism* (New York: Pluto Books, 2012); and Daniel Trottier and Christian Fuchs, eds., *Social Media, Politics, and the State: Protests, Revolutions, Riots, Crime, and Policing in the Age of Facebook, Twitter, and YouTube* (New York: Routledge, 2015). My thanks to Sarah Heidebrink-Bruno for her insights on digital activism.

21. See Solomon Northup, *Twelve Years a Slave: Narrative of Solomon Northup, a Citizen of New-York, Kidnapped in Washington City in 1841, and Rescued in 1853* (Auburn, N.Y.: Derby and Miller, 1853), *Documenting the American South*, http://docsouth.unc.edu; and Robert S. Levine, "*Uncle Tom's Cabin* in *Frederick Douglass' Paper*: An Analysis of Reception," *American Literature* 64, no. 1 (1992): 71–93. My thanks to Steven W. Thomas for directing my attention to Northup's reference to *Uncle Tom's Cabin*.

22. Sarah Jane Cervenak, "On Not Teaching about Violence: Being in the Classroom *After* Ferguson," *Feminist Studies* 41, no. 1 (2015): 223.

23. Joanna Brooks, "Working Definitions: Race, Ethnic Studies, and Early American Literature," *Early American Literature* 41, no. 2 (2006): 319; Simon Gikandi, "Rethinking the Archive of Enslavement," *Early American Literature* 50, no. 1 (2015): 82.

24. Gikandi, "Rethinking the Archive of Enslavement," 82.

25. Ibid., 83–84.

15. Merging Print and Digital Literacies in the African American Literature Classroom

Tisha M. Brooks

IN A RECENT LIBRARY WORKSHOP, co-led by the resident humanities librarian at Southern Illinois University Edwardsville (SIUE) and myself, I asked students in my African American literature survey course to peruse twenty-one print anthologies of African American literature and provided them with a worksheet of questions to answer as they reviewed their texts (see Appendix 15.1). The goal of the anthology perusal workshop was to help prepare students to create their own digital anthologies for the final course project. Much like a scavenger hunt, the workshop worksheet asked students to find key elements that are central to an anthology: the title, editor(s), table of contents, and the introduction. After they located these key elements, I asked them to determine the focus and purpose of the anthology. At the outset, this seemed like a straightforward set of tasks, but as students began their independent work, it quickly became apparent that many did not possess the skills necessary to locate the information I asked them to find. Some students sat staring at their closed book, wondering what to do next, and had to be encouraged to open the book to find the features listed on the worksheet. Others opened the text but were immediately lost—searching for the table of contents in the back and finding themselves unable to locate the name of the editor. Perhaps the biggest challenge was the question asking them to write down the focus and purpose of the anthology. Several students found the introduction but had no idea how to discover the focus or purpose. Once again, we had to encourage them to read the opening paragraphs of the intro in search of that information. By the end of the workshop, my understanding of the print literacy divide had grown tremendously. Although my class contained many students who had little trouble navigating these print anthologies, a significant number of students found it difficult to "read" these texts, and some even handled their book like a foreign object.

As educators, it would be easy on a first consideration to negatively evaluate these students' literacy skills and their intellectual capacity. However, given the unequal access students have to acquire such skills due to racial and economic disparities in education, we must move beyond a narrow consideration of this lack of traditional print literacy as the marker of intellect in our students. As Maryemma Graham asserts in her article "Black Is Gold," "the distinctions we make between types of writers, speakers, and readers encourage exclusion and invisibility. The preference for the ideal academic student reader or writer can blind us" to the alternative critical literacies and reading practices that students do possess.[1] For those of us who value a classroom space predicated on democratic practices of inclusion and critical engagement rather than on hierarchical practices of exclusion and silence, we must adapt to and recognize an evolving definition of literacy that is not tied strictly to a traditional and highly specialized canon of literature (i.e., print books).

Drawing on Graham's claim of technology as a tool capable of "promoting greater facility with literacies that operate beyond the classroom," I assert in this chapter that the use of digital pedagogy in the African American literature undergraduate classroom is imperative in order to bridge the gap between students' reading practices and our own.[2] More specifically, the privileging of print literacy skills, central to our study of literature, often leaves students who lack these skills feeling alienated and voiceless in the classroom. We must embrace democratic education that, according to bell hooks, "seeks to re-envision schooling as always a part of our real world experience, and our real life," enabling students to "experience learning as a whole process rather than a restrictive practice that disconnects and alienates them from the world."[3]

Given the exclusion and invisibility in the undergraduate classroom to which Graham and hooks attest, how can a digital pedagogy of African American literature create a more democratic and less exclusionary space? In particular, how can a digital pedagogy transform the classroom into a space where we invite students to use and further develop their own reading and critical practices, skills that demonstrate students' competence and intellectual capacity, alongside those literacy practices that are central to the study of nineteenth-century African American texts? If, as Matthew Kirschenbaum asserts, the digital humanities possess "a culture that values collaboration, openness, nonhierarchical relations, and agility,"[4] then a digital pedagogy that grows out of this culture of collaboration and openness, rather than hierarchy, is well poised to embrace and, more importantly, to bridge multiple literacies—those originating within the academy and those from without.

As the opening anecdote of the digital anthology workshop reveals, students in my English 205 course, Introduction to African American Texts, are particularly in need of such a bridge. Although this course fills general education and English major requirements, it is not a required course. This means students in the class have elected to take this course, and the overwhelming majority of students are *not* English majors. Moreover, students enter the classroom with little to no knowledge of nineteenth-century African American history. Consequently, many students are unprepared to succeed in this course, as they lack the print literacy skills and the historical grounding that are critical to traditional African American literary study.

In this course, I construct assignments and exercises around the use of several digital archives in and outside of class and through a final collaborative project in which students create a digital anthology of African American literature. These assignments encourage students to become knowledge curators and meaning makers. Further illustrating these pedagogical benefits, Joanne Diaz claims that digital archives invite "students to reconsider what a book is and how it functions as a series of editorial choices . . . and perhaps most important . . . can actually get undergraduates—and teachers—to work toward a clearer and more effective definition of close reading."[5] While students work closely with several archives throughout the semester, this chapter focuses on the digital archive of the Schomburg Center for Research in Black Culture, *In Motion: African American Migration Experience*, as I use it extensively over the first four weeks of class in order to introduce students to the historical context of late eighteenth- and nineteenth-century African American literature.[6]

Focusing specifically on the digital archive and digital anthology assignments that I use in the class, this chapter demonstrates the core function of digital pedagogy as a form of democratic education that enables students to bridge multiple literacies and historical gaps. Because of these divides, many students initially enter the classroom with anxiety—rooted in a fear of reading lengthy texts, especially historical works, which they find particularly alienating. Nevertheless, the digital archive and digital anthology assignments help bridge this divide by offering a "hands-on engagement" with learning and the opportunity to use technology as a tool for "real resistance and reform"—one that can "imagine, produce, and disseminate" knowledge, while shaping meaning in the world.[7] Through this democratic digital pedagogy, students take responsibility for their own educational journeys by working collectively with peers and with me to engage in meaning-making activities. These activities invite students to merge their own critical knowledge and reading practices from outside the classroom with knowledge and literacy skills gained from within the course. Enriching their own and their peers' learning and understanding of African American literature, this digital pedagogy leads students to a greater facility with and even a newfound enjoyment of nineteenth-century African American literature.

Searching for Meaning in the Digital Archive

Funded in part by a grant from the Institute of Museum and Library Services and with the support of the Congressional Black Caucus, the Schomburg Center's digital archive, *In Motion: African American Migration Experience* (AAME), was created in order to document the "thirteen defining migrations that formed and transformed African America."[8] The goal of the archive is to offer an alternative history of the presence of black peoples in America—one that reflects the complexity of their movements that were at times coerced, while at other times self-directed. Presenting these movements as "hopeful journeys," the archive showcases "resourceful and creative men and women, risk-takers in an exploitative and hostile environment." Published in 2005, the AAME digital archive "presents more than 16,500 pages of texts, 8,300 illustrations, and more than 60 maps" related to these various migrations, including the transatlantic slave trade and the domestic slave trade.[9]

At the beginning of every semester, I take a poll of my African American literature students to gauge how much they know about the transatlantic slave trade (otherwise known as the Middle Passage) and American slavery. Students consistently explain that they did not learn about the Middle Passage in high school, and their study of slavery consisted of a few paragraphs that focused on the Underground Railroad and the role of slavery in the Civil War. In short, students learned nothing about how slaves were produced or created, and they had little or no concrete sense of what slavery really looked like and how it impacted those who, as Frederick Douglass asserts, were "doomed to be witness[es] and participant[s]" within the institution of slavery.[10] The late eighteenth- and nineteenth-century texts that we read in the class, as well as the twentieth-century texts that revisit those earlier historical moments, cannot be read in a historical and social vacuum.[11] Therefore, the digital archive becomes an essential point of entry into these historically grounded literary texts. To facilitate this entry into the past, students spend one week exploring the archive before reading any literature and then an additional three weeks using the archive alongside primary readings and discussions of late eighteenth-, nineteenth-, and twentieth-century literature that focus on slavery and/or the Middle Passage (see Appendix 15.2).

During our initial class meeting, I introduce students to the AAME archive, demonstrating how to access it and explaining the kinds of artifacts and resources they will find there. I then ask students to explore the archive on their own outside of class, focusing specifically on the "Transatlantic Slave Trade" section. Accompanying their exploration of visual and textual resources, students also read an excerpt from the introduction to Marcus Rediker's book *The Slave Ship: A Human History*. Finally, after completing the archival exploration and the reading, students participate in a Blackboard discussion forum asking them to share a discovery they made about the Middle Passage. Encouraging their skills of observation, I prompt students with these questions: What aspects of the Middle Passage do you find significant, surprising, or strange? Explain why. What connections did you observe between the images and artifacts in the AAME archive and the reading? These discussion forum posts must be three hundred words in length and are always due the evening before our next class.

The goal of this assignment is to encourage students to determine how to find meaning in what they viewed or read, while also challenging them to make connections between written text and images. This is a relationship I try to encourage throughout the class, as many students are adept at reading visual images but often struggle with the close reading of written texts. Through a recurring series of in-class and out-of-class exercises, activities, workshops, and assignments, students begin to see the inextricable link between the assigned written texts and images in the archive (photographs, prints, visual art) and the ways in which words and images work together to reinforce their learning of the material.

During our next class, we follow up on this online discussion with students sharing some of their discoveries. Students are particularly interested in the instruments and devices used to discipline and imprison captives aboard the slave ship, how captives were packed on the ships, their forced dancing, and the common practice of throwing sick and dying people overboard to the sharks. Using the classroom's SMART technology, we view some of the artifacts they find most compelling and begin to discuss the value of the digital archive in light of the educational gaps with which they entered the course. From here, we deepen our conversation about educational gaps and historical silences about slavery and the Middle Passage through a discussion of Rediker's *The Slave Ship*. I ask students to share their experience reading this print historical text, which is always overwhelmingly positive. Students note again and again that Rediker's historical narrative reads quite differently from other history books that they have encountered. Rather than write what they see as dry and boring history, Rediker begins his story from the perspective of a young female captive who tries to escape being transported on a slave ship across the Atlantic. In many ways, this historical narrative is new for students and surprises them, as they have never learned about the West African side of the slave trade; nor are they familiar with the resistance of captives to being transported and just how much they were willing to risk to avoid being enslaved. But students are also pleasantly surprised at how this historical narrative engages them and helps them to connect with what they believe to be a very distant past. This opens the possibility for us to begin thinking about how Rediker constructs history differently both in terms of content and in terms of form. Through their viewing and reading of the digital archive and Rediker's text, students discover that there is no one perfect way of transmitting knowledge—engaging with both a print book and digital resources offers a far more expansive understanding of the past. Students comment that the digital archive enables them to "imagine, see, visualize, observe, and witness" everything Rediker writes about.[12] Hence, the digital archive literally functions as a bridge between their own historical and educational gaps and the print text, as the archive makes the print text real and tangible for them. Moreover, this archival assignment encourages them to make connections across media and reinforces the knowledge gained from the print source. This discovery becomes more significant once students begin working on their digital anthology artifacts, as it similarly enables them to bring print and digital worlds together to disseminate knowledge and produce meaning in the world.

Following this brief discussion of their reader response to the text, I offer a short mini-lecture on Rediker's introduction to ensure that students understand how his historical text contributes to and expands our perspective on the Middle Passage. The lecture centers around these three questions: (1) How does Rediker define the slave ship; (2) how did captives respond to and resist the violence of the slave ship; and (3) why does Rediker feel compelled to write what he calls "a human history?" I am interested in helping students think critically about the strategies used when representing the Middle Passage. Through this mini-lecture and discussion of Rediker's text, students begin to understand that some representations of the Middle Passage, regardless of intent, reproduce the violence of that event by continuing to dehumanize and objectify the bodies of African captives.[13] Though students are not explicitly aware of this reproduction of violence in their initial exploration of the archives, their responses to seeing the images reflect an overwhelmingly singular narrative of black bodies as victims of pain, trauma, and violence. The goal of this class is to help students become more critically aware of this singular narrative that, as Judalyn Ryan asserts, makes it difficult, if not impossible, to see the full humanity of black people as "bearers, shapers, and producers of culture."[14]

Using Rediker's excerpt as a critical lens, students participate in a visual analysis small-group workshop to examine images from the AAME digital archive that I have chosen: *The Slave Ship*, *Hold of a Ship*, *Punishment*, and *Bodies in the Sea*.[15]

These images reflect many of the specific aspects of the slave ship that students find most compelling. After viewing their assigned images, students work through several steps of a visual analysis exercise: summarize, observe, contextualize, and analyze. Although some of these rhetorical terms initially seem unfamiliar to students, they are often pleasantly surprised to discover that they engage in these steps all the time when they read images. Each term is followed with a clear directive that explains what they should do with the image to successfully complete each step, and students have no trouble following these instructions. The most difficult step, of course, is analysis, which is why I have them work in small groups. Some students get stuck because they are looking for the "correct" meaning. By working collaboratively, students begin to realize that multiple meanings are at work in visual images. This becomes even more apparent when small groups share their visual analysis with the entire class. Other students (not in their group) add to, expand, and, in some cases, revise their meanings. This collaborative meaning making forms a critical foundation for students before I send them off to complete the final assignment tied to this workshop—a short written argument about their image using the knowledge they gained from the in-class digital archive workshop and our mini-lecture on *The Slave Ship*. Engaging with a specific prompt, students write insightful critical responses to their image from the digital archive, weaving together the knowledge they have gained from the digital archive, Rediker's text, and our collaborative work in the previous class (see Appendix 15.3).

This work analyzing images in the digital archive has a profound impact on students' literary analysis and close-reading skills, as the exercise provides a framework for their literary analysis essays. Students are often surprised to discover that the steps for reading a visual and written text are quite similar: summarize, observe, contextualize, analyze. Since the steps are the same, students are less daunted when I ask them to analyze a literary text in class, and their formal essays that build on this in-class exercise offer a richer reading of the literary text. In the end, the visual analysis and archival workshops enable students to bridge the gap between the reading experience they bring into the classroom, in particular a facility with visual texts, and those critical reading and writing skills central to the study of nineteenth-century African American literature.

The foundational knowledge and analytical skills that students develop from their work with visual texts in the digital archive extends to and informs their work with written texts that focus on slavery, including Phillis Wheatley's 1773 poem "On Being Brought from Africa to America," Robert Hayden's 1962 poem "Middle Passage," and Frederick Douglass's 1845 *Narrative of the Life of Frederick Douglass*. With each of these print texts, students continue to explore digital archives, expanding beyond AAME to use the *National Archive* and *Documenting the American South* (*DocSouth*) as well. These archives ensure that students not only understand the historical context of the literature, but also that they are prepared to consider the ongoing challenges of representing slavery and the Middle Passage in the past and present.

With Frederick Douglass's *Narrative* in particular, we extend our discussion of representations of violence against black bodies to our conversation about nineteenth-century slave narratives. In order to introduce students to the central work of slave narratives, I have them review an online resource on the slave narrative to encourage students to consider some of the recurring features of the genre and the rhetorical strategies used to demonstrate the injustice of slavery and the humanity of enslaved people.[16] Using *DocSouth* to access Douglass's *Narrative* and supplementary resources, students gain additional historical and literary context about Douglass's life, his writing, and his role within the larger antislavery movement, which we review during our initial class discussion of the text.[17]

We focus specifically on the challenges of representing slavery and its violence through close study of the 1792 print titled *Punishment* in the AAME archive. This print informs our reading of the "blood-stained gate" scene in which Douglass witnesses the brutal whipping of his Aunt Hester when he is just a young child.[18] While Douglass's narrative portrays Aunt Hester being whipped by the plantation overseer as punishment for resisting his sexual tyranny over her body, the print similarly portrays a slave ship captain whipping a fifteen-year-old enslaved girl as punishment for her refusal to dance naked before the crew. Although students see a clear repetition between the violence of the slave ship and the violation of enslaved people in America, Douglass's claim that the scene of Aunt Hester's whipping "doomed [him] to be a witness and a participant . . . [in] the hell of slavery" is often difficult for them to fully comprehend.[19] Certainly, they understand why Douglass refers to himself as a witness to slavery, but understanding the inextricable link between witnessing slavery's violence and participating in it is a far greater challenge. Returning to the *Punishment* image offers an alternative way for students to engage critically with Douglass's claim, as the antislavery sketch similarly depicts this tension between witnessing and participating in the violence of slavery. Specifically, students read Douglass's viewing of Aunt Hester's beating in comparison with the enslaved women's witnessing of the whipping in the sketch. Viewing the sketch from the digital archive enables students to see the forced witnessing of violence on slave ships and plantations as a practice used to teach enslaved people their status as chattel and to ensure their submission to and, therefore, participation within what Douglass refers to as "the hell of slavery."

In addition to the visual representation of the captives' forced witnessing of and participation in violence aboard the slave ship, the painting also illustrates the ways in which the crew too became witnesses and participants and raises questions about how the print also positions its viewers as witnesses and participants in such violence. Some students, for instance, recognize that this violent display of the captain's power could also be intended for the white crew as well to discourage disobedience or worse mutiny. This conversation

Isaac Cruikshank, *The abolition of the slave trade Or the inhumanity of dealers in human flesh exemplified in Captn. Kimber's treatment of a young Negro girl of 15 for her virjen (sic) modesty* (1792), courtesy of Library of Congress Prints and Photographs Division, PC 1-8079, captioned in *In Motion: African American Migration Experience as Punishment*

about the complex web of power aboard the slave ship is important; it helps students understand the complexity of power within the institution of slavery as Douglass represents it in his text—an institution that turned everyone into either a willing or unwilling participant.

Saidiya Hartman's *Lose Your Mother* (2007) further illuminates the sketch's intended impact by linking it to abolitionist William Wilberforce's speech about the girl's violent death. According to Hartman, Wilberforce wanted to make his British audience "smell the stench of slavery and to feel the great misery condensed into the small space of the slave ship. He wanted them to envision the girl and to know what he knew: *we are all guilty*. What he wanted them to see was not the girl's disgrace but their own."[20] This intersection of the digital archive and Hartman's work of historical recovery leads students to a deeper discussion of what it means to be a witness and a participant in Douglass's *Narrative* and helps students understand the often tenuous mission of abolitionist texts to move their audience to action. Through our comparison of the *Punishment* sketch from the digital archive and Douglass's *Narrative*, students come to a larger understanding of the purpose of all slave narratives and abolitionist texts: to hold an entire country—even those who did not own slaves—accountable for ending slavery and its violence. Hence, the digital archive creates a bridge between Douglass's words and their potential meanings within the context of his *Narrative*, within the context of abolitionism in the nineteenth century, and within a larger conversation about representing the violence of slavery in the past as well as in the present. Ultimately these digital archival exercises push students to see themselves as agents in the world, not as passive consumers of the visual texts they witness but as critical readers, producers, and users of visual content who are capable of discerning the tenuous potential of all images to objectify or to humanize its subjects.

Creating a Digital Anthology of African American Literature

The time students spend engaging with the digital archives through visual analysis workshops, as well as in small- and large-group discussions, prepares them for the final project of the semester: creating a digital anthology of African American literature (see Appendix 15.4). Since the project is intended to offer a visually engaging representation of African American literature that provides viewers with access to primary and secondary resources related to the field, digital archives are one of the repositories that students use to integrate knowledge into their anthologies. If the goal of the various exercises, workshops, and activities in the archives throughout the semester is to push students to move from being mere consumers of knowledge to become critical thinkers who use the archive to make meaning of its artifacts and the history and literature connected to them, then the purpose of this final project is to push students a step further intellectually by challenging them to use those skills to create their own digital artifact that disseminates knowledge and creates meaning for their fellow peers but also for a wider audience. The digital anthology is a particularly useful assessment because it requires students to merge multiple literacies as they include visual and written texts from the digital archives in meaningful ways and demonstrate their ability to use print literacy skills to give structure and meaning to digital content.

For this final project, students work in teams of three for nearly the last five weeks of the semester. During this time, they attend four workshops in class as well as in the library and hold a team conference session with me to ensure that everyone successfully completes the project, which is broken up into five smaller assignments: the anthology perusal workshop, team contract/

proposal, digital anthology, presentation of digital anthology, and the anthology introduction.

This assignment begins with the anthology perusal workshop for several reasons. First, students need to spend time exploring print anthologies to discover the work anthologies do, why they are important, how they are organized, as well as some of the key features they contain. This is particularly important given that we do not use an anthology in this course—students access all primary readings online through Blackboard and digital archives. As my opening anecdote about this workshop reveals, this exercise is essential for bridging the print literacy divide that exists in the literature classroom, as my students come with a wide range of experiences in working with print texts. This workshop ensures that all students understand the value of having a clear sense of purpose and organization in their anthologies.

Not only does this workshop highlight the strengths of print anthologies, but students also become quickly aware of their limitations as well. During a candid discussion about print anthologies, students found these texts limiting because of the lack of images and visual references, the lack of color, and the inability to connect readers to the unending multimedia resources available online. Despite such drawbacks, students were also struck by the power of many of these anthologies that make radical claims about what African American literature is or isn't, claims about what an anthology of African American literature should or shouldn't be, and which voices it should or shouldn't include. In short, students discovered that anthologies can and should be critically engaged texts that have a profound impact on our world.

Merging their print and digital literacy skills, teams create digital anthologies that reflect their own arguments about African American literature and its relationship to our past and present world. A team of three students typically produces a digital anthology with fifteen to eighteen slides that consist of the following elements: anthology title page, statement of purpose, table of contents, primary source slides, and bibliography. Teams work collaboratively to determine the overall organization of the anthology as well as the content and design of primary source slides, which include the following elements: source title, publication date, brief excerpt from primary source, visual image to represent author and/or source, and hyperlinks to related digital artifacts and resources. Whenever I teach the anthology assignment, I offer students the option of using PowerPoint, Google Slides, or Prezi. For this particular class, every team chose PowerPoint to create their anthologies, as this technology is very user friendly, allows students to embed hyperlinked text, images, and video, and works well for group presentations. After deciding on their technology, students choose the primary selections to include in their anthologies, half of which must come from the course readings. Additionally, teams must also choose new selections, affording students the opportunity to revise and expand beyond the required reading. Given that students must justify their choices during their presentations and in their written introductions, this assignment also allows students to construct arguments about and to speak to the inevitable silences and gaps within the course reading but also in the larger canon of African American literature.

Through a series of in-class workshops that take place in the library, students work in their teams with the aid of the humanities librarian and myself to find additional primary texts from outside the course, as well as visual images and digital resources to represent and enhance the selected texts in their anthology.[21] The role of the librarian is central in these workshops for many reasons. First, the librarian ensures that we have physical access to all the anthologies of African American literature from the library collection, even those in storage and in the archives. Secondly, the librarian offers a formal research workshop to introduce students to invaluable search tools and online databases and teaches students how to navigate those digital tools, archives, and databases. Finally, the librarian provides much needed informal help to teams, as questions inevitably arise during the research process. Independent workshops scheduled in the library instruction rooms ensure that students have dedicated time to work with their teammates and have access to both the librarian and instructor to cover research and content-related questions. With an average class size of twenty-four students, having additional support means that students get their questions answered in a timely manner.

Although teams receive informal feedback throughout these workshops, I also formally meet with each team during a conference in which I provide more feedback on a rough draft of their anthologies, making suggestions for how to improve the clarity, organization, and visual strength of their projects. Lastly, teams present their projects in front of their classmates and other members of the SIUE community, offering the opportunity to demonstrate their oral communication skills and to receive comments from the audience about the strengths of their anthology and areas for improvement.

Students submit two written documents in addition to their final digital anthology: a team contract (collaborative) and an introduction (individual). Given that this is a collaborative project, students begin their teamwork by developing a team contract that also functions as a proposal for their digital anthology. The goal of this assignment is to give them some experience working together to produce a document that explains the focus, purpose, and significance of their anthology, as well as the selected texts that they will include in their project. Finally, students use the contract to document and divide the various tasks and responsibilities necessary for completing the project between all the members. This ensures that the workload is shared and helps me in evaluating each student individually based on the effectiveness of his or her contributions to the team. With this assignment, students begin the process of seeing themselves as editors—often a key moment of professional development for students. After completing and submitting their final anthologies, students construct an individually written introduction that offers a justification for their anthology and the specific texts they chose to include. While the team collectively determines the purpose and focus of the anthology, every member chooses three to four texts to include. Hence, the introduction offers an opportunity for students to explain how their individual selections contribute to this collaborative project. In the end, students produce a digital (visual), oral, and written explanation of and argument about African American literature, its key themes and voices, and the enduring value of the tradition from the past to the present.

The Digital Imperative

While the digital archival assignments aid students in bridging the historical distance between their twenty-first-century world and the historical context central to nineteenth- and twentieth-century African American literature, the digital anthology project offers students an opportunity to create a digital artifact that also does the difficult work of bridging the past and the present. Selecting texts that reveal continuities and intersections between the nineteenth century and later periods, students use technology in cogent and innovative ways to represent such historical continuities and repetitions.[22]

Moreover, in this final project, students demonstrate the multiple literacies that they have learned and expanded upon over the semester through their work with print and digital texts. The print literacy skills developed through their work with print texts ensure that the final anthologies have a clear focus, statement of purpose, and logical organization. When students combine these print, information, and technology literacy skills gained in the classroom and in library workshops with their own critical reading practices, their digital anthologies become visually engaging and useful as tools for research and knowledge exploration.[23] Perhaps most importantly, this digital project ensures students' ability not only to successfully navigate the literature classroom but to use those skills to bridge the multiple critical spaces (academic and non-academic) they already inhabit or will in the future.

Many scholars committed to a digital pedagogy recognize the revolutionary potential of technology that allows for a "shift towards more independent, student-led inquiry modes of learning" in which instructors "assume the role of co-collaborator."[24] While this new mode of learning inevitably disrupts traditional literary practice, it also opens up opportunities to engage in liberatory rather than oppressive pedagogical practices, as educators create a learning community in which students' ways of knowing become visible and integrated into the classroom rather than silenced and excluded.[25] This shift to a digital pedagogy rooted in partnership and collaboration does require greater effort on the part of instructors and students. However, Graham reminds us that if we remain fixed in our old pedagogical ways, we risk alienating students who

> have learned to construct meaning and indeed develop critical practices that rarely find space for discussion, let alone recognition inside the classrooms that they enter. . . . The foremost challenge we face in our critical and pedagogical practice is the ability of our current frameworks to capture the changing definition of what African American literature is and whom it serves.[26]

Though Graham focuses on African American literature specifically, her call for new pedagogical practices that reflect and respond to changes in the field must be located within a larger conversation about the meaning and relevance of literary study and of the humanities more broadly within higher education.

Recognizing the evolving needs of students studying African American literature, my own digital pedagogy similarly demonstrates that for the literature classroom to remain a viable space where all students can thrive, we must develop new modes of teaching that seek to build bridges across the many divides that exist for undergraduates. This includes the historical divide between the nineteenth century and our contemporary moment, the print literacy divide, as well as the divide between the classroom and the "real" world that bell hooks positions as a serious threat to democratic education. If the undergraduate classroom has increasingly become a space of alienation for students, then we must engage in a digital pedagogy that embraces multiple critical reading practices. As the digital archive and anthology assignments reveal, a digital pedagogy bridges the ever-widening gap between teacher and student as it resists divisive and hierarchical teaching practices through the cultivation of partnerships and collaboration that transform students' engagement with and relationship to the past.

The appendixes for this chapter, assignments by Tisha M. Brooks for an African American literature survey course, can be found at www.press.uillinois.edu/books /TeachingWithDH.

Notes

1. Maryemma Graham, "Black Is Gold: African American Literature, Critical Literacy, and Twenty-First-Century Pedagogies," in *Contemporary African American Literature: The Living Canon*, ed. Lovalerie King and Shirley Moody-Turner (Bloomington: Indiana University Press, 2013), 66.

2. Ibid., 57.

3. bell hooks, *Teaching Community: A Pedagogy of Hope* (New York: Routledge, 2003), 41, 43–44.

4. Matthew G. Kirschenbaum, "What Is Digital Humanities and What's It Doing in English Departments?," *ADE Bulletin* no. 150 (2010): 59.

5. Joanne T. Diaz, "The Digital Archive as a Tool for Close Reading in the Undergraduate Literature Course," *Pedagogy: Critical Approaches to Teaching Literature, Language, Composition, and Culture* 12, no. 3 (2012): 425.

6. I focus primarily on *In Motion: The African-American Migration Experience*, Schomburg Center for Research in Black Culture, New York Public Library, 2005, accessed March 26, 2017, http://www.inmotionaame.org/home.cfm. Students also work with the *National Archives*, accessed March 26, 2017, http://www.archives.gov; *Documenting the American South*, University of North Carolina at Chapel Hill, accessed March 26, 2017, http://docsouth.unc.edu/index.html; and *Africans in America*, PBS, accessed March 26, 2017, http://www.pbs.org/wgbh/aia/home.html.

7. Kirschenbaum, "What Is Digital Humanities," 59; Tara McPherson, "Introduction: Media Studies and the Digital Humanities," *Cinema Journal* 48, no. 2 (Winter 2009): 123.

8. "The African-American Migration Experience," *In Motion: The African-American Migration Experience*, http://www.inmotionaame.org/home.cfm.

9. "Introduction," *In Motion: The African-American Migration Experience*, http://www.inmotionaame.org/about.cfm?bhcp=1.

10. Frederick Douglass, *The Narrative of the Life of Frederick Douglass, an American Slave. Written by Himself, Documenting the American South* (1845; electronic ed., University of North Carolina, 2004), 6, http://docsouth.unc.edu/neh/douglass/douglass.html.

11. Course readings from the late eighteenth, nineteenth, and twentieth centuries include the following texts: Phillis Wheatley's poem, "On Being Brought from Africa to America" (1773); Olaudah Equiano's *The Interesting Narrative of the Life of Olaudah Equiano* (1789); Frederick Douglass's *Narrative of the Life of Frederick Douglass* (1845); Paul Lawrence Dunbar's "We Wear the Mask" (1895); Ida B. Well's anti-lynching pamphlet, *A Red Record* (1895); Robert Hayden's "Middle Passage" (1962); Alice Walker's "In Search of Our Mothers' Gardens" (1974); and Octavia Butler's *Kindred* (1979).

12. In previous classes, we did not explicitly discuss the form or structure of the digital archives, but I hope to do so in future classes to deepen student understanding of the impact of organization and structure in their own digital artifacts.

13. Rediker refers to this dehumanization as the "violence of abstraction," in which the experiences, lives, and subjectivity of captives are silenced and erased from the historical record. According to Rediker, this "'violence of abstraction'... has plagued the study of the slave trade from its beginning. It is as if the use of ledgers, almanacs, balance sheets, graphs, and tables—the merchants' comforting methods—has rendered abstract, and thereby dehumanized, a reality that must, for moral and political reasons, be understood concretely. An ethnography of the slave ship helps to demonstrate not only the cruel truth of what one group of people (or several) was willing to do to others for money... but also how they managed in crucial respects to hide the reality and con-

sequences of their actions from themselves and from posterity. Numbers can occlude the pervasive torture and terror, but European, African, and American societies still live with their consequences, the multiple legacies of race, class, and slavery." Marcus Rediker, *The Slave Ship: A Human History* (New York: Penguin Books, 2007), 12–13.

14. Judalyn S. Ryan, *Spirituality as Ideology in Black Women's Literature and Film* (Charlottesville: University of Virginia Press, 2005), 16.

15. "The Middle Passage: Image Gallery," *In Motion: The African-American Migration Experience*, http://www.inmotionaame.org/gallery/index.cfm?migration=1&topic =5&type=image.

16. Donna M. Campbell, "The Slave, Freedom, or Liberation Narrative," *Literary Movements*, Washington State University, accessed May 12, 2016, http://public.wsu .edu/~campbelld/amlit/slave.htm.

17. "Frederick Douglass, 1818–1895: *Narrative of the Life of Frederick Douglass, an American Slave. Written by Himself,*" *Documenting the American South*, http://docsouth .unc.edu/neh/douglass/menu.html.

18. Though the image is titled *Punishment* in the AAME archive, the print is cataloged in the Library of Congress Prints and Photographs Division as follows: Isaac Cruikshank, *The abolition of the slave trade Or the inhumanity of dealers in human flesh exemplified in Captn. Kimber's treatment of a young Negro girl of 15 for her virjen (sic) modesty*, 1792.

19. Douglass, *Narrative, Documenting the American South*, 6.

20. Saidiya Hartman, *Lose Your Mother: A Journey along the Atlantic Slave Route* (New York: Farrar, Straus and Giroux, 2007), 143.

21. Though I worked with students in another class, Autobiographical Practices, in spring 2014 on a similar project in which they created digital anthologies of African American autobiography, this was the first time that I had students attend formal workshops in the library. Special thanks to Lora Del Rio, the humanities librarian at SIUE, who made this key suggestion to move some of the workshops to the library and whose assistance during these workshops greatly increased the effectiveness of the project.

22. Although students can choose which periods to represent in their anthology, the overwhelming majority of teams decide to include selections from the late eighteenth and/or nineteenth centuries. This illustrates the profound impact of their archival work with this early period and demonstrates a tremendous shift in students' perception of early literature as "old" and "hard to read" to their understanding of the literature's significance to the larger African American literary tradition and to their understanding of black peoples' experience in America historically and in the present.

23. Students attend six workshops total over the final five weeks of the semester: three workshops in class and three workshops in the library.

24. Jennifer Howell, *Teaching with ICT: Digital Pedagogies for Collaboration and Creativity* (Melbourne: Oxford University Press, 2012), 5.

25. Paulo Freire, *Pedagogy of the Oppressed* (New York: Continuum International, 2002), 75. Here I specifically draw on Freire's concept of the "humanist, revolutionary educator" who works alongside students to "engage in critical thinking and the quest for mutual humanization."

26. Graham, "Black Is Gold," 56.

About the Contributors

The Editors

JENNIFER TRAVIS is professor and chair of the English department at St. John's University, where she teaches American literature and digital humanities. Her books include *Boys Don't Cry: Rethinking Masculinity and Emotion in the U.S.*, coedited with Milette Shamir (2002); *Wounded Hearts: Masculinity, Law, and Literature in American Culture* (2005); and *Danger and Vulnerability in Nineteenth Century American Literature: Crash and Burn* (2018). Among her journal articles, she has published on her work with students on the WikiNovels Project and has developed several new undergraduate and graduate courses on digital literary studies for her department and university. Her current work includes a Cambridge University Press collection on gender and American literature (coedited with Jean Lutes), and a book and online exhibit based on her research and collaboration with art historian Susan Rosenberg in the Davis Library, a New York City insurance archive.

JESSICA DESPAIN is an associate professor of English at Southern Illinois University Edwardsville and is the codirector of SIUE's IRIS Center for the Digital Humanities. She is the author of *Nineteenth-Century Transatlantic Reprinting and the Embodied Book* (Ashgate, 2014) and the lead editor of *The Wide, Wide World Digital Edition*, an exploration of the more than 170 reprints of Susan Warner's bestselling nineteenth-century novel. She has published several articles on the intersections of book history and digital humanities pedagogy both within and beyond the traditional classroom. DeSpain collaborated with faculty in education and STEM on the NSF-funded *Digital East St. Louis Project*, in which middle school students built a digital project about the history and culture of their city. She is currently the director of the

NEH-funded *Conversation Toward a Brighter Future* project, wherein middle and high school students participate in digital storytelling studios about the value of intergenerational relationships.

The Authors

NICOLE N. ALJOE is an associate professor of English and African American studies at Northeastern University and codirector of *The Early Caribbean Digital Archive* at NULab for Texts, Maps, and Networks. Her research and teaching focus on eighteenth- and nineteenth-century black Atlantic and Caribbean literatures with a specialization on the slave narrative. She has published essays in the *Journal of Early American Literature, African American Review,* and *Anthurium.* She is the author of *Creole Testimonies: Slave Narratives from the British West Indies, 1709–1836* (Palgrave, 2012), coeditor of *Journeys of the Slave Narrative in the Early Americas* (University of Virginia Press, 2014), and *Literary Histories of the Early Anglophone Caribbean: Islands in the Stream* (Palgrave Macmillan/Springer 2018). She is at work on a new project that examines the relationships between the development of slave narrative and the rise of the novel.

ELIZABETH ARGENTIERI is the special collections librarian at SUNY Geneseo's Milne Library. She has trained and worked closely with students in several courses to discover, digitize, and describe items for themed online exhibits they create using Omeka. She collaborates with professionals at other area cultural institutions in resource sharing, research assistance, and digitization projects such as the New York Heritage digital repository and the New York State Historic Newspapers website. Liz is a charter member of Rochester Regional Library Council's New York Heritage Local Steering Committee and its Digital Humanities Interest Group.

BLAIR BEST completed undergraduate degrees in theater and journalism at New York University in May 2018. She is a published journalist, and her honors thesis focuses on twentieth-century American female playwrights and the development of the female character.

TISHA M. BROOKS is an assistant professor of English language and literature at Southern Illinois University Edwardsville. Her scholarship focuses on African American literature, women's studies, and religion. As an instructor of literature and composition, Brooks uses digital resources and technology in the classroom to help students bridge gaps in historical, disciplinary, and experiential knowledge.

MADELEINE (MADDIE) G. CELLA is a recent graduate of New York University, where she double majored in drama and history. She recently finished her senior-year thesis in performance studies titled "Unknowable: The Nature of Truth in the Information Society." She is from the south shore of Massachusetts, and she hopes to pursue a career in law.

RATI CHOUDHARY is completing her undergraduate degree in drama at Tisch School of the Arts, NYU. As well as studying drama, she is minoring in both film production and producing and one day hopes to write and direct her own original material. She feels incredibly lucky to have been introduced to the digital humanities by Professor Robert Davis and hopes that others will find their research just as compelling as she does.

KAYLA C. COLEMAN is a working actor, singer, and activist from Philadelphia who is based in New York City. She graduated from New York University's Tisch School of the Arts drama department, with a minor in Africana studies, in May 2018. She plans to pursue a B.F.A. in performance and art as community engagement/activism in the near future. Her other hobbies include youth engagement, gardening, and cooking.

KEN COOPER is an associate professor of English at SUNY Geneseo, where he teaches courses in American literature and ecocriticism. He has published on Cold War fiction and is at work on a project concerning ecology and 1970s culture. He wishes to thank students in his Bioregional Literature class for their support of and contributions to *Open Valley.*

RYAN CORDELL is an assistant professor of English at Northeastern University and a Core Founding Faculty Member in the NULab for Texts, Maps, and Networks (https://web.northeastern.edu/nulab/). His scholarship seeks to illuminate how technologies of production, reception, and remediation shape the meanings of texts within communities. Cordell primarily studies circulation and reprinting in nineteenth-century American newspapers, but his interests extend to the influence of computation and digitization on contemporary reading, writing, and research. Cordell collaborates with colleagues in English, history, and computer science on the NEH- and ACLS-funded Viral Texts project (http://viraltexts.org), which is using robust data-mining tools to discover borrowed texts across large-scale archives of nineteenth-century periodicals. He is also a primary investigator in the Digging Into Data project Oceanic Exchanges (http://oceanicexchanges.org), a six-nation effort examining patterns of information flow across national and linguistic boundaries in nineteenth-century newspapers. Cordell is also a fellow in critical bibliography at the Rare Book School in Charlottesville, Virginia, and serves on the Executive Committee of the MLA's Forum on Bibliography and Scholarly Editing.

ROBERT DAVIS is an adjunct assistant professor at John Jay and Hunter Colleges, CUNY, and an instructor at New York University. His dissertation, "Performance and Spectatorship in United States International Expositions, 1876–1893," looks at audience behavior at world's fairs, sections of which have been published in *The World's Fair Reader* (2014) and *Classics in the Modern World: A Democratic Turn?* (2013). He has also published in *The Oxford Handbook of Greek Drama in the Americas* (2015), *Comparative Drama* (2011), and the *Journal of American Drama and Theatre* (2011, with Amanda Wrigley). He wrote *Broadway: 1849*, an interactive novel about managing a theater in antebellum New York City. Davis authored the essay on theater history with students in a fall 2015 sophomore honors seminar in the Drama Department of New York University's Tisch School of the Arts, titled The Digital Nineteenth Century.

BENJAMIN J. DOYLE is a PhD student in English at Northeastern University. His research focuses on early Atlantic world literatures, political philosophy, and the digital humanities. His dissertation project, "An Account of Uncommon Suffering: Early Atlantic Texts and the Fabrication of Human Rights (1640–1857)," examines the role of the extra-national subject in the historical formation of human rights law and literature in its modern, Western contexts.

AMY E. EARHART is an associate professor of English at Texas A&M University. She is the author of *Traces of the Old, Uses of the New: The Emergence of the Digital Humanities* (University of Michigan Press, 2015) and coeditor with Andrew Jewell of *The American Literature Scholar in the Digital Age* (University of Michigan Press, 2010). She has published articles and book chapters in venues including *Debates in the Digital Humanities, DHQ, Textual Cultures,* and *Scholarly Editing.* Earhart's students have completed classroom projects that have resulted in the publication of Alex Haley's "The Malcolm X I Knew," *Notecards from "The Autobiography of Malcolm X,"* and *The Millican "Riot" Project, 1868.*

DUNCAN FAHERTY is an associate professor of English and American studies at Queens College and the City University of New York Graduate Center. He is the coeditor of *Studies in American Fiction* and, along with Ed White, the co-curator of the *Just Teach One* digital humanities project housed at the American Antiquarian Society (http://jto.common-place.org/). He is the author of *Remodeling the Nation: The Architecture of American Identity, 1776–1858* (New Hampshire University Press, 2009), and his work has also appeared in *American Literature, American Quarterly, Early American Literature,* the *Los Angeles Review of Books,* and *Reviews in American History.* He is currently at work on a book about the Haitian Revolution and early U.S. print culture.

ERIC GARDNER is a professor of English at Saginaw Valley State University and the author or editor of five books including *Unexpected Places: Relocating Nineteenth-Century African American Literature* (Mississippi, 2009) and *Black Print Unbound: The Christian Recorder, African American Literature, and Periodical Culture* (Oxford, 2015). Two-time winner of the Research Society for American Periodicals Book Prize, he has published shorter work in venues ranging from *American Literary History* to *PMLA*, and he held a fellowship from the National Endowment for the Humanities in 2012–2013. He blogs at blackprintculture.com, and he is currently working on several projects surrounding black engagement with print during the Civil War and Reconstruction.

ELLA L. GILL is in her final year at New York University's Tisch School of the Arts. She spent her first three years at the Atlantic Acting School and is studying at Stonestreet Studios this year. She is interested in writing for the screen, writing music, and acting and is very excited to be included in this project.

CLAYTON GRIMM is a drama major and French minor at NYU's Tisch School of the Arts. He graduated in 2018 and hopes to continue his study of theater while pursuing a career as an actor.

CYNTHIA L. HALLEN is an associate professor of linguistics and English language at Brigham Young University. She applies knowledge from composition, lexicography, linguistics, onomastics, philology, rhetoric, stylistics, translation, and literary analysis to the field of Emily Dickinson studies. She is the chief editor of the *Emily Dickinson Lexicon*, an online comprehensive dictionary of all the words in Dickinson's poems. Her EDL website includes a searchable database of the 1844 second edition of Noah Webster's *American Dictionary of the English Language*, which Dickinson used for her poetic composition.

MOLLY O'HAGAN HARDY is director of the library and archives at the Cape Ann Museum. Previously, she was the director for digital and book history initiatives at the American Antiquarian Society. Her work, both as an exhibition curator and as a digital humanities project director, centers on the study and remediation of pre-1900 colonial and U.S. archival materials in the digital age. Her essays on these topics have appeared in *American Literary History*, *Debates in Digital Humanities*, *Early American Studies*, *Book History*, and *CR: The New Centennial Review*.

ELIZABETH HOPWOOD is a lecturer in English and the assistant director of the Center for Textual Studies and Digital Humanities at Loyola University Chicago. Her current book project focuses on technologies of taste and food production in nineteenth-century Atlantic World texts. Her work has most recently been supported by the American Antiquarian Society.

MALIN JÖRNVI is a recent graduate of Tisch School of the Arts, New York University. She is excited to continue her scholarship on the intersection of theory and practice within theater, film, and performance in the years to come. She is currently applying to graduate programs in cinema studies and philosophy, and she reviews female-made films for FF2 Media.

WYN KELLEY, senior lecturer in literature at MIT, serves as the associate director of the *Melville Electronic Library* (http://mel.hofstra.edu/) and is a research associate of the HyperStudio, MIT's digital humanities lab, working to develop Annotation Studio (http://www.annotationstudio.org/). She is author of *Melville's City: Literary and Urban Form in Nineteenth-Century New York* (Cambridge University Press, 1996) as well as *Herman Melville: An Introduction* (Wiley-Blackwell, 2008) and is coauthor, with Henry Jenkins, of *Reading in a Participatory Culture: Re-Mixing* Moby-Dick *in the English Classroom* (Teachers College Press, 2013).

PHILIP KENNER is a recent graduate of New York University, where he received his BFA in drama and English literature. After studying at Playwrights Horizons Theater School, he has developed a number of original plays and musicals alongside his peers and faculty. Kenner has written his senior thesis on the evolution of gay male identity on stage, and he plans to pursue a graduate degree in playwriting.

PATRICK KORKUCH is a senior undergraduate student at New York University, completing his BFA in drama. At NYU, he has been interested in the intersection of theater and technology and has taken courses in both fields. He plans to complete his premedical coursework and enroll in medical school postgraduation.

MAHAYLA LAURENCE is completing her BFA in drama at New York University. Her interests include theater, African American/African-diasporic literature, and comedy. She directs two comedy groups at NYU, Hammerkatz and Dangerbox. Her recent endeavors include a touring production of *Julius Caesar* to underserved communities in Manhattan and devising a new work with playwright Young Jean Lee (www.MahaylaLaurence.com).

JOANNA PISANO graduated from New York University's Tisch School of the Arts in December 2017. She received a Bachelor of Fine Arts in drama, as well as a minor in producing. In both fields, she hopes to utilize technology to further investigate the work being produced and create interactive communities for artists and audiences.

TIMOTHY B. POWELL is a faculty member of the religious studies department at the University of Pennsylvania and a consulting scholar at the Penn

Museum. Currently, he is the director of Educational Partnerships with Indigenous Communities (EPIC) in the Penn Language Center. He founded the Center for Native American Indigenous Research (CNAIR) at the American Philosophical Society and currently serves there as a consulting scholar. Powell is the author, most recently, of "Digital Knowledge Sharing: Forging Partnerships between Scholars, Archives, and Indigenous Communities" and "'The Songs Are Alive': Bringing Frances Densmore's Recordings Back Home to Fond du Lac Tribal Community College" (forthcoming). Over the years, he has successfully applied for and directed more than $3 million in grants to support digital repatriation in Indian Country.

TEAGAN RABUANO is an undergraduate student at New York University completing their BFA in drama with a double major in gender and sexuality studies. Their primary work has been in transgender studies and advocacy, working at organizations such as the National Center for Transgender Equality and being featured in *New York Magazine* and *them*.

ASHLEY REED is an assistant professor of English at Virginia Tech, where she teaches courses in American literature and digital humanities. She received her PhD in 2014 from the University of North Carolina at Chapel Hill and held a Mellon Postdoctoral Fellowship in digital humanities in 2014–2015. From 2007 to 2013 she served as project manager of the *William Blake Archive* and remains with the project as a consultant. She has published articles in *J19: The Journal of Nineteenth-Century Americanists*, *Digital Humanities Quarterly*, and *Essays in Romanticism*.

LAWRENCE G. RICHARDSON is currently completing a degree in acting and political science. He plans to attend law school in the near future and practice with a public law organization.

AUGUSTA ROHRBACH is the author of *Thinking Outside the Book* (University of Massachusetts Press, 2014), a meditation on the relationships between new media and the conventions associated with literature and the book. She also wrote *Truth Stranger than Fiction: Race, Realism and the US Literary Marketplace* (Palgrave, 2002), a study that establishes the slave narrative as a taproot for literary realism. Her work has been supported by a Bunting Fellowship at the Radcliffe Institute for Advanced Research, the W. E. B. Du Bois Institute at Harvard University, and research grants from the Library Company of Philadelphia, Smith College, and the Houghton Library. Her essays have appeared in *American Literature, Callaloo, New England Quarterly*, and *Prospects*. Currently, she is director of strategic initiatives in the Office of the Vice Provost for Research, Tufts University, and working on "The Gallows Diary of Mary Surratt, Presidential Assassin."

HALEY SAKAMOTO is a recent graduate of New York University's Tisch School of the Arts. She received a BFA in theater and is pursuing acting, writing, filmmaking, and music in New York City. She hopes to collaborate on compassionate and meaningful work in this divisive time of history.

CELESTE TƯỜNG VY SHARPE is the academic technologist for instructional technology at Carleton College, where she works on digital projects with faculty and staff across campus that infuse technology into the curriculum. She received her PhD in history from George Mason University for her born-digital dissertation project titled "They Need You! Disability, Visual Culture, and the Poster Child, 1945–1980," which examines how charitable organizations, disabled children and their families, and the public understood and shaped ideas about disability, identity, philanthropy, family, and the nation after World War II. She was a Penn Predoctoral Fellow for Excellence Through Diversity at the University of Pennsylvania and worked at the Roy Rosenzweig Center for History and New Media at George Mason University on a number of projects in the Education and Public Projects divisions. Previously, she has written on historical thinking, hybrid asynchronous learning for history courses, and iterative web writing.

VICTORIA K. SPROWLS completed her BFA in drama at New York University in May 2018. She enjoys listening to podcasts and making short films based on her life experiences. She can be found on Instagram (@viccckyg).

CATHERINE WAITINAS is professor of English at California Polytechnic State University in San Luis Obispo, where she teaches American literature. Her research centers on Walt Whitman, literary mesmerism, and literary pedagogy. She also works with students to create literary Open Educational Resources (OER).

ED WHITE is the Pierce Butler Chair of American literature at Tulane University. He is the coauthor of *The Traumatic Colonel: The Founding Fathers, Slavery, and the Phantasmatic Aaron Burr* (NYU Press, 2014) and the author of *The Backcountry and the City: Colonization and Conflict in Early America* (University of Minnesota Press, 2005) and *How to Read Barthes' Image-Music-Text* (Pluto Press, 2012). He has edited a new edition of Hugh Henry Brackenridge's 1792–1815 novel *Modern Chivalry* and, with Michael Drexler, has coedited *Beyond Douglass: New Perspectives on Early African-American Literature*. His work has also appeared in *Early American Literature, Early American Studies, PMLA, American Literature, American Literary History, American Quarterly, Studies in American Fiction*, and *Journal of the Early Republic*. He is currently working on a study of early U.S. literary conservatism.

EDWARD WHITLEY is an associate professor in the English Department at Lehigh University. He is the author of *American Bards: Walt Whitman and Other Unlikely Candidates for National Poet* (University of North Carolina Press, 2010) and the coeditor, with Joanna Levin, of *Whitman among the Bohemians* (University of Iowa Press, 2014) and *Walt Whitman in Context* (Cambridge University Press, 2018). Since 2004, he and Robert Weidman have codirected *The Vault at Pfaff's: An Archive of Art and Literature by the Bohemians of Antebellum New York* (http://lehigh.edu/pfaffs).

CAROLINE M. WOIDAT is a professor of English and coordinator of the American Studies and Native American Studies programs at the State University of New York at Geneseo. Her research and teaching focus on American women writers, Native American literature, captivity and migration narratives, and nineteenth-century social reform. She collaborated with Geneseo colleagues on "English Majors Practicing Criticism: A Digital Approach" (*Academic Commons*) and with members of the Council of Public Liberal Arts Colleges in *Hybrid Course Sharing in Native American Studies*, a Teagle Foundation grant project combining online instruction with on-the-ground mentoring to join faculty and students from multiple campuses into one community. Her publications include a Broadview Edition of Elizabeth Oakes Smith's *The Western Captive and Other Indian Stories* (2015) and essays in *Legacy*, *MFS*, *Twentieth-Century Literature*, and *Journal of American Culture*.

Index

Topics in the Digital Humanities

The University of Illinois Press
is a founding member of the
Association of American University Presses.

University of Illinois Press
1325 South Oak Street
Champaign, IL 61820-6903
www.press.uillinois.edu

Made in United States
North Haven, CT
31 August 2023

40955063R00178